AGGRESSIVE IN PURSUIT

The Life of Justice Emmett Hall

PATRONS OF THE SOCIETY

Aird & Berlis LLP

Blake, Cassels & Graydon LLP

Davies Ward Phillips & Vineberg LLP

Gowlings

McCarthy Tétrault LLP

Osler, Hoskin & Harcourt LLP

Torkin Manes Cohen & Arbus LLP

Torys LLP

WeirFoulds LLP

The Osgoode Society is supported by a grant from
The Law Foundation of Ontario

THE LAW
FOUNDATION
OF ONTARIO

The Society also thanks The Law Society of Upper Canada
for its continuing support.

AGGRESSIVE IN PURSUIT

The Life of Justice Emmett Hall

FREDERICK VAUGHAN

Published for The Osgoode Society for Canadian Legal History by
UNIVERSITY OF TORONTO PRESS
Toronto Buffalo London

Printed in Canada

ISBN 0-8020-3957-x

Printed on acid-free paper

Library and Archives Canada Cataloguing in Publications

Vaughan, Frederick
Aggressive in pursuit : the life of Justice Emmett Hall / Frederick
Vaughan.

Includes bibliographical references and index.
ISBN 0-8020-3957-x

1. Hall, Emmett M., 1898–1995.   2. Canada. Supreme Court –
Biography.   3. Judges – Canada – Biography.   4. Judges –
Saskatchewan – Biography.   5. National health insurance – Canada –
History.   6. Governmental investigations – Canada – History.
7. Canada – Biography.   8. Saskatchewan – Biography.
I. Osgoode Society for Canadian Legal History.   II. Title.

KE8248.H34V39 2004   347.71'03534'092   C2004-904039-1
KF345.Z9H34V39 2004

University of Toronto Press acknowledges the financial assistance to its publishing program of the Canada Council for the Arts and the Ontario Arts Council.

University of Toronto Press acknowledges the financial support for its publishing activities of the Government of Canada through the Book Publishing Industry Development Program (BPIDP).

For William C. Winegard, P.C., O.C.

Contents

Foreword

THE OSGOODE SOCIETY
FOR CANADIAN LEGAL HISTORY

This is the fourth biography of a Supreme Court of Canada judge published by The Osgoode Society and doubtless it is the most provocative. For Emmett Hall, as Professor Vaughan so persuasively demonstrates, was a different sort of judge – and a different sort of man. Appointed to the Court in 1963 by Prime Minister John Diefenbaker, Justice Hall proved every bit as flamboyant and controversial as the prairie populist who elevated him to the highest court of the land.

This judicial biography focuses on Hall's career as defence lawyer and civil litigator, his position as a civil-libertarian judge and advocate of the rights of minority groups, and his work on a series of royal commissions, most significantly the Royal Commission on Health Services. Always an individualist and possessed of a probing and disciplined mind, Hall made his own unique contribution to the judicial history of Saskatchewan and Canada.

The purpose of The Osgoode Society for Canadian Legal History is to encourage research and writing in the history of Canadian law. The Society, which was incorporated in 1979 and is registered as a charity, was founded at the initiative of the Honourable R. Roy McMurtry, a former attorney general for Ontario, now chief justice of Ontario, and officials of The Law Society of Upper Canada. Its efforts to stimulate the study of legal history in Canada include a research-support program, a graduate student research-assistance program, and work in the fields of oral history and legal archives. The Society publishes volumes of interest to the Society's members that contribute to legal-historical scholarship in Canada, including studies of the courts, the judiciary, and the legal profession, biographies, collections of documents, studies in criminology and penology, accounts of significant trials, and work in the social and economic history of the law.

Current directors of The Osgoode Society for Canadian Legal History are Robert Armstrong, Kenneth Binks, Patrick Brode, Michael Bryant, Brian Bucknall, Archie Campbell, David Chernos, Kirby Chown, J. Douglas Ewart, Martin Friedland, Elizabeth Goldberg, John Honsberger, Horace Krever, Virginia MacLean, Frank Marrocco, Roy McMurtry, Brendan O'Brien, Peter Oliver, Paul Reinhardt, Joel Richler, William Ross, James Spence, and Richard Tinsley.

The annual report and information about membership may be obtained by writing: The Osgoode Society for Canadian Legal History, Osgoode Hall, 130 Queen Street West, Toronto, Ontario. M5H 2N6. Telephone: 416-947-3321. E-mail: *mmacfarl@lsuc.on.ca*.
Website:: Osgoodesociety.ca

R. Roy McMurtry
President

Peter N. Oliver
Editor-in-Chief

Preface

Navigating the shoals, as every mariner knows – even when they are clearly marked on the charts – can be a tricky business requiring a good deal of concentration. No less difficult is the art of navigating the shoals of biography. Granted, the biographer is confined to the coordinates dictated by the subject's life, but most subjects of biography throw up reefs or barriers to block the passage of the determined biographer or, at least, make the passage difficult. In a certain sense it can also be said that the biographer betrays his or her subject by coming ashore and digging through the attic and into hidden trunks for papers and material that will 'spice' up the narrative. It is for this reason that it has been said that every great man has his disciples but it is Judas who writes his biography. Since, therefore, every subject of biography harbours a certain reluctance to be exposed, most biographers have to dig and pry into corners, looking for those indiscretions or lapses of propriety that will portray the man or woman 'as he truly was.' Indeed, it is almost de rigueur for biographers nowadays – with Lytton Strachey shouting over their shoulders that 'discretion is not the better part of biography' – to expose the unseemly side in their subject's life. Not everyone is as gifted as Strachey – who could sniff a scandal in every scented breeze – in uncovering the unseemly. And what if the biographer's subject does not have an unseemly side? What if the subject is, like the late Chief Justice John Cartwright, a man of uncommon virtue without any 're-deeming vices' for the prying eyes of the biographer to reveal to the reading public? It is universally acknowledged that it is easier to write about vice than about virtue. But, alas, Emmett Hall, while not a man of uncommon virtue, had very little vice – a little vanity and ambition, perhaps, but those qualities hardly set him off from the majority of men. Fortunately for this biographer, however, he did commit the occasional indiscretion, as the reader will see.

If, as Dr Johnson, the subject of the most celebrated pre-Strachey biography, said, 'nobody can write the life of a man but those who have eat [sic] and drunk and lived in social intercourse with him,' then there would be few biographies written. I did, however, talk with Emmett Hall intimately about his life and work for long hours over many years. What I encountered was a man who did not drink far into the night or carouse with casual bar friends and acquaintances; I found no evidence of midnight assignations with women of easy virtue, not even a taste for gambling. I found that he loved to play bridge with his friends but I have not been able to uncover a single instance where he cheated. He finessed, yes, but he never cheated. In brief, by the standards of vice, his was an unexciting life. To make the biographer's task even more difficult, Hall's life was almost exclusively wrapped up in the law; his closest friends were either judges or lawyers. Even his political friends were former lawyers. He had no passion for music or literature or the theatre; he enjoyed an occasional movie and theatrical performance but he was not a devotee of the stage or concert hall. Nor did he follow sports as a devoted fan. He was aware, of course, of the Grey Cup and showed an interest – from a safe distance – in the prospects of the Saskatchewan Roughriders. But, after all, he was from Saskatchewan where people take football seriously. His life was wholly in the practice of the law. Even his public service or 'good works' were an extension of his passion for the law. His aggressive character, accordingly, emerges gradually as we watch him in court both as a defence counsel and as a judge as well as a royal commissioner. By studying him in court in both personas – by following his line of reasoning as he developed a case before a jury, by entering closely into his reasons for judgments in numerous cases on the bench – I hope that the character of Emmett Hall as an aggressive advocate will emerge in all its colours. And that, after all, is the reason for biography.

However, I have had to navigate a number of shoals in the course of writing this biography. Hall attempted, for example, to steer me away from certain aspects that impinged upon his life as a lawyer and as a judge. He insisted that I not contrast his approach to judging with that of his Supreme Court colleague, Justice Wilfred Judson. Nor did he want me to relate his candid observations about matters relating to the inner workings of the Court. But I have stuck to the conviction that such matters not only serve to bring out Emmett Hall's character as a judge but also shed light on the daily dynamics that take place behind the invisible veil that screens the Supreme Court of Canada from the view of passers-by. On one occasion when I had reported in a law review article that he had become angry with his colleagues during the Truscott case, he angrily denied the claim. But I had witnessed him give full vent to his Irish temper in a conversation I had had with him on this highly publicized case. Clearly, he did not want me to report that he ever lost his temper with his colleagues – which he did frequently. One of the shoals.

Over the years I conducted many interviews and corresponded with leading contemporaries of Emmett Hall, from former law students and colleagues to Tommy Douglas and John Diefenbaker. Mr Douglas was – as no one will be surprised to learn – generous and gracious in his comments on Emmett Hall's contribution to medicare. He gave full credit to Hall for the establishment of our national health services. 'Without Emmett Hall's report it would not have happened,' he told me. My interview with John Diefenbaker, on the other hand, was less satisfactory. Unlike Tommy Douglas, Diefenbaker ordered my tape recorder out of his office. He wanted nothing recorded on tape. Unfortunately, Diefenbaker talked more about himself than about Hall; every time I tried to bring the conversation back to Hall, Diefenbaker would filter his response through an episode in his own life. There was no question in Diefenbaker's mind that any achievements in the life of Emmett Hall were due to his prescience in appointing him to the bench. Conversations with Hall's former judicial colleagues were equally fruitless: 'a good man, a wonderful judge, a loving father etc.' Not a single indiscretion escaped their lips (the lone dissenting voice was that of Justice Douglas Abbott, as the reader will see). I have incorporated the results of those sources into the narrative of this book. I must note, however, that this is not a 'life and times' book. Though I have attempted to place Emmett Hall's life – which began in 1898 and ended in 1995 – in the context of the leading events that took place in the history of Canada during those many years, my central focus is on the life in the law that was the core of this distinguished Canadian lawyer and judge. By watching how the disparate pieces of the life of Emmett Hall come together into a clear portrait of the man – who became a justice of the highest court in the land and a major contributor to the national health-care system of the nation – readers will, I hope, come to understand better how the Canadian judicial process works and how this one lawyer made a difference both on and off the bench.

Emmett Hall has been praised for his generosity and dedication to public service and other virtues. But he was, above all else, an aggressive advocate in his long life in private practice, on the bench, and as a mediator and royal commissioner. And this is the story of that man whose achievements have altered the lives of Canadians in many important ways – from elementary education to native land claims to criminal justice, from railway transportation to health services. Few Canadian judges have left diaries or memoirs in which they record their feelings about other lawyers or judges with whom they worked for years at the bar or on the bench. We do not have the equivalent of Felix Frankfurter's diaries where he was fully prepared to record his critical judgments on such of his colleagues as Harold Burton, Hugo Black, and William Douglas.[1] Speaking of Justice Harold Burton, Frankfurter wrote: 'He hasn't the remotest idea how malignant men like Black and Douglas not only can be, but are.'[2] These diaries put a human – albeit at times scarred – face on the inner workings of the Supreme Court of the United States. Emmett Hall did not leave a diary but I had the pleasure of listening to him for many hours talk about his colleagues on the Court, as well as about discussions that took place in the conferences following oral arguments. He expressed strong critical opinions of some of his colleagues, such as Gérald Fauteux. I have decided to include only those anecdotes and remarks that add to the narrative of this story of men – he was never on a bench with women colleagues – engaged in working the judicial process from the inside. Emmett Hall did not approve of my doing this and urged me to sanitize the draft manuscript. I refused to do so and incurred a measure of his displeasure. At one point I asked a member of the present Supreme Court of Canada to vet a passage relating to the last days of the late Chief Justice Robert Taschereau which Hall insisted that I delete from the text. That judge saw no reason for me to exclude it; so it remains in the text contrary to Hall's wishes. It is for these reasons that this book has been a long time aborning. I have laboured throughout to be both judicious and fair to a man and to a Court I hold in the highest esteem. Only the reader can say whether I have been successful or not.

I owe a large debt of gratitude to many people with whom I discussed parts of this book over the past thirty years: I am especially grateful to the late W. Kenneth Campbell, executive secretary at the Supreme Court of Canada, who was a treasure trove of information on the Supreme Court. I would also like to express my gratitude to Dr Harry Arthurs who, as dean of Osgoode Hall Law School, York University, invited me to spend the academic year 1976–7 as a visiting fellow of the law school. The bulk of the research for the first draft of this book was undertaken during that year. The congenial and professional atmosphere at Osgoode Hall Law School made the researching of this biography very pleasant as well as profitable. I am deeply indebted to many members of the Osgoode faculty for their assistance, such as Professor Neil Brooks (a former Supreme Court clerk to Justice Hall), Professor (now Mr Justice) Allen Linden, Professor (now Mr Justice) Sidney Lederman, Professor Pierre Patenaude, and Professor Stanley Beck. I should also like to thank Meg Kinnear, of the federal Department of Justice, for reviewing an early version of the manuscript and for making many suggestions for improvement. I am most grateful to Peter Oliver and the Osgoode Society for providing me with the funds to pursue archival research in Saskatoon in June 2003. I want to thank, too, Cheryl Avery, of the University of Saskatchewan Archives, for permitting me access to the Hall Papers and for providing me with help in locating several items relating to the life of Emmett Hall. As well, I want to thank Bruce Shepard, director of the Diefenbaker Centre, for permitting me to see the Diefenbaker correspondence with Hall. Illa Knudsen, the deputy local registrar of the Judicial Centre, Saskatoon, was also most helpful in tracking down certain material that was unreported. As usual, I owe a great debt to my old friend and colleague, Patrick Kyba, a Saskatchewan native and keen student of all things relating to his home province, for combing the draft manuscript for 'howlers' of fact and interpretation relating to Saskatchewan history. I cannot express the depth of gratitude I owe to Justice Horace Krever – a member of the Board of the Osgoode Society – who subjected the manuscript to a detailed critique; the time and attention he put into the task has saved me from many embarrassing mistakes. Finally, I am deeply indebted to my wife, Carol, for a mountain of help and advice over a number of years on this project. Without her help I would not have completed this book. I am, of course, solely responsible for any errors of fact or interpretation, to say nothing of the indiscretions.

AGGRESSIVE IN PURSUIT

The Life of Justice Emmett Hall

Justice E.M. Hall. Courtesy of the Supreme Court of Canada, CSS 195–Hall.

1

From Saint-Columban to Saskatoon

Emmett Hall's great-grandfather, James Hall, came to Canada with an Ulster regiment to fight in the War of 1812.[1] When the regiment was disbanded after the war, those who wished to remain in Canada were given land upon which to settle. James's wife, Alice Donnelly, emigrated from County Tyrone, Ireland, to join her husband on a tract of land near the small village of Saint-Colomban – an Irish settlement – about twenty-five miles northwest of Montreal between Lachute and Saint-Jerome, where they made a living as dairy farmers. Alice was a devout Catholic, while James was an Ulster Presbyterian. Whether he became a Catholic is not known. What is known is that the children, including Emmett's grandfather, were brought up staunch Catholics with deep affection for all things Irish.

Emmett's father, also named James, was born in Saint-Colomban in 1866, one year before Confederation. In 1892 James married Alice O'Shea, the daughter of a neighbouring farmer. Her family had come out from Ireland during the great potato famine migrations of the mid-1840s and had been one of the earliest Irish settlers at Saint-Columban. Emmett Matthew was born – the fourth of eleven children – on 9 November 1898 at Saint-Columban.[2] He remembered his early childhood as happy and carefree. Looking back over many years to those early childhood days in Saint-Columban, Hall recalled them in idyllic terms, a time of running free and playing with his brothers and sisters and the children of neighbouring farms. His parents provided a home that was warm and loving and devoutly Catholic. Most of their social life revolved around the local parish church where his mother was active and the Hall sons served as altar boys.

Emmett's father was active in local politics, serving at one point as reeve and as a member of the school board for nearby Saint-Canut. Emmett retained a clear recollection of his father as a stocky, powerfully built man, just under six feet tall, quiet and pleasant, who took things in his stride. While outwardly he appeared to be a rustic farmer, his son claimed that he was 'quite a philosopher in his own way. Actually had he had an opportunity for an education, he might well have become one.' James Hall was an avid reader; he read widely but had a special interest in Irish history. There is good reason to believe that the fourth son was named after Robert Emmet, the Irish patriot, who was hanged in 1803 for his abortive attempt to throw off the English yoke. Emmet had made a stirring speech of defiance from the gallows and quickly became a great hero among the Irish. As a result of his father's reading, the third-generation Halls grew up steeped in the history of English mistreatment of the Irish, especially during the dreadful potato famine when almost a third of the population of Ireland died from starvation.[3]

Education was of utmost concern in the Hall household. Emmett's mother, Alice, was determined that her children – who by 1910 consisted of five girls and four boys – would get a good education. She oversaw the homework of her children and encouraged them to read and take their studies seriously. According to Emmett, his mother instilled an enthusiasm for learning by her persistent encouragement. He remembered her as a gentle but firm teacher at home; most evenings during the week were given over to homework, the older children taking turns teaching the younger ones. Mother was ever vigilant and supervised while tending to the needs of the pre-school children. Emmett's father, meanwhile, gave example by reading and relating what he read to his children. It was, Hall recalled many years later, 'a happy home.'

Since the Hall's dairy farm was on the outskirts of Saint-Columban, not far from the little French village of Saint-Canut, the children were sent there to the French-speaking school. They were the school's only English-speaking students. As a consequence, the Hall children learned French at an early age, a fact Emmett always recalled with pride. He used his French in public with ease and facility for the rest of his life.

In the early 1900s it became clear to James and Alice Hall that their

Quebec dairy farm was not sufficiently productive to support their large family. The prospects of their children having to work in the factories and breweries of Montreal horrified Alice. Ever fearful of her sons succumbing to the allure of the bottle, she was deeply against alcohol in all its forms – no son of hers was going to work in a brewery or in distant Montreal where God alone knew what could happen to them. James Hall was a temperate man who liked an occasional drink but Alice was against taking chances with her children. The Hall parents saw and feared the magnetic attraction that Montreal held out to many rural young men and women and they were determined to protect their children from those urban enticements.

Montreal at the turn of the twentieth century was a vortex of industrial activity. Major construction was taking place everywhere: bridges, canals, electric street railways, factories, and shipping provided plentiful work for both skilled and unskilled, all overseen by the English financiers of St James Street. Along with the construction came not only smoke and dirt but also the debauchery that was to taint the reputation of Montreal for many years. Civil corruption soon began to characterize Montreal to such an extent that, by 1898, the year of Emmett Hall's birth, 'a new cry for clean government, a movement ... to recast the whole city charter,' arose.[4] And for the next decade it continued to dominate the political conversation of the city. The demand for clean government led to a royal commission under Justice Lawrence John Cannon the year before the Halls headed west.[5] James and Alice Hall observed all this with a mixture of awe and horror and decided that they did not want to raise their family near an emerging metropolis literally bursting with industrial activity complete with bars, booze, and brothels.

The Halls wanted a rural environment for their family, one that would at the same time provide educational opportunities beyond the elementary for their children. And so they discussed privately the alternatives to remaining in Saint-Columban. James and Alice pored over the newspaper stories about the new province of Saskatchewan that was offering farming opportunities to Canadians and foreign immigrants. The *Family Herald* and the *Weekly Star*, the two major newspapers available in Saint-Columban, advertised for settlers and pictured Saskatoon as the western town with the most potential for growth; there was even a promise to establish a university. From all appearances, Saskatoon seemed ideally suited to the hopes and ambitions of the large Hall family. But there was one other factor that caught the attention of the abstemious Alice Hall: Saskatoon had been founded in 1883 in part by the Temperance Colonization Society of Toronto, which promised to keep the new city free of the evils of alcohol. What more could they ask for? How far from the soiled blandishments of Montreal could they hope to get?

Accordingly, in the fall of 1909, James Hall went west on a harvesters' excursion to reconnoiter the land. He looked around and liked what he saw. He bought a quarter-section of land about five miles from the centre of Saskatoon and a few building lots not far from the university planned for a site across the South Saskatchewan River. Acre-lots of land on the banks of the South Saskatchewan were selling for $500 in 1910.[6] So James Hall must have gone prepared to buy and with sufficient capital.

It came as no surprise to the children to learn one February morning in 1910 that their parents had decided to sell the family farm in Saint-Columban and move to a new city called Saskatoon, way out in Saskatchewan. The children had overheard the frequent conversations of their parents on the prospects of moving to the west; the older ones were even encouraged to take part in the discussions. But the decision to leave was not an easy one; the Halls had deep roots in Saint-Columban, with many relatives and friends in the area. Evidently, the people of Saint-Columban continued to remember fondly James and Alice Hall long after their departure, for, at a celebration in 1936 to mark the one hundred and fiftieth anniversary of the founding of the town, the Halls were brought from Saskatoon as guests of honour for the occasion. It was a recognition James and Alice Hall cherished to the end of their lives.

ARRIVAL AT SASKATOON

Emmett was eight months short of his twelfth birthday when, on 5 March 1910, the Canadian Pacific Railway (CPR) settlers' train – consisting of three coaches of people and ten boxcars of cattle and household furnishings – left Montreal's Bonaventure Station. The trip by train from Montreal, by way of Ottawa, over the Great Lakes to Winnipeg, and on to its destination, Saskatoon, took five days. The coal-fired locomotives were required to stop for long periods of time for refuelling and other supplies and the cattle had to be fed and watered. The Hall children were enthralled by the whole excursion; the excitement of travelling by train through long stretches of forest towards a new home in far-off Saskatchewan was too overpowering for the young settlers to feel any discomfort, although they were sad to leave behind their friends in Saint-Columban. For the parents, however, the trip was long and at times uncomfortable; nine children – ranging in ages from three to fifteen years – were not the most congenial travelling companions for adults, especially in crowded train quarters.

The trip through northern Ontario and the Manitoba plains was uneventful; snow, pine, fir, and cedar forests became monotonous for the parents and the long flat prairies held no immediate charm in the lingering winter; the charm would come later, after a few seasons in the west. When the settlers' train approached Saskatoon, the young family thought that they had arrived in a beautiful, virgin land. The spring of 1910 was one of the warmest the prairie provinces had experienced; it was as if the elements had conspired on behalf of the fledging province of Saskatchewan to conceal its long winter harshness, with the aim of seducing the new settlers into sinking roots as quickly and as painlessly as possible. Emmett Hall recalled years later how the sun shone magnificently out of an enormous blue sky and the land appeared to his weary but excited young eyes to have no horizons in any direction. The high banks of the southwest bank of the South Saskatchewan River displayed a vast fresh green carpet of early spring brush foliage. The official temperature reported in the Saskatoon *Daily Phoenix* for 10 March 1910 was 53 degrees, but, to the settlers disembarking after a long trip from Montreal, it felt much warmer than that. Emmett said that, to his young mind, 'the temperature on the platform of the CPR station in Saskatoon on that March day in 1910 was 80 degrees.' The *Daily Phoenix* for 10 March 1910 reported with excitement the arrival, on 9 and 10 March, of a group of two hundred settlers from Montreal. The Halls from Saint-Columban, Quebec, were, of course, among them.

By 1910, the city of Saskatoon comprised about 12,000 inhabitants. In September of that year, the Board of Trade's *Saskatoonlets* brochure unabashedly proclaimed, in a pitch to young men and women, that there were 'no Old Inhabitants to Hinder Progress.' Indeed, the board boasted that the town had prospered in the previous ten or twelve years beyond the wildest dreams of its earliest settlers. The brochure trumpeted with evident pride the physical assets of the young city in 1910:

Three Railway Stations.
Eleven Mails received each day by Post Office.
Highly Modern Sewer and Water Systems.

17.65 Miles of Sewers.
18.80 Miles of Water Mains.
The Latest and Best Fire Equipment Procurable.
Three Fire Halls.
Two Hundred Fire Hydrants.
Municipal Light and Power Plants.
9.75 Miles of Concrete Sidewalks.
8.20 Miles of Wooden Sidewalks.

'All this did Enterprise and Public Spirit accomplish,' the brochure proudly claimed, 'in but six short years.'

These were clearly optimistic times in Saskatoon. The *Daily Phoenix* ran a special industrial issue during the Halls' first winter in Saskatchewan. One article announced loftily how the historic process itself was working to the unquestionable advantage of Saskatoon. The article, entitled 'Saskatoon, the product of a World Movement of Population, the Centre of Inland Empire,' claimed that Saskatoon belonged to the great family of Western cities. 'It is in the class with Cincinnati, St. Louis, Chicago, St. Paul, Minneapolis, Winnipeg ... It has all the natural advantages to become the largest farmers' city in America.'[7] Needless to say, real estate speculators, mainly from the United States, descended upon Saskatoon and did their utmost to foment land speculation. Land prices on Second Avenue, for example, soared from $300 for a twenty-five foot lot in 1903 to $300 for a front foot in the spring of 1909; by 1910, the value had risen to $440 a front foot and, by the fall, speculators were asking (and getting) $550. By late 1912, the same lot was valued at $1,900.[8]

Important public men vied with one another in predicting the future population of Saskatoon and Saskatchewan throughout those early years. Charles Powell of the Toronto Colonization Society, for example, predicted in 1911 that Saskatoon would have 100,000 citizens by 1917.[9] The Church Union Committee of Saskatoon was more modest, foreseeing 65,000 people by 1921.[10] President Walter Charles Murray of the new University of Saskatchewan, not to be outdone, was confident that the population of Saskatchewan would reach two million by 1931, at which time the University of Saskatchewan would rival the University of Toronto.[11] As it turned out, Saskatoon did not reach the 65,000-mark until 1955. But by then the real estate speculators had made their money and left Saskatoon.

Fatigued after the long train trip but excited about his new home town, James Hall gathered together his large family and they all walked with as much luggage as they could carry through the mud streets of the new city to a house on 28th Street West, about three blocks from the CPR train station. James had made arrangements to lodge his family there for a few months until the family house was built across the river near the site of the planned university. Emmett's father, although not a carpenter by trade, was skilled in the use of tools and soon had more work than he could handle. Though he longed to return to farming, he soon discovered that farming on the prairies was a far different thing from mixed farming in Quebec. In the west one went into either cattle farming or grain farming. Whichever one chose, it had to be in a big way, otherwise it would not pay; grain farmers tilled and sowed huge sections of land in order to make a living. And cattle farming likewise required large tracts of land upon which to graze large herds. Back in Saint-Columban, James Hall had worked a small mixed farm and he could feed his family on its produce. But that was in Quebec; out in Saskatchewan, things were different. For a time, Emmett's father tried to keep a small farm – the property he had purchased when out west for the harvest – and, as the same time, work as a supplier of sand and gravel for the construction of the new university. After assessing the scene and reluctantly coming to the conclusion that he was unsuited to prairie farming, James Hall went to work with the Canadian Northern Railway and stayed with the company the remainder of his working life. He retired in 1935. Although the Halls had the money from the sale of their farm in Quebec, they were far from rich. Indeed, for the first few years in their new home, the Halls lived in a 'genteel poverty,' as Emmett was later to describe conditions. But he never had the feeling of being destitute; he was no different than the other kids at school. He certainly remembered being warmly dressed and well fed; his determined mother saw to that.

One of the first surprises – shocks, one might say – the new arrivals experienced was the quality of elementary school education in the young city. The Halls quickly became conscious of a prejudice against anyone educated in Quebec. Most people they encountered thought that education in Quebec was backward and that the Hall children would be at a disadvantage in the schools of Saskatchewan. Emmett had five and a half years of school to his credit. But, since the Saskatoon school authorities were reluctant to concede that he and his brothers and sisters had learned much in Quebec, they decided that, despite his age, he should start in grade three. Hall recalled this affront with a chuckle many years later: 'That was the cockeyed idea they had in the west of how backward things were if you came from Quebec.' They all enrolled in the fall of 1910 in King Edward School, which has since been demolished to make way for the new Saskatoon city hall. It soon became apparent to their teachers that the new settlers from Quebec were far ahead of their younger classmates and indeed of many in senior grades; as a result, Emmett and John, his elder brother, vaulted into grade seven the next year. When his classmates discovered Emmett's fluency in French, they quickly dubbed him 'Frenchy.'

Emmett was a tall youth but never robust as a child. Since he was a keen student who had acquired his mother's passion for education, he did well in school. He was raised a devout Irish Catholic with the firm conviction that he should never fail to wear his faith in public. He made no effort to disguise his religious convictions either as a youth or later as a practising lawyer or as a judge. His early home life was centred to an important extent on activities at St Paul's Cathedral and St Joseph's Church. The family joined St Paul's parish immediately upon arrival in 1910, and his mother became an active member of the Ladies Aid and the Altar Society, as well as, in later years, the Catholic Women's League. The Hall children were brought up as strict and proud Irish Catholics prepared to take on all comers, secular and religious. Perhaps it is here that the seeds of Emmett's later aggressive manner were sown.

After completing elementary school, Hall enrolled in the Saskatoon Collegiate Institute and graduated in July 1916, at the age of seventeen. He decided to teach school during the summer of 1916 and, since he spoke French, he secured a teaching position in Boutin, in the Shell River District, northeast of Prince Albert. He had forty-five students from grade one to grade eight; he taught a half-day in French and a half-day in English. In those days it was lawful to teach in French in the public schools of Saskatchewan. Emmett Hall unwittingly found himself, however, in the midst of a furore over religion and language as soon as he first stepped into the classroom.

From the earliest days, the history of western Canada was embroiled in sectarian discord; the Anglo-Protestants of eastern Canada were hell-bent on ensuring that Catholic – and hence Quebec – influence not be extended into the new territories of the west. Naturally, the focal points were language and religion in the classrooms. Owing to the considerable influence of Bishop Alexandre-Antonin Taché, next door in Manitoba, the act creating Manitoba as a province in 1871 contained in section 22 the educational safeguards of section 93 of the British North

America Act, 1867. For almost twenty years, Manitoba enjoyed a dual system of public schools, Catholic and Protestant. But in 1890 the legislature abolished the old order and substituted a uniform system of public non-sectarian education.[12]

The dispute over Catholic education throughout the North-West Territories began as early as 1897 when Frederick Haultain, the first premier of the territories, had made the educational system almost exclusively English-speaking and Protestant. He was adamant that what had happened in Manitoba would not happen in the new provinces then emerging out of the territories. When the Laurier government passed the autonomy bill, in 1905, creating two provinces, Alberta and Saskatchewan, out of the North-West Territories, it annoyed leading Conservatives such as Haultain, who refused to become premier of either of the new provinces. Haultain wanted one province, not two. Rather than become premier, Haultain chose instead to become leader of the Saskatchewan Conservative Party, which he promptly renamed the Provincial Rights Party. He led the party into the election of 1905 on a platform opposing those provisions of the Alberta and Saskatchewan acts which denied the new provinces complete control over educational matters while providing at the same time constitutional guarantees to minority groups – including Catholics – that they would be able to establish their own schools.

Throughout the first provincial election in 1905, Catholics pressured Haultain to acknowledge their right to educate their children in publicly funded Catholic schools. Haultain waffled on the hustings, conceding only that he did not wish to abolish the separate schools which had been established in the French communities in the territories. He insisted, however, that the government have absolute control over its educational system. The matter quickly became bitterly partisan when Haultain publicly accused the Catholics of Saskatchewan of conspiring with the Liberals. He turned his guns on the Liberals with the assertion that they were attempting 'to barter the educational freedom of this Province for temporary political advantage.'[13] Despite Haultain's best efforts, the Liberal Party won seventeen and the Provincial Rights Party won only eight of the twenty-five seats in the new legislature. But, as Patrick Kyba has written, 'the issue of separate schools and their role and place in Saskatchewan society would remain to simmer beneath the surface of provincial politics until it erupted into a full-blown explosion of sectarian animosity two decades later.'[14] Haultain left politics in 1912 to become the first chief justice of Saskatchewan. He was succeeded to the leadership of the Saskatchewan Provincial Rights Party (which had returned to the old name of the Conservative Party in 1911) by Wellington B. Willoughby, who pursued Haultain's political agenda.

While these events were unfolding in Saskatchewan, Dalton McCarthy, an Orange bigot, spoke up and down the province of Ontario preaching the danger of French expansion and Catholic domination. He travelled west to Manitoba and discovered to his horror that in that province and in the new provinces of Alberta and Saskatchewan the French language was an official language in governments, courts, and schools.[15] From that moment on, the issue of French instruction in the schools of Saskatchewan became a bone of contention; indeed, the Orange Lodge made sure that language and religion remained at the centre well into the 1900s. One year after Emmett Hall's stint as a teacher, the Saskatchewan legislature passed legislation making English the only language of instruction in the schools, with no place whatsoever for either French on German (the German language was perceived as a greater threat than French to the dominant Anglo-Protestant community in Saskatchewan because of the large German-speaking population and the First World War with Germany). But Saskatchewan Catholics, especially in the predominantly French communities, were determined to teach their children their ancestral faith and language. Not surprisingly, Hall's sympathies were clearly with his Catholic faith and with the French population of Saskatchewan.

Emmett enjoyed immensely his brief teaching experience but he had other ambitions. He had often thought of becoming a lawyer throughout his last years in high school and, by the time he graduated in 1916, the idea had become a firm decision. As an aspiring lawyer, Hall was required to apprentice with an established firm where he performed all manner of minor legal tasks. In addition, he was obliged to attend classes at the new law school at the university before and after work at the law office. He was accepted as a student-at-law with the Saskatoon firm of Murray and Munro in the fall of 1916. One of the first things he did upon joining the firm was cash the post-dated cheque he had received for teaching that summer in Boutin. Rather than do so at a bank, Emmett decided to cash it through the firm's accountant. This turned out to be a wise decision because the cheque was not honoured by the bank. When the embarrassed Hall raised the issue with George Murray, the latter generously said that he would carry the cheque until the Boutin school district paid it. The school board honoured the cheque in due course, much to Hall's relief.

Hall's work for the Murray and Munro firm involved searching titles and learning how to prepare motions for court under the direction of George Murray. He later recalled that there was no task too menial for him. Murray made it clear that the newest addition to the firm was beginning at the lowest level of the practice of law and he was expected to learn the basics from the ground up. George Murray was a demanding tutor but he took a personal interest in his students and had a serious view of his responsibilities. Hall not only learned much about the law from Murray but he also borrowed his tutor's exacting manner. Those who later articled with him when he was established in his own practice testify that Hall was a 'demanding teacher.'[16] He maintained throughout his life that the training he received under George Murray not only provided him with a solid foundation in the minutiae of legal practice but also gave him a certain sense of 'what to look for' when handling cases. This sense was the one thing he often said an aspiring lawyer could not get from sitting in a classroom. And he remained permanently indebted to George Murray for taking him under his wing and guiding him. Murray, a Scottish solicitor, was a specialist in mortgage work, particularly for the Great West Life company. As a result, Hall became almost totally occupied in searching land titles during his time in Murray's office. The large emigration into the Canadian west during the early decades of the twentieth century generated a great deal of legal work in securing clear title to land.

Hall never got to know Munro because he was in France with the Canadian army and was killed in action a few months after Hall had joined the firm. With the addition of a Scottish lawyer by the name of Morrison, the firm became known for a time as Murray, Munro and Morrison. In actual practice, Murray and Munro was a branch office of the prestigious Winnipeg law firm of Munson, Allan, Laird and Davis.

After one year's articling with Murray and Munro, Hall decided that he should follow the course of many of his friends and volunteer for service in the Princess Patricia's Canadian Light Infantry. To his disappointment, he was rejected for military service when the medical examination discovered that he had full vision in one eye only. Emmett had always been aware of his defective vision, which must have been acquired in infancy because he had no recollection of ever injuring his eye or suddenly experiencing a loss of vision. In later life, he recalled how fortunate he was to be rejected by the army in 1917 because most of those young men from Saskatoon who had enlisted were killed in action.

Disappointed at the time that he could not follow his brothers and friends overseas, Emmett returned to Murray and Munro with the determination to excel as a lawyer. By arrangement with Murray, Hall was transferred to the Bence, Stevenson and McLorg firm. Three or four older students in that firm had been accepted for military service, leaving Hall as one of the few law students in town. This was a felicitous move for he became involved almost immediately in litigation, an aspect of law he soon grew to love. He worked closely day after day with A.E. Bence, senior partner in the firm and one of the leading counsel in Saskatchewan. Hall found Bence a severe teacher who worked him long, hard hours, but he learned a great deal about how to prepare a sound case for court.

The dominant figures on the College of Law faculty during Hall's tenure there were Dean Arthur Moxon, who had come to the university from Dalhousie University in Halifax as a professor of classics, Professor Ira McKay, and sessional lecturer J.W. Estey, who later became a justice of the Supreme Court of Canada. Classes were scheduled from 8 A.M. to 9 or 9:30 A.M. and resumed again at 5 P.M. Ira McKay was an especially good teacher who inspired his students to pursue justice as an ideal. He would frequently lecture from five o'clock in the evening through to eight without a break and without losing a single member of the class. He eventually left Saskatoon for McGill where he became dean of arts. The remainder of the day was spent in the law office of Murray and Munro and later, Bence, Stevenson and McLorg.

Students-at-law were not required to article during the summer months and Hall had the good fortune to secure a job with a federal government survey team. He had seen a notice at the university that the government was looking for summer survey workers. He applied and was accepted. The survey team's task was to locate and map all small bodies of water in central-northern Saskatchewan; the larger lakes had long before been mapped. The only appropriate means of transportation in those days was a horse, so he rode the township lines and section lines of northern Saskatchewan from May to the end of October on horseback. When he recalled that summer job years later, he would chuckle about how inept he was at first in handling the horse. 'I grew up on a small mixed farm as a boy in Quebec,' he would say, 'but didn't do much horseback riding.' He loved the idea of riding on warm summer days in search of small bodies of water, however, and in time he did learn how to ride.

He was a month late getting back to classes, much to the annoyance of the law school's administrators. But Hall was making money – $80 per month plus room and board – and aimed at returning with a nest egg. When he finally returned to classes, he had saved more than $400 – a princely sum for a student in 1917. This achievement demonstrated the kind of financial prudence that was to characterize him for the rest of his life. He had grown up in genteel poverty and intended never to return to it. He took a liking to money and began to accumulate it from the moment he entered his law practice.

The Hall family grieved sorely upon hearing the news that the eldest son, John, had died in the summer of 1918 on board ship en route home from the trenches of France. Emmett Hall recalled being told that his brother had died of an 'infection' but it is likely that he was a victim of influenza. For the fall of 1918 was the time when the infamous 'Spanish' influenza pandemic claimed the lives of thousands of returning soldiers. This strange bug swept throughout the world, killing more than forty million people, mainly healthy young men between the ages of twenty-one and thirty.[17] Many who had survived the fetid trenches of France and the ferocious battles of Mons, Ypres, Passchendaele, and Vimy Ridge died of the virus upon arrival home; those who did not fall victim spread the disease throughout the civilian population. In Saskatchewan alone, almost two hundred people died from this virus. The entire University of Saskatchewan was closed for several weeks in the fall of 1918 because of the flu; students were quarantined in residence and classes were cancelled. Emmett Hall was laid low with the disease and remained in bed throughout Armistice Day in November 1918; he was one of the fortunate ones and survived a disease that killed more people than were lost in the two world wars, the Korean War and the VietNam War combined. It was a scourge greater than the AIDS pandemic and it disappeared as mysteriously as it appeared. To this day virologists and other medical scientists do not know where the virus came from or whether it could strike again.[18]

When Emmett recovered from the flu, he returned to the university and helped stage a debate between the College of Arts and Science and the College of Law. The debate was held on 15 February 1919. The resolution was: 'Resolved that the complete nationalization of Canadian Railways is in the best interest of the country.' The affirmative was supported by a Mr Neeley and a Miss Sinton, representing the College of Arts and Science. John Diefenbaker and Emmett Hall were assigned to uphold the negative side for the College of Law. The combined talents of Diefenbaker and Hall were not sufficient, however, to win the debate on this occasion. In those days in Saskatchewan, when trains played a critical role in the life of the emerging agricultural community, there was a strong sentiment in favour of nationalization of railways. Out of this early association with Diefenbaker in law school emerged a relationship of mutual trust and respect that was to last almost a lifetime. Their wives, Edna Diefenbaker and Belle Hall, became friends as well. Over the years the two couples occasionally vacationed together.

Emmett Hall was the youngest among the law graduates – being not yet twenty-one – and was known as the 'boy graduate in law.' The biographical sketch in The Sheaf, under a picture of the young graduate on the page opposite a picture of Diefenbaker, contains the following observation on Hall: 'A "prince of good-fellows" and a terror to Freshmen, he has played a big part in his Year. His executive ability has been felt in many spheres of student activity – in the Law Students' Association, the Debating Society, and the SRC [the student common room], in which his works, nefarious and otherwise, will not soon be forgotten.'[19] One gets a clear picture of a determined undergraduate prankster whose good side freshmen were wise to cultivate. The biographical note ends with two observations: 'Pet Aversion: Lectures at 8:30 A.M. Favorite Occupation: Conspiring and planning for banquets at others' expense.' Despite, or perhaps because of, these character traits, Hall's college biographer wrote that 'when one possesses such ability as he does, no heights are insurmountable – in short, his future is assured.' Of John Diefenbaker, the class biographer wrote, after listing his extracurricular activities, that 'he has occupied a place which will be difficult to fill, and hereafter all transgressors of the Students' Code will breathe more freely when he relinquishes his position as custodian of justice.' But Diefenbaker would never relinquish that position. He always saw himself as the 'custodian of justice.' And it was he, as prime minister of Canada, who gave the country the Canadian Bill of Rights in 1960. The Sheaf recounts the results of a moot-trial in which Diefenbaker and Hall acted for the plaintiffs. The issue was the liability of trade unions for damages resulting through third parties losing profits to which they otherwise would have been entitled, had there been no strike. 'Professor Estey, who acted as judge, gave judgment in favor of the plaintiffs with costs.'[20] This was the first success at litigation the young classmates were to experience. 'Judge' J.W. Estey, incidentally, succeeded Justice John Henderson Lamont on the Supreme Court of Canada in 1944, becoming the second Saskatchewan lawyer to do so. Little could anyone know, on this occasion, that Emmett Hall would become the third Saskatchewan lawyer to sit on the highest court.

After graduation, the aspiring lawyer was required to write the bar-admission examinations. In Hall's time, students were required to write five examinations every year for three years while articling. The topics covered were similar to those found today in all law schools – civil and criminal procedure, property law, torts, tax law, constitutional law, and so forth. It was a tough regimen, perhaps even tougher than the process today. The examinations were prepared at Wetmore Hall in Regina under the direction of the benchers of the Law Society of Saskatchewan; the examination papers were sent to the University of Saskatchewan College of Law where the students were required to write them under an appointed supervisor. The examiner during Hall's three years was the Reverend Canon Smith, rector of the Anglican Cathedral of St John's on Spadina Crescent in Saskatoon. Hall recalled that Canon Smith would hand out the papers and say, 'Boys, you're on your honour,' and go about his business of reading and writing. At the end of the examination he would collect the papers and send them to Regina to be corrected by examiners at Wetmore Hall appointed by the Saskatchewan Law Society.

Following graduation from law school in 1919, Hall was offered and accepted a position with Bence, Stevenson and McLorg. By now, with the First World War over, efforts were being made to aid the men returning from active duty. The Federal Parliament passed the Soldier Settlement Act in 1917[21] for the purpose of assisting soldiers who wished to settle on the land as farmers. They received loans for the purchase of land, stock, and equipment. The loans varied in amount but rarely exceeded $5,000; they were made without interest for the first three years and at a rate of 5 per cent thereafter. From its inception, the Soldier Settlement Board was administered by the minister of the interior, James A. Lougheed of Alberta.

Under the terms of the act, Saskatchewan was divided into two districts: Prince Albert district, under the administration of W.S. Woods, and the Regina district, administered by M.A. Wood.[22] By the end of 1921, 4,927 men had accepted the opportunity to farm the land in Saskatchewan under the terms of the act. The board disbursed a total of $19,425,234 in Saskatchewan between 1919 and 1921. This amount constituted 24 per cent of the entire $80 million set aside throughout Canada for that period under the scheme.

Since McLorg was a veteran, he became the solicitor for the Soldier

Settlement Board of Saskatchewan. Bence, Stevenson and McLorg had plenty of work and Hall became involved in searching titles and calculating loans under the Soldier Settlement program. A branch was opened in the office just for Soldier Settlement work and Hall was given almost total responsibility for that part of the firm's business; it was an enormous task for the young, new, and not fully fledged lawyer. Frank McLorg was supposed to have directed the project as of 1 May 1919, but he wanted to marry a girl he had met while serving in England. After a brief meeting with Hall where he outlined how he expected Hall to do the job, McLorg left for London that summer. The parents of McLorg's fiancé objected to their daughter marrying him and following him back to the Canadian west. After several months of negotiations with his bride's parents and the repeated pleadings of their daughter, Frank McLorg was married in England in late August 1919. 'With poor Frank distracted by all this,' Hall recalled years later, 'I was left in charge of the Soldier Settlement work for four months, having a hell of a time.'

The original Soldier Settlement Act of 1917 applied only to Canadian ex-servicemen.[23] In 1919 the act was amended to allow soldiers from other parts of the British empire to take advantage of loans if the board judged them fit for farming in Canada. Hall's job was to disburse the money once the ex-soldier provided the appropriate documents of entitlement. In addition to disbursing several million dollars, he had to make sure that the title to the land was clear and the new owner duly registered. The average legal fee per loan was $20.58.[24]

It soon became apparent to other lawyers in Saskatchewan that the Bence firm had a hold on a lucrative monopoly, and they were not about to sit back and watch from the sidelines. Solicitors in and around Prince Albert, North Battleford, and Humboldt raised a rumpus and protested to members of Parliament that the monopoly was unfair, and the disbursement of public funds of such a magnitude should be spread around. Ex-servicemen who were returning to practice after an absence of several years took special umbrage. Hall acknowledged in later years that the monopoly of work on the Soldier Settlement scheme was, indeed, unfair. He always felt uncomfortable reaping the benefits of the windfall because of not having served overseas as so many of his contemporaries had. In early September 1919 the work was divided into several districts. A lawyer ex-serviceman, E.S. Wilson, set up his office in Humboldt and was chosen to handle the Soldier Settlement work in the Humboldt district; he came to Saskatoon to recruit assistance. Since Hall had, by all standards, more experience than anyone else, Wilson persuaded him to come with him to Humboldt. Hall found the newly established but mainly German-speaking community – northeast of Saskatoon – to his liking. The German residents of the area were devout Catholics who had brought with them a group of Benedictine monks from the American mid-west, and these monks quickly established a monastery which became the focus of the community's spiritual life. Also to his liking was the fact that there was a strong Liberal presence in Humboldt. The young lawyer enjoyed talking politics with his friends, one of whom was John Diefenbaker, who at this time was practising in Wakaw, not far from Humboldt. Hall's family political loyalties prompted him to gravitate towards the Liberal Party and he soon began to take part in the politics of the town. In 1921 he nominated John Angus MacMillan, a Wadena lawyer, for the federal Liberal nomination. MacMillan, a transplanted Nova Scotian, had served as mayor of Wadena in 1917 but vacated the office that year to assume a seat in the provincial legislature for Wadena. He lost his first bid for Parliament in 1921 but ran on two subsequent occasions until he was finally elected, in a by-election, in 1933.

During this period in Humboldt, Hall also struck up a friendship with Dr Harry Fleming, another active Liberal Party supporter. Fleming was a prominent member of the Humboldt Catholic community and became a good friend to Emmett. Though only four years Hall's senior, Fleming was to act as a mentor to the new lawyer. Fleming was himself elected to Parliament as a Liberal in the election of 1935. He was re-elected in 1940 but died two years later, on 5 November 1942, by which time Hall had settled into a practice in Saskatoon.[25] What the Bence firm thought of Wilson absconding with the young lawyer is not known. Hall never revealed what the reaction was when he told McLorg of his intention to follow Wilson to Humboldt. Clearly, Wilson must have made the move financially irresistible. Money always figured prominently in Hall's calculations and measure of success.

Emmett Hall left the Wilson firm in 1921 to join J. Harvey Hearn in Wadena. Whatever prompted him to move, once again, is not known. He claimed years later that there was 'no particular reason for the move.'[26] But, regardless of the reason, the move was especially fortuitous for it brought him in contact with the firm's legal secretary, Isabel Mary Parker of Humboldt. After a brief courtship, Emmett and Belle were married in a small ceremony in Saskatoon on 26 June 1922, two months after he had been admitted to the bar at the age of twenty-two. Isabel Parker had been born in Sydney, Nova Scotia, of Newfoundland parents who came west the same year as the Halls left Quebec. She was a petite and beautiful woman with a keen intelligence and sense of humour. And she also had a great deal of style; she dressed impeccably and never appeared in public without being properly attired for the occasion. All who knew her over the years of their long and happy marriage attest that she had a spine of steel, and a tongue that could cut through cant and humbug like a razor. She called Emmett to order whenever he wandered into indiscretion in conversation with other people, 'Emmett!' she would say sternly bringing him to heel. She could also cut a strip off formidable men, such as John Diefenbaker. When Diefenbaker remarried after the death of his first wife, one of Belle's closest friends, she never forgave the dismissive way Diefenbaker treated her memory. She would bristle with resentment whenever the subject came up. On those occasions it was Emmett who would try to calm her down with a gentle, 'Now, Belle.' With that, the subject was changed. But the look on Belle's face made it clear that the resentment towards Diefenbaker on this matter, at least, was deep. According to her son, John, who became a distinguished orthopaedic surgeon at the Hospital for Sick Children in Toronto and later a professor of orthopaedics at Harvard Medical School, 'Mom was the disciplinarian in the family.'[27]

Hall remained with the Hearn firm until January 1923, when he opened his own firm in Humboldt. But, as he soon discovered, Humboldt's population of approximately 2,000 people offered little opportunity of a law career. So the young couple returned to Wadena where, in 1924, Emmett purchased the Hearn firm. Harvey Hearn sold the firm to Hall in order to relocate to Saskatoon. How Hall could afford to purchase the Hearn firm is a mystery; he certainly could not have had much money so early in his career. From subsequent events, however, it can be assumed that Hearn provided the newly fledged lawyer with a generous mortgage or a flexible payment schedule. Hall settled down to practise in Wadena for two years and then went to Prince Albert for another year in an effort to make a living. What Belle, by this time with one child, thought of these moves, is not known; she never commented on the early years of her married life. But it must have been a time of great anxiety. Five years of wandering back and forth from town to town – Saskatoon to Humboldt to Wadena back to Humboldt to Wadena to Prince Albert – testify how difficult it must have been for a young lawyer to establish a practice in rural Saskatchewan those years.

As fate would have it, Harvey Hearn once again called on Emmett Hall to join him in his practice, this time in Saskatoon as a partner. Hall could not resist the opportunity; he had had enough of wandering 'in the wilderness,' as he later put it. And, besides, the prospect of practising in Saskatoon was too good to pass up. One can only speculate at the jubilation that Belle must have experienced upon hearing of Hearn's offer. Emmett accepted the invitation and immediately set off, in 1927, with Belle and their son, John, for Saskatoon. Saskatoon was to remain home for the Halls until his appointment to the Saskatchewan Court of Queen's Bench in 1957. Actually, Saskatoon would always remain 'home' for he and Belle would return to Saskatoon upon his retiring from the Supreme Court of Canada in 1973.

Since a great portion of Hearn's practice involved the United Farmers of Canada, it is not surprising that he would want someone with Hall's past experience with the Soldier Settlement Board to join him in practice. The United Farmers had been established a year before Emmett joined the Hearn firm and quickly became an important force in the west. But the organization wanted strong legal assistance to push its grievances, especially against the CPR, which, it insisted, was gouging farmers with high freight rates. Hall's Settlement Board experience had put him in touch with a large number of farmers throughout Saskatchewan and he was familiar with their problems. To Hearn, Hall must have been the perfect man for the job. But there were likely other motives in play that prompted Hearn to seek out Hall to join him in his Saskatoon practice, for, a short two years after he became familiar with the work of the firm, Harvey Hearn abruptly quit the practice of law and left to live permanently in California. Obviously, he must have discussed the matter with his young associate, but is it too much to assume that Hearn had planned all along to pass his major client safely into the hands of Emmett Hall and then quietly leave town? It is difficult to believe that Hearn could have made such an important decision without having thought about it for a long time. Be this as it may, Hall quickly established a solid and lucrative practice upon the foundations laid by Harvey Hearn.

2

At the Bar of Saskatchewan

Emmett Hall settled into his practice in Saskatoon in 1927 and was to remain there until 1957, when he was appointed chief justice of the Saskatchewan Court of Queen's Bench, a promotion that required him to move to Regina. A few short months after joining the Hearn firm, Hall took on a case that would lead to his first appearance before the Supreme Court of Canada. The case was *Schofield v. Glenn and Babb*[1] and it involved the long-festering dispute between ranchers and grain growers that dominated a good part of rural life in Saskatchewan in the early 1920s. The ranchers wanted to ensure that Saskatchewan developed a large livestock industry, that of neighbouring Alberta, and this necessitated, in their minds, an 'open range' policy for the grazing of their large beef herds. Grain farmers, on the other hand, wanted to see the land made safe for large-scale wheat production. The cattle farmers had sufficient influence in the Saskatchewan legislature that they were able to secure the passage of two acts which placed the onus on grain farmers to ensure that cattle roaming free upon the range did not fall victim to various farm hazards, such as by eating too much grain or by falling into wells. The first act, the Act Respecting Open Wells and Other Things Dangerous to Stock,[2] was passed in 1920 and stipulated that 'no person shall have or store on his premises ... any kind of threshed grain accessible to stock or any other person which may come or stray upon such premises when lawfully running at large.' The second act, Stray Animals Act,[3] specified that wells and excavations must be protected by fences of precise dimensions in order to ensure that cattle or horses did not injure themselves while grazing on the open range.

Three days after Christmas, 1925, five horses belonging to Charles J. Schofield strayed onto the grain farm owned by Edgar E. Babb and leased by Robert J. Glenn in Swift Current. On the property was a wooden granary in which 245 bushels of wheat were stored. The horses kicked a hole in the granary and ate a large quantity of wheat. The result was that one of the horses died and the four others 'were damaged.' Schofield sought compensation in court, claiming that the Open Wells Act made Babb and Glenn responsible for the loss of the one horse and for the injuries sustained by the other four. The case was tried by a jury in the fall of 1926 before Chief Justice G.J. Brown of the Saskatchewan Court of King's Bench. After hearing arguments for both sides, Chief Justice Brown instructed the jury that it need only find that Babb and Glenn had kept the granary in reasonable condition and that there was no negligence on their part. Babb and Glenn had introduced evidence that the granary had been carefully inspected and repaired before being filled with grain the previous summer. The jury deliberated for an hour and returned with the verdict that Babb and Glenn had met the requirements of the Open Wells Act and hence were not responsible for the injuries to the horses.

Schofield and the Saskatchewan Ranchers' Association were not satisfied with the trial verdict and accordingly instructed their lawyers to appeal the decision to the Saskatchewan Court of Appeal. The case came before the Court of Appeal on 15 March 1927.[4] The court at that time consisted of Chief Justice Sir Frederick Haultain and four associate justices, one of whom was Justice John Henderson Lamont, who was to be elevated to the Supreme Court of Canada a year later. The court issued a judgment on 31 March 1927 reversing the trial verdict. This judgment was written by Justice Lamont, who ruled that the trial judge had erred when he instructed the jury that it was sufficient to decide whether Babb and Glenn had taken reasonable care. 'The Section [4 of the Open Wells Act] does not say anything about reasonable fitness of the granary, but it does say that the grain must not be accessible to stock.'[5] Since Babb and Glenn had grain on their property and it was accessible to stock, they had a strict liability under the act and were responsible for the injuries sustained by the animals. Lamont concluded that the clear and explicit meaning of the act must be given effect 'no matter how hard or arbitrary the enactment may appear to be.'[6] As the Saskatoon *Star* reported, 'the effect of this [decision] was that every farmer in the province who kept grain over the winter and any municipality where stock was permitted to run at large, became an insurer of such stock. This was considered a serious situation by the United Farmers of Canada, Saskatchewan section. It meant that a man held his grain at his peril.'[7]

Babb and Glenn instructed their lawyer, P.H. Gordon, to appeal the decision to the Supreme Court of Canada. If the Court of Appeal judgment were permitted to stand, it meant that grain farmers in Saskatchewan would be placed in an almost impossible position. How could a wheat farmer possibly ensure against livestock kicking holes in their granaries and gaining access to stores of wheat? The Court of Appeal judgment extended the grain farmer's responsibility beyond reasonable care to strict liability. The grain farmers rallied behind Babb and Glenn and hired Emmett Hall, then aged twenty-nine, to represent their case in the Supreme Court of Canada. He was chosen because he was well known to them through his work for the United Farmers. Hall was clearly excited about the prospects of representing prairie grain growers before the highest court in the land. He prepared himself by studying with great care the trial and appeal court judgments. By early February 1928, he was ready to present his case to the justices of the Supreme Court of Canada. He was confident that he could persuade the Court to reverse the judgment of the Court of Appeal and restore the verdict of the jury trial.

He left Saskatoon by train on 12 February 1928 and arrived in Ottawa two days later on the 14th. As it happened, he travelled to Ottawa on the same train as Schofield's counsel, C.E. Gregory, a prominent Regina lawyer. Gregory spent the trip informing the young lawyer from Saskatoon that he was wasting his time going before the Supreme Court because Justice Lamont, the author of the Saskatchewan Court of Appeal judgment, had just been appointed to the Court and that the Court would not, out of courtesy, reverse on the very first occasion a lower court judgment of a new colleague. Those words of advice made no impression on the young lawyer. He checked into the Chateau Laurier Hotel upon arrival in Ottawa and prepared himself mentally for his first appearance before Canada's highest court. He recalled years later that Gregory's gratuitous warnings only stirred his bile and made him spend the better part of the night before his court appearance steeling himself for the challenge.

Emmett Hall arrived early the next morning at the Supreme Court building, which in 1928 was situated on the west driveway to the Parliament Buildings, just off Wellington Street at the head of Bank Street. The building had been a stable years before and was converted hastily into the quarters for the new Supreme Court of Canada after 1875 when the Court was established by an act of Parliament.[8] That act had not provided for the construction of a building for the Court or, indeed, facilities of any sort. Until Parliament designated the abandoned stone stable at the head of Bank Street, the Court had to make do with the use of the Railway Committee Room of the House of Commons in the main Parliament Buildings. The converted stable itself was barely adequate as the Court's first home: the roof leaked and the library had only a few books, mostly cast-offs from local firms – during the first years of its existence, the Court's first registrar, Robert Cassels, went begging for books, especially British and Commonwealth law reports. Nevertheless, the Court remained in the renovated stable for sixty years (the building was demolished in 1952 and the site is now a Parliament Hill parking lot). It might be argued that the dilapidated facilities reflected the respect with which the government and the public at large accorded the Supreme Court in those days. After all, how could the Court be said to be *supreme* when its decisions could be overturned by the Judicial Committee of the Privy Council, which sat in London and was composed of British law lords? Indeed, many litigants in important cases bypassed the Supreme Court of Canada and appealed directly to the Judicial Committee from a provincial court of appeal. Not until 1946 did the Court move to its permanent quarters farther down Wellington Street on a promontory overlooking the Ottawa River.[9] And it was not until three years later, in 1949, that the Parliament of Canada abolished appeals to the Judicial Committee.

When Emmett Hall appeared before the Supreme Court in February 1928, the Court consisted of Chief Justice F.A. Anglin and six puisne judges: Justice Lyman Poore Duff, who was later to become chief justice and one of the greatest Canadian jurists, Justice Pierre B. Mignault, Justice E.L. Newcombe, Justice Robert Smith, Justice Thibaudeau Rinfret, and Justice John H. Lamont. Since the *Babb and Glenn* appeal was from a Saskatchewan judgment of Justice Lamont's, he was prevented from sitting on the appeal.

Hall robed in the barristers' lounge and took his place in the Court armed with his notes and several volumes of Saskatchewan reports and statutes which he would need for his oral presentation. When the Court opened, the chief justice greeted the young lawyer and invited him to come up in front of the bar, a position usually reserved for those lawyers who had been appointed as King's (or Queen's) Counsel. Schofield's lawyer, C.E. Gregory, was a King's Counsel, and therefore properly within the inner bar. Hall was being accorded a courtesy.

Hall began by stressing that the Open Wells Act and the Stray Animals Act placed clear responsibility on the grain farmers to ensure against cattle injuring themselves on their land. But, he suggested, the acts should be construed as to impose *reasonable* responsibility and the defendants, Babb and Glenn, had taken reasonable care to comply with the provisions of the acts. He emphasized that it was a 'standard of care' issue, that Babb and Glenn had acted responsibly in the steps they took to ensure that the granary was soundly constructed and in a condition of good repair. He drew heavily upon the trial level instructions to the jury by Chief Justice Brown of the Saskatchewan Court of King's Bench and argued that these instructions were a correct construction of the intention of the Open Wells Act. As one might expect, the young lawyer was a little nervous; however, he was enormously pleased by the approach of the Court – no one badgered him, nor was he hurried in any way. Much to his surprise, he enjoyed this first appearance before the Supreme Court of Canada. At the conclusion of his presentation, he felt satisfied; he thought that he had done well, although, of course, he could not be certain how the Court had received his arguments.

Gregory, for his part, argued that the judgment of Justice Lamont in the Saskatchewan Court of Appeal should stand. He insisted, as had Lamont, that the act did not present the implied escape of 'reasonable care.' As Hall expected, Gregory played to the fact that Lamont, a new appointment on the Supreme Court bench, deserved the courtesy of his colleagues' support on the first appeal of one his earlier rulings.

The unanimous decision of the Supreme Court was announced on 5 March 1928 when Hall was back in Saskatchewan immersed in other legal work. The judgment of the Court was written by Justice Robert Smith – an Ontario judge elevated to the bench one month after Lamont had been appointed – who began by noting that the case turned on the construction to be placed on the clause 'accessible to stock' of section 4 of the Open Wells Act. 'The real meaning to be attached to those words,' he continued, 'must be arrived at by consideration of the mischief that the statute was intended to remedy and the provisions of the statute as a whole.'[10] It was clear to the Court that the statutes imposed an obligation upon farmers to prevent stock from being injured or destroyed by the *obvious* danger of open wells or excavations or grain openly accessible to cattle. Justice Smith concluded his judgment with the claim: 'Reading the statute as a whole, I am of the opinion that it is clearly indicated that the phrase "accessible to stock" in Section 4 has a qualified meaning, and calls for only such reasonable protection against access by stock to stored grain as men of ordinary sense would judge to be reasonably fit to prevent access to it by stock.'[11] Since Hall had convinced the Supreme Court of Canada that Babb and Glenn were 'men of ordinary sense' and that they had taken 'reasonable protection against access by stock' to their grain, they were not liable for damages. The Court accordingly reversed the judgment of the Court of Appeal and restored the trial verdict. The Saskatoon *Star* reported in a headline: 'Schofield Ordered to Pay All Costs.' And so, contrary to the warning of Hall's train companion, the Supreme Court did overrule Justice Lamont's Court of Appeal decision.

Hall was naturally elated when word reached him by telegram in Saskatoon the day the judgment was announced: he had won his first case before the Supreme Court. The United Farmers of Canada were, of course, even more delighted. For Schofield and the ranchers, it meant the end of their domination of land-use policy in Saskatchewan.

DROUGHT AND DEPRESSION

The 'open range' case earned Emmett Hall the high praise of legal colleagues as well as of grain farmers throughout Saskatchewan. But neither he nor the grain farmers spent much time savouring the victory. For in the year before the Great Crash of 1929, Saskatchewan farmers were beginning to see signs of an impending drought. While the crop of 1928 was good, the weather forecasts were predicting little moisture. Little did Saskatchewan farmers know in the summer of 1929, however, that they would soon find themselves in the cruel grip of the twin pincers of drought and economic depression. Most people on the Canadian prairies had experienced drought from time to time: it was the price one paid for living and farming in Saskatchewan. But no one could recall being hit so hard by both drought and depression at the same time. It mattered little that the causes of the impending depression were not home-grown, but rather global in scope. According to Goronwy Rees, a leading authority on the Great Depression, agriculture was at the epicenter of the great economic collapse:

The insatiable demands of the belligerent countries for food and raw materials during the war had engendered a vast expansion of agriculture throughout the world, and the application of modern science and technology had increased agricultural productivity and reduced costs to an unprecedented degree; the combine-harvester and the tractor, the improvement in and increased use of fertilizers and insecticides, the breeding of new strains of wheat and other crops, all contributed to an immense increase in world agricultural production. From 1926 onwards the prices of agricultural products had been falling continuously if not disastrously; in the summer of 1929, as the industrial boom reached and passed its peak, they underwent a sickening and catastrophic fall.[12]

Canadian and American farmers were caught up in the post–First World War boom and borrowed and mortgaged to meet the demands placed on them. In so many respects, prairie farmers became victims of their own success. They were devastated, however, when the tidal wave of the Wall Street collapse rolled over them. 'The fall in commodity prices,' Rees notes, 'which continued throughout the depression, produced some of its most calamitous features, reducing entire communities and entire nations to near subsistence level.'[13] No one in Saskatchewan took consolation from the knowledge that the collapse of farm income and the foreclosing of farm mortgages were part of a world-wide phenomenon. Farmers in Saskatchewan could no longer feed their families. As J.L. Granatstein has written: 'Though the Depression affected the whole country, some regions were hit harder than others. The worst by far was Saskatchewan. In the 1920s that province was among the most prosperous farming communities in the world; by the 1930s it was among the least, for the Depression there was aggravated by natural disaster – grasshopper, rust, drought and drifting soil. No province was so completely dependent on one staple as Saskatchewan. And as the market for wheat collapsed, so did the entire economy.'[14] A full 66 per cent of farmers in Saskatchewan were thrown on relief in the Great Depression. For the first time ever, scurvy appeared on the prairies. Drought combined with high winds to drive tons of Saskatchewan topsoil to North Dakota and the American Midwest.[15] Out-migration of destitute farm families began to strain relations with neighbouring provinces. Manitoba and Alberta flatly told Saskatchewan farmers to stay home – there was no room for them. The call for federal government assistance fell, for the most part, on deaf ears. Conditions were simply terrible; Saskatchewan had never experienced anything like it before.

Lawyers, like everyone else, were laid low by the Depression which lasted until the boom brought on by the Second World War. Yet, during those 'hard times,' as Emmett Hall called them, he experienced a 'piece of good fortune.' He became associated with the defence of insurance claims, acting for the C.M. Brewster Insurance company in Saskatoon. His brother Mike was the manager of the company and he steered work to his brother. In addition, Emmett did work for the Massey Renwick Insurance company. 'The group had their western Canadian head office here in Saskatoon and my office was right next door, so that I had a small fee on practically every automobile case and that kind of thing in Manitoba, Saskatchewan, Alberta and B.C.'[16] Indeed, Hall's connection with Renwick Insurance made him one of the luckiest lawyers in Saskatoon, allowing him to lay the foundation of a very successful practice. By the time the Renwick company moved its head office to Winnipeg in 1938, Hall's firm had become well established and Hall's own reputation was clearly on the rise.

Yet, in the early years of the Depression, even Hall struggled. Years later, when reflecting on those days, Hall admitted that he helped support with money two members of his family who were less fortunate than he was. And he added after a pause: 'Belle resented that.'[17] The impression left by that laconic afterthought was that his wife believed that members of his family took advantage of him. There was no question about it: he was a 'soft touch.' But there was no way he could refuse to help his own family in those hard times. Belle, however, knew how tight things were. The first years of the Depression were 'hard dollar days' for the Halls. An exchange of letters between Hall and Diefenbaker between 1929 and 1931 reveal just how tight financially Hall was. In November 1929 Hall wrote to Diefenbaker asking for a personal loan: 'Being very hard up yesterday and having to raise money to save myself from being closed out in more ways than one, I took the liberty of drawing upon you for the sum of $60 ... I would ask you to meet this draft and raise hell with me afterwards.'[18] Diefenbaker obviously honoured the draft but had to write Hall for repayment in May 1931: 'I would be very much pleased if you would forward me cheque covering monies advanced by me to you some time ago.' And again, in May 1931, Hall wrote to Diefenbaker: 'I regret exceedingly that I could not meet that cheque yesterday. Would you send it through Monday or Tuesday and I will see that it is ok this time?' An exasperated Diefenbaker waited until October to send off a demand for repayment: 'Please arrange to let me have $100 on account at once. This is very urgent and I must ask that you do so.' If Belle knew of these exchanges, she must have been a little more than anxious.

BALLOTS AND BURNING CROSSES

Hall had little time to bask in the afterglow of his victory in *Babb and Glenn*, for the political atmosphere throughout Saskatchewan was then beginning to assume a distinctly ugly tone. In the two years leading up to the general provincial election of 1929, the Ku Klux Klan had moved west from Ontario into Saskatchewan, and the Conservative party appeared eager to exploit the discontent that the Klan fomented.[19] Indeed, the Klan was to shape the course of the Saskatchewan Conservative Party for a decade following the election of 1929.[20] As Patrick Kyba has written about the election of that year: 'The 1929 campaign was among the most bitter ever fought in Saskatchewan. The Conservative party knew that it could not defeat the [J.G. 'Jimmy'] Gardiner government by pitting its promises against the Liberals' record of economic achievement or the government's close links with the organized farmers' movement. The Conservatives needed an issue which transcended traditional economic concerns if they were to break up the long-standing coalition of Catholic, European immigrant, and Protestant Anglo-Canadian farmers which had guaranteed Liberal success so often in the past.'[21] They found an issue deep within the bigotry aroused by the Klan. As Kyba explains: 'The Conservative party maintained a discreet distance from the Klan, but its spokesmen had no hesitation in directing the emotions aroused by the Klan into political channels. Conservatives charged that the government had pandered to the province's Catholic and European minorities in order to win votes ... and that the premier [Gardiner] had allowed Catholicism to infiltrate the public school system.'[22] Emmett Hall, who would always remember vividly the election of 1929, claimed that 'the involvement of the Klan was ... much more significant than [the Kyba] article would appear to indicate. There is no doubt that the Provincial Conservative Party in many constituencies worked hand in glove with the Klan in that election.'[23] The strategy worked: the Conservatives wrestled control of the provincial government from Gardiner's Liberals.

According to Constance Backhouse, Saskatchewan was the Ku Klux Klan's 'most successful base outside of the United States.'[24] The Klan targeted 'Roman Catholics along with the Chinese, Blacks, and Jews, as the focus of their venomous tirades and intimidation. Klan literature spewed vitriol about the Pope, priests, and nuns, charging them with kidnaping children, murdering babies, and a host of spectacular pornographic sexual acts. The Klan began to register surprising success in

Saskatchewan, signing up an estimated 25,000 members across the province.'[25] Andrew MacKinnon, a prominent Regina Catholic lawyer, felt the Klan's sting when he ran for a seat in Parliament in the general election of 1926.[26] MacKinnon had successfully defended Yee Clun, restaurateur, against the city of Regina's refusal to grant him a licence to hire white women in his restaurant. His victory was not looked upon favourably by the people of Regina. The prejudice against Chinese Canadians was strong at this time and the Klan exploited the prejudice to the detriment of Andrew MacKinnon's reputation.

Hall was, of course, fully aware of the swirl of political events around him; in later years, he would recall them as disturbing but exciting times. 'I was young and the issues were important.' To no one's surprise, least of all his own, he found himself in the thick of things, both as a lawyer and as a Catholic. Shortly after defending Babb and Glenn, he was called to defend Gerald Dealtry, a movie projectionist at a local Saskatoon movie theatre, against the chief Klan organizer in Saskatchewan. When he was not at work showing movies, Dealtry was busy putting out a small penny newspaper called *The Reporter*. And when J.J. Maloney, a Ku Klux Klan organizer from Ontario, came into Saskatchewan to help organize the Klan, Dealtry wasted no time denouncing the newcomer and his evil designs.[27] On 22 October 1927 *The Reporter* greeted Maloney upon his arrival with unequivocal, blazing denunciations: 'WELL-KNOWN HATRED BREEDER COMES TO TOWN' and 'EX-CATHOLIC CLERIC SPREADS LIES AND ILL FEELING.' And if that were not sufficiently clear, Dealtry said of Maloney in bold print: 'HE IS A LIAR.' Those were strong words at any time in Canadian history; but in Saskatchewan in 1927 – when the embers of racial and religious bigotry were being fanned by opponents of Jimmy Gardiner's ruling Liberal Party – they were more than sufficient for a charge of libel. Today, there are three types of libel in the Canadian Criminal Code: blasphemous, defamatory, and seditious.[28] Blasphemous libel relates to religious speech or writing which reviles or ridicules religion; defamatory libel is defined by the Criminal Code as 'matter published, without lawful justification or excuse, that is likely to injure the reputation of any person by exposing him to hatred, contempt or ridicule, or that is designed to insult the person of or concerning whom it is published.' Seditious libel is defined as the act of writing or speaking words that contain a 'seditious intention,' that is, an intention to raise disaffection and discontent among Her Majesty's subjects or to promote the unlawful overthrow of the government. But in 1927 the libel laws were not as precisely set out as they are today. The 1927 Criminal Code listed two kinds of libel: seditious and defamatory. Seditious libel was defined as 'a libel expressive of a seditious intention.'[29] Defamatory libel was defined as 'matter published, without legal justification or excuse, likely to injure the reputation of any person by exposing him to hatred, contempt or ridicule, or designed to insult the person of or concerning whom it is published.'[30] Then, as now, most libel cases were brought in the civil courts as suits for damages; one who claimed injury to his or her reputation became the plaintiff, and the author of the publication became the defendant. Maloney brought an action against Dealtry for seditious libel. However unusual, it was possible for a person to commence a private prosecution under the Criminal Code, but one ran the risk of losing control of the prosecution because the attorney general had the right to take over the conduct of the proceedings.[31] The fact that Maloney prosecuted on the grounds of seditious libel illustrated the intensity of passions in religious matters throughout Saskatchewan on the eve of the 1929 provincial general election. It also illustrated how loose the law on sedition was at this time.

Seditious libel laws are primarily intended to prevent citizens from inciting by oral or written word the violent overthrow of the government, but they could, in 1927, extend to those who through speech or print caused 'ill-will and hostility between different classes.' Since there was no way that Dealtry's condemnation of Maloney could be construed as incitement to overthrow the government, the case against Dealtry was based on the claim that his newspaper attack on Maloney constituted an attempt to incite hostility between Catholics and Protestants throughout Saskatchewan.

J.J. Maloney had been born in Hamilton, Ontario, of devout Catholic parents. From his earliest years, the young Maloney had expressed an interest in becoming a Catholic priest. He studied for the priesthood first at St Jerome's seminary in Kitchener, Ontario, and then later at the Grand Séminaire in Montreal. Some time during his last years in the seminary, Maloney soured on all things Catholic and he became associated with the Presbyterian Church and the Orange Lodge. In short order, he took on the role of an itinerant bigot, travelling to the west ready and willing to expose the machinations of the Catholic Church. He was an electrifying speaker with a clear focus on Mackenzie King and Jimmy Gardiner, both of whom, he claimed repeatedly, were stooges of the Catholic Church. He arrived in Saskatchewan in May 1927 and set about immediately to denounce Jimmy Gardiner. At Alsack during the 1929 election, Maloney charged that the Gardiner Liberals had allocated 80 per cent of the funds budgeted for orphanages in Saskatchewan to Catholic institutions, while the Protestant orphanage at Indian Head received a 'miserable six hundred dollars.' 'Perhaps this in part explains,' he concluded, 'why Mr. Gardiner prefers a black shirt to a white robe.'[32] The charges were, of course, completely false.

Dealtry came to Hall, a Catholic and grand knight of the Knights of Columbus, for assistance. Hall willingly accepted the case and, with the assistance of his partner, Harvey Hearn, defended Dealtry before Mr Justice Donald McLean and a jury in Saskatoon on 24 January 1928. The Saskatoon *Star* described the proceedings as 'one of the greatest legal battles fought in the Saskatoon court house.'[33]

Counsel for Maloney argued vigorously that Dealtry's attacks on his client were offensive at the best of times and, in the context of Saskatchewan in 1928, dangerous to the public order. He argued that a halt had to be made quickly to the kind of inflammatory charges Dealtry was making in *The Reporter*. In support of his argument, he cited the *Sentinal and Orange and Protestant Advocate*, a journal that provided Maloney with extensive coverage. The editors of this organ of the Saskatchewan Orange Order provided an account of how a Catholic priest in Lusela had ripped one of Maloney's posters off the post office bulletin board and how one Catholic hotel owner refused to rent Maloney a room because of the hatred that the likes of Dealtry had whipped up against him. Maloney's lawyer read further from a *Sentinel* story of how, at a public meeting in Evesham a 'papist heckler' sparked a fracas. When Maloney put the heckler in his place, the 'heckler' unleashed a profane oath at the speaker, who 'jumped clear over the piano and made for the individual who suddenly disappeared.'[34] Maloney's lawyer drove home the theme that Dealtry's explosive journalism provoked public disorder and, hence, constituted seditious libel.

Hall undertook Dealtry's defence, which consisted of frequent citations from Maloney's own paper, *The Freedman*. He quoted Maloney's claim that lax immigration laws, which permitted Catholic immigrants from eastern Europe to settle in Canada, were the direct result of the presence of twenty-seven priests in the Immigration Department in Ottawa. Hall countered this charge with evidence from the federal department that the allegations were false. He ridiculed Maloney's claim that the campaign to have *O Canada* proclaimed the national anthem was part of a Roman Catholic plot. All of this evidence and much more was presented to prove the *truth* of Dealtry's claims that Maloney was 'a liar and a man in whom little or no trust should be placed.' As for the Klan, Dealtry had claimed without equivocation that it was 'founded by fakers and financed by fools' and he was determined to stand by that assessment. Hall's defence was two-pronged: first, he refuted the claim that Dealtry's writings promoted public uprising against the established order, and, second, he maintained that what Dealtry said was, in fact, true: Maloney was a liar. On the other hand, Maloney's lawyers argued, successfully as it turned out, that the truth or falsehood of Dealtry's writings had nothing to do with the matter. The only relevent fact was that Dealtry's inflammatory writings had caused a public fracas. The jury was persuaded and rejected Dealtry's defence and found him guilty of seditious libel; he was fined $200 and forbidden to publish such material in future.

Strange as it appears today, the Canadian Criminal Code provisions relating to sedition were not finally sorted out until 1951 and the *Boucher* case.[35] Until that time, the Code defined seditious intention as, among other things, one that was likely 'to promote feelings of ill-will and hostility between different classes' in the community. The definition was so broad as to include any negative comments made by one person about another group of citizens. Boucher, a Quebec Jehovah's Witness, had been convicted for publishing a pamphlet of four pages in which he denounced the 'Godlessness of Quebec' and took several shots at the Catholic Church. The Supreme Court of Canada, led by Justices Ivan Rand and John Cartwright, overturned Boucher's conviction and made it clear that individuals could engage in heated exchange in the Canadian public square without fear of being charged with sedition. Since the *Boucher* case, seditious intention is more closely tied with the intention to overthrow the government by violent, illegal means. Today, with *Boucher* as the controlling precedent, Dealtry would not have been found guilty.

Hall's role in the Dealtry case was not overlooked by the Klan. One dark fall evening a few weeks after the trial, the Klan held fire-lit ceremonies across the South Saskatchewan River on the university grounds, not far from the CPR bridge, during which it hanged Hall in effigy. Years later, Hall would recall the event with a chuckle, commenting: 'I think that was the first honour I ever received.' At the time, however, it was far from a joking matter.

DEFENDING THE TREKKERS

In 1935, with his volume of cases mounting, Hall decided that he needed help and took on Percy Maguire as a partner. Maguire had graduated from the University of Saskatchewan College of Law and was known around Saskatoon as a solid black-letter lawyer. He was the perfect fit: he was good at doing the solicitor side of the practice while Hall was preoccupied with litigation. The two were to practise together for the next twenty-two years; the partnership was dissolved when Hall was appointed to the Court of Queen's Bench. The only other major addition to the Hall and Maguire firm occurred in 1949 with the arrival of James Wedge, Hall's son-in-law. Hall assigned him the task of handling the lucrative but controversial divorce work of the firm. Wedge had been raised a Protestant but became a Catholic when in 1944 he married Marian Hall, Emmett's and Belle's only daughter. There is every reason to believe that Emmett, at least, did not approve of Jim Wedge. Marian reported years later that Wedge had courted her for a full year before her father would speak to him. Relations at the office were professional but far from cordial. As one law clerk opined many years later, 'during those early years, Hall treated Jim Wedge badly.'

Also in 1935, Hall was called upon to assist in the defence of a group of men from the work camps of British Columbia popularly called 'trekkers,' who were arrested for rioting in Regina on their way to Ottawa where they had hoped to place their grievances directly before Parliament. These men were widely denounced in the press as 'communists' and 'troublemakers.' But, for the most part, they were hungry, unemployed workingmen who wanted help from their government. At the time of the Regina riots, newspapers across the country were filled with the story of how these desperate victims of the Depression had banded together and were heading for Ottawa.

In 1932, as a part of his effort to assist unemployed men throughout Canada during the Great Depression, Prime Minister R.B. Bennett had established 'relief camps' in various parts of the country.[36] They were placed under the authority of the Department of National Defence because, as the prime minister explained, the army 'had the equipment, tents, and they had the personnel, and the experience with respect to housing and caring for considerable numbers of people and for rationing them with proper food.'[37] Men who sought relief in these camps were obliged to work eight hours a day and received twenty cents for each day's work. As one might expect, medical and sanitary conditions in some camps were less than adequate. Those in the interior of British Columbia were apparently worse than most elsewhere in Canada. The British Columbia relief camp workers attempted to do something about the appalling conditions by setting up grievance committees. But, when these committees tried to present their grievances to the military commander, they were blacklisted and driven out of the camps. They were branded as 'communists' bent on organizing camp workers into communes, with the hope of eventually overthrowing the Canadian government. There was no question that some members of the relief camp committees were associated with the Workers' Unity League, an organization with its head office in Toronto, which was pressing hard at the time for unionization of labour throughout Canada and was generally known to be associated with the Communist Party.

The Conservative government of the day – and indeed not a few Liberals – was fully determined not to buckle under to the demands of 'communists,' 'anarchists,' and 'reds' in the relief camps. The problem appeared well in hand, thanks to the military discipline imposed by the army throughout the camps, until Christmas Day, 1934, when twelve hundred British Columbia workers assembled in Vancouver. For a month they petitioned Premier T.D. Pattullo for aid. At length, C.B. Griffiths of the Provincial Relief Association promised, with the backing of Premier Pattullo, that the province would establish an inquiry into the workers' complaints. Satisfied with this promise, the workers returned to their camps. And there they waited throughout the winter without further word from the government of British Columbia. By March 1935, the Vancouver branch of the Workers' Unity League decided to call a conference of relief camp workers in Kamloops for 9 and 10 March. The workers held a peaceful meeting and voted to press their demands upon the government. One of their members, a man named Cumber, was chosen to represent the workers; he later led forty men to Vancouver. The police forced the delegation into a Vancouver restaurant and arrested them; Cumber was charged with receiving relief under false pretenses; he had changed his name in order to get into other relief camps because he had been blacklisted.

Meanwhile, in Ottawa, the minister of national defence, Grote Stirling, was keeping a close eye on events in British Columbia. He warned the government and Parliament that there was a 'red' element operating in British Columbia and that it was determined to spread radical views throughout the relief camps. In an attempt to assure members of Parliament that he had matters firmly in control, Stirling announced at the end of March the formation of a commission to investigate complaints about the relief camps. The commission was headed by an ex-judge of the British Columbia Supreme Court, W.A. Macdonald, with businessman C.T. McHattie and the Reverend E.D. Braden as the other members. After two months spent visiting 46 relief camps and interviewing 277 relief camp workers, the Macdonald commission submitted its report to Stirling on 6 June 1935. The report commented favourably on relief camp conditions and was unsympathetic to the workers' complaints.

The British Columbia strikers became increasingly frustrated; no effort appeared to bring relief or even recognition of their grievances. Over a thousand strikers gathered in Vancouver in April and, after waiting for two months, decided to 'trek to Ottawa.' The strikers boarded boxcars and began their journey east; they received friendly cheers and food supplies at various stops along the line. It became evident that the camp workers, or 'trekkers' as they began to be called, had the support of the general population. The railway police made no effort to stop them along the way. On 14 June the trekkers reached Regina. In Ottawa, the seriousness of the matter was becoming increasingly apparent to the prime minister. After meeting with his cabinet, Bennett set out to stop the trekkers at Regina. Accordingly, the government ordered the trekkers off railway property and threatened to prosecute them if they refused to leave. At the same time, Bennett sent to Regina two cabinet ministers, R.J. Manion, minister of railways and canals, and Robert Weir, minister of agriculture; they were to confer with the trek leaders as personal representatives of the prime minister on behalf of the government.

Manion and Weir persuaded the trekkers to stop in Regina and to send a delegation of eight, headed by Arthur Evans, to meet with the prime minister and his cabinet in Ottawa. The representatives of the trekkers met with the prime minister and several members of his cabinet in Ottawa on 22 June 1935. A transcript of the interview reveals the contempt in which Bennett held the trekkers and how he attempted to intimidate their representatives. To say that there was no meeting of minds would be an understatement. The trekkers outlined their demands for relief of conditions in the relief camps but Bennett sat in stony silence throughout, showing no sign that he was affected by their litany of grievances. The trekkers then made a tactical error by indicating that their major demand was for 'a genuine system of social and economic insurance according to the provisions of the Workers' Social and Unemployment Insurance Program.'[38] This was a demand that Canadian socialists had made many times before but Bennett, the Conservative, was unyielding. His main response was to say that the matter was a provincial concern.

The final demand was for the right to vote. Bennett dismissed this request with the claim that 'every worker has the right to vote if he comes within the provisions of the Franchise Act, and if he does not, he has not.'[39] A worker could vote, that is, if he could fulfil the property-ownership requirements of the act, requirements that excluded most of the trekkers. The meeting ended with a stern lecture from the prime minister on the evils of communism and how the government was determined to resist it. The trekker representatives left Ottawa for Regina dejected and at a loss to know what to do next. Bennett had conceded nothing; later, in the House of Commons, he branded the trekkers as part of an organized communist conspiracy.[40] Having been scolded as wayward schoolchildren and labelled as subversives, the dejected Evans and his colleagues arrived back in Regina on 25 June. The next day, the government cut off all aid to the men, leaving them hungry and desperate.

The Bennett government was resolved to break the trek and accordingly declared an emergency under the War Measures Act. On the morning of 27 June, the government instructed the commissioner of the Royal Canadian Mounted Police (RCMP) to arrest the trek leaders as soon as possible. When the RCMP assistant commissioner in Regina, S.T. Wood, asked Ottawa repeatedly what law the trekkers had violated, he received no reply. Commissioner Wood refused to arrest the trek leaders. The government still appeared determined to arrest the leaders but found no legitimate grounds upon which to do so. Those grounds, however, were not long in coming.

On 1 July 1935, after more than two weeks of sitting idle, hungry, and frustrated in Regina, the trekkers assembled for a Dominion Day rally in the Regina Market Square and listened to speeches by Evans and other leaders. By early evening, one could sense that something was going to happen; the police – the RCMP and the Regina police force – were out in large numbers; some in plain clothes infiltrated the crowd, others were in uniform and mounted. When RCMP Inspector Walter Mortimer blew his whistle at 8:17 P.M. – the signal for his undercover agents to seize the trek leaders – chaos erupted. Police charged from all directions with sticks raised. The trekkers reached for weapons with which to defend themselves; one Regina plain-clothes police officer – Detective Charles Miller – was killed in the ensuing mêlée. The fracas continued for some time until the police were finally able to restore order.

The police arrested one hundred and thirty trekkers and several of the many Regina citizens who had turned out to support the trekkers. Of these, thirty-three were brought to trial for 'unlawfully, riotously, and in a manner causing reasonable fear of a tumultuous disturbance of the peace, assemble together, and being so assembled together, did there and then make a great noise; and thereby began and continued for some time to disturb the peace tumultuously.'[41]

By this time, Jimmy Gardiner's Liberals were back in power, having crushed the Tories in the provincial election of the previous year. Gardiner issued a lengthy and bitter press release on the day following the riot. He claimed that the federal Conservative government of R.B. Bennett had botched the trek affair from the beginning through mishandling and incompetence.[42] He accused the federal government of a 'preconceived plan' to stop the trekkers in Regina and not earlier. This decision, Gardiner charged, placed the citizens of Regina at the flashpoint of a federal problem. The people of Regina and the Saskatchewan government had been friendly to the trekkers; it was the federal government that had caused the riot. Gardiner, a fiercely partisan Liberal, would place himself and his party on the side of the aggrieved workers on the eve of the federal general election of 14 October 1935, the election in which he himself was elected to Parliament and in which the Liberal Party under William Lyon Mackenzie King was returned to office. The Great Depression proved the undoing of Bennett's Tory government and the trekkers had played an important role in its demise.

P.G. Makaroff and Emmett Hall, both of Saskatoon, were retained to defend the thirty-three trekkers. Of those thirty-three, Joseph Belaback was under sixteen years of age and was tried in Juvenile Court, where he received a six months' suspended sentence. Seventeen of the accused received 'stay of prosecution,' a court order calling a halt to further judicial proceedings. Charges against two were formally withdrawn; thirteen were found guilty, and eight of those were sentenced to hard labour in the Regina jail. Jack Wedin, a labourer from Alberta, received the longest sentence – eighteen months' hard labour. In addition to being charged with rioting a – general charge covering all the accused – Wedin was charged and convicted of wounding police officer J.H. Gibbons; he received fifteen months for rioting and three months for wounding Gibbons. The trek leaders, six in number, including Evans, were not charged with rioting but under section 98 of the Criminal Code: that is, 'with membership in an unlawful organization, to wit, the Relief Camp Workers Union.' On 28 February 1936 the attorney general of Saskatchewan withdrew charges against Evans and the other leaders for lack of evidence.

The handling of the relief camp trekkers constituted a sorry chapter in the history of the Canadian right to peaceful assembly. Hall and Makaroff argued to little effect that the police had led a premeditated attack on an orderly gathering. They showed that the police had used excessive force and wielded wooden clubs eighteen inches long with which they inflicted injury on a few of the trekkers; Wedin, for example, received facial lacerations and was taken to the General Hospital for treatment. To the end of their lives, Hall and Makaroff believed that no riot would have occurred had the police not rushed the crowd with the intention of arresting the trek leaders.

After rereading the transcript of the interview with Prime Minister Bennett and the efforts of the government to have the leaders arrested, one is inclined to agree with Hall that the trekkers were simply 'a bunch of unfortunate teenagers and men who were not much more than teenagers. They were made the victims of conditions that existed in Canada through no fault of theirs.'[43] Those trekkers not arrested left Regina on 4 and 5 July by passenger train. The federal government reluctantly paid $31,257 for fares, meals, and two trains to Vancouver. And thus ended the notorious Regina riots of 1935.

Hall's part in this episode gained for him few new friends, and even made it difficult for him to retain some of his old ones. 'Friends who used to call and invite me to dinner every time I came to Regina suddenly didn't know who I was,'[44] he commented years later. But this did not last long; in due course he re-established all his former social ties. In any case, the trial – covered so extensively in the national press – did help make Emmett Hall's name widely known throughout the country.[45]

But 1935 was a milestone year in the career of Emmett Hall for other reasons. That May, at the age of thirty-seven, he was appointed King's Counsel. Clearly, Hall must have been in good standing in Liberal Party circles or else he would never have become a KC at such an early age. Without Premier Gardiner's approval, he most certainly would not have received the honour. Then again, it would have been difficult for him to have been overlooked since there were thirty-four lawyers awarded the honour that year in Saskatchewan. The *Star-Phoenix* account of the appointments concluded with the comment: 'According to reliable information obtained from the Legislature Building, this will be the last long list of K.Cs to be appointed. From now on Legislative restrictions on the number to be appointed will likely be brought down, limiting the number to two a year, or not more than eight every four years.'[46] But in 1935 it rained KCs and Emmett Hall got one of the five designated for Saskatoon.

SCRAPBOOK RECORD

Emmett Hall kept a scrapbook of newspaper clippings of cases he argued before the courts from the 1930s until the 1950s. The cases ranged from personal injury actions to contested wills to murder charges. He argued cases at all four Saskatchewan court levels. A review of these cases shows him, usually as defence counsel, pitted against such notables of the Saskatchewan bar as Walter Tucker, later to become a federal cabinet minister and chief justice of the Supreme Court of Saskatchewan; John Diefenbaker, later to be prime minister of Canada and the one who would name Hall chief justice of Saskatchewan and, later still, a puisne judge of the Supreme Court of Canada; and Gilbert 'Bert' Yule, a Saskatoon lawyer who sparred with Hall through thirty years of practice. All in all, the clippings reveal Hall as the virtual embodiment of Lord Brougham's description of an advocate: a person single-minded in pursuit of his client's cause to the exclusion of all other things. Brougham had written, a hundred years before Emmett Hall became a lawyer, that 'an advocate, by the sacred duty which he owes his client, knows in the discharge of that office but one person in the world, that client and none other. To save the client by all expedient means – to protect that client at all hazards and costs to all others and among others to himself – is the highest and most unquestioned of his duties; he must not regard the alarm, the suffering, the torment, the destruction which he may bring upon any other.'[47]

By this time, Hall was beginning to acquire a reputation as a combative courtroom performer. Not infrequently was he reprimanded by a judge for his courtroom manner. On one occasion, in 1939, he challenged an opposing lawyer, Harry Ludgate, in an action for unstated damages. Hall heatedly charged Ludgate with defaulting on an earlier agreement to introduce a certain piece of evidence. The two lawyers turned on one another in a shouting match. Justice Embury of the Court of King's Bench called the attorneys to silence and warned that 'my learned friends are not going to play fast and loose in this court and get away with it. I have quite enough to do in conducting this court without acting as referee in a prize fight.'[48]

In the trial of Eric Keely, charged with manslaughter, in a motor-vehicle accident, the presiding judge, H.V. Bigelow, repeatedly objected to Hall's questioning tactics. One newspaper story headline read: 'Defence Counsel Rebuked by Judge in King's Bench.' Judge Bigelow objected especially to Hall's address to the jury, in which he said that his client was not dissolute. The judge instructed the jury to disregard the statement since there was no evidence brought in its support. After the jury retired, Hall objected to what he called His Lordship's 'facetious' remarks about his address to the jury. Judge Bigelow said that Hall was knowingly misleading the jury as to how far Keely's truck was from another parked vehicle when Keely, according to one witness, noticed it. The evidence showed that the distance between the parked truck and Keely's at the time of first visual contact was 2,160 feet, about 500 feet more than the figure Hall insisted on using. The crown argued that Keely had sufficient time to apply the brakes to his vehicle and failed to do so because he was travelling too fast at the time. Hall was determined to undermine the crown's insistence that Keely had been travelling too fast. He claimed that Keely did not have time to apply the brakes; that was why he consistently reduced the figure for the distance involved. He did not deny that Keely struck the parked truck owned by E.H. Bakke, killing Ole Stenerson, who had been assisting with repairs to the Bakke truck. But he claimed that the truck was parked in such a position as to make it impossible for Keely to react in time to prevent the accident. Hall was at least partially successful inasmuch as the jury returned with a verdict of not guilty of manslaughter but guilty of reckless driving. His aggressive manner, however, had produced a sharp exchange with Justice Bigelow, who criticized the way in which he had cross-examined a witness. Hall objected to the judge's comments on his behaviour as well as his instructions to the jury. The judge had claimed that Hall had 'gloated' over Mrs Annie Forsyth, a crown witness. Hall snapped back that 'it was not uncommon for counsel to draw inaccuracies between present and former statements of witnesses to the jury's notice.' Justice Bigelow quickly rebuked the young lawyer for impertinence.

Few cases show Hall's combative courtroom manner more than the Charmbury inquest into the death of Ernest Markwart in 1939. Hall acted for Robert Charmbury, who had struck and killed Earnest Marwart with his car. Marwart, seventeen years of age at the time, was riding his bicycle along Highway 12, north of Prince Albert. The *Star-Phoenix* reported that 'the inquest was marked by several altercations between E.M. Hall, K.C., and Coroner A.F. Malloy, M.D., and at one time the coroner called upon the police to keep order in the court.' Hall kept raising objections when the crown counsel questioned Charmbury about the speed he was travelling and other matters relating to his handling of the car. The coroner told Hall to refrain from interfering with the inquiry with his persistent objections, remarking pointedly that 'he had no privileges in this court.' When Coroner Malloy told him to sit down, Hall intimated that he intended to continue. The coroner responded, 'I am running this court, please sit down.' Hall shot back: 'I won't.' The coroner then called upon the police to preserve order. After sparring with J.M. Goldenberg, who was appearing for the crown, Hall conceded that it was not proper for him to appear to be cross-examining the witness at a coroner's inquest. But he was determined to defend his client. The feud between the two lawyers settled down for a time but, with the appearance of another witness, Hall was heard to mutter something about 'persecution.' Goldenberg reacted angrily, and, once again, the *Star-Phoenix* reported, Hall and the crown tussled until the presiding coroner, called them to order.

After one and a half hours' deliberation, the jury found that Marwart had died as a result of injuries sustained in the accident, which, it noted, 'could have been avoided had proper precaution been taken by the driver of the car.' Charmbury was accordingly arraigned on a charge of manslaughter. After appearing at a preliminary hearing before Magistrate J.T. Leger, the court found that there was insufficient evidence to commit Charmbury for trial by a higher court.

However, the victim's mother, Mathilda Wegeler, brought a claim for damages against Robert Charmbury and John Craig, the owner of the vehicle, in the amount of $4,500 for the loss of her son. Emmett Hall defended Charmbury and Craig.[49] The trial took place before Mr Justice H.V. Bigelow in the Court of King's Bench. After four hours of deliberation, the jury found that, while the defendants had been negligent, there was contributory negligence on the part of the boy. Mrs Wegeler was assessed costs.

'QUEEN OF THE UNDERWORLD'

In another case, not long after the Markwart trial, Hall defended Bessie Johnson, who was arraigned on charges relating to robbery and safe-cracking. The newspaper clippings give a fairly detailed account of the trial. While not exactly a Bonnie and Clyde robbery saga, the case involved love, life on the run, and robbery. Alas for poor Bessie, her 'Clyde' ratted on her and turned king's evidence. At her trial for breaking and entering before Justice H.Y. McDonald in the Court of King's Bench, Terrence W.D. Kelly, her erstwhile accomplice and lover, became a crown witness. Emmett Hall, acting for Johnson, had Kelly admit on cross-examination that he had turned king's evidence in the hope that he would be released on parole. 'Clean-shaven, and with his hair neatly parted, the witness explained how he and two other men, George Warren and John Small, both of whom are serving terms in the Prince Albert Penitentiary, had robbed the office of the Quaker Oats Company warehouses at Vanscoy, Delisle and Laura, south of Saskatoon, last Fall and how the accused woman had driven the car in which they had travelled and had shared in the loot they had taken.'[50] If ever there was a luckless gang of robbers it was this one. The Quaker Oats grain-elevator safe contained the princely sum of $300, a gold piece valued at $10, a $2-gold piece, and a diamond ring. After a trip to Edmonton, Alberta, the trio returned to Saskatchewan by way of Leduc, where they looted another Quaker Oats grain-elevator safe and came away with $10 in cash. Disappointed with the meagre take, the gang headed for the Quaker Oats warehouse, where they proceeded to rifle the safe and came away this time with $368 in bills and silver. Buoyed by their new-found wealth, the three robbers headed back home by way of Rosetown but, on the way, the car broke down about eight miles from Zealandia. After waiting a day for the car to be repaired, the robbers continued their journey south towards Calgary, where Mrs Johnson stayed a couple of days before returning to Saskatoon. The three male members of the gang, Kelly, Small, and Warren, later returned to Saskatoon but were arrested for a string of break and enters and were convicted and sent to the Prince Albert Penitentiary. Bessie Johnson visited Kelly several times when he was in prison and exchanged romantic letters with him.

Hall had Kelly admit that he had had a romantic relationship with Bessie Johnson. After having Kelly portray himself as a double-crosser, he called as witnesses for Bessie Johnson the two other members of the gang, George Warren and John Small. Both testified that Bessie Johnson did not know of the illegal entry into the Quaker Oats building in Vanscoy. Warren told the court that he, along with Small and Kelly, had entered the building and that Bessie Johnson did not go with them. Warren also swore that Kelly had borrowed Bessie Johnson's car for the trip to Vanscoy and that Bessie was not involved in the robbery. The witness also testified that, while Bessie Johnson had driven the three robbers to Edmonton, they had not told her of the Vanscoy burglary. She became aware of the heist only when Kelly asked her to see if she could sell a diamond ring that they had taken from the Quaker Oats safe. Kelly had tried unsuccessfully on two previous occasions to sell the ring but was unable to do so. On the return trip back to Saskatoon, Kelly, Warren, and Small broke into a grain-elevator safe in Flaxcombe and stole a rug, a hammer, and a wrench. Under Hall's questioning, Warren insisted that Bessie Johnson had no part in this escapade, that she 'was asleep in the car' at the time of the offence. Warren also testified that, when the trio took the safe in Delisle and cracked it, only to find a mere $10, Bessie Johnson was asleep in the car then, as well. She awoke, he said, when the car broke down near Rosetown. When Hall asked whether Bessie Johnson had received a portion of the stolen goods, Warren insisted that she had not received anything from any of the robberies. Hall got him to admit that Bessie Johnson was not even present when the stolen property was later divided between the robbers.

On cross-examination, the crown prosecutor, R.F. Hogarth, had Warren admit that he had a long string of convictions going back to 1932 in Tacoma, Washington, where he received a suspended sentence and was deported back to Canada. Warren testified that he was a painter by trade but that he had not been employed since 1931. Yet he resolutely insisted that Bessie Johnson was asleep in the car at the time of the Flaxcombe robbery. Hogarth next called John Small to the witness box. However, he, too, insisted that Bessie Johnson had nothing to do with the robberies in Vanscoy.

The crown then called William Arnold, who was involved in the threshing business. He stated that he not only knew Bessie Johnson but was known as 'her man.' He also testified that he remembered hearing about the diamond and that it was in the possession of Bessie Johnson. He testified further that she had asked him if he knew how she might sell the ring. He said he told her that he didn't know where she might sell it. In an effort to tie Bessie even more closely to Kelly, Hogarth read two letters by Bessie to Kelly. They were of an affectionate nature. In one of the letters Bessie wrote to Kelly, 'Don't forget, I am queen of the underworld.'

In addressing the jury, Justice McDonald noted that it was not suggested that the accused took any active part in entering any building, but that was not necessary to be guilty of the offence. The judge explained to the jury that, if it found that Bessie Johnson had helped the trio of men, that they used her car and that she drove them, then she was just as guilty as they. Justice McDonald noted that the main evidence against Johnson came from Terrence Kelly. He also noted that Kelly's evidence had been amply corroborated by Warren and Small, both creditable witnesses. The judge further pointed out that the evidence for the defence was a complete denial that Bessie Johnson was at Vanscoy on the night of the robbery and that it was for the jury to determine whether she had a part in the robbery. The defence had also argued, observed the judge, that Bessie was asleep on each occasion when robberies were taking place. The judge told the jury that it was up to them whether to believe that she was asleep at the time. The fact that Bessie Johnson had also given a false name to the jeweller who extracted the diamonds from the ring in Edmonton was noted as well. The judge asked whether an honest person would leave a false name and address. Justice McDonald discounted the allegation made during the trial that the police promised early parole to Kelly in exchange for his testimony against Johnson. Parole was a matter, he noted, beyond the authority of police departments to give; it resided with the federal Department of Justice. To no one's surprise, the jury found Bessie Johnson guilty. Justice McDonald sentenced her to two years in Portsmouth penitentiary for women near Kingston, Ontario.

Hall's clippings on this case contain an item from the *Star-Phoenix* titled 'No Further Jail Term.' This short, half-column piece related that Terrence William Bernard Kelly would not have additional jail time added to the eighteen-month term he was already serving as a result of his guilty plea to seven additional charges. Magistrate J.T. Leger expressed the opinion that Kelly had shown that he 'had decided to change his habits' and that he did not wish to place any obstacles in Kelly's way. The magistrate went on to note that he had been impressed with the evidence given by Kelly in the preceding trial against Bessie Johnson. The judge 'felt that the young man had decided to change his habits and seemed ready to wipe out his debt to society and begin again. He could see no gain in adding to the time the prisoner must serve.' In speaking for the crown, R.F. Hogarth pointed out that the prisoner had been of great assistance to the police and to the crown in the case against Bessie Johnson. Emmett Hall was annoyed to read the plaudits extended to Kelly at his trial. He thought Bessie Johnson deserved at least as much consideration or leniency as Kelly had received.

HALL v. YULE, A FALLING FLAGPOLE, AND MURDER

The scrapbook also reveals the protracted courtroom rivalry between Emmett Hall and Gilbert 'Bert' Yule throughout many years of their practices in Saskatoon. As early as 1939, Hall and Yule had begun to lock horns in court. The two were bound to clash because they were so much alike in temperament: Yule was as passionately committed to his client as was Hall to his. Hearing Hall describe Yule was to hear him describe himself. He said that Yule became 'completely immersed in any case ... at times you had the feeling that he may have lost sight of some aspects of it because he was so determined that he was right. The mere fact that a judgment was against him was of no consequence.'[51] There was no question in Hall's mind that Bert Yule was 'the toughest opponent that I had through the years.'[52] Despite the courtroom rivalry, the two men were friends; they lived two doors apart on Poplar Crescent and their wives were very friendly. 'We always had a good time when we went to Ottawa together but we could slug it out in court without getting into any real difficulties.'[53]

The two lawyers frequently appeared in court, as they did when, in another motor-vehicle case, Gwenda Lloyd sued John A. Milton, the driver of the car, and Dr W.H. Derkson, the owner of the car, for damages she had sustained in a 'pleasure drive' with John Milton. Yule acted for Gwenda Lloyd and Hall acted for Derkson. The trial judge dismissed the action on the ground that no gross negligence or want of misconduct had been shown by the driver of the car, that both the plaintiff and the first defendant knew that they were using the car improperly. The judge ruled that Gwenda Lloyd had proved no damages. He issued his judgment without hearing the defence.[54]

Gwenda Lloyd instructed her lawyer, Bert Yule, to appeal the case to the Saskatchewan Court of Appeal. On appeal, Yule was successful in overturning the trial judge's decision and Gwenda Lloyd was awarded $1,393.40 in damages.[55] Dr Derkson instructed Hall to appeal the decision to the Supreme Court of Canada. Hall did not go personally to Ottawa for this appeal; he retained, instead, T.N. Phelan to argue the case. Bert Yule, however, argued the appeal himself.[56] After hearing from both counsel, the Supreme Court, presided over by Chief Justice Lyman Poore Duff, concurred in the finding of the trial judge who had dismissed Miss Lloyd's action for damages. Emmett Hall had won again over Bert Yule.[57]

One of the more bizarre cases in the 1930s in which Hall participated involved a malady called 'litigation neurosis.' In 1938 Mrs Eva Harvey of Saskatoon was walking down Twenty-First Street in front of Woolworth's store and received a blow on the head that knocked her out. At the inquiry into the event, she swore that she could remember nothing about it until later in hospital. She testified that, since the accident, she had experienced constant head and body pains, sleeplessness, and weakness of memory. It turned out that Mrs Harvey was struck by a flagpole that Mrs Sydney Aird Hogarth had struck as she attempted to park her car in front of the Woolworth's store. Mrs Harvey sued the city of Saskatoon and Mrs Hogarth. F.H. McLorg, in whose firm Hall had once worked, acted for Mrs Harvey. He brought Dr Lloyd Anderson forward to give his expert opinion as to Mrs Harvey's medical condition as a result of the accident. The doctor testified that Mrs Harvey was suffering from a neurosis resulting from the accident as well as a neurosis over the approaching trial. He labelled the latter condition 'litigation neurosis.' He then suggested that no one could judge which, the physical injury sustained or the worry over the lawsuit, had the greater influence on Mrs Harvey's continuing poor health since the accident. Dr Anderson's expert testimony was confirmed by the testimony of Dr Lorne H. McConnell, a brain specialist who had attended eighty-nine head-injury cases in his career. He had examined Mrs Harvey and expressed the opinion that she was, indeed, suffering from 'litigation neurosis' and that she was not a malingerer.

A Court of King's Bench jury found Mrs Hogarth not to blame for the accident, but the city was held responsible because it had not kept the curb in good repair. Indeed, it was shown in court that the sidewalk was found to be broken and in need of considerable repair. The jury awarded Mrs. Harvey $4,200 in damages.[58] The city, in turn, sued Woolworth's store to recover the money it was obliged to pay Mrs Harvey. Emmett Hall and Carl Niderost, who had graduated from law school one year before Hall, appeared for the city. They argued that, according to the City Act, section 606, the city was entitled to have a 'remedy-over' against a third party in respect of an obstruction placed by such third party. In a jury trial before Justice J.F.L. Embury in the Court of King's Bench, the judge expressed the view that 'it shocks one's sense of justice to find that such legislation apparently permits one who is guilty of a wrong to be able to escape the consequences of that wrong by holding some third party liable.' This, he concluded, represented 'an entire derogation of the principles of the Common Law.' Hall argued that, barring the determination that section 606 of the City Act was *ultra vires* the powers of the legislature of Saskatchewan, the course of 'remedy-over' was available to the city. He argued for a judgment that would find negligence on the part of the Woolworth company in erecting a flagpole, when it had been clearly proved that the curb was in a condition of disrepair. In short, the defendant should have anticipated the accident. Carl Niderost added that the city should be entitled to a judgment against the Woolworth company even though a jury had previously found that the injuries inflicted on Mrs Harvey had been caused through the disrepair of the curb and sidewalk. The broken flagpole was produced and inspected by Justice Embury, the jury, and H.R. Hunking, manager of the Woolworth's store. Ten feet in length, it was an inch and a half through. It was broken off about five inches from the bottom end which stood in the sidewalk socket. Hall had Mr Hunking take the stand, where he admitted that he saw a car driven by Mrs Hogarth enter a parking space in front of the store and heard the flagpole strike the sidewalk. He did not see it strike Mrs Harvey. He gave the opinion that the car 'seemed to be going a little too fast for parking.' The store manager further testified that the pole in question had been used in the same location many times over the previous ten years.

McLorg had the city engineer admit that the curb at the point of the accident was broken away at the time and had not been replaced. In an effort to establish a case for negligence against the city, McLorg had the city engineer testify that the sockets for the flag poles had been installed almost thirteen years previously by the Great War Veterans' Association. The sockets were eleven inches from the edge of the curb when initially installed but, at the time of the accident, owing to the curb's deterioration, were only about six inches from the edge of the sidewalk. Despite his reservations over the fairness of the city suing to recoup its loses, the judge agreed with Hall's contention that section 606, granting 'remedy-over,' was valid in law. The judge accordingly ordered Woolworth's to indemnify the city's losses.

In another case in the late 1930s, Hall demonstrated his courtroom skill in a murder trial. Alvin J. Carr was charged with the murder of Henry Podmoroff, his thirty-seven-year-old neighbour. The trial took place in the Court of King's Bench in Humboldt before a jury of six. While the number of jurors required in capital cases is today – and has been for many years – twelve, a jury of six was permitted in the newly settled western provinces, where finding twelve jurors would have been difficult.

Podmoroff had been found dead on his hayrack shortly after noon, 25 July, on the Quill Lake road with gun shot wounds in his chest. Police investigations eventually led them to Alvin Carr, who gave a statement that he had shot Podmoroff by accident while talking to him on the side of the road. RCMP ballistics testimony established that the gun in Carr's possession had, indeed, fired the shot that killed Podmoroff. Hall cross-examined Corporal Mason-Rooke, the RCMP ballistics expert, by questioning him about the safety features of rifles in general. The officer admitted that 'at best safety features of rifles were imperfect.' Hall had the officer admit, further, that even an expert would occasionally have the weapon discharge accidentally under certain conditions. This was all he needed to introduce the theory that Carr's gun had in fact gone off accidentally. And he demonstrated his theory for the jury by cocking the rifle at a half-way point so that, while it appeared to be on safety, it was actually capable of being fired.

Senior prosecution counsel, G.M. Salter, in addressing the jury, argued that the jury could return with a conviction for murder, as the crown originally sought, or a verdict of manslaughter. A third option would be to convict Carr on the lesser, but still serious, charge of careless use of a firearm. With delight, Hall quickly pounced on the crown's movement away from the murder charge, which carried the death penalty. The mere fact that the prosecution would suggest the possibility of a reduced verdict was all he needed to press his case for acquittal. But, rather than urge the jurors to accede to the invitation to find a lesser verdict, he told them that they should focus on the seriousness of the charge of murder as laid by the prosecution and not accede to the crown's reduction scenario. In his address to the jury, Hall stressed the 'reasonable doubt' duty that lay upon jurors and reinforced his arguments by playing up the doubts the crown had raised with the suggestion that, if not murder, then perhaps manslaughter was an appropriate verdict, and if not manslaughter, then careless use of a firearm. It was the kind of tactic he revelled in.

After four hours of deliberation, the jury reported to the judge that it had found Alvin James Carr 'not guilty of the willful murder of Henry Podmoroff.' Emmett Hall had won another case and it did much to enhance his reputation throughout Saskatchewan as an effective defence lawyer.

'PLACIDITY OF CLUBMEN'S MEET RUDELY DISTURBED'

Emmett Hall's aggressive manner was not restricted to the courtroom, as we learn from an incident that occurred in October 1936, when A.A.

MacLeod, a member of the Communist Party of Canada and later an Ontario MLA, was invited to speak to the Saskatoon Kinsmen Club. MacLeod incurred Hall's wrath in open forum. MacLeod, who had been chairman of a delegation of communists to the world peace conference in Brussels, spoke in Saskatoon of the atrocities under Generalissimo Francisco Franco in Spain. Hall sat sullen throughout the main portion of these remarks but interrupted angrily when MacLeod claimed that the Spanish election of 1936 was similar to the 1935 election in Canada. Unable to contain his anger, he thundered his objections, to the embarrassment of most Kinsmen present. He publicly challenged the right of MacLeod, who, he charged, represented communists, to 'enlist sympathy here which they could not get otherwise than under false colours.'[59] From the *Star-Phoenix* account of the exchange, Hall was the loser. The story appeared under the headline: 'Placidity of Clubmen's Meet Rudely Disturbed by Political Argument.' But Hall cared little about being censured in this manner. Someone had to speak out against such blatant communist propaganda. In those years prior to the Second World War, there was a climate of compromise and appeasement. He was not a compromiser or an appeaser.[60]

WAR COMES AGAIN

Throughout the late 1930s, prairie newspapers – like others or the continent – watched anxiously the rise of German military power under Hitler. The threat of another war in Europe was clear. In an editorial titled 'British Troops in France Again,' the *Star-Phoenix* explained, in a tone of naive optimism, that the need for British troops in 1939 was not as critical as it had been in 1914. 'France is said to have 8,000,000 troops, all well trained, and the line facing Germany is about 250 miles long.' The newspapers in Saskatchewan tracked closely Britain's efforts under Neville Chamberlain to avert war. Letters-to-the-editor during those days deplored the prospects of another war against Germany. People were shocked, therefore, when on 1 September 1939 the *Star-Phoenix* announced in large, bold type: 'GERMANS RAID WARSAW.' The front page of the paper contained several stories on how 'the German War Machine Moved Rapidly,' introducing its readers to the terrifying results of Germany's new tank strategy, the 'blitzkrieg.'

On the home front, *Star-Phoenix* headlines reported that the War Measures Act had been proclaimed at Ottawa and that the government of Mackenzie King was 'Summoning Units of Non-Permanent Militia.'

It also noted: 'Saskatoon Units to Report at Armouries this Evening.' When Britain declared war against Germany, the newspaper blared the news in huge print on the first page. It also ran pictures of London demonstrators calling for Churchill to be brought into the Chamberlain cabinet. Chamberlain promptly obliged. On 6 September the *Star-Phoenix* announced that recruiting was going well in the area with the opening of a Second Avenue recruiting office. 'Fifty Volunteer for Service Here during Forenoon,' the paper proclaimed.

The one bright item of news almost lost in the array of articles on the beginnings of the Second World War was provided by the grain crops which were said to be 'largest since 1928.'[61] The *Star-Phoenix* reprinted an item from the Calgary *Herald* that proudly announced the end of the 'Western Exodus.' The story went on to say: 'It looks as though the emigration from the Prairies may be over. Crops have come back again; the livestock industry is in healthy condition; gardens are yielding heavily; grain companies are putting big staffs to work.'[62] On 9 September, just a day before Canada declared war on Germany, the *Star-Phoenix* proclaimed that a 'Golden Torrent of Wheat Flows from Saskatoon.' The contrast between the return of good economic times after the ravages of the Depression, however, was overshadowed by the reality of war. The young men who had produced those bumper crops – and looked forward to the good times they would bring – were now being called to leave their farms and ranches and answer the call to arms.

On the day following Canada's declaration of war, the *Star-Phoenix* gave a full account of the debate in Parliament over the government's decision.[63] The paper noted that the only party not to give full support to the war effort was the CCF. Its leader, J.S. Woodsworth, member of Parliament from Winnipeg, along with three Quebec members, voted against the motion to proclaim war. M.J. Coldwell, member of Parliament for Rosetown-Biggar, Saskatchewan, stated that the remaining CCF caucus would support economic aid to Britain but not conscription or the sending of an expeditionary force.[64] These parliamentary proceedings caused bitter debates throughout Saskatchewan, where the CCF had been born and was deeply rooted. Entire families and communities were divided between M.J. Coldwell's pacifism and loyalty to the British empire in its time of need. But there was no such divide in the Hall family; they were solidly on the side of active service. As much as Emmett Hall resented the idea of conscription, he firmly supported Canada's participation in the war and spoke frequently on patriotism.

At a meeting of the Fourth Degree Knights of Columbus, in Edmonton, Alberta, on 1 July 1945, he talked of 'patriotism as a moral duty for Catholics.' Immediately upon Canada's declaration of war, Hall enrolled for formal military instruction himself in the use of the Lee Enfield rifle. More to the point, he signed the approval form for his only son, John, to join the Royal Canadian Air Force (RCAF) at the age of seventeen. It is hard to believe that the decision to approve of John's entry into the air force did not cause considerable, anxious debate in the Hall household. No one is privy to what took place, but Belle was undoubtedly an enthusiastic participant in the decision to send her boy to war at such an age. She was a forceful woman and a formidable mother. In the end, John Hall served as a pilot in the RCAF and survived the war to become one of Canada's outstanding orthopaedic surgeons.

THE EMBARRASSMENT OF ALGER HISS

Emmett Hall was active in the Bar Association of Saskatchewan as well as the Canadian Bar Association (CBA) during the pre-war years. Later, in the 1940s, he served as CBA vice-president for Saskatchewan. In 1942 he was chosen to become a member of a CBA committee that had been given the task of surveying the legal profession throughout Canada. The study was to cost $50,000 and was financed by the Rockefeller and Nuffield Foundations and by the CBA itself. The committee was charged with interviewing lawyers throughout the country as to the major sources of their income, the nature of their specialty, and to what extent they were engaged in litigation. It was also instructed to look into the methods of practice employed across Canada and examine the qualifications of judges of all ranks and their age at retirement; review the relation of lawyers to the public, including services of a non-legal character, such as election to provincial legislatures and Parliament; and investigate the state of legal services available in rural areas as well as the plight of those who were unable to pay for legal representation. It was an important and comprehensive mandate. The director of the committee was C.P. McTague, a retired Ontario Supreme Court justice and former chairman of the federal Labour Relations Board. Its other members, in addition to Emmett Hall, were N.A.M. MacKenzie, president of the University of British Columbia; F. Cyril Jones, principal of McGill University; Professor J.A. Corry, chairman of the Canadian Social Sciences Research Council; A.N. Carter, of Saint John, New Brunswick, president of the Canadian Bar Association; V.C. MacDonald, dean of Dalhousie University Law School; and J.C. Higgins, treasurer of the Law Society of Newfoundland. Hall was delighted to be chosen to serve on such a distinguished panel, and his appointment testified to his growing reputation in the legal profession of Saskatchewan and Canada.

In the course of its preliminary work, the committee was especially pleased with the financial assistance of the Carnegie Foundation in New York. As an expression of gratitude, the CBA passed a resolution in 1943 thanking the Carnegie Foundation for its support. The person at Carnegie with whom the commission had been dealing and to whom the letter of appreciation was addressed was none other than Alger Hiss. In subsequent years, Hiss would become the object of a major loyalty-security investigation under the probing eye of Senator Joseph McCarthy and Congressman Richard M. Nixon – and prompted in no small part by the Gouzenko espionage revelations in Canada in 1949. Hall remembered that members of the CBA committee worried among themselves and wondered if their letter of gratitude would ever surface as testimony to Hiss's good character. It never did, to the relief of all members of the committee. Hall often said that he could not understand why some enterprising journalist had not uncovered that embarrassing incident. But no one did. Years later, after the Soviet Union collapsed and its archival records became accessible to Western journalists, it was established beyond doubt that Alger Hiss had, indeed, been an active agent of the Soviet government of Joseph Stalin, much to the mortification of his determined defenders.

Unfortunately, and to the disappointment of committee members, the survey into the legal profession in Canada was overtaken by the hostilities in Europe. The committee disbanded before the end of the war, without fulfilling its mandate or filing a report.

The flow of Emmett Hall's life was interrupted on 5 June 1943 with the death of his mother, Alice, at the age of sixty-nine. She was then living with her daughter, Mrs J.J. Scissons, in Saskatoon; her husband had died five years earlier, in October 1938. At the time of Alice Hall's death, nine of her eleven children were still surviving. Two children, John, a sapper with the Canadian engineers, had died in 1918, and a daughter, Helen, had died in 1928. The nine surviving family members gathered for Alice Hall's funeral at St Joseph's Church at 9 o'clock on Monday, 9 June, for the funeral Mass. All but four of her twenty grandchildren were present. The four were unable to attend because they were on active duty in the Canadian armed services.[65]

HALL v. YULE: ROUND TWO

Meanwhile, back in court in 1944, Hall and Bert Yule locked horns again in the case of *Wolfe v. Giesbrecht*, which involved an accident caused by the alleged negligent operation of an oil truck. Hall won for his client, Wolfe, at the trial but lost to Yule in the Court of Appeal.[66] He then persuaded his client to appeal to the Supreme Court of Canada. In the fall of 1945, the Supreme Court heard the appeal and ruled, once again, in favour of Yule's client. Hall had argued that the trial judge erred in his instructions to the jury. Justices Estey and Kellock were not impressed and ruled for a unanimous Court to uphold the Saskatchewan Court of Appeal decision reversing the trial judgment. Score another one for Bert Yule. In passing it should be said that the only time Hall and Yule acted together was in the case of *Williams v. Anderson and Anderson*, in 1947. And they won.

The courtroom rivalry, however, between the two leading lawyers in Saskatchewan continued throughout the 1950s. In 1950, for example, Hall and Yule were at it again in an action for divorce. Irene Ada Couch sought a divorce from her husband, Norman, on the ground of adultery, the only ground for divorce at the time in Canada. On this occasion Hall won for Irene Couch by parading witnesses who testified that they had actually caught Norman in bed with the wrong Irene. Witnesses testified that Irene Walsh, with whom he had been having an affair for some time, fought with Irene Couch months before the adulterous episode was discovered and that there was no doubt that on the night in question Irene Walsh was in bed with Norman Couch. The judge issued a *decree nisi*, to become absolute in three months. He also awarded monthly support to Irene Couch in the amount of $80 and $22.50 per month for each of the three children.

In 1952, five years before Hall went to the Court of Queen's Bench as chief justice, he tussled with Yule in Surrogate Court before Judge V.R. Smith over the contested will of Mrs Lily May Taylor. The papers billed this case as 'unique in Saskatchewan legal history.'[67] Local legal authorities agreed that the only case approaching it was the *Harms* case in Regina in 1942 which was eventually resolved in the Judicial Committee of the Privy Council, in London, in 1946.

Mrs Taylor had died in hospital on 17 March 1951 and left an estate of $264,398. W.W. Ashley, known as a 'pioneer real estate dealer' in Saskatoon,' was named in the will as residuary legatee as well as executor. When the will became known to the nephews and nieces of the deceased aunt, they took steps to contest the will. Once again, court watchers saw Hall and Yule spar with one another. Hall acted for Mrs Taylor's next-of-kin and Bert Yule acted for Ashley. Under the terms of the will – after disbursing small amounts of money to nieces and nephew totalling $74,000 – Ashley, as residuary legatee, stood to inherit $190,000. This angered the family. They thought that Ashley had un-duly influenced the childless aunt to their detriment. Ashley had been a long-time business adviser to Mrs Taylor and vigorously contended that the terms of the will were precisely what Mrs Taylor had instructed and that the will itself had been properly witnessed.

Bert Yule introduced Mrs Tracy E. Fells, who had lived with the ailing Mrs Taylor as a practical nurse in her home for more than a year before Mrs Taylor went to hospital and died. Yule had Mrs Fell give a portrait of Mrs Taylor, showing that she was a penny pincher who could account for every nickel of her wealth; indeed, she never paid Mrs Fell a cent despite the fact that the nurse had been hired on a promise to be paid fifty cents an hour. Fell also testified that, while she never discussed business with her, she knew Mrs Taylor confided frequently in Ashley. Mrs Taylor even suggested that Mrs Fell make a will and that Ashley would be the one to see that it would be done properly. She further testified that Mrs Taylor had little regard for her nieces and nephews. Yule then put Ashley on the stand and asked him about the will. He testified that it was drawn up on 28 June 1950 and was witnessed by his secretary, May Thaine, and a Mr Cameron. Yule then called Fred George Morrison, who testified that he was a witness to a codicil Mrs Taylor made to her will; he said that he had seen Mrs Taylor 'make her mark' on the codicil and that he witnessed it while she lay in bed in hospital. Gordon Frith, business manager of the City Hospital, also witnessed the codicil and said he had seen Mrs Taylor make her mark. 'He did not think Mr. Ashley had guided her hand. Mrs Taylor appeared able to hear what was said.' He went on to say that 'she had made her mark with the left hand, guided by Mr. Ashley. Her right arm was incapacitated, as she had been given intravenous injec-tions there.'

The *Star-Phoenix* then records: 'Monday afternoon, Mr. Ashley was subjected to a gruelling two-hour cross-examination by Mr. Hall.' One would have to sympathize with Ashley, for anyone who knew Hall would verify that he displayed a fierce demeanour on cross-examina-tion. His cross-examination of Ashley brought several 'stormy objec-tions from Mr. Yule.' When Hall asked Ashley when he knew he was to be the major beneficiary of the will, he replied that he had no indication prior to making out the will that he would benefit from it. He also volunteered the comment that Mrs Taylor had said more than once, 'I don't want to give too much to my nieces and nephews, because I think they might spend it foolishly and it might go to their heads.' He admitted that Mrs Taylor had paused for about two minutes before naming him as residuary legatee. Then Hall asked Ashley pointedly: 'After naming the other bequests, which totalled $66,500, did you not know she had not even started to get rid of her estate? That she had some $200,000 more to dispose of?' Ashley replied that he did not know that she had that kind of money. Hall shot back: 'Well, you knew her affairs intimately. You had just filled out her 1949 income tax return a short time previously. Did you not know that Famous Players had offered her $100,000 for the Daylight Theatre?' Ashley said that he knew nothing about the offer. When Hall asked him how much value he would place on the Daylight Theatre, Ashley responded that he would estimate its worth at about $60,000 or $70,000. 'Then why was its value listed as $50,000 in the will?' Hall demanded. Ashley replied that 'that was the figure we settled on for tax purposes.'

Hall continued to grill Ashley about Mrs Taylor's bank accounts and the interest she had earned on $10,000 in bonds. He then asked Ashley about what value he placed on Mrs Taylor's home on University Drive. Ashley gave a figure of about $10,000 or $12,000, to which Hall replied: 'I am not suggesting that you're not human, Mr. Ashley, but didn't these things pass through your head while she was deciding about a residuary legatee?' Ashley said weakly: 'I can't remember.' Hall then turned to what Ashley said after the will was made out. He said that Mrs Taylor had volunteered the comment that 'the government will take a lot of it. And you can have the rest.' When asked how he replied to this remark, Ashley said: 'I said "Thank you."' Hall asked incredulously: 'You knew you were getting thousands of dollars ... long pause ... and all you said was "thank you"?' Ashley replied that he actually said to Mrs Taylor, 'Thank you very much.' To this Emmett Hall asked facetiously: 'Did you stand up to say it?' 'No,' was Ashley's reply.

When Hall turned to another will Ashley admitted drawing up at about the same time he drew up Mrs Taylor's, Bert Yule objected strenuously, claiming that the examination was not relevant to the issue before the court. But Hall was able to establish that Ashley had drawn up a will of an elderly man who died in hospital shortly after he made out Mrs Taylor's will, that the man had named Ashley residuary legatee, and that Ashley had received $6,000 as a result. This line of questioning again drew 'stormy objections' from Bert Yule. But Judge Smith allowed Hall to continue, accepting his promise that the questioning would throw light on Ashley's credibility. Hall proceeded to question Ashley about his conversation with one of Mrs Taylor's nieces, Mrs Ella Fagan, who expressed surprise that Mrs DeGeer, a good friend of Mrs Taylor's for more than thirty years, had not been included in the will. When Hall asked Ashley whether he had promised Mrs DeGeer she would get something if he won this trial, Ashley firmly denied that he promised her anything.

When Hall finished his cross-examination, Bert Yule rose and asked Ashley what exactly Mrs Fagan had said after the will had been read. 'Well, she did appear to wish her aunt had left her more but she said, "Well, I guess that's Aunt May's wish and that's the way it will have to be."' Yule then asked whether Mrs Taylor had ever mentioned Mrs Fagan to him previously. Ashley replied that Mrs Taylor had mentioned her on several previous occasions and had expressed the view that she was her favourite niece. But she also said that 'Mrs Fagan had so much money she didn't know what to do with it.'

Yule concluded the session by asking Dr A.L. Caldwell, Mrs Taylor's doctor, whether she was of sound mind during her stay in hospital. 'I would say,' the doctor replied, 'that she was capable of giving instructions as to her will the morning of June 28, 1950.' Yule concluded his defence of Ashley confident that the will would stand and that his client would be acknowledged as the residuary legatee. But he was in for a surprise, for Hall called to the witness stand Stephen Lett, a handwriting expert from Vancouver. The *Star-Phoenix* reported that Bert Yule was caught off guard by this turn in events.[68] 'It was understood that if Lett could prove that Mrs. Taylor's will had been tampered with in any way after its execution, regardless of the intent, the will could be declared invalid,' the paper explained. Hall's tactic caused a furore in the court. Bert Yule at one point 'jumped to his feet ... and said heatedly: "Under what instructions can counsel for one side obtain possession of documents concerned in a litigation without letting counsel for the other side know about it?"' But Judge Smith replied that Bert Yule knew that Hall had asked to have the will photocopied. Why would he ask for it if he had not intended to have it examined by an expert? the judge asked rhetorically. After trying desperately to show that Emmett Hall had acted improperly by providing a photocopy of the will to Lett, Yule, 'nonplussed,' called for a brief recess. 'Mr Ashley has been charged with the most despicable type of fraud, and I think we should have a chance to counter the arguments,' he pleaded in frustration. Before granting a short adjournment, Judge Smith said to Yule: 'I must say I'm not taken by surprise, I thought it was quite obvious something of this nature would be coming up from the groundwork laid previously. What I'm concerned about is whether the issue is relevant in this case. I'm inclined to rule that it is relevant.' Judge Smith recessed the hearing for ten minutes.

Hall argued that Lett's testimony was highly relevant to the case inasmuch as 'the residuary clause of the will does not set forth the true intent of Mrs. Taylor as contained in the instructions for the preparation of the will.' Hall knew that, if he could show that those who signed the will had used different ink and that their signatures were executed at different times, he would be successful for his clients. When Lett was asked to take the stand, Hall asked him pointedly: 'From your examination of the will, would you say the name of Mr. Ashley as it appears on page three of the will is written in the same ink as that on page one?' Bert Yule and his co-counsel, A.M. McIntyre, according to press reports, seething at Emmett Hall's tactics, waited for the reply. 'My considered opinion is,' replied Stephen Lett firmly, 'that the two inks are different. The ink on page one is of a definite bluish tinge. On page three it has a slate-colored tinge.'[69] Hall knew that he now was in a strong position to prove that the will had been tampered with. He quietly asked Lett to demonstrate his investigative methods to Judge Smith and invited Bert Yule to look on. Lett produced a small flashlight and a lens with which he said he found the best results in his work. After the demonstration, Lett stated that the signature of Ashley as executor showed 'definite evidence of two inks being used. It obviously was written first in bluish ink then traced over with the slate-colored ink.' He then volunteered that no man can write two signatures so identical that one could be superimposed on the other and that it was obvious from his examination that one of the signatures had been traced.

When the trial resumed the next day, the *Star-Phoenix* ran a story headlined: 'Will Hearing Ends Abruptly; Surprise Finish as Parties Agree to Settle out of Court.'[70] Apparently Emmett Hall and Bert Yule had got together and, after one full day of negotiating, reached the conclusion that 'this litigation which promises to be prolonged and expensive should come to an end.' Bert Yule had met with his client and advised him to settle out of court. He warned Ashley that Emmett Hall was likely to drive home to his disadvantage the fact that two inks were used in the will. It was the kind of technicality that had broken many wills. Ashley at length agreed and Yule informed the court that his client was withdrawing his application to probate the will and that the two sides had agreed to settle the dispute out of court. Judge Smith informed the parties that, regardless of the settlement they might reach out of court, the charitable bequests would not be prejudiced. He reminded the parties that Mrs Taylor had bequeathed $5,000 to the Grace United Church and $2,500 each to St Andrew's College, Saskatoon, the Saskatoon Salvation Army, the Saskatchewan Red Cross, and the Orange Orphanage at Indian Head. He adjourned the case until 13 June 1952.

The parties returned to court briefly on 28 May when Hall had discovered the name and whereabouts of the missing nephew who had been adopted out of the family years previous. The *Star-Phoenix* reported the news under the headline: 'Will Case Delayed to Check Another Likely Beneficiary.'[71] Judge Smith had no alternative but to adjourn the case until Hall could ascertain whether the missing nephew would agree to join his relatives in the out-of-court settlement. Judge Smith accordingly reminded the litigants and their counsel that they were expected back in court on 13 June. When the court reconvened on that date, the judge was informed that the missing nephew had agreed to join his relatives in the out-of-court settlement.

The two parties met many times over the next four months and, after reviewing the evidence and court proceedings, came to the conclusion that the will drawn up by Ashley was airtight. Hall simply could not break the fact that Mrs Taylor was of sound mind when she wrote the will and added the codicil. Accordingly, on 11 September 1952, the court ruled that 'It is ordered and adjudged that Lily May Taylor was, at the time of the execution of the codicil to the said Will, dated 3rd day of March 1951, of testamentary capacity and that the said Will and Codicil were duly executed in compliance with the requirements of the Wills Act, being Chapter 110 R. S. S. 1940.'[72] The court did rule, however, that all costs were to be paid 'out of the residuary estate of the said Lily May Taylor.' At least Ashley had to pay the costs of the trial and proceedings. Score one more for Bert Yule for it was he who manoeuvred the issue out of court and into settlement. He knew that, if the case had remained in court, Hall would have capitalized on Ashley's use of two inks to make him out as a villain. He might have broken the will. But Hall also knew that he was in Surrogate Court before a single judge without a jury and that such tactics were not likely to work in the circumstances. Hall was better before a jury, where he could turn on his powers of forensic rhetoric. With no forum for these powers here, he relented and Mrs Taylor's will stood. It is not recorded how much Ashley actually won in the final disposition of the assets; he was removed as executor and replaced by the Toronto General Trust company. Nevertheless, Ashley won a considerable windfall.[73]

Emmett Hall's long courtroom rivalry with Bert Yule reached its climax in 1955, two years before he went to the Saskatchewan bench, with a case involving eggs and doughnuts that went all the way to the Supreme Court of Canada. The Canadian Doughnut company of Toronto had successfully sued the Canada Egg Products company for breach of contract to supply 100,000 pounds of powdered egg yolk and 10,000 pounds of powdered egg albumen. The Saskatchewan Court of Queen's Bench had awarded Canadian Doughnut $54,483 damages for breach of contract. The Saskatchewan Court of Appeal dismissed the appeal and the Supreme Court of Canada upheld the Court of Appeal's decision. Hall had acted on behalf of the successful doughnut company and, once again, Bert Yule found himself on the losing side.

KASPAR BECK AND THE MINISTER OF NATIONAL REVENUE

The entire city of Saskatoon and the countryside for miles around buzzed with the news. The Department of National Revenue had seized the six and a quarter sections of land belonging to Kaspar Beck. The land was to be sold at auction and the proceeds were to defray Beck's tax debt of $28,623 for the years 1941–5. At long last, this 'land hog,' as many around Saskatoon called Kaspar Beck, would finally be done in. Not a few Saskatoon businessmen borrowed money for the auction; everyone knew that the farms of Kaspar Beck were in top condition and had the latest farm implements. And everyone wanted a share of the spoils.[74]

But this was not the story of a farmer who had accumulated large tracts of land through fraud or intimidation. This was the real-life story of a hard-working farmer who had been born into the German community in Odessa in 1884. He left Russia in 1909 for the United States with his young wife, Katharine, and the next year – the year so many people like the Halls went west – they came to Saskatchewan. With the money he brought with him from Russia, a nest egg of $1,300, he purchased a half-section of land in Allan Township, thirty miles southeast of Saskatoon. Kaspar and Katharine knew that only one thing was certain: if you had the clear title to land, you could pass it on to your children. Their experience in Russia made them distrust governments; Kaspar was made to serve in the army in 1899 after the Russian government had promised that the children of the German community in Odessa would not have to do so. This distrust turned to hatred and suspicion of all government authority in 1919 when his father had died and his land was confiscated by the new government of the Soviet Union. All government agencies became synonymous with thieves in Kaspar's mind and he took precautions to ensure that he would not be robbed by them. Wanting nothing more than to be left alone to work the land and raise a family, he and Katharine built a sod house on their half-section and had their first child, a son, that same year; eventually they replaced the sod house with a frame one and added children regularly from that time on.

All through the First World War – which seemed as distant from the Beck farm as the planet Jupiter – Kaspar and Katharine toiled on the land. By 1918, Kaspar had acquired an entire section, paid for in cash. He had also, by that year, acquired six more children: Eva, Marcus, Rose, Tony, Caroline, and Joseph. In the 1920s, Beck increased his land holdings a quarter-section at a time, while also increasing his family even further. Katharine bore her last child – the seventeenth – at the age of forty-four. Nature had set a limit on how many children Kaspar Beck might acquire, but it did not say how much land he could own. As late as 1950 he was determined to acquire more land so that he could bequeath a good portion to each of his children. By 1951, Kaspar Beck had acquired six and a quarter sections of first-class farm land. Since this large family meant that he had to guard every dollar carefully, Beck sent his two younger single daughters into Saskatoon to work as domestics with the strict instructions that they were to bring every nickel home.

Kaspar Beck ruled this large family and farm operation like a feudal lord; he did not give salaries to any of his children but paid all their expenses. They all shopped at Lehrer's Ltd in Saskatoon and were instructed to charge all their purchases to his account. On the day of his death, the Beck account was $1,800. The amount might appear large for even a family the size of Kaspar Beck's, but the store manager knew that Beck would pay the account promptly – he always did. Indeed, Beck rarely borrowed money; he saved until he could afford whatever he wanted, whether the latest machinery or groceries (which he always bought in bulk for the entire family) or clothing for his children. Only once, during the hard days of drought in the late 1930s, did Beck have to borrow to make ends meet. Roy Weninger, the secretary of the Rural Municipality of Allan, recalls that 'Kaspar Beck never took any relief during the depression and wouldn't allow his children to take family allowances. The only time he borrowed any money was in 1937 when things were very bad. He got a rural loan of two hundred and thirty-five dollars for seed grain. He paid it back promptly plus seventy-seven dollars in interest. Later half the interest was refunded.'[75]

But Beck was not a stingy man. He would frequently take as many as twenty of his children and grandchildren – who by 1951 amounted to twenty-six – to Joe Yee's Victoria Cafe in Saskatoon and let them order whatever they wished. Beck resented deeply one thing only: government interference with his determination to raise his family the way he wished. That meant keeping them home from school whenever he needed their help on the farm – which was frequently. As a result, none of his children ever got beyond grade five. They did, however, learn to read and write English, something Kaspar Beck had never learned. All his business dealings in Saskatoon and in the surrounding area were done through his sons or daughters; he would question or answer in German and they would translate into English.

All went well on the extensive Beck farm till January 1947. That was the year Kaspar Beck was fined one hundred dollars for failing to file his income tax returns for 1945. No farmer in Saskatchewan was able to pay income taxes in the 1930s owing to the Depression and drought; but things got better in the 1940s. With the coming of good times, Saskatchewan farmers began, once again, to file income tax returns. But not Kaspar Beck. Giving money to the government made no sense whatsoever; he had taken nothing from the government so why should he have to give any of his hard-earned money to them?

However much sense this attitude made to Kaspar Beck, it made no sense to the Department of National Revenue. Nor did it make any sense to those farmers who looked with envy upon Beck's enormously efficient farm operation. When word of Beck's delinquent income taxes became public knowledge, many people wrote letters to the editor of the Saskatoon *Star-Phoenix* complaining that Beck should be made to pay promptly for the privilege of living in the Canadian democracy. They were bitter letters, not without a certain amount of bigotry. But Kaspar Beck simply did not understand such matters. And so he ignored them.

He also ignored the fine of one hundred dollars. Income taxes made no sense at all and Beck found support in his views in the speeches of

Roger Smith, a crank who toured Saskatchewan telling people that Canada was illegally formed in 1867 and that they should withhold all payment of income taxes. Such drivel was all the confirmation Kaspar Beck needed.

In time – by 1950 – matters turned worse; the Department of National Revenue had calculated that Kaspar Beck's back taxes amounted to $28,634 for the years 1941–6. Department officials failed every time to make Beck understand what the issues were. To him, his eldest son Roy recalled, all National Revenue accountants 'were a bunch of sharpies who were wanting his money for themselves.'[76] Beck fought these sharpies with a series of lawyers but they either gave up exasperated or he dropped them. He was advised to mortgage a section of land in order to raise the money needed for back taxes, but he resolutely refused. With tears in his eyes, he would sit clutching his deeds. He believed that no one could touch his land because he had those deeds. And he was living in Canada, not Russia.

Beck tried everything. He even had his lawyer appeal to the minister of national revenue, Dr James McCann. On 26 September 1950 Dr McCann wrote saying that his department had gone as far as it could. If Beck did not show immediate intention to pay the outstanding taxes and fine, his lands would be confiscated and sold at auction and the proceeds would go to the federal treasury towards defraying the taxes.

The date set for the auction was 24 October 1950. All Saskatoon and the surrounding area were talking about the upcoming sale at public auction of twenty-four quarter-sections of land and a lot in Allan. Shortly after it was announced that Beck's farm land would be auctioned, the *Star-Phoenix* ran a lead story sympathetic to Beck and pointed out that, if his lands were sold, all his children and grandchildren – fifty-four in total – would be thrown off the land which they had worked so hard for more than forty years. The story prompted more angry letters from 'English-speaking, tax-paying citizens' and also from outraged veterans of two world wars who had fought against the Germans and were proud to pay their taxes. The atmosphere was charged with bitterness and resentment. And Kaspar Beck became more confused as events unfolded. He did not know what to do or to whom to turn.

Sheriff Basil P. Boyce seized Beck's six farms, scattered over six sections, on 24 October 1950 and conducted the auction in the Saskatoon court house. More than a hundred people packed the courthouse ready to get a quarter-section of the land. Before beginning the auction,

Boyce recounted the efforts of the Department of National Revenue and how all attempts at settlement had failed – even a last-minute attempt to have Beck transfer his property to his sons. This would have dispersed Beck's liability for taxes and given his sons and daughters an opportunity to meet the debt. Beck appeared willing until late in the evening of the previous night. At a meeting in Saskatoon with W.A. Gilchrist of the Department of National Revenue, who had the transfer documents ready for Beck's signature, Beck suddenly ran from the room with his eyes filled with tears. Despite the efforts of five sons, he was not found till dawn, wandering the deserted streets lost in a daze. Everything was being taken from him; the legal and accounting technicalities made matters worse; he could cope with the land and the elements but he was lost in a jungle of words and documents which he could not comprehend.

The auction took place as scheduled. The bidding began on a quarter-section of land for which Beck had paid $2,500. Sheriff Boyce said that the auction would cease the moment the amount of $28,623 was realized. The first quarter-section went for $100. It quickly became apparent that little of Beck's land would remain. Another quarter-section of land went for $1,100 – Beck had paid $5,000. A whole section for which Beck had paid $14,080 sold for $8,321. And another quarter-section went for $200 – more than $2,500 less than Beck had paid for it. Most people at the auction were prepared to pay a reasonable and fair price. But not all the people at that auction were reasonable or fair; there was a group of speculators who had agreed not to bid against one another and they purchased lots at ridiculously low prices.

Beck attended the auction accompanied by his aging wife who had worked side by side with him for almost half a century. Twice during the auction, Beck tried to read a statement in German; and twice he was warned by the sheriff that if he attempted to interrupt the proceedings he would be forcibly removed. At the end of the auction, Boyce announced that the total amount acquired was $22,100 – more than $6,300 short of the assessed tax debt. And that was on property which on the open market could have commanded at least $50,000.

Beck, despite his confusion, knew now that if he hoped to reclaim his land he had to have the advice and assistance of a good lawyer; he went through a list of possibilities and at length turned to Hall. Hall had, of course, followed the case in the press and was delighted with the prospects of representing Beck. Years later, he recalled talking with Beck and how suspicious he was; he had never trusted anyone outside his own family. It took all of Hall's resources of personality to earn Kaspar Beck's trust, but earn it he did. Beck gave to Hall power of attorney and he set about his new task with all his considerable energy. It was just the kind of legal battle most lawyers relish.

Since all the sales at the auction had to be confirmed by the court, Hall encouraged Beck not to give up hope. But Beck was too shattered to understand what confirmation by the courts meant. A week after the trial, Hall met with the Saskatchewan Mediation Board, a provincially appointed board designed to settle disputes between parties; Beck had been left with nothing as a result of the absurdly low sale price of his property and his children were being dispossessed. Hall urged all purchasers to waive their rights in order that he could effect a more equitable settlement with the Department of National Revenue. But only three of the purchasers – all farmers – came to the board meeting. H.W. Warren, chairman of the board, thanked the farmers for their public decency and willingness to waive their rights to Beck's land. He also said that he would see to it that the other purchasers – who paid less than a quarter of the market value – would not be permitted to take title to those lands. Warren spoke eloquently of the virtues of the Beck family, who, if the auction prices were permitted to stand, would be expelled from the land they all worked so hard to cultivate.

In April – almost six months after the auction – the crown made an application for confirmation of the sale in the District Court before Judge V.R. Smith. The sale was now formally before the court. To most observers, the case against Beck was airtight. Even Hall thought it would be difficult. He studied Saskatchewan's Executions Act[77] and found that the Department of National Revenue had made one mistake – but that was all he needed.

Hall rose in court and presented his case in three points: first, the Department of National Revenue had failed to advertise the property in accordance with the manner prescribed by the Executions Act; second, the lands were sold at a grossly inadequate price; and third, the southwest quarter of section 11 was not advertised for sale at all. Hall protested that the auction was 'a farce under the guise of law.' The Executions Act clearly and explicitly required, he emphasized, that the property be advertised in the newspaper *nearest to the site of the property*. This had not been done. Gilchrist had advertised in the Saskatoon *Star-Phoenix*, not the weekly newspapers which were published at Viscount and Watrous. The Viscount *Sun* was clearly nearer to the site of the lands.

W.A. Gilchrist responded that he knew well that there were two weekly newspapers but that the combined circulation was insignificant; for example, he argued, in Allan itself the *Star-Phoenix* sold fifty-three copies while the Viscount *Sun* sold only one. He argued that it made more sense to advertise in the *Star-Phoenix* than in the small weekly papers. But Hall replied – holding a copy of the Executions Act – that the law stated clearly that the land *must* be advertised in the newspapers nearest to the property to be sold; there was no room, he continued, for the kind of interpretation Gilchrist was putting on the statute. Gilchrist argued to no avail. Hall had a hold on the kind of technicality that had been known to break much greater cases. Judge Smith accepted Hall's arguments and declared the sale of the Beck lands invalid. Those speculators who had borrowed money to finance their purchases of the Beck land were, of course, outraged at the decision. They had been told that the case against Beck was solid and that they had little to worry about.

Kaspar Beck returned to his home still confused but a little more secure. Hall had told him of the possibility that the Department of National Revenue might appeal the decision, but that made no more sense to him than the tangle of proceedings, sales, and court action up to now. A month after the successful hearing – 3 May 1951 – Kaspar Beck was at home sitting on the porch looking out over his land when he saw two well-dressed men approach the house. Thinking that it was another delegation from the Department of National Revenue, Beck ran to the cellar crying, 'They'll never leave me alone.' Mrs Beck admitted the two men and discovered that they were not from the government but were representatives of an oil company offering to buy up drilling rights on farm land throughout Saskatchewan. Most of the farmers considered the terms of the agreement reasonable and the compensation generous. Mrs Beck went to fetch her husband from the cellar and found him bathed in blood from self-inflicted wounds; Kaspar Beck had attempted suicide by striking himself on the head with an axe. Fortunately, the wounds were not serious and easily bandaged.

The couple came upstairs and met the two men; Beck explained through his wife's broken English that he had fallen and cut his head. He listened to the two men and, uncharacteristically, consented to sign the drilling agreement. The two men left and Kaspar Beck began to rage: 'They tricked me into selling my land. They have tricked me.' Kaspar Beck was clearly emotionally exhausted and could not be calmed. He sat up most of that night with Katharine brooding over the loss of his lands. He urged his wife to send the children to school, remarking that 'times had changed.' The next morning, May, 4 1951, when Katharine awakened, Kaspar was not there; she called to him, but there was no answer. She went out into the garage, and there she found her husband: he was hanging by a rope from a rafter.

Kaspar Beck never knew that the Department of National Revenue had decided not to appeal Judge Smith's decision to disallow the sale of his property. The estate was eventually settled by giving one-third of the land to Katharine and two-thirds to the children. It was the very thing that Kaspar Beck had worked so hard to achieve.

JOHN PETLOCK ON A CHARGE OF MURDER

It was common knowledge throughout the Melville area farm community that the Petlock brothers were at war with one another. John Petlock was not only on bad terms with his brothers but was constantly feuding with his mother, as well. The brothers had long been at one another's throats over entitlement to property and farm machinery but relations between them had worsened upon the death of their father a few years earlier. The unfortunate mother was left with an inheritance of $11,000 and the three unruly sons. As long as the father was alive, the internecine war rarely went beyond a shouting match. But, after the father's death, the mother was unable to stop the flow of bad blood between the brothers and herself. A few days before the tragic event that was to unfold, John Petlock had visited his lawyer P.J. Dielschneider in Melville to explore the prospect of suing his mother over the ownership of some farm machinery.

In October 1955 neighbours heard gunshots coming from the Petlock farm and called the police. When police arrived to investigate, they discovered a gruesome scene: five people had been shot dead. The police discovered in the garden the bodies of the mother and her son Mike's wife, Angeline. Upon entering the back door of the house, police found the dead body of Mike. In the bedroom they discovered the bodies of two infant children slain in their cribs. The only one of the family nowhere to be seen was brother John. The police put out a call for John Petlock's arrest.[78] A week later, acting on a tip, he was discovered living in a rooming house in Edmonton.[79] Police returned him to Melville and placed him under arrest. Petlock arranged to see his lawyer, P.J. Dielschneider, who visited him in prison and advised him to engage the services of Emmett Hall, with whom he had articled years before.

Petlock repeated to Hall and Dielschneider the story he had told the police upon arrest: he was working in a field not far from the family house and he heard gunshots. When he investigated he encountered his brother Mike carrying a rifle. According to John, he tried to take the rifle from his brother, but Mike refused to give it up. The two tussled and in the course of the struggle the gun went off, killing Mike. Having wrestled the rifle from his brother, John shot Mike several times. He then dragged Mike's body into the house. A few moments later, he said, he discovered the bodies of his mother and sister-in-law lying in the garden. He told police and, later, his lawyers that he had not noticed the bodies of the two infants in the bedroom. After seeing the blood-splattered children's room, John said that he panicked and took off in Mike's car, in which he found luggage filled with clothing and what later turned out to be the mother's $11,000 inheritance money. John told police that the clothing and the money clearly meant that his brother Mike had killed their mother and the others and had planned to take off with the money. Fearing that no one would believe his story, John fled the scene.

Dielschneider consented to work with Hall in the preparation of the defence and during the trial. The two lawyers worked on the case throughout the winter of 1956. They first moved to have the trial postponed until the spring in order to allow them time to prepare Petlock's defence as well as to permit public outrage over the incident to subside.

Since John Petlock had admitted to the police that he had, in truth, killed his brother, there was no way Hall could argue that the police had the wrong man. The two defence lawyers huddled for long hours and finally arrived at the only plausible line of defence for their client. As improbable as it sounds, Hall was convinced that he had a firm hold on a plea of self-defence. He sent Dielschneider to the scene of the crime to look for further evidence, but Dielschneider was ordered off the property. Hall questioned John Petlock in jail and became committed to freeing him. Few cases absorbed him emotionally as this one appears to have done. Certainly, few cases would remain as imprinted on his mind as the Petlock case. Not even the Truscott trial in the Supreme Court displaced the Petlock case in his recollection. He had become convinced in his own mind – and remained convinced to the end of his life – that John Petlock had killed his brother Mike in self-defence.

Early in the trial Hall focused on the testimony of Sergeant Minor, the RCMP officer who was in charge of the investigation. Minor felt the iron blows of Hall's questioning throughout his lengthy time on the stand. 'When Mr. Hall cross-examined a witness it was like a sledge hammer coming down on a peanut,' wrote one contemporary who had seen him in action.[80] The first thing he did was to have Minor admit that he had formed a 'theory' about where Mike had been killed. 'I formed a theory as the investigation progressed,' he said. Hall drew him out: 'And it became your theory that Mike was killed in the kitchen?' 'That is correct,' replied Sergeant Minor. This admission was crucial to Petlock's defence because Hall knew that theories are vulnerable to other theories. So he laid the foundation of a substitute one of his own which he would, in due course, set before the jury in an effort to discredit Sergeant Minor's theory. But before doing that, Hall turned to the thoroughness of Minor's investigation. He asked the police officer whether he had made 'a very thorough search of the kitchen.' Minor replied: 'Yes, I made a very thorough search of the kitchen.' 'Can you say you made an inch-by-inch search of the kitchen?' Hall pressed. 'Well, no. I wouldn't say that I took a magnifying glass and went over it inch by inch.' Hall shot back: 'I didn't ask if you used a magnifying glass. I asked if you made an inch-by-inch search of the kitchen.' He then asked the sergeant: 'If the bullet was fired, if that happened in the kitchen, you expected to find the bullet in the kitchen?' 'That is correct,' replied the Sergeant. 'Did you find it?' 'No I did not,' replied Sergeant Minor. So, Hall proceeded, 'Sergeant Minor had found no bullet or casing in the kitchen where he was determined to locate the fatal shot that killed Mike Petlock.' Hall had sent P.J. Dielschneider to the farm a second time; there, Dielschneider and an assistant chipped off a piece of the cement steps leading to the kitchen. The forensic laboratory in Regina confirmed the presence of human blood in the cement. Hall was slowly but steadily building his 'theory' that the evidence proved that Mike had been killed outside, not in the kitchen as Sergeant Minor's 'theory' proposed. He pressed the police officer hard, asking him why had he not taken photographs of the outside area where John Petlock claimed he had wrestled with his brother. Minor had no answer. He now had all the ammunition he thought necessary to convince the jury that the police 'theory' was wrong and that the hard evidence proved that the critical encounter between the two brothers took place outside and that John Petlock had defended himself against the rage of his brother, who had killed his own mother, wife, and two infant children.

Armed with the admission that the police 'theory' did not fit the hard facts, especially the presence of blood on the cement steps, Hall addressed the jury for almost two hours. He began by inviting the all-male jury to view the case as a large jigsaw puzzle which he and the jury had been called to assemble in the interest of justice. 'The task of putting a jigsaw puzzle together is, generally, perhaps hard enough, but where you have missing pieces, it adds to the difficulty, does it not?' he asked rhetorically. 'Where you have pieces that have been distorted, it adds to the difficulty. Where you have pieces that have been jammed by one or other of the witnesses, then the task becomes more difficult again. And you may even have pieces that have been turned around, so that you are not able to really define the correct margins or determine whether it fits into the right side of the case or the left side, or the top or the bottom, because its edges have been frayed.'

Hall went looking for those missing, distorted, or frayed pieces. He began by suggesting that the police, in their determination to have the facts fit their theory, had excluded certain fine details or overlooked certain important facts. There was no question that there had been a fight between the two brothers. No one denied that. And brother Mike was killed in the fight by the rifle Mike brandished. Hall claimed that the grass where Mike and John clashed showed all the signs of a scuffle. But the police ignored this detail. Why? he asked the jury. Hall suggested that perhaps the police were hiding something. If not, why was Dielschneider ordered off the property by Ednot Petlock, another of the brothers, when he was sent to examine the grass and surrounding area for bullet casings? Ednot was convinced that John had murdered Mike's entire family and he would not cooperate with John's defence counsel. Police, however, could not find evidence linking John with the murder of his mother and the other members of Mike's family. He was charged solely with the murder of his brother Mike.

Focusing on what the police had failed to do, Hall said to the jury: 'What a wonderful thing it would have been if a photograph had been taken before anything was moved. But no photograph was taken.' He then began to cast doubt upon the manner in which the police behaved in the course of collecting evidence against John Petlock. He invited the jury to scrutinize the evidence and theory of the prosecution: 'Sergeant Minor formed a theory as to what had happened, and gentlemen, it is now of supreme importance that everything from here on – in terms of the police evidence – be judged in the light of that theory that was formed. Because is it not the fact that in our own (your own) ways of life we proceed at times from certain theories or standpoints? Is it not the way with us all as part of our human characteristics, that having formed an opinion, we release it very slowly and we will stick to it – sometimes through thick and thin – regardless of the fact that, to other people, it may sound silly.'

Hall knew that he had a difficult case so he laboured hard to sow the seeds of doubt in the minds of the jurymen. He insisted on raising questions about the police theory that Mike had been killed in the kitchen. All he needed to secure the release of his client was 'reasonable doubt.' And he was determined to get it by proving that Mike had been shot outside and that his body was dragged into the kitchen after the fatal quarrel. 'If Mike was not killed in the kitchen, then where does all this evidence lead you? The whole house of cards comes crashing down, insofar as the police case is concerned.' One of the photographs the police had taken at the crime scene showed that Mike Petlock's body had been dragged. 'The pattern of the blood which flowed from Mike's body on to the mat, on to the floor, fixes the pattern there showing that that mat and Mike reached that location at the same time,' Hall emphasized. He then moved on to show that the kitchen revealed no signs of struggle, and, above all, he posed one central question: If Mike had been shot in the kitchen, where were the empty bullet casings? The police admitted that they had looked for empty casings and had found none. But they had found three empty casings outside. Was this not proof that Mike was killed outside?

He returned to the fact that the police had failed to explore a part of the backyard where, he maintained, John and Mike had struggled. This, he concluded, was a critical mistake. Once again, he emphasized the fact that his colleague, P.J. Dielschneider, was prevented on the first of two attempts from making a search. This was because, he insisted, an independent search might lead to evidence that would embarrass the police. Furthermore, he reminded the jury, the police themselves still persisted in refusing to examine that part of the yard. Why? he asked repeatedly. And then he answered his own question: 'Because it did not fit the preconceived theory of the police and prosecution.' Hall kept driving home the point that the facts and the police oversights left reasonable doubt as to John Petlock's guilt.

As the trial progressed, Hall became visibly more intense. Towards the end of his lengthy address to the jury he asked: 'Does it not appear to you, gentlemen, that Sergeant Minor is just a little too anxious?' 'I am not suggesting,' he feigned, 'that he would wilfully do anything to bring about the unlawful conviction of a man, but don't some of us get a little too exuberant about our work, and feel that our reputation may be at stake and feel that we must fill up the gaps as we go along, lest it be considered that the prosecution failed by reason of something that he did not do?' Then he added: 'Gentlemen, I do not suggest that it arises in that way' – but, of course, that was exactly what he was suggesting. The 'villain' was Sergeant Minor, or, more precisely, the sergeant's theory. Hall concluded his defence of John Petlock with the following words: 'My suggestion to you, gentlemen of the jury, is that this prosecution must fail because the mistake that was made was that original mistake made by the prosecution of coming to a wrong theory and then closing the mind to anything else, and everything since that day has been done to support that theory and what does not fit with that has to be discarded.'

The judge instructed the jurors that they alone had the full power and responsibility to pronounce upon the guilt or innocence of John Petlock. They could find him guilty or not guilty of the murder of his brother Mike; or guilty or not guilty of manslaughter. Or they could acquit him of all charges. The jury deliberated for four hours and at length emerged with a verdict: John Petlock was guilty of manslaughter of his brother Mike. Hall listened impatiently as the judge sentenced John Petlock to seventeen and a half years in the federal penitentiary at Prince Albert. He was sure that he had sown the grounds for reasonable doubt and, hence, established sufficient reason for acquittal.

There is no question that Hall's was a masterful defence in the face of overwhelming evidence against Petlock. The crown, clearly, held the trump card: John Petlock admitted that he had shot his brother *several times* after the initial occasion during the struggle. The crown emphasized repeatedly to the jury that John Petlock had shot his brother, not once in a struggle, not accidentally, but several times in a rage. That fact not even Hall's determined defence could obscure or diminish. And so John Petlock went to prison for manslaughter. But he went to prison only after Emmett Hall's determined defence, which was at least sufficiently successful to have the jury convict his client of manslaughter and not murder, as the crown had sought.

Hall appealed the sentence as excessive but to no avail. The Court of Appeal declined to alter the sentence. John Petlock – who was a model prisoner – was eventually released after serving eleven years in the Prince Albert federal penitentiary. He died a few months after his release in January 1967. And Emmett Hall, to the end of his life, stubbornly held to the conviction that John Petlock had received a raw deal.

IN CLASS WITH PROFESSOR HALL

During his busy law practice, Hall found time to lecture at the Saskatchewan College of Law for ten years, between 1948 and 1958. He was a severe presence in class, impeccably dressed and in total control of his lectures on criminal procedure. Not blessed with a strong voice, Hall, nevertheless, commanded the attention of his audience. He instilled a sense of urgency into the matter at hand and brooked no inattention. As one of his former students recalled, he frequently appeared overbearing and intolerant of questions that challenged his interpretations of a given statute or point of law. 'But, by damn,' he confessed years later, 'he was most often right, as much as we resented his domineering manner.'[81] This same student built up enough courage on one occasion late in his third year of law school to approach Hall – who, by the mid-1950s, was at the peak of his reputation as a leading defence lawyer – and asked him whether he could article in Hall's firm. Hall told the student to come and see him in his office the next day.

After agreeing to accept the student, Hall announced that he would pay him $75 per month. There was no prior discussion of the matter. It was a straight take-it-or-leave-it proposition. This was clearly below the going rate at the time; most articling students were receiving $100 per month. The student, who had completed his arts degree and was about to be married, responded that the going rate was $100 and that he thought he should receive the going rate. Hall erupted in an outburst, just as he did in class when challenged. 'God damn it, what the hell do you think you're worth?' he scolded. 'You don't know a damn thing about the law. I teach my students who come here for their articles. My students don't come here to spend their time in land title offices. They get a training from me, and a damn good one. You're only worth $75.' He continued in this vein for some time, outlining how the student would learn from his experience at Hall's firm. At length he stopped. The student – nervous and certain now to be dismissed – asked simply: 'Do I get $100 or don't I?' 'God damn it. It's no skin off my back whether you get $100 or $75. Take your $100. See if I care.' That ended the interview and on those terms the young man began his articles in Hall's firm. Hall never once recalled the event or let it affect his relationship with the young man, who later became a professor of law. Indeed, they became life-long friends. Hall was not one to hold grudges; once an issue was settled, he put it behind him.

As the young law student was soon to discover, Hall was, most often, right. He received an education as an articling student unlike that experienced by most students. Hall quite literally took his articling students under his wing; he had them present in interviews with clients, and he showed them how to prepare a case with exactitude – what to look for, what to anticipate in opposing counsel's arguments, when to compromise, and when to settle out of court. These were lessons a young man could not hope to learn until he had the experience of years in practice. But Hall gave his students the benefit of his own experience. One other lawyer who articled years later with the Hall firm, Robert McKercher, recalled how Hall would focus his attention in a given case, looking for the one point on which to win it. 'He used to say,' McKercher related, 'there's only one point in the lawsuit and you either win or lose it on that.'[82] He worked hard and he expected his students to work just as hard. He had little or no time for small talk. Anyone who dared to enter his office in search of idle chatter would encounter the knitted brow of his displeasure and make a quick exit.

SCRAPBOOK OVERSIGHT

One aspect of Hall's practice that is conspicuous by its absence from the scrapbook was his abortion and divorce work. For a Catholic, these were exceedingly contentious issues, subject to the heavy weight of formal church disapproval. Divorce was forbidden to Catholics and anyone who had an abortion or participated in performing one was subject to immediate denial of the sacraments and excommunication. It was not doctrinally clear, however, whether the ecclesiastical prohibitions extended to legal defence work. Most Catholic lawyers simply refused to handle divorce cases and fled from abortion work with horror. It came as a surprise, therefore, in 1945 when Hall agreed to defend Dr H.A. Matheson on charges that he had procured abortions for five women. Hall poured his energies into this case by consulting with a leading gynecologist at Queen's University Medical School in Kingston, Ontario. His vigorous defence was successful and Dr Matheson was cleared on all courts. The court victory did little to enhance Emmett Hall's reputation in the Catholic community of Saskatoon, but he defended himself on the grounds that every accused person was entitled to the best legal defence possible. The fact that he himself did not approve of abortion had nothing to do with his duty to accord the best defence to his client. His aggressive nature rose to the surface in such circumstances. On this issue – the right of an accused to the best legal defence – he would give quarter to no man. And he defended himself with force before the censure of both lay and clerical Catholic critics.

Hall used the same line of argument in defence of his firm's divorce practice, which was handled principally by Jim Wedge. Presumably, Hall thought that divorce work would be less of a burden on the conscience of this convert from Presbyterianism. As it turned out, the Hall and Maguire firm handled most of the divorce work in the city of Saskatoon during and following the Second World War. In Hall's papers there is a note from a nun expressing her disapproval of him because, she said, 'he defends too many drunks.' But business was good and Hall and Maguire were beginning to make real money. And his iconoclastic reputation did not prevent Hall from serving on the board at St Paul's Hospital or the Catholic school board. Much of the corporate work the Hall-Maguire firm did for Catholic causes was done free. Emmett Hall was clearly adept at working both sides of the street.

THE HALLS AT HOME

As Hall's practice became more successful, the family assets grew correspondingly. After renting a number of houses in Saskatoon for several years, Emmett and Belle decided that it was time they settled into more permanent quarters. So in 1940 they purchased a large three-storey house with five bedrooms on Poplar Crescent. It was to be their home until Hall went to the bench. Poplar Crescent was 'a sedate street of tree-shaded mansions adjacent to the river, the closest thing that a city scarcely forty years old could offer in the way of a preserve for the *nouveau* elite.'[83] This house was transformed in due course into a comfortable home by Belle's impeccable taste and efforts.[84] The increased space was especially welcomed because it provided Emmett with a quiet office in which he could work almost every evening. Like many lawyers, Hall spent long hours at home poring over documents, preparing cases for court, and doing a thousand things required of him by his practice as well as his school board and hospital duties. But the extra space was especially treasured by Belle, for, ever since she and Emmett had moved back to Saskatoon, her mother lived with them. The new home made it possible for Mrs Parker to have a good deal more privacy and space of her own. She lived with the Halls for thirty years. It is easy to imagine that Belle, who had witnessed her father's desertion, was determined that her mother would have a warm and comfortable home. As one of her old friends commented: 'Belle had artistic features about her. She knew how to arrange flowers, and she was always fixing furniture and buying different things for the house.'[85] As well, Belle was ever ready to take care of the children of in-laws when anyone became ill; the large house provided the ideal forum for these generosities. It was in every sense a happy home, with visible signs of the family's Catholic faith. But Belle ran the house and disciplined the children, seeing to it that they did their homework. As her son John recalled, 'Mother was the disciplinarian. Dad was always an easy mark as far as my sister and I were concerned. He was the softer of the two, which is quite in contrast to his public image.'[86]

The large house was also an important venue for social gatherings of professional friends and visiting dignitaries. As Hall's career at the bar continued to rise, so, too, did his circle of professional friends in the Saskatchewan bar as well as in the Canadian Bar Association. Not infrequently, he would invite a visiting judge or prominent lawyer home for dinner and an evening of fine drinks and good conversation. He would also invite members of the school board back to the house for extended rehashings of board business, especially if he had become agitated over something that had gone contrary to the way he wanted. It was during these years – from the late 1930s to the early 1950s – that Hall became intensely active in Catholic hospital and Catholic school board issues. In 1937 he was called upon to extricate the Catholic school board from a mess caused by some poor real estate investments. The board was about to lose one of its schools to creditors. Hall stepped in and saved the day for the school board. This experience led him to serve on the Catholic school board for twenty years. He never had to contest an election to the board since he was acclaimed at every election. Emmett took an active role in the affairs of the school board both locally and province-wide. He served as chairman of the board for ten years and as president of the Catholic School Trustees of Saskatchewan for seven, and he was responsible for convincing the Catholic trustees to merge with the public school trustees. Hall was on this, as on all the other boards he was to serve on, a strong presence. As Bill Reid, a long-serving member during Hall's tenure on the school board, observed years later: 'Emmett was not a lovable character in his younger days. He was not domineering exactly, but he was almost arrogant in his aggressiveness ... He's a humbler and milder man [now] than he used to be.'[87]

To say that Emmett Hall, in the years before his appointment to the bench, was active in matters beyond the practice of law would be an egregious understatement. Besides his work with the Catholic school board and the trustees association, he was chairman of the lay advisory board of St Paul's Hospital (he would remain a member of the St Paul's board while chief justice of Saskatchewan). He was, as well, the president of the Saskatchewan Law Society, a member of the University of Saskatchewan Senate, and a part-time lecturer in criminal procedure in the College of Law. And, as if this were not enough to keep him busy, he was an active member of the Knights of Columbus, the Kinsmen Club, and the provincial and national executives of the Canadian Red Cross Society. Is it any wonder that his son and daughter could say that they did not see very much of their father around the house when they were growing up? Belle raised the children and provided the home support for a man who was driven by a love of the law and public service.

3

Legal and Political Ambitions

As with many lawyers, Emmett Hall harboured political ambitions for a time but they were always secondary to his primary aspiration to go to the bench. His father had been a vocal supporter of the Liberal Party since his arrival in Saskatoon; most Catholics voted Liberal in Saskatchewan in those days. Following in his father's footsteps, Emmett gravitated to the Liberal Party and soon became widely known as an important Liberal voice in Saskatoon. According to Walter Tucker – a leader of the Saskatchewan Liberal Party who eventually became an MP and, still later, chief justice of Saskatchewan – 'by the time he [Hall] opened an office in Saskatoon he was regarded as a good Liberal – good enough to feel that when the place on the bench held by Turgeon [a French-speaking Catholic] became vacant he felt he should receive the appointment.'[1] Tucker stated: 'There had been a tradition in Saskatchewan that there should be two RCs on the high courts of Saskatchewan [Queen's Bench and Court of Appeal], one French and the other non-French,' and that Hall felt strongly that as a Catholic and bilingual he was entitled to be considered.'[2] There is no question that Hall had made his ambitions known to well-connected people in the Liberal Party. But the leading Liberal in Saskatchewan was Jimmy Gardiner and, when Adrien Doiron was appointed to replace Turgeon, Hall blamed Gardiner. 'Emmett Hall was clearly upset,' Tucker acknowledged, 'but if a French Canadian had not been appointed, French Canadians in Saskatchewan – and indeed in all Canada – would be *very* upset.'[3] Tucker claimed, however, that the federal minister of justice, Ernest Lapointe, made the appointment without consulting Gardiner. 'I was therefore really surprised when a cabinet minister told me that the first Gardiner knew of the appointment was when he read about it in the newspapers. Apparently Ernest Lapointe, the minister of justice, had gone ahead and put it through without clearing it with Gardiner.'[4]

But most people active in Saskatchewan politics thought that Gardiner had used his influence or had put forward Doiron for the federal appointment. Tucker knew that Hall had often spoken of his 'good chance' at getting the appointment and believed that he never got over his anger at Gardiner. 'It was also generally believed that when he left the Liberals and joined the Conservatives it was because he was badly treated by the Liberals and particularly Gardiner,' Tucker conceded.[5] Even close personal friends such as Dr J. Francis Leddy believed that Hall had quit the Liberal Party because he was denied the appointment to the bench that went to Doiron. Yet Emmett Hall resolutely denied to the end of his life that there was any truth in these allegations. When told of Leddy's comment, he exploded: 'It's a damned lie.'[6] Hall's own words on this matter are contained in a letter to the author: 'I actually left the Liberal Party in or about 1924. I did not actually join the Conservative Party until the early 1940s when a group decided to throw in their lot with Mr. Diefenbaker and to do everything to help him head the Conservative Party.'[7] Jimmy Gardiner may well have treated him badly but Hall did not leave the Liberals for the Conservatives because of the Doiron appointment. There were enough reasons for one such as Hall to leave the Liberal Party in these years of William Lyon Mackenzie King, when westerners generally were becoming vocal over the neglect of their interests and ambitions. In any case, Hall was never an ideologue and, hence, was capable of changing his political affiliation. And, as we shall see, he put the interests of Saskatchewan ahead of a rigid allegiance to any political party.

Apart from an unsuccessful bid for a seat on the Saskatoon city council in 1937, Emmett Hall's principal foray into elective politics occurred two years after the Second World War. In the fall of 1947 he sought and secured the Progressive Conservative nomination in the rural district of Hanley – surrounding Saskatoon – for the provincial election scheduled for 24 June 1948. One newspaper advertisement for this election featured a picture of Hall, not yet fifty years of age, over a caption that read: 'People Are Always Saying: "Why Do Our Best Men Not Offer Themselves for Election?"' It went on to say that the electors of Hanley had an opportunity to vote for and elect a man of impeccable credentials in the person of Emmett Hall. His platform was stated boldly in four points:[8]

1. Freedom of religion – he will oppose discrimination of every kind, religious or racial.
2. The right of the working man to a just and living wage for himself and his family, and for labour to participate in the management of industry and in its profits.
3. The right of Western Canada to a square deal in the Canadian Federation – particularly in regard to freight rates, prices, use of Hudson Bay Railway, irrigation projects, etc.
4. Eliminating bureaucracy and regimentation and restoring self-government in Saskatchewan.

Most of these issues were standard prairie election themes that all three major parties in Saskatchewan – Liberals, CCF, and Progressive Conservatives – supported. But the second item on Hall's list reveals just what kind of Conservative he really was. The ideas of labour-management industrial councils and profit-sharing were far from traditional conservative policies; if anything, they were closer to traditional progressive policies long viewed with suspicion by Conservatives. Hall, however, supported both, and he did so comfortably as a Conservative. But the Saskatchewan Tory has always been a unique breed of political animal; the eventual success of the CCF in Saskatchewan owed much to the defection of former Conservatives to that party instead of to the Liberals. Hall was clearly a member of the progressive wing of the Progressive Conservative Party and in this he had more in common with Alvin Hamilton than with John Diefenbaker. (Little did he realize in 1948 that the greatest opposition to labour-management industrial councils would come from the labour movement itself.)

Hall threw his boundless energies into the 1948 election campaign; he visited every corner of the Hanley constituency and talked with hundreds of people. Much to his surprise, he enjoyed himself; for the first time in his life, he stopped strangers and asked them to support him in order that he could serve them in the provincial legislature. Everyone he met showed him genuine interest and pledged to vote for him. He was clearly exhilarated by the prospects. He felt he was sure to win.

On the eve of the 24 June election, the Saskatoon *Star-Phoenix* featured a large advertisement authorized by the Saskatchewan Progressive Conservative Party, then led by Premier Rupert Ramsay of Saskatoon. It announced in bold type the names of four candidates who were seeking election in the rural areas outside Saskatoon. Those names were: for Tidale, William Hayes, farmer; for Wilkie, O.A. Bentley, farmer; for Rosetown, Alvin Hamilton, schoolteacher; and for Hanley, Emmett Hall, barrister. The advertisement also announced a ten-point program for the province. This program clearly bore the stamp of Emmett Hall, especially in points one and four. Point one promised a 'decrease in school taxes on land and property by increasing the government grants for local school costs from the present 25 per cent to a 50 per cent minimum'; the fourth point pledged the government to 'the improvement of Saskatchewan's Health Services by special grants to hospitals having building troubles, or to hospitals losing money, because of operational difficulties.'⁹ But there was nothing in the program about labour-management councils or profit-sharing, two items set out in Hall's own political advertisements.

This election campaign introduced Hall to a cause for which he would fight strenuously for many years to come. On the evening of 23 April 1948, two months before the election, Hall gave a radio address on station CFQC Saskatoon on the subject of the South Saskatchewan Irrigation and Power Project. The address showed not only how well he had done his homework but how fiercely partisan he could be when the occasion required.

Saskatchewan wheat production since 1940 had been about 210 million bushels a year. These were clearly boom times, but every farmer's memory could be jogged back to 1937, just ten short years before, when the total Saskatchewan wheat production amounted to a scant 37 million bushels, for an average of 2.7 bushels per acre. The farming techniques were identical throughout the boom and bust periods, the one variable being moisture. All farmers are at the mercy of the elements; however, when the entire economy depends upon a single crop, the impact of crop failure is devastating. Small wonder that Saskatchewan farmers were excited about talk of an irrigation project which would stabilize moisture and ensure a continuous high wheat production, to say nothing of the electric-power potential of the dams.

Emmett Hall reminded his radio audience of these economic realities as well as the fact that, between 1931 and 1944, Saskatchewan had lost 243,000 people through migration to other parts of Canada. These people had left Saskatchewan 'literally for greener fields,' he said. Quoting the recently published report of the Royal Commission on

Dominion-Provincial Relations – the Rowell-Sirois report – Hall drove home the point that something had to be done. The report said: 'The Prairies are threatened to become a classic example of an area doomed to chronic depression. Drought was the final blow, for it prevented resort to the traditional defense of the average producer – expansion of production. The bare statistics cannot convey the full measure of the Western Debacle, with its shattering blows to living standards, to adequate nutrition, to health services, to educational standards, and to individual hopes and dreams and ambitions.'[10]

Hall pleaded for a constructive conservation policy, one that would remove the recurring problem of drought. 'We have the water,' he emphasized. 'Each year there flows through the prairies sufficient water to insure adequate soil moisture to most of the area threatened by drought – but it flows in its course to the sea – through the North and South Saskatchewan rivers – unharnessed – of little service to man or beast.'[11] It was time, he said, to harness the Saskatchewan waters and not permit them to flow through to Hudson Bay unused.

With not a little irony, Hall drew his listeners' attention to the fact that it was an easterner, John R. MacNichol, Progressive Conservative MP for Davenport (Toronto), who had until then done more than anyone else to keep the problem before the eyes of Parliament and the public. MacNichol, a Toronto engineer, had developed a deep interest in the prospects of harnessing prairie waters in the interest of breaking the threat of drought. His efforts in the House of Commons finally began to pay off when the government under Mackenzie King ordered the Prairie Farm Rehabilitation Authority to undertake a study of the proposals. The Saskatoon *Star-Phoenix* ran a lead editorial on 15 January 1947, in which it sang the praises of John MacNichol. 'The visits to the West of Mr. John R. MacNichol, the member of parliament for Davenport (Toronto), brings something of the old vision back in new terms. Would he not after all, turn three million acres into a wonder garden of the West? Does he not see a hundred towns and cities rising where the short grass struggles to exist? Is it not true, as he says, that 56,000,000 tons in motion flows between the banks of the Saskatchewan, doing nothing for us except add to the weight of water and ice in Hudson Bay?'[12] The engineers' interim report was filed in Parliament on 8 July 1947. The author of the report, G.L. Mackenzie, was chief engineer of the Prairie Farm Rehabilitation Authority, and he had an American engineer, Major-General H.B. Ferguson, as chief consultant. The main recommendation of the Mackenzie report was that a damming of the South Saskatchewan River eighteen miles upstream from Outlook was feasible and practical. Such a dam would store enough water to ensure the recurring irrigation of 500,000 acres of farm land in an area on both sides of the Saskatchewan River from Riverhurst to Saskatoon, and extending out from Dinsmore and Milder on the west to Kenaston and Hanley on the east.

Hall showed how the residents of Hanley would benefit from such a project by translating its impact into dollars and cents: 'Twenty-nine years ago some 17,000 acres around Taber, Alberta, were all but deserted by their original settlers. Values dropped to less than $15.00 per acre. Today the price is $150.00 per acre. The area through irrigation has been transformed into a rich, lush oasis. In the Lethbridge Northern Irrigation District an area of 360 square miles (10 townships) has been changed from harsh, dry and thinly populated prairie, scarcely capable of supporting life, into a garden-land. The number of farms has increased in those 10 townships from 300 to 900; population has grown from 1,500 to 10,000; there are grade schools, electric lights and better roads. The average return is $24.00 an acre as against $12.00 for the entire province.'[13]

Eric Knowles, news editor of the Saskatoon *Star-Phoenix*, wrote a lengthy article about irrigation on 24 July 1947. In the lead paragraph he described an annoyingly familiar landscape:

'We traveled down a prairie road. On one side, as far as the eye could see, stretched a flat, dead land on which nothing grew but a little sage and some sparse grass. On the other side of the road there were good farmsteads, crops of wheat, oats, barley, flax, rye, alfalfa, sweet clover, peas, beans, corn, potatoes and garden truck galore. There were horses, dairy cattle, beef cattle, hogs, sheep, and poultry. There were trees, flowers, shrubs. The soil on the one side of the road varied not one iota from that on the other side, a soils expert said. The one side of the road was dead because it got insufficient rainfall. The other side gave abundant life because man had brought it water – irrigation!

That, in a nutshell, is a picture of the Eastern Irrigation District of Alberta with only two variations. In some areas both sides of the road were irrigated and both sides blossomed. In other areas, there was no irrigation and both sides of the road were dead.[14]

If Alberta could do it, why couldn't Saskatchewan? Hall asked his Hanley constituents. He concluded his radio address with the charge that the CCF government (which had come to power in June 1944) had not pressed sufficiently hard for the enormous project. Hall promised that he would bring all his energies to bear on the matter as a Progressive Conservative member of the legislature.

But, unfortunately, Hall could not have chosen a worse time to run for the provincial legislature on the Progressive Conservative ticket. Not only did the party take a thorough drubbing at the polls in 1948, it was destined not to hold a single seat in the legislature until 1953, when it won a seat in a by-election. That achievement was short-lived, for the party was to lose its single seat in the general election three years later. That was the first seat the Tories had won since 1929. Indeed, the Saskatchewan Progressive Conservative party held only two seats in the legislature in the thirty years between 1934 and 1964.[15]

The odds were clearly against both Hall and the Saskatchewan Progressive Conservative party. His defeat in Hanley was a tremendous personal blow. His son John and friends of the family recall that the experience left him almost in a state of shock. He sincerely believed that all the people he had met in Hanley who had responded favourably to his request for support would in fact vote for him. When the votes were counted, he found that he had placed third in a field of four candidates. He had received 1,025 votes, while Robert Walker, the successful CCF candidate, had received 2,417. The Liberal candidate, Clayton Pascoe, was a close second with 2,366. Years later he would say: 'I couldn't believe that people would say that they would vote for you and then not do so.'[16]

It was the last time Emmett Hall was to run as a candidate for elective office.[17] But it was not the last time he was to campaign actively for the Progressive Conservative Party in Saskatchewan. Nor did he leave behind the matter of irrigation. On 23 February 1949 he spoke on radio station CFQC on behalf of the federal Progressive Conservative Party. Not only did he return to the subject of irrigation, but he identified a villain in the person of Jimmy Gardiner, federal minister of agriculture and 'the boss of the Liberal machine in Saskatchewan,' as he put it.

Jimmy Gardiner had campaigned on behalf of W.A. Boucher, the federal Liberal candidate for Rosthern in a by-election held on 25 October 1948. The vacancy had been created by Walter Tucker, who had resigned his seat in Parliament to become leader of the provincial Liberal Party. In his campaigning on behalf of the Liberal candidate in Rosthern, Gardiner had promised a speedy beginning of the irrigation and power development on the South Saskatchewan River near Outlook. 'He led everyone to believe that the job was to be done immediately,' Hall reminded his radio audience, and that Gardiner, as representative in the Cabinet for Saskatchewan, 'was going to see that it was done.'[18]

But, Hall said, the speech from the throne read on 26 January 1949, at the opening of the fifth session of the 20th Parliament, contained not a single reference to the South Saskatchewan water conservation and power project. Gardiner had betrayed Saskatchewan again. Hall read the text of the speech from the throne and saw that it was more than simply a matter of the South Saskatchewan River project not receiving the attention it deserved; rather, the speech clearly showed that a western Canadian project had lost out, once again, to an eastern Canadian one. In this instance, the government of Canada, under Prime Minister Louis St Laurent, had decided that the St Lawrence Seaway was to receive priority over the Saskatchewan irrigation and power project. More salt was rubbed in western wounds by the government's decision to rank the Trans-Canada Highway higher than Saskatchewan's need for irrigation and electric power. Hall believed that the Liberal government of St Laurent had deliberately consigned Saskatchewan to the fate of periodic drought and good times, to boom and bust, with all the inequities that entailed.

The economic future of Saskatchewan depended on irrigation for its primary industry and electric power for its manufacturing or secondary industry. So it was only to be expected that Hall and the Saskatchewan Progressive Conservative Party were beside themselves with frustration.'How long can the cities of Regina and Moose Jaw go without an adequate water supply? How long must this vital project remain a political football? The exodus of people from Saskatchewan continues because people will not stay to be dried out year after year, to see the crops planted with high hopes in the spring weather and die for lack of moisture.'[19]

Hall took special delight in pointing out Jimmy Gardiner as a party to the betrayal of the Saskatchewan irrigation project and urged that he be replaced as the spokesman for the province. 'Saskatchewan has one vigilant, able and loyal spokesman at Ottawa, Mr. John Diefenbaker, the member for Lake Centre; the man Mr. Gardiner is so anxious to have defeated that the order has gone out from Saskatchewan's Liberal Caesar: "Beat John Diefenbaker at all costs." The Liberals have gerrymandered his seat – they will stop at nothing to defeat him. Why? Because John Diefenbaker has in season and out been fearless in his criticisms of the Government, fearless in the interests of Saskatchewan and Canada as a whole.'[20]

In the federal election of June 1949 Prime Minister St Laurent visited Saskatchewan and gave the standard vague assurances that the irrigation project would be undertaken in the future. The Liberals won fourteen of Saskatchewan's twenty seats; the CCF won five, and John Diefenbaker won the sole Progressive Conservative seat in the province. Yet, despite the Liberal's success in Saskatchewan, there was no action on the irrigation project.

On 9 February 1953 Hall once again spoke on radio about the evils of the Liberal government in Ottawa and the callous neglect of the South Saskatchewan River project. The Liberals were still dangling the project before the people of Saskatchewan; they even appropriated $250,000 for the project in 1948, when its cost was estimated at $60 to $70 million. 'At this rate it will take 30 to 35 years to do the job at Mr. Gardiner's rate of progress, ' Hall commented sarcastically.[21] He reviewed the long list of delays since 1947 and the favourable Mackenzie report. The crowning delaying tactic came in 1951 after the opposition parties in Parliament became outraged at the government's failure to include in the estimates an appropriation for the Saskatchewan dam. Prime Minister St Laurent responded to the pressure with the appointment of a royal commission to look into the matter. The commission was instructed to inquire[22] 'whether the economic and social returns to the Canadian people on the investment in the South Saskatchewan River Project would be commensurate with the cost thereof; whether the said project represents the most profitable and desirable use which can be made of the physical resources involved.' In short, the government was instructing the commission to inquire whether the Canadian people supported the Saskatchewan project. The terms of reference were clearly negative; further, there was no western representative on the commission and Dr John A. Whitsoe, a major consultant to the commission, was an eighty-three-year-old scientist from Utah who was known to be in poor health. Hall called the commission a 'ruse' and 'a red herring across the Liberal government's trail of failure' to implement its promise to build the dam. To make matters worse, the chief commissioner, Dr T.H. Hogg, was also too sick to do anything for about six months. (Hall remained convinced that his illness was politically induced by the evil machinations of Jimmy Gardiner.)

The Hogg commission visited Saskatchewan in 'a hit and miss

fashion' (Hall's words) throughout 1952. It held a lengthy hearing at Outlook, the proposed site of the dam, and heard numerous briefs from farmers of the area calling for the construction of the dam. Only Dr. Whitsoe appeared to be persuaded that the dam was necessary and he said so at Outlook. Unfortunately, Whitsoe died in December 1952, before the commission's report was made public. There is a great deal of mystery surrounding the fact that Dr. Whitsoe's signature appears on the final report recommending against the construction of the South Saskatchewan River Project as economically unsound. Hall and many other Saskatchewan Conservatives were convinced that Whitsoe wrote a minority report but that the government suppressed it. If such a minority report existed – and there is no evidence that one was ever written – it has never surfaced. Critics of the commission also believed that Whitsoe had been pressured into signing the majority report.

The Hogg report concluded that irrigation was not necessary in central Saskatchewan, a conclusion that raised the hackles of even Jimmy Gardiner. He called the report the 'silliest thing he had ever seen.'[23] Yet, as Hall told his radio audience, 'the man who appointed the Commission, the Prime Minister, says he needs time to study the silly thing.'[24]

Despite Jimmy Gardiner's repudiation of the report, he was able to rally all his Saskatchewan Liberal members of the Commons to vote against a motion tendered by John Diefenbaker, on 30 January 1953, calling for the immediate construction of the dam. All Saskatchewan Liberal members, under Gardiner's leadership, voted against the motion. 'Oh yes,' Hall told his listeners, 'the Saskatchewan members of Parliament are for the project in Saskatchewan but they vote against having it dealt with in Ottawa.'[25]

The death of the Outlook dam was sealed by the Hogg report's conclusion that the cost of construction would be $250 million (the report of the consulting engineers claimed that it could be done for $118 million). Hall saw this larger figure as a distortion designed to turn people in other parts of Canada against the project, as it clearly did. Eastern newspaper editorials protested that $250 million was exorbitant. 'That thought has been planted deep in the Canadian mind and will be difficult to eradicate. Taxpayers in Ontario, Quebec, the Maritimes and elsewhere will have to be re-educated after their being made the victims of this propaganda,'[26] Hall told his Saskatchewan audience. What hurt most was that the government was spending hundreds of millions of dollars on the St Lawrence Seaway and not a penny on

Saskatchewan. 'Why?' he asked 'Why is it that we of all Canada cannot be permitted in the national interest to fulfil our destiny? We cannot do that without power and without irrigation.'[27]

Hall had become deeply absorbed by this issue in the 1950s, and he was eager to work on behalf of John Diefenbaker, whom he called 'the only authentic voice of Saskatchewan.' His efforts throughout Saskatchewan on behalf of Diefenbaker contributed to the Conservative's electoral success – however limited – in the 1957 election in his home province: Diefenbaker was able to win, besides his own, two other seats in Saskatchewan that year. The Liberals won four seats and the CCF won ten. But John Diefenbaker was called upon to form a minority government. He then took advantage of the political momentum un-leashed in 1957 and swept the country in the general election the following year, taking all but one of the seventeen Saskatchewan seats. Hall had contributed his share to the success of John Diefenbaker and the Progressive Conservative Party of Canada, and he revelled in his friend's personal triumph.

As fate would have it, Hall's decision to support John Diefenbaker throughout those long years in the wilderness was a wise one. For, shortly after he became prime minister of Canada in 1957, Diefenbaker appointed Hall to the Saskatchewan Court of Queen's Bench and set in motion a chain of appointments – on royal commissions and on the bench – that would shape his life for the next forty years.

4

On the Bench of Saskatchewan

Emmett Hall, accompanied by his wife, Belle, left Saskatoon for Regina on 4 October 1957 to be sworn in as chief justice of the Court of Queen's Bench for Saskatchewan. He was named by Prime Minister Diefenbaker to succeed Chief Justice J.T. Brown, who had died the previous April. Hall was formally notified of his appointment to the bench in a letter from the deputy minister of justice. The day he received the official notice he also received a phone call from the prime minister telling him to expect the letter and to congratulate him.[1] He knew that he was going to be appointed because, as he said, 'my appointment was forecast some three months before in a call from Mr. Diefenbaker, but the Order-in-Council was not passed until either September 30 or October 1.'[2]

On 4 October, the lieutenant governor of Saskatchewan, W.J. Patterson, administered the oath of office in a ceremony at Government House in Regina. A reception for the new chief justice following the swearing-in ceremony was attended by leading political figures of all parties, lawyers, judges, and businessmen. Hall was not yet fifty-nine years of age. Greetings from all across the country and from abroad flowed in to express congratulations to the new judge. George Drew wrote from London, where he was Canadian high commissioner; he praised the appointment and wished Hall his very best. Prime Minister Diefenbaker wrote a personal note a few days later, saying, 'I shall only say in comment that I believe the best possible appointment was made and also that I have every confidence that you will be an ornament to the

Bench of our Province.'³ At the time of his appointment, the Court of Queen's Bench consisted of seven judges: the chief justice and six puisne judges. Chief Justice Hall's colleagues on the court were justices G.E. Taylor, Adrien Doiron, S. McKercher, H.F. Thompson, R.T. Graham, and C.S. Davis.

The relocation to Regina was not something that Belle looked forward to; she loved her home in Saskatoon but she knew that there was no alternative to the move. It meant, of course, leaving behind family. Their son John was off pursuing graduate studies in orthopaedics and making a solid name for himself as a surgeon at the Hospital for Sick Children in Toronto and later at Harvard Medical School. However, their daughter, Marian, and her husband and children were still in Saskatoon. (Marian had graduated from the University of Saskatchewan in 1944 and would return to study law in 1961 after her four children had grown up. After practising law for a few years, she was appointed first as a judge of the Magistrates' Court and later as a judge of the Court of Queen's Bench.) One of the most painful decisions Belle had to face as a result of the move to Regina was to place her mother in a nursing home in Saskatoon. This Belle did with care but deep regret; she took consolation, however, in the fact that Marian and her family were able to visit the aging 'Granny Parker.' Nevertheless, it was not easy for Belle.

The Halls bought a house in the fashionable old crescent area of Regina close to the centre of the city, just north of the Wascana Creek. It is a beautiful area of Regina complete with old elm trees and three-storey stately homes. It has also long been the preferred location for the professional and wealthy burghers of the capital city. Life soon became a carbon copy of their life in Saskatoon: professional colleagues dropped in, visiting judges were entertained, and other members of the bar and bench of Saskatchewan found a ready welcome. Hall joined the Assiniboia Club, an exclusive male-only club in Regina, and when he discovered that the club refused membership to Jews, he began a firm behind-the-scenes campaign to undo the affront. At length he was successful in having the ban quietly abandoned. When he went to Ottawa three years later, as a member of the Supreme Court of Canada, he undertook a similar campaign to end discrimination against Jewish membership in the Rideau Club. He was successful in that endeavour as well.

Since he was not one to waste much time celebrating, Hall immediately set about his new job as chief justice. In a letter to the deputy minister of Justice, W.R. Jackett, he informed him officially of his oaths and attached certified copies. He also added: 'I met with the other judges and found that they are really short handed with the sittings at Moose Jaw scheduled for tomorrow (October 8) with no judge in Moose Jaw tomorrow morning.'[4] He discovered quickly that 'the Court lists were very much in arrears and two or three sittings of the Court had been postponed because there was no judge to preside for them. Two of the judges were ill and that was the reason.'[5] As a result, three days after being sworn in, the new chief justice was on his way to Moose Jaw and his first trial as a judge. 'The first case I heard on becoming C.J.Q.B. in 1957 was one of several divorce cases.' As he later recalled, 'I was sworn in on Friday in Regina and went to Moose Jaw at the beginning of the next week. I heard several cases then went to Saskatoon for the Friday weekly court and back to Moose Jaw to complete the list the following week.' The hectic schedule made it difficult for him to return to Saskatoon and wind up his partnership business. 'It was a matter of five or six weeks' before he was able to do so.[6]

Many people in the legal fraternity of Saskatoon opined that Hall would not be a good judge because they thought his aggressive manner would make him impatient and unwilling to listen. Fortunately for both bar and bench, these misgivings proved to be groundless. Hall was determined from the first day to listen intently to counsel; he had in his lifetime appeared before too many judges who appeared not to listen, including the legendary Frederick Haultain.

The administrative responsibilities of the chief justice of the Court of Queen's Bench are demanding. Not only is the occupant charged with the responsibility of administering – with the assistance of his colleagues – the rules relating to pleadings, practice, and procedures of that court, but he or she is also charged with superintending the district courts of the province. The chief justice must see to it that the Queen's Bench sittings are scheduled, that judges are available, and that there is no undue backlog of cases awaiting trial. One of Chief Justice Hall's first administrative decisions was to convince his colleagues to revise the tariff of fees paid to lawyers appearing before the court. The tariff had not been revised for years and was far below the fees in neighbouring provinces. The new chief justice revised the fee upwards about 30 per cent and did away with the requirement that lawyers submit detailed bills of costs. In its stead, Saskatchewan adopted the Alberta practice of having lawyers submit a simple bill of one amount. Needless to say, this made him popular throughout the practising bar of Saskatchewan.

In addition, Chief Justice Hall set about with Justices McKercher and Harold Thompson to revise the Rules of Court. This took a great deal of concentrated effort, but they completed their work in due course; the new rules were ready for promulgation in December 1960. He also appointed a committee to revise the Crown Practice Rules.

During the summer of 1960, less than three years after he had been appointed chief justice of the Court of Queen's Bench, Hall became embroiled in a controversy with the attorney general of Saskatchewan, R.A. Walker, the very person who had defeated him in the 1948 provincial election. The dispute was over the assignment of district court judges and at its centre was Judge J.H. McFadden, who for several years had sought, unsuccessfully, a transfer from Melville to a larger urban centre, either Saskatoon or Regina. In August 1960, Hall wrote the attorney general explaining the matter: 'I am sure you will agree that Judge McFadden could be moved from Melville. I concede that at present there is not nearly enough work for a judge at Melville. The difficulty with Judge McFadden is that he will not consider leaving Melville unless he has a guarantee that he will be designated either immediately or later to Saskatoon. In other words he wants to impose his own terms. He has been soliciting a change from Melville to a larger centre on each occasion a vacancy occurred in a larger centre. He sought Yorkton, Moose Jaw, Regina and now Saskatoon. I have not found it possible to conscientiously approve of his translation to the busy Judicial Centre of Saskatoon.' Unfortunately for the chief justice, the attorney general had announced to the press that 'Judge McFadden will be taking up residence in Saskatoon' and would be serving as district court judge for the Battleford-Kerrobert-Kindersley-Wilkie circuit.[7] Indeed, on 11 August 1960, McFadden was officially notified that he was 'hereby authorized to act as District Court Judge for the Judicial Centre of Saskatoon' from 3 September.[8] On the same day, Judge McFadden received another letter from the deputy attorney general stating that McFadden was 'hereby authorized to act as District Court Judge for the Judicial Centres of Battleford, Wilkie, Kerrobert and Kindersley from September 3 next and until otherwise advised, in addition to your other judicial duties.'[9] The 'other judicial duties' presumably referred to Judge McFadden's duties in Saskatoon.

Emmett Hall bristled at this clear intrusion, as he perceived it, into his administrative responsibilities. When he pointed out to the attorney general that the chief justice was responsible under the statutes for assigning judges their judicial duties, Walker replied: 'I assured him

[Judge McFadden] that he could be designated by the Chief Justice as one of the judges for the Saskatoon judicial centre or *I could authorize him to act in that judicial centre pursuant to subsection (8) of section 8 of the Act.*'[10] This attempt to make an end run around him prompted Hall to write the minister of justice for Canada, E. Davie Fulton. In a lengthy letter the chief justice outlined the dispute over McFadden's efforts to be transferred to Saskatoon from Melville and how Walker had defended his right to assign judicial duties by appealing to subsection (8) of section 8 of the District Court Judges Act. He made the case that there is 'a void in the legislation, both Provincial and Federal, in that nothing is said as to where any District Court Judge should reside. I can designate the Judicial centre at which the Judge shall act but cannot direct where to live.'[11] It is interesting that, while Hall did not address explicitly Walker's threat to use the power under subsection (8) of section 8, he made it clear to Minister of Justice Fulton that a revision of the act removing that provision would help to solve his problem.

In addition to this request for revisions to the District Court Judges Act, Hall made it indelibly clear that his reasons for not wanting McFadden on the Saskatoon district court were substantive. 'I am firmly convinced that Judge McFadden has neither the judicial ability nor the energy to do the work required of a District Court Judge at Saskatoon.'[12] He went on to say that the Saskatoon district centre required two full-time 'competent' judges and that McFadden was clearly not, in his judgment, able to handle the administrative responsibilities of the position.

The flurry of letters back and forth between Hall, Walker, McFadden, and Fulton lasted into the fall of 1960. McFadden put his house in Melville on the market and rented an apartment in Saskatoon. After all, he had been informed by the deputy attorney general that he was to sit as a district court judge in Saskatoon. But on 22 August, Hall wrote the attorney general about 'Judge McFadden's refusal to serve the Judicial Districts of Battleford, Wilkie and Kerrobert on a temporary basis unless given a guarantee that he would be designated to act at Saskatoon and an assurance that he would be left there until his term of office expired.' The chief justice would have none of this and stubbornly resisted.

In one sense, the more serious dispute between Walker and Hall was that relating to the number of district court judges required. In the same letter to Davie Fulton in which he complained about McFadden's incompetence, Hall noted that the Saskatchewan lieutenant governor had issued an order-in-council reducing – as vacancies occurred – the number of district court judges in Saskatchewan to twelve. He went on to explain: 'With Judge Nay's retirement there will still remain 13, so unless the number is increased by another order-in-council no one can be appointed to replace Judge Nay, nor for that matter Judge Hanbridge of Prince Albert who retired August 1st, nor Judge Smith of Saskatoon who died in May.'[13]

In another letter to Davie Fulton later in October, Hall stated that he was prepared to discuss the matter with his old friend, the prime minister. Hall had suggested to the attorney general of Saskatchewan that Prince Albert should have a resident district court judge. And he took up this matter with the member of Parliament for Prince Albert, Prime Minister Diefenbaker. But Diefenbaker refused to intervene and left the matter to Fulton, who sat on it for a long time in the hope that the two men in Saskatchewan would work out their differences.

The tussle between Hall and Walker continued when the chief justice pressed the attorney general for more district court judges. Hall had requested that an additional judge be appointed to handle the workload for the Battleford-Wilkie-Kerrobert-Kindersley district since McFadden had changed his mind about taking on those responsibilities. The attorney general replied to Hall that 'the fourteen judges we now have are more than enough to take care of the present requirements.'[14] Walker included a statistical breakdown of the workload of district court judges over the previous ten years. He was having none of Hall's badgering. 'There is no statistical evidence, ' he wrote the chief justice, 'of an overall increase in the total volume of work done by the District Court in the past ten years. And in 1959 Judges Mill, Hogarth, Smith and Friesen took 41% of all the District Court trials in the province and did 32% of all the Surrogate Court work.'[15] And, as if this were not sufficient to dampen the chief justice's push for more judges, the attorney general offered the observation that the 'present judges have an extremely light workload.' As proof of this sweeping indictment, Walker appended a statistical record of the judicial workload of judges across the province. 'Judge McFadden of Melville in 1959 conducted only two District Court trials, (criminal and civil), out of 354 for the province. He dealt with 72 out of 4,157 probate applications, Judge Stechishin of Wynyard conducted only one trial out of the 354 and handled 85 out of 4,157 probate applications. Judges Campbell and Thompson of Estevan and Weyburn, who between them also carried Arcola, handled together 19 trials and 411 probate applications. Judge Hooge of Moosimin handled 2 trials and 128 probate applications. Judge Hebert of Gravelbourg (who, of course, has now retired) presided over 3 trials and 149 probate applications in Gravelbourg and Assiniboia.'[16] The attorney general concluded: 'It is therefore clear to me that, with the present jurisdiction which the court has, twelve is the optimum number of judges.'

The attorney general did concede that he had been pressing the federal government to enlarge the criminal jurisdiction of the district courts. But, until those changes were forthcoming, Saskatchewan would have to make do with the current roster of judges. The implication was clear: Chief Justice Hall must get on with the business of assigning judges. With a barely concealed threat, Walker ended his lengthy letter to the chief justice with the words: 'If the administration of justice in the District Court in circuit 'F'collapses because of the lack of a judge at a time when the total number of judges in the province exceeds the optimum number, then I will have no choice but to explain to the legislature how such a situation came into being, and I am sure that the Legislature will insist upon vesting in the government the power to prevent such a thing from happening in the future.' Walker, of course, said that he 'felt obliged' to send a copy of his letter to Davie Fulton.

The official correspondence between Walker and Hall on these matters conceal a deeper conflict beneath the surface. Both the Saskatchewan attorney general and the new chief justice were men of strong will. Walker was a member of the CCF government of the day and Hall had never been sympathetic to that party's cause, to put it mildly. As one appointed to the bench of Saskatchewan by a Progressive Conservative prime minister, an old classmate, and a friend, Hall was 'officially cordial' with Walker but did not think too much of him. As one associate recalled years later, Hall 'disliked him intensely and had no use for him.'[17] But Emmett Hall never revealed his distastes openly. He was far too politically astute for that; he always kept his channels of communication open. Still, there was undeniable tension between the two men. How could there not be, given their past encounter in the 1948 election?

Hall's administrative duties did not prevent him from involvement in hearing cases. In the summer of 1958 – just a year after being sworn in as chief justice – he presided over a bankruptcy trial[18] in which the Seiberling Rubber company claimed that it was a 'secured creditor,' within the meaning of the Canadian Bankruptcy Act,[19] against the bankrupt estate of Michael Sklar. Seiberling had won a judgment two years earlier in the Court of Queen's Bench against Sklar for the sum of

$14,431.57. The case before Hall now was whether Seiberling, which had a judicially confirmed claim against Sklar before the executors of Sklar's estate filed bankruptcy, was indeed a 'secured creditor' and therefore held a first claim on the assets of the Sklar estate.

After hearing from counsel for both parties, Hall studied the Canadian Bankruptcy Act, and particularly its definition of a secured creditor. As well, he reviewed the most recent precedents, especially one upon which the Seiberling company depended. He contrasted the reasoning of the *Williams*[20] case with his own understanding of the Bankruptcy Act and reached the conclusion that 'Seiberling Rubber Co. was not a secured creditor.'[21] He anchored his reasoning on a 1928 Privy Council decision[22] and dismissed the application with costs. The chief justice concluded: 'I cannot agree with the *Williams* decision which appears to me to be contrary to the Privy Council' in the *Lowe* case. Seiberling Rubber appealed this decision to the Saskatchewan Court of Appeal. In the Court of Appeal, Chief Justice William Martin wrote the unanimous judgment of the court affirming the reasoning of Hall's Queen's Bench decision.

In light of his own private practice, Hall was especially alert to novel dimensions in criminal cases. In the fall of 1958 he presided over the *Hnedish* trial, where the central issue was whether a confession given by the accused to a police officer following his arrest was admissible. The crown proposed to question the accused as to the truth of his confession.[23] When a 'trial within a trial' occurs, the procedure in Saskatchewan is to have the witness already giving evidence be resworn. When police arrested John Hnedish on suspicion of committing a crime, they claimed that, when they entered his room at 6:00 A.M., Hnedish was fully awake; they took him to an interrogation room where they questioned him at length and had him sign a statement. When the crown attorney introduced this 'confession,' Hnedish's counsel, P.G. Makaroff – with whom the young Emmett Hall had defended the Regina rioters in 1935 – objected, claiming that Hnedish had been asleep at the time and remained under the influence of sleep during the interrogation; in short, Hnedish was drowsy and had unknowingly signed an incriminating confession.

The court refused to allow the crown to cross-examine on the grounds that the settled jurisprudence of the time was that the object of a 'trial within a trial' is to discover not whether the confession is true but whether it is voluntary and hence admissible as evidence. Chief Justice Hall wrote that 'only the jury can pass upon the truth or weight of the confession and then only on evidence lawfully before it.'[24] Turning to the controlling precedent, which was the 1941 English case of *Rex v. Hammond*,[25] he remarked: 'Having regard to all the implications involved in accepting the full impact of the *Hammond* decision which can, I think, be summarized by saying that regardless of how much physical or mental torture or abuse has been inflicted on an accused to coerce him into telling what is true, the confession is admitted because it is in fact true regardless of how it was obtained, I cannot believe that the *Hammond* decision does reflect the final judicial reasoning of the English courts ... I am left with the conviction that because its foundation is on so insecure a footing as the *obiter dicta* of *Hammond's* case I cannot follow it or accept it as good law in Saskatchewan.'[26] And then he added: 'I feel that when the point comes squarely to be decided, another court will take a hard look at the whole question, including the implications above mentioned and others.'[27]

As one might expect, Emmett Hall was at his best in criminal cases. In the case of *Regina v. Phillips*,[28] Otto Phillips had been tried before a justice of the peace and found guilty of impaired driving. Phillips was without a lawyer and refused to plead guilty. He was convicted of violating section 223 of the Criminal Code of Canada and fined $50 plus $23.90 court costs. Phillips was given until 31 December to pay the fine or go to jail for thirty days; he paid the fine on 30 December 1957.

Two months later, on 25 February 1958, Phillips retained counsel and made an application to the Court of Queen's Bench claiming, first, that the original conviction was invalid because it did not disclose the nature of the offences; and, second, that the justice of the peace lacked jurisdiction. Crown counsel argued that section 682 of the Criminal Code prevents such cases arising by *certiorari* (a writ calling for a higher court to review the proceedings in a lower court). The code says:

No conviction or order shall be removed by *certiorari*
a) where an appeal was taken, whether or not the appeal has been carried to a conclusion, or
b) where the defendant appeared and pleaded and the merits were tried, and an appeal might have been taken, but the defendant did not appeal.

Chief Justice Hall noted that the Criminal Code required in Phillips's case that the charge be in writing and under oath and that, in the case of two or more charges, they be set out in separate counts and disposed of in turn. Phillips had been charged on two counts but was tried as if there was only one.

Hall concluded: 'It follows therefore that the information was bad in law and also the conviction.'[29] As to whether the Criminal Code prevented him from reviewing the case, he asked: 'Does it follow that by reason of Section 682 of the *Criminal Code* this court is powerless to act? In my opinion, Section 682 is not a bar where the proceedings are invalid *ab initio* [from the beginning].'[30] Hall had ordered up – as is required by *certiorari* – all the records from the court of Kerrobert prior to giving his judgment – and he found what he had suspected: a shoddy trial. That was all he needed; he had clear jurisdiction to scrutinize the validity of proceedings of the inferior court, and he found them wanting. The chief justice ruled accordingly that 'the fine and costs paid by Phillips should be returned to him.'[31] The amount involved might be small, but the legal principle was important.

In hearing appeals from inferior court judgments, Chief Justice Hall was fair to the judges but he demanded attention to detail. On one occasion in 1959, he was called upon to review the remarks of a Regina police magistrate who had allegedly uttered comments from the bench which were said to be prejudicial to an accused; he was also thought to be biased and had allegedly confirmed his bias by imposing an excessive bail. Counsel for the accused made an application to the Court of Queen's Bench for a writ to prohibit the magistrate from trying the accused.[32]

When the case came before Chief Justice Hall, he reviewed the court transcript and listened to the testimony of a newspaper reporter and that of Magistrate W.M. Elliott himself. It was confirmed that the magistrate had said at the trial that 'while this accused may be as innocent as the driven snow, nevertheless I know from my own experience that some of this security salesman stuff has been a terrible racket in this province. This has been a serious problem and should be cleaned up.' It was further established that the magistrate and counsel for the accused had exchanged words in anger. Hall summed up his views gently but firmly:

I have studied these transcripts and with regret I must say that they indicate a departure from that essential quality of impartial detachment which would be the hallmark of every judge or magistrate in respect of every cause that comes before a court. I do not suggest that the learned magistrate was being consciously biased or prejudiced but he permitted himself to be misled into fixing

excessive bail by the representations made to him by counsel for the Crown
and by linking Jackson's [the accused] arrests of stock salesmen a few days
before and by his personal experience as to 'this security salesman stuff being a
terrible racket in this province'.[33]

He concluded by restating the fundamental principle of Canadian
jurisprudence: 'Every accused has an inherent and constitutional right
to a fair trial by an impartial court and that means a court without any
preconceived notions or ideas respecting the necessity of suppressing
certain types of offences as distinct from others. I do not think that this
is a right which can be maimed because it is one which goes to the root
of the proper administration of justice.'[34] Hall accordingly granted the
application to prohibit Magistrate Elliott from presiding at the preliminary hearings on the three remaining charges against Jackson.

Ever since his involvement in the Trekkers' case, Hall maintained a
vigilant eye on police procedures; he insisted that they follow the
required forms precisely. On 4 October 1960 the Regina police obtained
two warrants to search the office and residence of Morris C. Shumiatcher,
a Regina lawyer, on suspicion of his having committed an offence.[35]
Counsel for Shumiatcher, A.W. Embury and E.J. Moss (one of
Shumiatcher's partners), argued that the warrants were improperly
granted and urged that they be quashed. Chief Justice Hall agreed with
Shumiatcher's reasoning that the magistrate who issued the warrants
did not have judicial cause for doing so and that the warrants were too
vague because they 'left to the discretion of those executing the warrants as to what should be seized.'[36]

Since it became evident to the police that the court was going to
quash the search warrants, they applied to another magistrate, L.F.
Bence, for two more search warrants. Bence issued the warrants and all
parties were back in court the next day. One can sense the annoyance in
Hall's judgment in this second attempt to ransack Shumiatcher's office.
He found it even easier to quash these warrants since the magistrate
could not possibly have had judicial reason to grant them – the first two
warrants were technically in effect at the time he granted the second
pair. Further, the detailed nature of the second set of warrants made it
impossible for the police to decide what to take or not to take. 'In my
view,' said the chief justice,

the new warrants cover a broader field than the first warrants and are even
more open to objection ... I can hardly conceive that in a law office such as that

of Shumiatcher, Moss and Lavery, in which no suggestion of wrongdoing has been suggested against the partners Moss and Lavery or against Mrs. Shumiatcher, it would be possible for a peace officer executing the warrant to know just what to seize. I do not think it was ever contemplated by Parliament that under the search warrant authorized by Section 429 of the *Criminal Code*, 1953-54, ch. 51. those executing the warrant would have *carte blanche* to open and to read the private papers of clients and of partners in the hope of finding something therein that might in the sole judgment of those searching have evidentiary value relevant to the charges made against Shumiatcher.

The second set of search warrants were accordingly quashed, with costs to the applicants. But that did not end the case of *M.C. Shumiatcher v. The Attorney General of Saskatchewan*. Nor was it to be the last time that Hall was to preside over a matter involving Morris Shumiachter.

Shortly after the *Schumiatcher* case, Emmett Hall was informed by telegram that he had been appointed chief justice of the Saskatchewan Court of Appeal, effective 1 March 1961. The news came as no surprise because he had been in touch with Diefenbaker, who had informed Hall of his intentions of elevating him to the position of chief justice of the province. Four months after being appointed chief justice, Hall took part in the official opening of the new courthouse in Regina.[37] On 22 June 1961 the new chief justice and the Court of Appeal moved into spacious new quarters following a ceremony presided over by W.G. Davies, the minister of public works. Hall made a few remarks on this occasion but the formal address was given by the attorney general, R.A. Walker.

A few days after moving into his new quarters, Hall found himself presiding over a criminal charge against Morris Shumiatcher. Shumiatcher and two associates, Walter W. Luboff of Saskatoon and Thomas S.C. Fawcett of Ottawa, were charged under the Criminal Code of Canada with unlawfully conspiring to commit an indictable offence, namely: 'unlawfully by deceit, falsehood or other fraudulent means, to defraud the public of property, money or valuable securities.'[38] The court read the indictment against Shumiatcher and found that it was not sufficiently detailed as required by the Criminal Code. The code states: 'A count shall contain sufficient detail of the circumstances of the alleged offence to give to the accused reasonable information ... and to identify the transaction referred to.' Chief Justice Hall, agreeing with Justice E.M. Culliton, said in his judgment: 'No reason was given why the Crown elected to convey as little detail in the information (indictment) as was done here. And when the information was challenged as being invalid, the Crown could easily at that time have laid a new information giving the detail lacking in the first information, but instead it has chosen to stand firm and to insist on proceeding on an information that appears to have been studiously prepared to give, at best, the minimum of detail to the person accused.'[39] This simply would not do, said the chief justice, for the additional reason that 'an accused person should be able to tell from the information or indictment the precise nature of the charge against him. That principle has been carried into the Canadian Bill of Rights.'[40] Hall then cited the relevant sections of the Bill of Rights, which had been passed by Parliament less than two years previously. He let it be known that he considered the new Bill of Rights to place a special responsibility upon the police and the judiciary. 'The prosecution, acting in the name of the sovereign, is, in my opinion, under a specific duty not to circumvent or negative this positive injunction of the Parliament of Canada. The courts, too, must be vigilant in seeing that the provisions of the Canadian Bill of Rights are not breached, ignored or whittled away.'[41]

Hall genuinely believed that, as a judge, he was obliged to ensure that the Canadian Bill of Rights was implemented. He never swerved from that conviction, as his career on the Supreme Court of Canada was later to confirm. During the *Schumiatcher* case, Emmett Hall wrote a handwritten letter to John Diefenbaker on the work of the court as well as the political events of the day.[42] He stated: 'We haven't issued our judgment in Schumiatcher but it is being typed. We are allowing the application to quash the information on grounds that the charge is not identified. In addition I think it is bad as violating the Bill of Rights. Am enclosing a copy of my separate judgment on that point as I know that it will interest you. The judgment will be handed out next week when other judges are here to sign it.' Commenting on a case before the court and revealing details before the judgment was announced was, of course, thoroughly improper. And it would not be the last time that Hall breached the rule of propriety.

Diefenbaker and Hall were determined to bring the new Canadian Bill of Rights to bear upon the law and practice of Canadian life. Hall, who was to remain convinced for the rest of his life that the courts had not applied the Bill of Rights as enthusiastically as they might have, took every opportunity to let Diefenbaker know that he was taking his responsibilities in these matters seriously. He knew that Diefenbaker liked to hear that. In fact, however, Hall never had an opportunity to make a significant use of the Bill of Rights while on the Saskatchewan bench, despite his widely acknowledged support for it. As he was to find out when he reached the Supreme Court of Canada, the problem was only partly the unwillingness of judges to apply the terms of the Bill of Rights. Also to blame were the confusing terms of the Bill of Rights itself. The Canadian courts were instructed under the terms of the federal statute – which applied only to federal areas of jurisdiction – to 'construe and apply' and 'construe or apply' its provisions 'so as not to abrogate or infringe' the stated rights and freedoms. The mandate was not clear; few judges believed that the act gave them authority to strike down acts of Parliament. As Peter Russell has observed, the Canadian Bill of Rights was 'a very weak instrument.'[43] Russell adds that 'the Supreme Court judges did not sense that the Bill of Rights gave them a clear mandate from the Canadian body politic to enforce its terms against the political branches of government.'[44] Similarly, Peter Hogg describes the approach of Canadian courts to the Bill of Rights as 'timid.' 'He notes that 'in the 22 years that elapsed between the Bill's enactment in 1960 and the Charter's adoption in 1982, the *Drybones* case[45] was the only one in which the Supreme Court of Canada held a statute to be inoperative for breach of the Bill.'[46]

But Hall clearly thought that he brought a freshness of perspective to the bench and this was nowhere more apparent than in the case of *Thomas v. Thomas,*[47] which he heard in September 1961. That case was an appeal from a judgment of Justice McKercher of the Court of Queen's Bench which refused the application of Mrs Thomas to have the family farm and chattel mortgages sold and the sum divided equally between herself and her husband.

When the case came before Chief Justice Hall on appeal, he, along with Justices D.A. McNiven and E.M. Culliton, noted that since the beginning of the marriage on 2 November 1952, until its dissolution seven years later on 2 October 1959, both parties contributed equal money towards the purchase of seven quarters of land – at a price of $40,000 – and the necessary farm equipment. Mr Thomas argued that the relationship was not a partnership but a marriage and that his former wife had no claim to direct a sale and division of the assets. He was successful with this line of argument before Justice McKercher and the court majority, but not before the new chief justice. Hall came to the conclusion that Mrs Thomas had indeed established to the court's satisfaction that their marriage arrangement also included a de facto and de jure partnership agreement and thereby could legitimately appeal to the provisions of the Saskatchewan Partnership Act.[48] 'In my view,' said the chief justice, 'the learned trial judge should have allowed ... [that] the joint undertaking constituted a partnership and that the Plaintiff [Mrs Thomas] was entitled to seek the relief provided by the Partnership Act.'[49]

Hall further reasoned that, when Mrs Thomas advised her husband that she did not intend to return, she thereby served effective notice dissolving the partnership – as is required under the terms of the Partnership Act. The chief justice said in his conclusion:

As the Plaintiff has established that this partnership has been dissolved, the appeal will be allowed. The matter will be referred back to the Court of Queen's Bench for the necessary directions to wind up the partnership in accordance with the provisions of The Partnership Act. While I feel compelled to make this order, I strongly urge the Plaintiff and Defendant to use every effort to settle their business difficulties by agreement. It appears to me that in respect to their partnership undertaking, there is no real difference between the parties and there should be no obstacle to a mutually satisfactory settlement. If the parties fail to heed this suggestion, and the court is compelled to direct a sale of the assets, there is every likelihood that both parties will end up with little or nothing.'[50]

MR DIEFENBAKER'S ESCORT

Everyone in Saskatchewan knew, of course, of the close friendship between Emmett Hall and John Diefenbaker and that the friendship continued after he went to the bench. But not a few lawyers in Saskatoon and Regina thought that it was not quite proper for the chief justice of the Court of Queen's Bench, and later of the court of Appeal, to squire the prime minister around town when he came to visit. Hall brushed aside those strictures; he never hesitated to show publicly – however inappropriate – his support for the man who shared so many of his own aspirations for Canada and the fact that he was now a judge was not going to stop him. On the occasion of the fiftieth anniversary of the University of Saskatchewan, Emmett Hall introduced the prime minister at the banquet. After singing John Diefenbaker's praises and recalling how as a newspaper boy Diefenbaker met Sir Wilfrid Laurier in 1910, he concluded: 'It cannot be wrong to speculate that Sir Wilfred [sic] was attracted to the eager boy before him and always conscious of Canada's destiny and of his own prophecy may well have said to himself: "Is this the boy who will one day take up where I am leaving off and carry to fruition my vision of Canada in the 20th century?" and was this thought communicated to the boy? Who knows – but, Mr. Chairman, Ladies and Gentlemen, this we do know that the man I now have the pleasure to introduce is the man who has the ability, the vision and the opportunity to lead Canada on the road to its destined greatness in the coming decades of this century, our own John Diefenbaker.'

John Diefenbaker openly basked in the warm glow of such praise, however fulsome. But one had to wonder how he, a Conservative partisan to the core, appreciated being told that he was destined to live out the dreams of a Liberal prime minister. It did not matter; he happily accepted all such accolades and was settled in the conviction that he deserved them. And Emmett Hall knew that better than most people and stroked the 'Chief's' ego on every public occasion. Much to the chagrin of some.

5

The Birth of National Medicare

On 23 November 1962 Prime Minister John Diefenbaker appointed Emmett Hall to the Supreme Court of Canada. He was chosen to replace Justice Charles Holland Locke from British Columbia who had retired in September 1962. Hall's appointment to the nation's highest court came as no suprise; he had been in frequent contact with the prime minister and knew that he was being considered as a replacement for Justice Locke. Emmett and Belle had discussed the prospects of moving to Ottawa many times in preparation for the call. When it came they were ready to make the move. With the burden of the chairmanship of the Health Services commission in tow, the Halls travelled to Ottawa where, in the presence of his wife and members of the court, Emmett was sworn in as a puisne judge of the Supreme Court of Canada by Chief Justice Patrick Kerwin. While Emmett was clearly excited over the prospects of living in Ottawa, at the centre of national politics, and serving on the Supreme Court, Belle was less thrilled; for her, the move meant living farther away from her family and making a home in a city where she knew few people. But she realized that Emmett wanted this appointment and gave him her full support.

Hall's professional activities following his appointment to the bench were not all judicial in nature; in fact, it was while he was serving on the court that he also became one of the country's royal commissioners. In this regard, Hall owed much of his success on commissions of inquiry to experiences he had had prior to his appointment to the bench in

Saskatchewan. His first experience came in 1956, when he was appointed to the board of conciliation established to settle the dispute between firemen on diesel locomotives and the Canadian Pacific Railway. He was appointed to this board by federal Labour Minister Milton F. Gregg on 7 May 1956, on the recommendation of the CPR. The board was chaired by J.C. Anderson, a county court judge from Belleville, Ontario; the union nominee on the board was Senator Arthur W. Roebuck.

The dispute involved a practice known as 'featherbedding,' in this case the continued use of firemen on diesel-powered trains long after trains ceased to use coal-fired boxes. *The Financial Post*[1] ran a short satirical account of the role played by the fireman, whose job used to be to shovel coal, on the CPR's *Canadian*: 'There's a fireman on the CPR's track, transcontinental diesel passenger train, *The Canadian*. One gets on at Ottawa, "works" the two hour, 111 mile trip to Montreal. Here's his job: He gets paid for 15 minutes before pull-out time, 7:30 P.M. He (a) looks in, (b) checks his watch, (c) looks at the bulletin board, (d) inspects the part of the cab he's to ride in, and (e) helps the engineer with a brake test. Every 20 minutes he pushes a button on a boiler providing steam to the coaches behind. He watches the road ahead being watched by the engineer. At Montreal, he sits for 1 hour while the train is unloaded, backed up to the Glen yard. His pay: just under $14 an hour. In the month he'll earn slightly more than $500.' What could be greater proof of 'featherbedding' than that? asked the writer.

The issue of 'featherbedding' was the first major conflict in Canada between management and labour over automation and, accordingly, attracted a lot of attention. The impact of technological development had been felt throughout Canada in many industries and the problems it introduced were becoming more acute each year. The effect of technological development had changed the character of work for many people, and their unions were understandably concerned. New machines were doing jobs formerly performed by men and unions were strenuously resisting retraining programs for the displaced workers.

The steam locomotive soon became obsolete with the introduction of the more powerful and more efficient diesel engine. There was no doubt as to the place or importance of the fireman in the old steam locomotive; he shovelled coal by hand and thus produced the power to run the engine. A century earlier, before coal was widely used, the train fireman was assisted by a 'wood passer' whose job it was to hand wood to the fireman. When coal was later introduced, the 'wood passer' was phased out; the fireman, of course, remained. Now, with the introduction of the diesel engine, the fireman's role became redundant, and, quite naturally, the railway companies attempted to phase out the fireman since his position, like that of the 'wood passer' before him, had become obsolete. But times had changed since the days of 'wood passers' and the new era brought with it the power of unions. Unlike the 'wood passers,' the firemen belonged to a strong union, the Brotherhood of Locomotive Firemen and Enginemen, and the union refused to permit the firemen to be phased out abruptly.

The railway companies, especially the CPR in this case, were saving a large amount of money through the introduction of diesel engines: in 1955 the CPR had saved $18 million in locomotive repair expenses.[2] Between 1952 and 1956, the company had reduced the number of its mechanical employees by some 2,750, largely owing to the introduction of the diesel engine. The CPR believed that it should be able to operate diesels in freight and yard service without the firemen in the cab. The company claimed that it could save a minimum of $5.4 million in the first year of such a program. The union protested that it was not opposed to automation, but that it wanted to be consulted before employers used automation as an excuse for ruthless dismissals. The union also believed that the presence of firemen in diesel cabs contributed to the safe operation of the trains – a view that it had great difficulty supporting.

The Anderson board concluded, after hearing lengthy arguments from both sides to the dispute, that the CPR should be permitted to operate locomotives in freight and yard service without a fireman in the cab. But the board also recommended that the company not be permitted to strike the firemen off the payroll 'merely because of the large savings which automation offers, and in circumstances under which by not even the greatest stretch of the imagination could it be considered any fault of their own ... [that] is a much too exacting and far-reaching sacrifice to expect experienced firemen to be called upon to bear in the name of technological change.'[3] Despite his role as spokesman for the railway interests on the board, Hall was not disposed to see employees treated unfairly; this conviction went back many years to his father's experience with the CNR in Saskatoon. James Hall was never laid off because he had seniority but he saw many of his fellow workers dismissed without notice before unions entered the scene. Hall never forgot his father discussing this matter at the dinner table. The Anderson report pointed out that, if the company were permitted to operate without firemen in diesel cabs, 1,050 firemen would be put out of work immediately. The board accordingly recommended that 'the Company continue to employ all firemen (helpers) who are at the date of the new agreement on the firemen's roster and who have passed their engineer's qualifications and/or attained three years seniority as firemen.'[4] The Anderson report recommended that the role of the firemen in diesel trains be phased out gradually in order to provide the existing firemen with seniority time in which to achieve promotion to enginemen; others without seniority were to be absorbed into other jobs with the company.

To the board's disappointment and surprise, the union refused to accept its recommendations and called a strike; the CPR came to a halt throughout Canada. The strike lasted for several weeks, until Parliament ordered the strikers back to work and appointed a royal commission to look into the matter. This commission, under Justice R.L. Kellock of the Supreme Court of Canada, was appointed on 17 January 1957 – exactly one month after the Anderson report was submitted to the minister of labour. In addition to Justice Kellock, the commission consisted of Justice Campbell C. McLaurin, chief justice of the Trial Division of the Supreme Court of Alberta, and Justice Jean Martineau, puisne judge of the Court of Queen's Bench for Quebec.

The Kellock commission sat for one full year and covered the same material as the Anderson board. It surprised no one, especially the members of the Anderson board, that the Kellock commission came to the same general conclusions as the earlier report. Kellock's commission concluded, as had the Anderson board, that 'firemen are not required on diesel locomotives on the Canadian Pacific in either freight or yard service.'[5] The commission also concluded that the existing firemen (those with seniority) be phased upward or into other jobs with the company. Justice Kellock submitted his report on 18 December 1957, one year and one day after the Anderson board had submitted its report. And, once again, the union refused to accept the findings, the CPR came to a standstill, and Parliament ordered the strikers back to work. In time, after much haggling and pressure from the government, the union came to accept the recommendations of the Kellock commission. The cost to the Canadian taxpayer was, of course, considerable.

THE USE AND ABUSE OF JUDGES

Unlike in the United States, where it is the very rare exception,[6] in Canada judges are frequently asked to preside over public inquiries.

Many in and outside of the legal profession have questioned this use of judges.[7] As a report on the appellate jurisdiction of the Supreme Court of Ontario, prepared under the direction of a former Ontario Supreme Court justice has observed, the use of a judge as a royal commissioner may expose him or her 'to unwarranted criticism reflecting unfavourably on the image of the court and lessening the public appreciation of the judiciary.'[8] The Canadian Judicial Council has expressed its qualified approval of judges conducting public inquiries; the council's minutes for 25 September 1978 record the passage of a resolution stating that 'no invitation to carry on work that falls outside a Judge's judicial functions should be accepted by a Judge unless the invitation falls squarely within section 37 of the Judges Act.' Still, there can be no doubt that, depending on the terms of reference, a royal commission assignment can involve a judge in controversial issues of public policy, to say nothing of bitter disputes steeped in political partisanship. Many have argued that a judge is no more qualified to participate in contentious public-policy matters than anyone else. But a stronger argument against using judges as royal commissioners is that it necessarily cuts into the amount of time they may spend doing their work as judges – that is, hearing cases, searching for reasoned solutions, and writing sound judgments. After all, if their job as judges is a full-time one, it should command their undivided attention.

If Hall was conscious of the possibility that the time spent on public inquiries could affect his performance as a Supreme Court Justice, he never showed it. But it is physically impossible for a person to do two jobs well. One of the tasks is bound to suffer to some degree. Just how much Hall's own judicial duties suffered can be seen from a review of his work on the Supreme Court of Canada during the period he co-chaired (with Lloyd A. Dennis) an Ontario committee charged with studying that province's public educational system. This committee was established on the 10 June 1965 and released its final report to the public three years later, on 18 June 1968. During those three years, Hall's time on the Supreme Court in terms of cases on which he sat and judgments he wrote was as follows: in 1966 he participated in fifty-five cases and wrote eight judgments; in 1967 he participated in forty-six cases and wrote thirteen judgments; in 1968, the year the report was submitted, he participated in seventy-six cases and wrote ten judgments. If we contrast the above statistics for the year 1968 (keeping in mind that the year's cases were heard in 1967, in the heart of the commission's work) with the performance of the two other justices of the Supreme Court for the same year, we find the following: Justice

Roland Ritchie (Hall's immediate senior in the Court) participated in seventy-seven cases and wrote sixteen judgments; Justice Wishart Spence (his immediate junior on the Court) participated in seventy-three cases and wrote twenty judgments; and Justice Hall participated in as many cases as both Ritchie and Spence but wrote fewer judgments (in fact, he wrote 50 per cent fewer than Justice Spence). Looking back to 1966 (the Supreme Court Reports covering opinions delivered from October 1965 to October 1966), one finds parallel statistics; in that year Justice Hall participated in fifty-five cases and wrote eight judgments; Justice Ritchie sat on fifty-seven cases and wrote thirteen judgments; and Justice Spence sat on forty-eight cases and wrote twelve judgments.

The year following the Hall-Dennis report, Emmett Hall sat on sixty-seven cases and wrote twelve judgments. One can only conclude from the fewer number of judgments written during the time he served as royal commissioner that his work on the commission was a distraction. To some extent, at least, the time spent as committee co-chair reduced his effectiveness as a justice of the Supreme Court of Canada. This is not to say that he was entirely ineffective or that he neglected his Supreme Court duties. His dissent in the Truscott case, which was decided in 1967 – when he was winding down his Ontario education inquiry – more than testifies to the thoroughness of his sense of responsibility and his attention to details during this time. The wonder is that he was able to do so much Court work while serving on the education committee.

Emmett Hall clearly enjoyed his work on such public inquiries; he liked, especially, the public recognition and approval. Until recently, judges went about their tasks quietly in the shadows of anonymity. The chance to conduct a public inquiry, however, brings the judge out into the public limelight and Hall enjoyed that more than many other judges. On occasions when he spoke on the subject of judges serving off the bench on public boards, he would begin or end his remarks with lines from A.P. Herberts's 'Sad Fate of a Royal Commission':

> I am the Royal Commission of Kissing
>   Appointed by Gladstone in '74
> The rest of my colleagues are buried or missing;
>   Our minutes were lost in the last Great War.
> But still I'm a Royal Commission,
>   My task I intend to see through,
> Though I know, as an old politician,
>   Not much will be done if I do.[9]

Hall's experience on royal commissions prompted him to speak in 1972 – one year before leaving the Supreme Court – about 'Royal Commissions as Part of the Legislative Process.'[10] Strange as it struck some observers, he remarked on that occasion that he foresaw the eventual demise of royal commissions. 'I think it may be said,' he claimed, 'that the expansion and better utilization of special Standing Committees of Parliament and of Legislatures will limit resort to Royal Commissions quite markedly.'[11] He looked upon this development with favour. He pointed to the 1977 report of the House of Commons justice and legal affairs subcommittee on the penitentiary system in Canada[12] – under the chairmanship of Mark MacGuigan – as an example of the quality of investigation he hoped and expected from parliamentary committees. Unfortunately, he went on to observe, other committees, such as the standing committee on public accounts, do not have the staff or power to investigate matters adequately, thereby reducing their effectiveness. The best these committees can do is point to a major problem and then recommend that a royal commission or a public inquiry be set up to pursue the matter in greater detail. If the committees of the House and Senate had broader investigative powers, he noted, the need for royal commissions would be reduced. But he clearly thought that royal commissions could continue to play an important role in the development of public policy and the resolution of important public issues. And, despite his comments about the value of parliamentary committees of inquiry, he believed that the possibility for impartial study was greater in royal commissions than in most legislative committees.

HEALTH SERVICES COMMISSION

At 10:30 A.M. on 5 January 1961, Chief Justice Hall was presiding over a jury trial in Regina when the registrar, F.H. Sparling, entered the courtroom and handed him a note. The note read: 'Prime Minister Diefenbaker called. He would like you to return the call when you are free.' Hall adjourned proceedings at an appropriate point a few minutes later and returned to his chambers. He telephoned the prime minister and got through at once. 'Emmett,' said Diefenbaker, 'As you probably know, the Canadian Medical Association has been pressuring me to establish a royal commission to assess the health needs and the resources of Canada. And I think that you – in the light of your experience on hospital boards – should be the one to head such a commission. What do you say?' Hall, understandably taken aback by such a large request, equivocated somewhat: 'You'll have to give me a little time to think this over, John. I'll have to see to what extent such a Commission will interfere with my judicial duties here in Saskatchewan.' Diefenbaker said he understood, but he wanted an answer as soon as possible. The two chatted briefly about family matters for a moment or two and the prime minister concluded by saying: 'I'll be in touch with you a little later. I hope you will agree to take on the job.'

Chief Justice Hall returned to his courtroom and the trial proceeded until 12:45, when he adjourned the court for lunch. He then walked in the cold to the Wascana Club, pondering the prime minister's request; he knew that it would be an enormously important assignment, one that he could not refuse unless he had major reasons for doing so. And he could think of none: he thought that he could continue to perform his judicial duties, but he would like to see the terms of reference for the commission before he consented to serve. These were his thoughts when, upon entering the lobby of the Wascana Club, he heard the lead story of the CBC radio one o'clock news: 'Prime Minister Diefenbaker has just announced the appointment of Chief Justice Emmett Hall of Saskatchewan to head a Royal Commission inquiry into national health services. Other members of the Commission will be announced in a few days.'

Hall's reaction was one of stunned amusement. 'The bastard!' he mumbled through a smile as he made his way into the dining room. It was not long before he was being congratulated on his appointment. Little did his well-wishers realize that he had not even had the opportunity to refuse the appointment. He enjoyed the episode immensely, until he began to realize that he would have to head a commission of members as yet unnamed and with terms or reference as yet unknown to him. Also, since Hall was chief justice of Saskatchewan, he was not permitted to receive a stipend or honorarium for his time and effort. Unlike consultants and research staff and other commissioners who received salaries or stipends, Hall received expenses only.

Reaction to the appointment of Emmett Hall as chairman of the royal commission was, by and large, favourable. As the Regina *Leader-Post* noted in an editorial entitled 'A Sound Appointment,' 'Chief Justice Hall's services during the coming year will be missed – a situation that calls into question the popular procedure of naming senior judges as chairmen of Royal Commissions. In the present instance, however, the Chief Justice's personal suitability for the task coupled with his experience, overshadows this chronic objection.' The Saskatoon *Star-Phoenix*, for its part, welcomed Hall's appointment enthusiastically. After recounting his experience in health matters – he had served as chairman of the board of St Paul's Hospital and as an adviser to the Dominion Conference of Catholic Hospitals – the *Star-Phoenix* claimed that the 'appointment of Chief Justice Hall to probe the facts of the national health scene is a first step towards taking the social question of health services out of the realm of party politics.'[13] At the time of his appointment, Hall was president of the Saskatchewan Red Cross Society and a director of the National Red Cross Society. In light of his past experiences, it would be difficult to imagine anyone who better possessed the requisite qualifications for the task. More to the point, the leaders of the CCF (or the 'New Party,' as it had begun calling itself since 1959), both in Saskatchewan and in Ottawa, were convinced of his open-mindedness. T.C. Douglas said a decade later: 'We knew that Emmett Hall would approach the issue of medicare with an open mind. And we knew that he would support the establishment of a national health care program once he looked at the facts. He followed closely our efforts in Saskatchewan to introduce a public health care program. Mr. Diefenbaker couldn't have chosen a better man.'[14]

Not everyone was as convinced that Hall would be an impartial or non-political royal commissioner. Was he not a Conservative supporter and close personal friend of Diefenbaker's? Moreover, though Hall was not known to be sympathetic to socialized medicine, he personally supported some form of medical insurance. He never forgot the impact for good that the 'municipal doctors' program had on the life of Saskatchewan during the Great Depression. Under that program, doctors had been paid by the province and, as a result, people in need were not denied medical services. Hall believed that without the program, which he saw as an important 'forerunner to medicare,'[15] Saskatchewan 'would not have survived through the Depression.'[16] Perhaps, some feared, this was evidence of pre-conceived views on the subject of health care? There was another concern. His son, John, then an orthopaedic surgeon at the Hospital for Sick Children in Toronto, kept his father in touch with the problems of health care. But, some asked, was he too close to the doctors and insurance companies?

As well, when in 1946 the Saskatchewan government drafted Canada's first compulsory hospital program, Hall was legal adviser to all the private hospitals in the province; he took an active part in the negotiations during the formative years of this first medicare program in

Canada. But, as T.C. Douglas recalled later, 'Emmett Hall was by no means a convinced proponent of medicare or any form of government sponsored pre-paid medical insurance plan when he was named royal commissioner. The one thing he had going for him was his reputation as a fair-minded man. We all knew that if he had a chance to study closely our pilot program in south Saskatchewan, that Justice Hall would see the virtue of such a plan. He is simply that kind of man. If he can be persuaded by the facts, then he will change his views.'[17]

However much he may have been surprised by the way in which Diefenbaker announced his appointment as royal commissioner, Hall was fully aware that John Diefenbaker was planning to appoint such a commission for he had been in touch with him on health matters ever since he became prime minister in 1957. There can be no doubt that he played an important role behind the scenes in keeping hospital matters in Diefenbaker's mind.

Writing from the Court of Queen's Bench in mid-April 1958, shortly after the landslide Progressive Conservative victory, Emmett Hall began by congratulating Diefenbaker on his 'wonderful victory.'[18] 'It was,' he went on, 'a magnificent achievement from one end of Canada to the other; but to me the results here in Saskatchewan [Diefenbaker's Tories carried sixteen of Saskatchewan's seventeen seats] are the most remarkable and in my judgement your most personal.' Hall went on to say that it 'was a strange feeling to stand on the sidelines and have no part in the contest. At times it was hard to keep quiet.' Indeed, it must have been painful for Hall to be neutralized as a judge, denied as he was the right to campaign and even the right to vote, in those pre-Charter days, during the federal election campaign of 1958, when the Tories from coast to coast could taste victory. The best he could do was watch the television speeches and news reports and 'exchange talks with the [F.L.] Bastedos [Lieutenant Governor of Saskatchewan] and one or two others.' What pained him most was that he was obliged to celebrate the results alone: 'The isolation of the Bench is a reality at such a time.'

But the main purpose of Hall's letter was to inform Diefenbaker that he had just returned from Ottawa and a meeting with the executives of the Catholic Hospital Conference of Canada and the five bishops who constituted, under the chairmanship of Bishop Joseph F. Ryan of Hamilton, the Episcopal Commission on Hospitals. The meeting was called to discuss the Hospital Insurance and Diagnostic Services Act of 1957. That act, passed by the Liberal administration of Louis St Laurent, authorized the Canadian government to contribute towards the cost of programs, administered by the provinces, that provided hospital insurance and laboratory and other services in aid of diagnosis. But the act excluded any depreciation allowances.

Hall reported in his letter that Diefenbaker would be receiving a request from Father F. Smyth, executive secretary of the Canadian Conference of Catholic Bishops, for a meeting with the prime minister and the minister of health, Waldo Monteith, to discuss the plight of private hospitals. 'The question [of increased financial aid] is one of vital importance to private hospitals,' he emphasized. 'We think it is one of life and death to the private or Sister Hospitals in the long run.'

The remainder of the long letter recounts the abortive efforts of Hall and the Canadian Catholic Hospital Association in the fall of 1956 to have Paul Martin, at the time minister of health, agree to include the interest of capital debt and a depreciation allowance. The letter shows how friends try to bring pressure to bear on public officials. Hall stated:

Arrangements were made in August and September 1956 to have a delegation meet Paul Martin in an effort to have him include interest on capital debt and a reasonable depreciation allowance in the cost sharing formula. After considerable delay, he agreed to meet a delegation in January 1957. The delegation was arranged and included representatives from the Canadian Hospital Association. Dr. Turner of Montreal was to be the spokesman. I went from Saskatoon, Mr. Pickering from Winnipeg and others from practically every province.

We went to Martin's office and there learned that he was away – we were received by the Deputy Minister and got nowhere. We did however protest Martin's failure to see us. (I have no personal knowledge of this but, I understand that someone, perhaps Archbishop Lemieux of Ottawa, got in touch with St. Laurent and it was thus arranged that Martin would personally meet the delegation two weeks later, which he did, only this time I was not present because it was impossible for me to return to Ottawa so soon – Court of Appeal, I think).

The second meeting was as fruitless as the first except that Martin asked the Hospitals 'to trust him,' but insisted on going ahead with his bill excluding interest and depreciation. The Conference was in no mood to 'trust' Martin particularly after Archbishop Pocock and he had a rather spirited interview.

The bill came before the House and I was instructed by the Conference and Archbishop Pocock to brief Davie Fulton [at the time a member of the opposition] fully on the subject, which I did.

Then during the 1957 election the Canadian Hospital Association and the

Catholic Hospital Conference held their biannual meeting in Saskatoon in May ... Martin didn't come near the meeting although he passed through Saskatoon that day. The Deputy Minister was there.

The meeting, particularly the Catholic Conference meeting, spent a great deal of time discussing the question of interest and depreciation and I took advantage of the occasion to acquaint those present, as representative of the nursing Sisterhoods in Canada, of the attitude of Martin and the St. Laurent Government on the question.

This letter is getting too long and becoming an imposition on your good nature. But the whole problem is as acute and as serious as it was in 1957. Our hospitals are concerned that Mr. Monteith has accepted the view point of his Deputy and officials because when he met with representatives of the provincial departments of health last November or December he told them in effect that the only change [contemplated was] to bring it [the act] into effect July 1st rather than January 1st, 1959. I know, of course, that he was not dealing with hospital representatives or with the question of interest or depreciation but more particularly with T.B. and mental health patients which the provincial people wanted covered by the Act.

He concluded the letter with a request for a meeting with Diefenbaker in Saskatoon when the prime minister was in town the next month to receive an honorary degree from the University of Saskatchewan. 'I'll have my manuscript [on the hospital question] with me and could fill any gaps in the foregoing narrative and illustrate to you in terms of St. Paul's of Saskatoon how impossible it will be for a private hospital to rebuild or stay alive over a period of years if compelled to operate on a cost only budget that excluded interest and depreciation in the computation of "cost" for "payment of service purposes."'

In a postscript to the letter, Hall could not resist passing on to his old friend and confidant a little Saskatchewan political gossip. 'I hear gossip these days,' he wrote, 'of some who would like to lead the provincial P.C. party. Sandy McPherson is definitely interested. Told me about it a few days ago; the position has become attractive.' Both Hall and Diefenbaker were more than conscious that, a few months earlier, it would have been impossible to give away the leadership of the Saskatchewan Progressive Conservative Party. As John Diefenbaker liked to remind his audience, in his early years as a politician in Saskatchewan, 'the only protection for Tories on the prairies came from the game laws.'

The long letter illustrates how deeply concerned Hall was about hospital and health services. Diefenbaker's reply, dated 21 April 1958, was cordial and contained a promise to have a chat with Waldo Monteith. He said: 'I am looking forward to seeing you in Saskatoon at the Convocation. I will just be there for a day. Naturally I am pleased that the degree is going to be granted to me by my Alma Mater but I would so much like to have had it as the first rather than the tenth ... I am sorry I missed you when you were here and am glad you saw Bill and Sally Thorvaldson. With regard to the hospital question, I will take it up with the Minister at once.'[19] There is no evidence showing that Hall's intervention in this matter had any effect. The act was never amended to include interest on capital debt or a reasonable depreciation allowance.

On 27 May 1961 Diefenbaker wrote to Hall placing the issue of the health commission in the context of Premier T.C. Douglas's plans and aspirations. He explained:

I will try to get the announcement of the Royal Commission on Health made on Tuesday. I think there is a foundation for your ideas as I have had reports that Premier Douglas intends to announce the introduction of a Health Insurance Plan in the Province.

The fact that he is not going to give up the Premiership until November would give support to the idea that he will have a Fall session and bring in legislation to act as a boost in his federal ambitions.[20]

Diefenbaker did not have to be particularly perceptive to realize that T.C. Douglas was about to introduce health-insurance legislation; he had promised it from his earliest days in politics. Nor was it a coincidence that, upon being elected premier in 1944, Douglas also retained the health portfolio.[21] One of his first acts as premier and minister of health during the summer of 1944 was to announce the appointment of a commission to survey provincial health needs. He appointed a distinguished professor of public health, Dr Henry E. Sigerist of Johns Hopkins University, to head the commission, which was composed of several other outside consultants and representatives of the medical, nursing, and dental professions in Saskatchewan.

After a number of public hearings throughout Saskatchewan, the Sigerist commission reported on 4 October 1944. The report portrayed the sorry state of health services in rural Saskatchewan and recommended the establishment, in a series of steps, of 'a system of socialized medical service on a provincial scale, that will guarantee the people the basic services they need, and which they are entitled to at all times.' The

Douglas government adopted the commission's report and divided the province of Saskatchewan into several 'health districts,' with a pilot project announced for the Swift Current district. The machinery was set in motion in short order. By the passage of the Saskatchewan Hospitalization Act in 1946, state-financed medicine gained a toehold in Canada.

The Canadian Medical Association (CMA) knew of premier Douglas's intentions to expand the program and hence began to press the federal government to establish a royal commission into the state of health services throughout Canada. The CMA was confident that, if it had the opportunity of presenting its case – for a doctor-sponsored insurance scheme – to the nation in a widely publicized forum, the people of Canada would reject national, 'socialized' medicine. The CMA also hoped that the national commission would incline Tommy Douglas to postpone his intention to extend medicare throughout the province of Saskatchewan. Many people in Saskatchewan, Hall among them, were skeptical of this province-wide medical scheme, to say nothing of a national scheme. But no one foresaw the bitterness of the attack by the medical profession on the Douglas government's plans to follow through on its intention to extend medicare throughout Saskatchewan. Aided by the deep pockets of the American Medical Association, the CMA launched a media campaign condemning 'socialized medicine,' with a full panoply of predictions ranging from how doctors would flee Canada in droves to how Canadians would not be able to choose their own doctors to total hospital chaos. It did Douglas's cause for government-financed health care little good for his enemies to point out the fact that Dr Sigerist was a known admirer of the Soviet political system and had spoken glowingly of the Soviet medical system, which he held up as the ideal model that every country should emulate. (Little did anyone know at the time how false this propaganda was. One of the most startling discoveries that attended the fall of the Soviet Union in 1989 was the primitive state of Soviet medicine.) In any event, the controversy over Saskatchewan's experiments in health care continued through the late 1940s, all of the 1950s, and even the early 1960s. It culminated with the Saskatchewan government's passage of a Medical Care Act, providing universal medical insurance to all of the province's residents, in late 1961, along with a bitter – and unsuccessful – doctors' strike when the act came into force in July 1962.

Hall was determined to conduct his commission with utmost impartiality. He refused to be intimidated by the heated rhetoric being served up in Saskatchewan. One of his first tasks was to put together a research team. He made numerous inquiries which eventually led him to ask Bernard Blishen, a professor of sociology at the University of British Columbia, to serve as research director. In February 1961, Blishen was in his university office when his telephone rang. Without identifying himself, the caller asked: 'How would you like to be research director of the Royal Commission on Heath Services?'[22] Blishen blanched and asked who was calling: 'Chief Justice Emmett Hall. I've just been appointed Royal Commissioner to head an inquiry into the state of health services in Canada. Are you interested in the job?' Blishen replied that he would like to discuss the matter with his wife and colleagues before answering. Hall consented and expressed the hope that he would receive a favourable reply in a few days.

Blishen spoke to a number of his university colleagues and almost to a man they recommended that he *not* take the job. 'It will be a whitewash,' most replied. 'After all, he's a Diefenbaker stooge.' By that time, the other members of the royal commission had been announced: W. Wallace McCutcheon,[23] vice-president and general manager of Argus Corporation; Alice Girard, supervisor of nursing at St Luke's Hospital in Montreal; Dr David Baltzan, a Saskatoon general practitioner who had cared for Diefenbaker's mother for a number of years before her death; Dr Arthur Van Wart of Fredericton, New Brunswick, past president of the CMA; Dr C.L. Strachan, a dentist from London, Ontario; and Professor O.J. Firestone, an economist at the University of Ottawa.

The commission was hardly designed to instil confidence in those Canadians – mainly CCFers and Liberals, both of whom had recently endorsed a national health-insurance program – who hoped that Canada would soon have a national health service administered by the government. As one cynic at the time put it, 'putting the prospects of a national medical care scheme in the hands of that Commission – composed as it is of the past president of the C. M. A. and the head of the Argus Corporation – is like asking Colonel Sanders to protect your chicken farm.'

But the more Blishen thought about Hall's offer, the more he liked it; if nothing else, the job would certainly be a challenge. And, besides, he had never been involved in a royal commission before, so why not this important one? He called Chief Justice Hall in Regina and told him that he was ready to come to Ottawa and direct the research team. Looking back ten years after the report was published, Blishen, dean of research at Trent University in Peterborough at the time, recalled that it was truly the greatest experience of his life to work with Justice Hall. 'I learned so much from that man – and he demanded at times the impossible. We would argue fiercely sometimes to the point that on one occasion I told him I couldn't work with him any more. Hall was absolutely stunned: "Why not?" he asked. "Don't take these things personally."'[24] He assured Blishen that there was nothing personal in his attempts to sharpen his research efforts or establish precise points of detail. The commission had a major responsibility and it would fulfil its obligations to the letter. As Blishen remarked:

If one thing can be said about that commission it is that it was Hall's – and no one dared attempt to influence him or pressure him. When he had studied the evidence and came to a conclusion, by damn, it was time that the other commissioners had also come to a conclusion. And if it was not the one Hall had reached, the dissenter had better be able to support his conclusion with precise facts. No vague doubts would do; he would turn on a fellow commissioner and defy him to produce good reasons for his dissenting views. It is not without significance that there was no minority report from this commission. Hall was especially hard upon those commissioners who didn't do their 'homework.' He would sit on them and prod them mercilessly. In short, he was nothing short of a slave driver. But we learned not only to respect him, but to love him.[25]

At the time of this interview, the only picture adorning Blishen's university office wall was a signed photograph of Justice Hall during a hearing of the royal commission on health services.

The Hall commission conducted public hearings in fourteen cities including the capitals of all the provinces and the Yukon Territory. It received a total of 406 submissions – eighteen of which were submissions from private citizens; the rest came from provincial governments, medical associations, nursing orders, labour unions, insurance companies, university departments, and medical schools. It was the task of Blishen's research team – assisted by R. Kohn, three economic consultants (C.H. Berry, J. Boan, and J.J. Madden), and ten researchers – to study and digest these submissions. The commission also conducted its own studies, especially relating to the cost of establishing a comprehensive health-service program.

Blishen's research staff was required to present a written précis on each aspect of the commission's work. Hall would study carefully each one of these documents overnight and the next day return it to Blishen with questions or suggestions for improvements. On a draft copy of a press release relating to drugs, Hall frequently noted in the margin, 'not clear,' and inserted a comma here and deleted a phrase there. In the case of another draft press release, on 'Dental Manpower in Canada,' Hall cut out one whole paragraph with the marginal notation, 'unrelated.' And he remembered every major and minor correction. 'If I forgot to add a comma,' Blishen later recalled with a smile, 'he would call me in and say: "I told you I wanted a comma there."'

But Hall was also a good team manager. On one occasion during the last days of the commission's work, O.J. Firestone – a man who all too often showed both fire and stone – entered Blishen's office and demanded something; after a round of heated exchanges, Blishen ordered Firestone from his office, which was next door to Hall's office. Once he had cooled down, Blishen regretted his action. Who was he to throw a commissioner out of the research office? Downcast and not a little embarrassed by his hasty action, Blishen went to Hall's office to explain what he had done. He sheepishly explained: 'I just threw Professor Firestone, one of your commissioners, out of my office.' Emmett Hall looked up from his desk and replied simply: 'It's about time, isn't it?' He then smiled.

More than any other member of the commission, O.J. Firestone, at the time a professor of economics at the University of Ottawa, struck fear in those who appeared before it. Frank Walden, a reporter with the Vancouver *Sun*, writing of the commission's visit to Vancouver, said that Firestone, 'of all members of the commission, attempts to put each group that appears before him on the spot about a state health insurance scheme.'[26] As for W. Wallace McCutcheon, 'he seldom speaks except on financial matters,' Walden noted. But McCutcheon was soon to leave the commission to take up a position in the Senate.

The Hall commission came under fire not only from the CMA but from some members of Parliament. Frank Howard, a New Democratic Party member of Parliament for Skeena, British Columbia (by now the CCF had been transformed into the present-day NDP), charged in the House of Commons that the commission was doing 'a hatchet job on behalf of the medical profession and the government.'[27] Nothing could have been further from the truth, as was confirmed when the CMA appeared before the commission at the University of Toronto on Wednesday, 16 May 1962. When Firestone said that the commission was attempting to make complete medical services available to the majority of Canadians, Dr G.E. Wodehouse objected to the implication that such services were not already available. He was prepared to acknowledge the need for better facilities for medical education and – in some locations – more hospitals, but he objected to a government plan to regulate the practice of medicine. Wodehouse proceeded to outline the main features of the CMA health plan contained in a brief of more than one hundred pages. The brief recommended that foremost attention be given to personnel, education, and research, aimed primarily at expanding the supply of doctors and other health workers and increasing the number of hospital beds for cases of physical and mental health illness, as well as providing home care and other programs. On the financial aspects of the question, the CMA brief urged private medical-service insurance and additional tax assistance for those unable to pay for their own medical care; federal health services for those – mainly Indians and Inuit – living in remote northern regions; and federal government inducements for physicians to locate in more rural areas.

Dr Wodehouse went on to say that the medical profession had spearheaded pre-paid medical insurance over thirty years ago. It was 'malarkey' to suggest that health insurance is a new idea, he said. He gave the impression that the CMA had a firm hold on the facts relating to health services in Canada. At one point he said testily: 'Doctors have produced schemes representing sensible, practical, economical and dignified methods of providing medical care.'[28] He made it clear, to the point of arrogance, that the doctors knew more about the problem and, above all, the solutions required than the lay people at the meeting. Justice Hall leaned forward, eyes narrowed in irritation, and asked in a quiet but firm tone: 'I trust you were not including members of this Commission in your remarks.' Dr Wodehouse apologized for giving the impression that he was including the lay members of the commission – which, of course, he had intended to do. Justice Hall tried to smooth the ruffled feathers of the doctors with the comment, 'I think this discussion may prove fruitful, even if a little irritating or annoying to you gentlemen. The way in which you defend your premises will indicate the soundness of your plan.'

The Canadian Medical Association did have a plan, which it presented to the commission in four major points:

1) That, for the 1,520,000 persons, or approximately 8% of Canada's population who may be adjudged to be medically indigent, tax funds be used to provide comprehensive medical insurance on a service basis.

2) That a system for the provision of prescribed drugs be instituted for the

above mentioned group whose medical services insurance is underwritten from public funds.

3) That for persons in economic circumstances just superior to the identifiable indigent we recommend the application of tax funds on proof of need to permit the partial assistance which they require.

4) That approved carriers of medical services insurance be selected from the plans now in operation under voluntary auspices or from plans now providing social assistance medical services to provide insurance cover for those persons aided from public funds.[29]

These points left no doubt that the CMA's plan was for a private-sector insurance scheme building on the private insurance plans currently in place. Those Canadians who could not afford one of the available plans could, after taking a 'means test,' apply for government financial support. The national medical association, representing the majority of Canadian physicians, made it clear in its report to the Hall commission that it had thoroughly researched not only the medical aspects of the issue – including how best to maintain the doctor-patient relationship – but also the economic and public-policy dimensions. What the CMA was saying in effect was: We know the problem and we have done all the research and here is the scheme that you should recommend to the Government of Canada. As Malcolm G. Taylor, a research consultant to the commission, wrote many years later, 'It was almost impossible [for the CMA] to believe that the RCHS [Royal Commission on Health Service], which had been appointed at the CMA's request, would not have almost automatically perceived the superior wisdom of the CMA approach.'[30] The CMA thus found itself on a collision course with the royal commission, which had been established to assess these very issues.

This Toronto meeting between representatives of the CMA and the royal commission was tense and at times bitter. Not only did Hall serve notice to the CMA that his commission was competent to fulfil the mandate assigned to it, but he destroyed once and for all any lingering impressions that this commission was in the pocket of the medical profession. CMA members immediately became aware that the Hall commission was a formidable body and one they could not hope to dominate or deflect from its responsibilities. On several occasions, Hall told the doctors that their answers amounted to propaganda; what he and the commission wanted was factual support. And the doctors were not producing it. The CMA did not comprehend that the commission had been studying the whole range of medical problems for five months and was fully aware of the many discrepancies in the doctors' brief. The commission members would not settle for rhetoric or propaganda. They were tired of doctors talking down to them.

But not only doctors took an interest in the work of the royal commission. The Health Services Commission received over three hundred submissions from all across the country from those who had long staked a claim in the national debate over social policy for Canadians. As P.E. Bryden has noted in her comprehensive study of social policy in Canada between 1957 and 1968:

The usual participants in the health-insurance debate presented their opinions – the medical associations, insurance industry, labour unions, and business associations ... The Canadian Labour Congress argued for a system that was 'universal in application and comprehensive in coverage' and one that would 'present no economic barrier between the service and those who need it.' In accord with its belief in the 'freedom of the individual' and its opposition to 'the introduction of a socialized medicine' scheme in Canada, the executive council of the Canadian Chamber of Commerce recommended that 'Canadians place a higher priority on budgeting for health care and in particular avail themselves of an appropriate plan to assist in defraying the costs of medical care.'[31]

As Bryden has also pointed out, several of the provincial governments, especially in Alberta, British Columbia, and Ontario, were actively exploring ways of coming to grips with medical-insurance schemes, with a focus primarily on the idea of private insurance carriers aided somewhat by the provincial treasuries. These three powerful provinces had kept an eye on what had happened in Saskatchewan and did not like what they saw: doctors striking and bitter public debate over 'socialized medicine.' To the surprise of many federal and provincial Liberals, however, the lesson from Saskatchewan was not only that the medical profession was not sufficiently powerful to block a medicare plan but also that medicare was extremely popular with voters. It was so popular in Saskatchewan that the provincial Liberals – who had opposed Douglas's 'socialized medicine' – promised in the election of 1965 'not to change the existing Medicare legislation by as much as a comma.'[32] The Hall commission thus held its hearings across the country in the midst of this vocal and often acrimonious national debate over medicare. But, to its credit, the commission remained aloof from the 'overheated political environment' and went about its work patiently and methodically.

By the mid-way point in the public hearings, the commissioners were becoming convinced that a government-supported medical scheme was the only answer to the problem that faced the nation. It was not what the CMA wanted to hear. 'We do not subscribe,' the CMA representatives stated to the commission in Toronto, 'to the introduction of universal, compulsory, tax-supported comprehensive medical services insurance under Government auspices and we feel that public funds should not be applied to the self-supporting in the area of medical insurance.'[33] At every opportunity, the CMA spokesmen pointed to Britain and claimed that the Hall commission was leaning in that direction. The CMA representatives said that they 'would oppose even the leeway given to provinces to institute a compulsory plan from federal funds.' It became obvious to both parties that the doctors and the commissioners were on opposite sides of the issue. The CMA did everything it could to cast doubt on the idea the Hall commission was beginning to float: a nation-wide, government-financed health-care system.

Indeed, the national professional medical associations, representing a large number of physicians across the country, became the main antagonists before the Hall commission. When Dr R.G. Gilbert, president of the Canadian Anesthetists Society, appeared before the commission in Ottawa in March 1962, he incurred the displeasure of the commission's chairman. Hall was not getting direct answers to his questions. Gilbert's brief claimed that the best form of remuneration for anesthetists was through direct patient-to-doctor payments. He said that, if the government interposed itself between the patient and the doctor, anesthetic services would deteriorate. Hall asked in what way their services would deteriorate if the doctors were paid by the government. He also wanted to know what the essential difference was between payment through doctor-sponsored voluntary plans and payment through a government plan. When Dr Gilbert attempted to skirt the issue, Hall firmly directed him to answer the question: 'I have asked you a question which you are free to deal with or not as you see fit. But don't try to transpose it into something else and suggest you are giving me an answer to my question.'[34]

In private, Hall fulminated at 'those damn doctors. They think they know everything; all I hear is propaganda and not a shred of evidence to support their opposition to a government sponsored plan.'[35]

The first volume of the commission's report was released to the public in June 1964. It was almost a thousand pages in length and contained two hundred recommendations aimed at establishing what the commission called 'A Health Charter for Canadians.' The first and most fundamental recommendation was:

That the Federal Government enter into agreements with the provinces to provide grants on a fiscal need formula to assist the provinces to introduce and operate comprehensive, universal provincial programmes which should consist of the following services, with the provinces exercising the right to determine the order of the priority of each service and the timing of its introduction:

Medical Services
Dental Services, for children, expectant mothers, and public assistance
    recipients
Prescription drug Services
Optical Services, for children and public assistance recipients
Prosthetic Services
Home Care Services

In addition we propose a complete reorganization and important changes in the Hospital Insurance programme.

Although nursing services are not dealt with as a separate service, it is obvious that they constitute an important element in hospital and home care programmes. We believe it was essential for the effective co-ordination of health resources that nursing be administered as an integral element by each of these services.[36]

This principal recommendation made it clear not only that the scheme was to be provincially operated and assisted by federal funding but that was it to cover all parts of the country. The succeeding recommendations indicated that the prepaid medical scheme proposed in the Charter was not to be state medicine; rather, it was based 'upon freedom of choice, and upon free and self-governing professions and institutions.'[37]

The principles that provided the foundation of the entire report are enunciated clearly in the opening pages of volume one. And it is there that the report's humanitarianism emerges full blown. After reviewing the current condition of health services thoughout Canada – only 50 per cent of the population had adequate medical insurance, and the situation was particularly bad in the north and other remote areas – the commission concluded that it was unconscionable for a nation of great resources not to meet the challenge. The report noted pointedly, as if to forestall criticism, that 'a nation that in 1962 spent $756 million on cigarettes and tobacco, and $973 million on alcoholic beverages can afford the programme which would involve an additional $466 million in 1971'[38] or $20 per year per capita. The Hall report stated its basic philosophical premises clearly: 'Although we recognize that resources are limited, and individuals cannot expect to receive unlimited amounts of health care, the value of a human life must be decided without regard to whether the person is a producer or not. Health services must not be denied to certain individuals simply because the latter make no contribution to the economic development of Canada or because he cannot pay for such services. Important as economics is we must also take into account the human and a spiritual aspects involved.'[39]

Despite the humanitarian foundations, the proposed Health Charter strove to base its findings on hard economic data. After establishing the enormous amount of productive man-hours of time lost because of poor health – confirmed by the Canadian Sickness Survey of 1951– and other statistics revealing how many Canadians had been rejected for military service during the Second World War – the report emphasized the economic advantages to be gained from a healthy nation. The Gross National Product – suffering a 3.1 per cent loss on account of poor health – could rise appreciably if the Charter were put into operation as proposed. The increase in productivity would contribute to offsetting the costs of the program. One thing was clear to the commissioners: an unhealthy population was more costly in the short and long run. The commission was accordingly proposing what it considered to be a sound medical program which would redound to the material well-being of the entire nation.

The commissioners believed that their Health Charter was not only economically sound but medically sound as well. As the report stated: 'We are opposed to state medicine, a system in which all providers of health services are functionaries under the control of the state. We recommend a course of action based upon the social principles and the cooperation and participation of society as a whole in order to achieve the best possible health care for all Canadians.'[40]

The commission's program had Hall's stamp on it: it was a combination of impatience and compromise. The commissioners were determined that their report not be viewed as a white paper from which governments could pick and choose the ideas they liked. It was a coherent, unified proposal: take out one part and you weakened the entire edifice. It was impatient to the extent that it called for immediate government action on its single and comprehensive proposal. Witness the tone of the following: 'It follows that the advisory and planning councils we recommend in Chapter 2 should be agreed upon and chosen following a Federal-Provincial Health Conference *which we urge should be called within six months* by the Federal Government. The responsibility for leadership must be accepted by the Federal Government and plans made so as to ensure that every phase of the development of the programme is consistent with its over-all objective. The unity of the programme and its application to all Canadians must be safeguarded.'[41]

This all but constituted an ultimatum. But the Health Services Commission had reviewed existing conditions in health services throughout Canada and saw no course of action other than the one it proposed. Despite the major role governments – both federal and provincial – were being asked to assume, the Health Charter made it clear that the primary responsibility for health resided with individuals and, as a result, they should contribute to the plan. But Hall's commission rejected the proposal that the program be voluntary for the simple reason that it could not be funded adequately under such a formula. It would have to be universal, covering all citizens in order that all would contribute to the health needs of the entire nation.[42] And it rejected emphatically the application of a 'means test' recommended by the CMA.

Further, the report urged an immediate federal initiative to provide new facilities for training more doctors, nurses, and medical-dental assistants, even though education fell squarely within the constitutional authority of the provinces. The two-volume report (the second volume was released to the public on 18 February 1965) contained a total of 256 recommendations covering all aspects of health services – diagnostic, preventative, curative, and rehabilitative – and both physical and mental illness, including disabilities, and everything from minor surgery to alcoholism to drug addiction. Each phase or aspect of the report was anchored in carefully documented studies.

REACTION TO THE REPORT

Public reaction to the Hall report, as it quickly became known, was generally favourable, especially in the national press. Only the Canadian Medical Association roundly scorned the report, saying that if it were accepted, health services would be put in a 'straightjacket.'[43] Dr A.D. Kelly, general secretary of the CMA, was particularly critical of the manner in which the report made it difficult for a physician to practise outside the program. The CMA proposed that a patient who paid into the national health-care program but consulted a physician outside the program be reimbursed the amount the government would have paid the doctor had he been a part of the program. In Hall's mind, such a procedure would have weakened the unity of the program, and hence he deliberately made it unattractive. The Health Services Commission had studied carefully health programs and practices in other countries, including the United Kingdom, France, Holland, Sweden, Switzerland, Austria, Italy, the United States, the USSR, Australia, and New Zealand. The commissioners were fully convinced of the weak links in those systems and were not about to provide one in their own plan.

In January 1965, Hall, who had been appointed by Diefenbaker to the royal commission when he was chief justice of Saskatchewan and continued on with his duties after being appointed to the Supreme Court of Canada in 1962, tendered the final volume of his report to the Liberal government of Prime Minister Lester B. Pearson, which had replaced the discredited Diefenbaker government two years earlier. The response of the government was cautious and tinged with a little annoyance. The minister of health, Judy LaMarsh, reacted testily, calling the timetable as stated in the report 'unrealistic and precipitate.'[44] But LaMarsh was minister of health for a party that had won the 1963 election on a platform which had endorsed a universal health-insurance scheme. LaMarsh said, with an obvious back of her hand to the Diefenbaker-appointed commission, that she felt it was possible to deal with the national health problems in a more modest fashion than that proposed in the Hall report. She did promise to move quickly on the construction of five new medical schools as proposed by the commission. Yet, at the same time, the minority Liberal government was in the throes of negotiating a final agreement with the provinces on the Canada Pension Plan, and so, as P.E. Bryden has noted, 'action on health insurance had to wait.'[45] There can be no doubt that the Liberal government was serious about a national-health program and liked a great deal of what it saw in the Health Services Commission's report. As early as October 1961, Lester Pearson had announced that 'we will ensure, through a medical care plan, that no Canadian family goes without adequate health services or is financially crippled as a result of costly illness.'[46] But the principal issue became one of timing. The country had just gone through an intense national debate over a new flag and a national pension plan. Could it risk an explosive debate over medicare in the midst of a general election? Leading party strategists, such as Keith Davey and Walter Gordon, finance minister and chair of the national campaign committee, wanted to use the Health Services Commission's report as an excuse to call an early election.[47]

The formal response of Prime Minister Pearson was contained in a letter to Hall on 7 January 1965: 'Just a note to thank you for bringing over two copies of the second and final volume of the report of the Royal Commission on Health services. I would like to take this opportunity to thank you, the members of the Commission and the staff for the outstanding work performed. The Report of the Commission is indeed a monument reflecting your devotion to duty and thoroughness of approach to a vast and complex subject.'[48]

The Saskatoon *Star-Phoenix* reported Judy LaMarsh as expressing doubts as to the cost estimates of the report but also a guarded determination to proceed with the plan. 'Expenditures of this magnitude may only be considered within the overall structure of our sources of revenue,' she said.[49] The newspaper reported that Manitoba Premier Duff Roblin wanted the prime minister to call a federal-provincial conference to discuss national economic priorities in relation to resources. To determine whether the country could afford the plan proposed in the Hall report, Roblin felt that 'a discussion of the national economic priorities surely must come first. We can only decide about health when we are also considering pensions and education.' He wanted the tax sources to be allocated between the governments 'on a logical appreciation of the priorities and the phasing required by the best use of our resources.'[50] Hall saw no such need. His report pointed firmly in the direction of action; he had done all the study necessary. That was why the commissioners had spent forty-two months studying the economic and financial problems. It was obvious that Roblin had not studied recommendations 190 to 200, which dealt explicitly with these problems.

The Quebec College of Physicians and Surgeons greeted volume two of the report with a point-by-point rejection of the recommendations. The only point the Quebec College agreed with was that relating to the eventual availability of medical care for all Canadians. The College was particularly concerned that the Hall recommendations be studied carefully before being implemented; and, above all, that those recommendations be implemented gradually. It opposed flatly the principal recommendation calling for a single provincial commission administering medical insurance; this suggested that medical care be funnelled through prepaid provincial programmes, federally assisted and coordinated. The Quebec College proposed that the provincial, regional, and municipal advisory councils be drawn from the medical profession and the public; these were to be *advisory* only. At the same time, the Quebec College wanted these councils to be *administrative bodies*, independent of governments and comprised of doctors, insurers (government or private insurance companies), and the public (including voluntary associations, business, university, labour, and other associations).

The Quebec College of Physicians and Surgeons feared that universal medical coverage would result in an increase in demand for medical services. This increased demand would put pressure on physicians to provide services without giving them control over the services themselves. As Dr Victor C. Goldbloom, vice-president of the College, said: 'Physicians could be required under such a procedure to prescribe only drug A and drug B for patients in X category.'[51] Hall saw no grounds for these fears. The commission's proposal for a universal medicare program provided for the utmost freedom; it urged that the system must be nation-wide but not monolithic, coordinated but involving large elements of freedom of choice for everyone from patients and doctors to provincial governments and the councils of the federal territories.

One of the most pointed chapters in the Hall report drew attention to the fact – not widely known or appreciated at the time – that considerable medical research in Canada had been financed through grants from the U.S. government and American private foundations. The Hall report bluntly told the Canadian government that that was an intolerable arrangement. Hall called upon the federal government to increase its support for medical research substantially. With this particular proposal, the Canadian Medical Association found nothing to quarrel.

The report stressed that there was no intention to interfere with the manner in which physicians traditionally treated their patients. 'The physician continues in private practice,' the report made clear. 'He renders the service which in his judgement his diagnosis indicates. The state does not interfere in any way with his professional management of the patient's condition nor with the confidential nature of the physician-patient relationship ... Only the manner of receiving payment is altered. No one can seriously suggest that any one method of receiving payment is sacrosanct or that it has any therapeutic value,' the report observed. The report went further and added that the elimination of the financial element from the medical practice might have a beneficial effect upon the doctor-patient relationship.

It quickly became evident to the government and to the medical profession that this report was unlike any other royal commission report. Not only did it issue instructions to the government, it also attempted to meet every conceivable objection to its major proposals – as to content, timing and scope. And, furthermore, it soon became equally clear that Hall was no normal royal commissioner. In an editorial titled 'At Last the Right Advocate,' the Toronto *Globe and Mail* noted that 'too often in the past, Royal Commissioners have put their signatures to their final report and gone off breathing sighs of reliefs to other pursuits. They have left their work like a stone monument, immobile and vulnerable to hammers and chisels in other hands. Justice Hall is ready to defend the integrity of his report. If his example is followed, Royal Commissions may cease to be a means for government to evade or smother an issue. There can be few regrets for that.'[52] To ensure that this royal commission report did not end up on the back shelves of government offices, Hall sent copies of it to every organization that had appeared before the commission; to all governments, provincial and municipal; to all bishops of all denominations; to businessmen; and to a wide range of associations involved directly or indirectly with health. There was no way this report could be ignored because too many people knew its contents. He was determined to defend it publicly and privately.

And defend the report Hall did – to the eternal chagrin of Judy LaMarsh who complained, not unreasonably, about the propriety of a justice of the Supreme Court of Canada giving speeches on major policy matters. However much Hall protested in his opening remarks that 'I am not here tonight as an advocate to defend the recommendations of the Royal Commission on Health Services,'[53] that is precisely what he did.

Not surprisingly, Hall was asked to give numerous speeches on the report. He was invited to give the keynote address to the National Conference on Health Services in Ottawa on 28 November 1965. That speech was entitled 'Implications of a Health Charter for Canadians.' On other occasions, such as the meeting of the Community Welfare Planning Council of Winnipeg on 4 January 1965, Hall outlined the general content of the Health Charter and answered the critics. He passed up few opportunities over the next few years to speak directly to physicians in an effort to make them understand that the program he proposed was not only necessary but workable. He wanted especially to communicate to physicians that the program would not interfere with their ability to practise medicine as they had always done. But he insisted that the program would not work without their active and enthusiastic endorsement. For these reasons he willingly accepted an invitation to speak at a Winnipeg luncheon of the College of General Practice of Canada on 5 April 1965. At that event, he avoided any discussion of the political and economic aspects of the report, confining himself to the medical recommendations. This was a wise choice, as Dr G.R. Diehl, president of the College of General Practice of Canada, observed in a letter thanking Hall for his speech.[54]

Recognition from many sources poured in upon Emmett Hall after his report was released. One letter was from Dr Alexander Robertson, executive director of the Milbank Memorial Fund in New York. The letter read:

Over two years ago, when I was a Professor of Social Medicine at the University of Saskatchewan, I had the pleasure of meeting you and of presenting evidence to your Commission from more than one group.

At that time, I admired tremendously the thoroughness, interest, and open-minded concern with which you and your fellow Commissioners were examining the health problems of Canada.

With my great respect, I should like now to express to you my admiration for the courageous and far-reaching report which you have recently published. Those of us who make the study of health services one of our professional activities could perhaps disagree with some of your recommendations in a minor fashion; no one can fail to be impressed by the tremendous care with which your document has been produced and the social implications which it holds, not only for Canada, but for the Americas.

That kind of compliment pleased Hall immensely and he shared it with his commission colleagues. The Hall report was soon to be read widely throughout North America and abroad, and the response to it – with the exception of that of the medical associations – was invariably one of praise for its thoroughness, courage, and vision.

Justice Hall was chosen to receive the Bronfman Medal of the Public Health Association of the United States, its highest award for achievement in public health. The award was presented in San Francisco on 3 November 1966. The citation accompanying the award read in part:

'The Hall Report will stand as one of the major, influential documents in the history of world health, an enduring monument to the judgment and helmsmanship of Mr. Justice Emmett Hall.'[55] And it was not the only such distinction conferred upon him as a result of his royal commission work. One distinction that, to the end of his life, he prized beyond others was an honorary doctorate of medicine conferred on him by the University of Ottawa on 23 October 1966. It pleased him especially since it was the first time such a degree had been conferred in Canada.

On 1 June 1965 Justice Hall was invited to give the Donald Fraser Memorial Lecture at the annual meeting of the Canadian Public Health Association in Edmonton. His lecture was entitled, 'Whither Public Health.' He spoke on this occasion of the plight of the Canadian native peoples, stating bluntly that 'we, as a nation, have failed our Indians and Métis.'[56] The result of his inquiry into the medical services available to Canadian native peoples distressed him deeply. The royal commission had recommended an imaginative plan for organized flying health circuits, not unlike judicial circuits. 'It would bring regular visits several times a year, by health personnel to the scattered communities and the Yukon and Northwest territories.'[57] He went on to say that the 'eventual solution must result in employment opportunities for the people of the North if the region is to become more than merely a base for weather stations, scientific outposts, or defence installations manned by personnel on a temporary basis.'[58]

Alternative proposals for private schemes usually invoked Emmett Hall's displeasure, for he believed that all alternative proposals had been carefully considered by the commission and rejected. What irked him most was the fact that they often amounted to economic veils over ideological postures. Hall was never a socialist and had as much respect for hard work and individual initiative as anyone, and he insisted that these private qualities were not in any way jeopardized by the commission's Health Charter.

The Canadian Medical Association held a special symposium on 'The Hall Report from Various Points of View' at its 98th annual meeting in Halifax on 18 June 1965. One paper presented on that occasion by Professor R.B. MacPherson, a McGill economist, was entitled 'The Hall Report from the Point of View of an Economist.'[59] MacPherson presented an alternative plan for the payment of personal health services which he claimed was 'far simpler than most others.'[60] His major premise was that the 'average family not only has sufficient income to provide for the necessities of life, including normal health care, but also enough money left over to permit some considerable savings.' This conclusion was based on the fact, he said, that the average Canadian family income was approximately $6,500 per year. He saw no reason why such families could not afford to pay 5 per cent of their gross income on health care – that would amount to about $325 per family. This figure was slightly lower than the Hall report's calculations of annual premium costs of $346.50 per family (for 1963).

MacPherson recognized that there would be those who could not afford to pay $325 per year. He noted, however, that in 1961 only 13 per cent of Canadian families had cash incomes below $2,000, and he was optimistic that the Canadian economy would soon bring these people up to a higher level of income. MacPherson predicted that the national economy would grow by 7 per cent annually; this forecast was considerably higher than that of the Hall commission, which estimated a growth rate of 4.6 per cent annually between 1966 and 1971, and also that of the Economic Council Canada, which predicted an annual growth rate of 5.5 per cent. His conclusion was that it was reasonable to say that 'most Canadians can, or will shortly be able to pay for normal medical expenses or the premium on health insurance whether obtained from the government or private companies.'[61] If this is true, he asked: 'Why the controversy over the recommendations of the Hall Commission?' His answer was that we must not increase the tax burden – such as the Hall report would by way of premiums – because an increased tax burden would seriously jeopardize the prospects of economic growth. In MacPherson's mind, the Hall program ran the risk of producing 'the largest group of healthy but untrained and unemployed individuals in the world.'[62] These comments challenged directly the economic foundations of the report. MacPherson wanted any system of medical service to include a fee for service: 'When services are free, extravagant and wasteful use all too frequently results.'[63] He noted: 'If we believe in a system of free enterprise, we also support the principle that the traits of independence and self-reliance in the individual can best be developed by leaving him with responsibility for meeting normal living expenses, including that of medical care.'[64] Needless to say, these sentiments, appropriately robed in economic statistics, were grist for the CMA's mill. The association clung stubbornly to the conviction that only a private, physician-sponsored, and physician-administered insurance system would serve all Canadians well.

MacPherson's plan was to permit each individual wage earner to pay

Emmett Hall as a young man, c. 1930 (family photo)

Railway Conciliation Board, 1956. Left to right: Judge T.C. Anderson;
E.M. Hall, QC; Senator Arthur Roebuck, QC (photo by Newton)

Saskatchewan Court of Appeal, 1962. Left to right: Justice R.L. Brownridge, Justice E.M. Culliton, Chief Justice E.M. Hall, Justice Mervyn Woods, Justice Percy Maguire, Mr Fred Sparling, registrar (Saskatoon *Star-Phoenix* photo)

Emmett and Bell Hall with Fr Anthony Hall, OMI, preparing to meet the pope, Rome, July 1962 (Vatican photo service)

Health Services Commission, Hotel Vancouver, 21 February 1962.
Left to right: Chief Justice Emmett Hall, M. Wallace McCutcheon,
Dr Arthur Van Wart, Dr C.L. Strachan (Canadian Press photo)

Sr B. Dorais, SGM, with Hon. Emmett M. Hall unveiling portrait in
boardroom, 1963 (Artist: L. Torramen Alemson; Saskatoon *Star-Phoenix* photo)

His Excellency Victor Poano (left), ambassador extraordinary and plenipotentiary of Peru to Canada, presented his letters of credence to the deputy governor general of Canada, the Hon. Emmett H. Hall, puisne judge of the Supreme Court of Canada, in Ottawa on 4 August 1964. On the right, is Mr A.J. Pick, Head of the Latin American division of the Department of External Affairs (National Film Board of Canada, No. 64-5128)

Hall-Dennis committee at work. Ottawa, October 1965
(Roy Nichols, 225-1009)

Ninety-fourth annual meeting of the American Public Health Association,
3 November 1966, in San Francisco. Bronfman prize recipients and Bronfman
lecturers (left to right): Dr Bernard G. Greenberg, Dr Eveline M. Burns,
Justice Emmett M. Hall, Dr Abraham Horwitz (Action Photo Service, 3-7077)

Hall and Dennis presiding act, 1967. Left to right: Dr E.J. Quick,
Lloyd Dennis, Hon. E.M. Hall, D.W. Muir (Roy Nichols 225-1009)

Signing of *Living and Learning* document, 10 June 1968. Left to right:
(front row) Mrs R.W. Van Der Flier, Lloyd Dennis, M.P. Parent;
(back row) Dr G.W. Bancroft, H.G. Hedges, J.K. Crossley, Hon. Emmett M. Hall

Shortly after his retirement from the Supreme Court of Canada, Emmett and
Bell Hall relaxing at son John's cottage, Lake Muskoka, Ontario, c. 1974
(family photo)

full medical expenses up to 3 per cent of his net income; expenses beyond this and up to 8 per cent of his net income would be shared by the individual and the state. In addition, the individual should seek medical insurance from private insurance companies. When the cost of medical services exceeded 8 per cent, MacPherson claimed that the state should assume a much larger measure of responsibility. Where governments were supposed to get the funds for such a program was not something that MacPherson addressed. The CMA was, of course, impressed with MacPherson's alternative to the Hall report, which called for a government-financed and government-administered program. Hall dismissed the MacPherson alternative as undesirable and unworkable.

CONCLUSION

However heated at times the debate over medicare has been since 1965, Canadians have come to believe, as national opinion polls attest, that their publicly financed medical system embodies their most cherished values and represents their country's finest achievement. We all owe a debt of gratitude to Emmett Matthew Hall, for, without him, Canada today would not, in all likelihood, have a national health-care program. Certainly, Tommy Douglas held that view of Hall's role in bringing medical services to all Canadians. Nor did Emmett Hall forget to acknowledge the role played by the former Saskatchewan premier. In a 1971 letter to Douglas, Hall said: 'I think your greatest and enduring accomplishment was the introduction and putting into effect of Medicare in Saskatchewan. Without your program as a successful one in being, I couldn't have produced the unanimous report for the Canada-wide universal health recommendations in 1964. If the scheme had not been successful in Saskatchewan, it wouldn't have become nationwide. Generations to come will be your debtors.'[65] The fact that the two leading figures in the crusade – for such it was for Douglas – to provide necessary medical services to all Canadians, regardless of their ability to pay, came from Saskatchewan no doubt suggests something fundamental about the political culture of that province.

Bill C-227, 'An Act to authorize the payment of contributions by Canada towards the cost of insured medical care services incurred by provinces pursuant to provincial medical care insurance plans,' was debated in Parliament throughout the fall of 1966. On 8 December the bill received third reading in the House of Commons. After several attempts to amend the bill were defeated, the House, under the guiding hand of Allan MacEachen, minister of national health and welfare, voted to adopt a national health care scheme based on the Hall report. The vote in favour was almost unanimous, with only two members voting against the bill.[66] It was a proud day for Emmett Hall. Indeed, it was one of the crowning achievements of his life.

When the bill was debated in the Senate on 13 December 1966, one of the most vocal critics was none other than former commission member Senator Wallace McCutcheon. He told his Senate colleagues that 'I regard this bill as essentially a further unwarranted intrusion by the federal Government into fields of provincial jurisdiction. If the federal Government had said, we will contribute to the cost of medicare plans – to use that term – as developed by each province in accordance with what it considers the needs and requirements of its people, I probably should not be speaking here tonight.'[67] He denounced the bill as 'one more evidence of the new socialism. The new socialism is based on the philosophy that government – and it seems particularly true of the federal Government – knows better what should be done for the people than the people know themselves.'[68] McCutcheon went on to say that several provinces, such as Ontario and Alberta, had perfectly sound plans in place and saw no reason to replace them. 'Why do we have to proceed on the basis that the federal Government knows better than the governments of, say, the Province of Ontario and the Province of Alberta, as to what should be done for their citizens in a field which is primarily the responsibility of the province?'[69] A few other senators, such as Senator Orville H. Phillips, a dentist, expressed similar views about the 'drift towards socialism and its effect on Canada's development.'[70] He took his seat but not before taking a shot at Stanley Knowles, whom he described as 'setting himself above God with his socialistic blessings.' The bill was sent to the Senate's standing committee on banking and commerce, where it was eventually reported out without amendment on 16 December 1966. When Emmett Hall learned of McCutcheon's comments, he replied with a gesture of dismissal: 'Damn fool! He didn't stick around to hear the evidence we heard. What does he know about it?'

6

Reforming Education in Ontario

It would not be far off the mark to say that the history of public education in Ontario since the Second World War has been one long series of internal studies and royal commissions heaped on ministerial inquiries in a never-ending effort to reform the system. Indeed, education has been called 'Ontario's preoccupation.'[1] One professional educator describes the period from 1945 as 'years of rapid change, sharp shifts in direction, at times, tumultuous conflict.'[2]

Immediately following the war, the Conservative government of Premier George Drew established a royal commission under Justice John Andrew Hope to study the primary and secondary school needs of the province in anticipation of the 'baby boom' as well as new post-war industrial needs.[3] This commission took five years to report. But while the Hope commission was slowly making its way through the brambles, the Department of Education was becoming increasingly impatient to provide local school boards with an opportunity to suggest changes in the educational curriculum of the province. At the same time, battle lines were slowly emerging between 'progressive' educators and 'traditional' teachers. The former were fired by the writings of professional educators in the United States such as Ivan Illich, whose progressive ideas were set out in his books *De-Schooling Society*[4] and *Celebration of Awareness*.[5] Illich's ideas had caught the attention of key educators in Canada. These devotees of progressivism denounced traditional schools as factories with curriculums that demanded factory-like efficiency, destroying the continuity of life and stifling 'creativity.' 'The curriculum reflected distinctions between learning and doing, between child and adult, between the academic and the "real" world.'[6]

Traditional teachers, on the other hand, armed with the provocative *So Little for the Mind*,[7] published in 1953 by Saskatchewan university history professor Hilda Neatby, countered with a strong plea for a confirmation of traditional teaching methods and curriculums. Neatby ignited a firestorm of controversy over education in the public schools from one end of the country to the other. The response to her scathing indictment of Canadian public education was nothing short of venomous. The Saskatchewan minister of education, Woodrow Lloyd, angrily dismissed Neatby for having dipped her pen in poison, not ink.[8] Few – if any – Canadian books on education have struck a chord as deeply as Neatby's. The public airwaves during the winter of 1954 were dominated by *So Little for the Mind*; everyone was discussing it – at private parties and public meetings. Parents, teachers, and educators at all levels devoured the book and reacted to the extent that they had been roasted. The Toronto Public Library in 1954 cited it as the most frequently borrowed non-fiction book for that year. Professional educators, led by Dr John Long, director of educational research at the Ontario College of Education, dismissed the book as 'not worth a nickel.' Dr D.C. Smith, inspector of schools at Nelson, British Columbia, characterized *So Little for the Mind* as 'an almost hysterical diatribe.' But Neatby had her friends. Like a cavalry riding to the rescue, a formidable posse of academics came to her defence. Historians such as A.R.M. Lower, with political scientists R. MacGregor Dawson and Eugene Forsey riding shotgun, aided by philosopher George Grant, circled the wagons and defended the beleaguered Saskatchewan history professor. Little did she know it at the time, but Neatby had stirred a battle that was to rage until the arrival on the scene – in Ontario, at least – of J.R. McCarthy as deputy minister of education. A committed progressive, McCarthy quickly began to surround himself with like-minded disciples.

When the Hope commission finally tabled its report in 1950, it gave great comfort to traditionalist teachers and drove progressives to despair. It recommended, to no one's surprise, that the province invest in new schools at both the elementary and secondary levels of instruction. In terms of curriculum, the Hope commission reaffirmed that the primary schools were designed to educate all the young people of the province in the basic skills of reading, writing, and arithmetic. The high schools were given the mandate to prepare the minority among the students who showed a propensity for university education; the remainder were encouraged to enter the vocational schools or go directly into the workforce. A central feature of the reforms was the introduction of province-wide examinations – known as 'departmentals' – at the end of grade 13. At the time, the academic curriculum was rigid and uniform throughout the province, with only the very brightest scoring high enough to go on to university. The Hope report was embraced by W.J. Dunlop, who became minister in 1951. 'W. J. Dunlop,' reports one educational historian, 'denounced progressivism and declared that every trace of it would be rooted out of the schools.'[9]

These Hope commission-inspired reforms dominated the Ontario school agenda for the next decade but continued to meet with considerable opposition along the way, especially from within the Department of Education itself, where the progressives had begun to encamp. The continuing dissatisfaction with the public school system boiled over, once again, into the public arena, so much so that in 1962, under Education Minister John Robarts, the province undertook another formal review of the primary and secondary educational process and devised a plan, which was soon called 'The Robarts Plan,' whereby those students who scored high on the 'departmentals' at the end of grade thirteen would go to university and students destined for the trades or other non-academic careers were directed towards the newly established community colleges. These colleges taught the mechanical skills for the trades and other careers, such as commercial arts. The Robarts plan constituted little more than tinkering with the structures put in place by the Hope commission. Needless to say, the progressive educators were not pleased.

The Robarts two-stream system was, in fact, quite successful until the parents of those who were denied admission to university began to complain that the system was unfair. Provincial politicians started to feel the heat and voices were heard in the popular press urging the government to address the growing demands for greater access to university. One of the principal obstacles to this ambition was, of course, the dreaded 'departmentals.' They stood as a rigid barrier to large-scale university admission. So they had to go. In March 1966 William Davis, the minister of education, announced that the 'departmentals' would be eliminated in 1967.[10]

At the same time, while all this was going on, the atmosphere was charged by the demands from the Catholic separate school boards for increased funding for the burgeoning enrolments in their elementary and high schools. Until this time, public funding was available to separate schools up to grade ten; grades eleven to thirteen were funded by the parents of those students who attended the schools. With the growth in student population across the province, the demands of Catholic teachers and parents also increased, thus adding a sectarian element into the movement for reforms to the public educational system.

Responding to the mounting pressures from schools and parents, John Robarts, now premier, and his minister of education, William Davis, decided in 1964 that the time had come for a complete re-evaluation of the entire primary and secondary school system in Ontario. But who was to undertake such a formidable task? When William Davis called a meeting of his top departmental advisers early in the fall of 1964, he outlined his plans for a study of the public school system in Ontario. He explained that he wanted a man who was prominent in the educational community and beyond repute. His deputy minister suggested the name of an outstanding educator but the minister's attention was caught when Dorothy Dunn, assistant superintendent of curriculum for the province, suggested the name of Justice Emmett Hall.[11] Davis responded enthusiastically but thought that it would be difficult to get him to accept the appointment. The more the group discussed the alternatives to Hall, the weaker they all looked. By the end of the two-hour meeting, Davis was convinced that he ought at least to approach the Supreme Court justice.

While standing in his Supreme Court chambers in early March 1965, Emmett Hall received an unexpected telephone call from the Ontario minister of education. Davis explained that the government of Ontario wished to undertake a thorough review of elementary and secondary education in Ontario. The minister told Justice Hall that it was the unanimous recommendation of his senior advisers that he be asked to lead such a study. Hall demurred, noting that he did not know whether it would be proper for him to undertake such an assignment so soon after his royal commission report on health services. He asked for time to think the matter through, and promised to let the minister know of his decision within twenty-four hours.

It had been less than eight weeks since Hall had submitted the second volume of his royal commission report. But he found that he had enjoyed the public limelight and was still bathing in the after-glow of the public approval heaped upon him in the press for his work on the royal commission. After sounding out several of his colleagues at the Supreme Court – most of whom grumbled about the wisdom of a member of the Court taking on another major extrajudicial assignment – Hall agreed to head the study. Education had been one of his principal interests – since his days on the Saskatoon Catholic school board and with the Saskatchewan Catholic Trustees Association, so why pass up an opportunity to sit on such an important commission? But, according to Court administrator Ken Campbell, members of the Court were not pleased; several bluntly complained that Hall was on an ego trip. Emmett Hall disregarded the objections of his Court colleagues and informed William Davis that he would take on the commission.

Hall biographer Dennis Gruending claims that Hall took up the Ontario educational study out of a sense of duty to his church.[12] He contends that Hall considered the education committee as an opportunity to exert pressure on the Ontario government to extend financial support to all thirteen years of Catholic education in the province. Nothing could be further from the truth. The fact that the committee's final report never once addresses the issue weighs against such an hypothesis. Had this been one of Hall's motives, it is scarcely credible that he did not pursue it aggressively, as was his custom with causes he championed. There is no question that Hall personally supported the extension of full funding to all levels of Catholic education in Ontario, but the mandate of the provincial committee was a call for thorough curriculum reform, not financial restructuring. The call for curriculum reform from kindergarten to grade 13 was enough for any one committee to handle. And so the Ontario committee refused to be side-tracked by demands that it address the Catholic funding issue.

It is entirely understandable, however, that members of the court should have resented Hall's taking up another public commission of inquiry so soon after the Health Services report was submitted. But the fact that he was free do so without the collective consent of the Court points up a weakness in the administrative structure of the Court itself. Is it conceivable that he could assume major extrajudicial responsibilities without the consent of the chief justice? Unfortunately, the chief justice was Robert Taschereau, who was not at the peak of his abilities in 1965. When discussing this matter a few years later, Hall impatiently brushed off all objections with the claim that he had duly informed the Court of his decision to lead the ministerial committee. Not surprisingly, several of his judicial colleagues, such as Douglas Abbott, Gérald Fauteux, and Wilfrid Judson, never warmed to Emmett Hall as a colleague.

Hall was originally asked to chair, single-handed, this ministerial committee, but one day in late November 1965 – not long after the committee had begun to hold public hearings – he fell ill while hearing a case before the Court. He experienced severe pains in his head and could not make it back to his chambers unassisted. The fear of not knowing what was happening gripped him; it was obviously not a heart attack because all the symptoms were wrong. But was it a stroke? The thought filled him with horror. Hall was in his sixty-seventh year at the time. Doctors were summoned and he was given a thorough examination. It turned out that he had not suffered a stroke but a severe migraine. His doctor son, John, rushed to Ottawa and conferred with the attending physicians. When he recovered – which he did fully in a few days – Hall returned to his Supreme Court duties and set about to organize himself for the Ontario education committee. His son wrote him shortly after his return to work urging him to slow down. The long handwritten letter said:

Frankie and I are most relieved to know that your illness is not as serious as was feared at first. We hope that by now you are well on your way to recovery and that you will take this episode as just exactly the thing it is – a warning.

You are much too valuable to us and to the whole country to end your days like Joe Kennedy, unable to do anything you want to do, let alone everything. I wish you could give serious consideration to resigning from the Education Commission. By keeping up the present pace you may accomplish a lot in a year or so, but not as much in the long run, as if you pace yourself and do a little less at a time, but more in a lifetime.

You have already done more for your family, friends and country than anyone else I know; and I really feel that you should now take a little time to enjoy it. Most men of your age would consider the duties of the Supreme Court Judge quite sufficient – besides, if you think the education brief couldn't be done without you, reflect on what would have happened if your warning had been a little more pointed!

You could still hold yourself available to the commission as a consultant and I am certain that even in that role you would be forceful enough to shape the report the way it should be. Someone else not only can but should do the back breaking work of compiling the report and spare the man who most lawyers I know agree is the ablest Judge on the Supreme Court.

Whatever your decision, you may rest assured of my continuing admiration, love and respect.[13]

Only a source as close to him as his son could have persuaded Hall to inform the Ontario minister of education that he would have to have some assistance. He called William Davis and asked that a co-chair be appointed. Davis named Lloyd A. Dennis, a Scarborough elementary school principal and curriculum adviser, who had originally been appointed as secretary and research adviser for the committee. Dennis willingly and enthusiastically assumed the role as co-chair. The choice was a happy one: from the start, Hall liked Dennis, whose boundless energy and effervescent personality infused the entire committee. His expertise in education allowed him to assume a large share of the committee's work.

The Ontario education committee, which was formally established on 10 June 1965, consisted of a total of twenty-four people representing a wide spectrum of university, high school, and elementary school teachers and trustees, as well as representatives of the Ontario Teachers Federation and the teachers' colleges. Two university presidents – Dr G.M. Ross, president of York University, and Dr J.F. Leddy, an old Saskatoon friend of Emmett Hall's who was now president of the University of Windsor – also served on the committee at Hall's request. In addition, there was one representative from the Franco-Ontario school system, Léopold Séguin. Two members of the committee, Sister Alice Marie, of the Congregation of St Joseph and the London separate school board, and M.P. Parent, former trustee of the Ottawa separate school board, provided input from the separate school system of the province. It was a large committee but necessarily so because of the scope of its mandate. The last thing this committee needed was to be accused of neglecting some part of the public educational system in Ontario.

The committee was formally instructed 'to make a careful study of the means whereby modern education can meet the present and future needs of children and society.'[14] It would be difficult to imagine a broader mandate. And it was just the kind of task Emmett Hall liked the most. It did not fetter his team unduly and left the committee free to pursue its task in whatever direction the inquiry took as it progressed. Both Hall and Dennis felt strongly that the committee should consult widely and be open to directions prompted by the dynamics of the consultation process itself.

The Hall-Dennis committee, as it inevitably became known, criss-crossed the province of Ontario hearing submissions from teachers, parents' groups, and other interested parties. It even sent some of its members to canvass the education practices of places like Sweden and Japan. The committee was convinced that the research had to be exhaustive because there was a great deal at stake: proposals of major educational reforms that would shape the future of Ontario for generations to come. But one other issue ought not to be overlooked: the Hall-Dennis committee was never out of sight of the Ontario Department of Education. J.R. McCarthy, the deputy minister, and his senior advisers – all progressive educators – kept a close eye on the workings of the committee. In fact, as Eric Riker has pointed out, the committee was 'initially structured in a way that was wanted by the department; its agendas and working papers were prepared by the department's staff; almost all of the expert testimony during the early stages of its work was provided by the department; and finally, a number of its members were close associates, or former teachers and professors, or members of the department's curriculum branch.'[15] 'Without question,' Riker concludes, the Hall-Dennis committee 'was clearly biased before its work even commenced' and 'the consensus that emerged in fact reflected a basic view that was wanted.'[16]

'THE TRUTH SHALL MAKE YOU FREE'

As with the report of the Royal Commission on Health Services, Emmett Hall gave careful attention to the wording of the committee's final report, released in June 1968 and entitled *Living and Learning*. That included the title of the report's opening chapter – 'The Truth Shall Make You Free' – which Hall thought encapsulated the substance of the report. Lloyd Dennis saw otherwise; he did not like the heading – it was too biblical for him – but he lost out to his co-chair, who adamantly insisted that it remain. Hall reviewed the various drafts of the report and approved or disapproved of every sentence; he found this an easy task for he found much to approve and was deeply sympathetic to the progressive thrust of the report. The earliest briefs submitted by the ministry advisers had convinced him that the only way to achieve genuine reform of Ontario's educational system was to refashion and redesign the way courses were packaged and taught throughout the province's schools. He embraced the concept, essential to the commission's report, that learning was a voyage of discovery and that the pace of discovery should be set by the individual student, not by a process imposed from above.

Hall's imprint on this report can be identified in its first pages, where the committee stated that 'the underlying aim of education is to further man's unending search for truth. Once he possesses the means to truth, all else is within his grasp.'[17] This is a clear extension of the heading 'The truth shall make you free.' But it is the only time that the report ever concerns itself with 'truth.' Indeed, the very next sentences state that 'wisdom and understanding, sensitivity, compassion, and responsibility, as well as intellectual honesty and personal integrity, will be his guides in adolescence and his companions in maturity,' not the quest for 'truth.' Hall may have won his way with the title, but Lloyd Dennis and his fellow progressives won out in the restatement of the 'key to open all doors.'[18] The aims of progressive education dominated the report and were couched in sentiments that Emmett Hall could easily endorse; he was very much taken by the excitement promised by progressive education, especially when so many of the submissions to the committee confidently promised unprecedented results.

His Catholic background led him to endorse the continued public support of aid to non-confessional and separate schools but, much to the annoyance of separate school representatives who appeared before the committee, he stubbornly resisted attempts to have his report support the extension of full financial support beyond the junior high school level. Both Hall and Dennis – never one overly sympathetic to separate schools – would not permit this committee to be deflected from its central mandate to reform the curriculum of the public schools of Ontario. Nevertheless, the refusal to give formal consideration to the extension of funding in the separate school system appeared to many in Catholic educational circles as a serious oversight, however deliberate. Many in the Catholic community found it difficult to comprehend how the committee could have excluded from the ambit of its broad mandate a large segment of the province which constituted, in fact, an integral part of the 'public school system.' The refusal to consider full funding was even more puzzling when one considers that the work of the committee would affect the curriculum of the separate schools as well as the others. This issue raised questions about the effectiveness of Dr J.F. Leddy, a devout Catholic and staunch supporter of separate schools, and particularly about the role played on the committee by Sister Alice Marie and M.P. Parent, both of whom were there precisely to represent the interests of the separate school system. The best Emmett Hall would say when he was pressed on this matter was: 'We didn't want to get involved with that hot potato.' This was hardly an adequate response to such a major oversight. But, in retrospect, it may well have been the most prudent thing to do, for there is no doubt that had the committee recommended the extension of full funding to Catholic schools, that issue would have become the major focus of public debate and shifted attention away from the central curriculum reforms being recommended. It must be remembered that *Living and Learning* was the unanimous report of the entire committee. There was no dissenting or minority report. If the Catholic members of the committee had felt as strongly on the issue of funding as many members of the Catholic community, why did they not express their reservations in a minority report? Robert T. Dixon reports in *Catholic Education and Politics in Ontario*[19] that 'the Catholic members on the Hall-Dennis Commission in 1967 had seen the implications of the commission's emerging philosophy of a continuous, non-graded progress from kindergarten to grade 13. In this mindset, ending the separate school system after grade 10 seemed illogical. Furthermore, if kindergarten to grade 12 were recommended as the basic education for students of all abilities, then, in the minds of the Catholic leaders, separate school truncation would be unjust.'[20] They were prepared to submit a report that contained a powerful argument sub rosa in favour of extended funding to separate schools and let it germinate, with obvious benefits to Catholic school supporters. There is no question that separate school funding was still an explosive political issue in Ontario at this time. To no one's surprise, separate school funding became an issue in the Ontario election of October 1971, which returned a Progressive Conservative government under William Davis with 78 of the 117 seats in the legislature. Davis had run on a platform that promised *not* to extend funding to separate schools. It was not until 12 June 1984, thirteen years later, on the eve of his departure from politics, that Davis reversed himself and promised to introduce legislation that would extend full funding to Ontario Catholic students. This decision – made, it would appear, without consultation with senior party members – left the Conservative Party in high dudgeon and permitted the Liberal Party under David Peterson to form a majority government on the promise to make good Davis's promise.[21]

In the final report, Hall's influence was evident in the call for the improvement of health services in schools and formal instruction in such matters as alcoholism and drug addiction as well as 'sexual ethics.' It is significant – and no accident – that the report does not refer to sex education but to 'sexual ethics,' emphasizing, by clear implication, that children should be instructed in sexual morality and not simply in sexual hygiene. Not a few members of the committee balked at this but Emmett Hall wanted it and he got his way. But his victory was more show than substance, for there is nothing in the body of the report to indicate the content of such instruction, beyond saying that the 'curriculum should educate the pupil in ethical values and ensure his moral development.'[22] 'Ethics' is merely listed as a senior-year option after 'Choral Singing' and 'Comparative Religion.' Once again, Emmett Hall seems to have been sandbagged whenever the committee conceded to his specific requests.

There can be no doubt that this report contained a great deal that everyone could applaud: the genuine effort to encourage pupils in elementary and secondary schools to pursue their full potential; the desire to make learning as enjoyable as possible and free from the old tyrannical whims of taskmasters; the provision for slow learners; the emphasis on the total learning environment; the concern for native peoples. All of these issues pervaded the report and elicited immediate editorial approval. Above all, many observers welcomed the report as a formal repudiation of the rigidity that had dominated education in Ontario. The fear of failing the 'departmentals' and thus being barred from university was pervasive throughout the schools and, with the growth in population, affected increasingly larger numbers of students. More and more, parents were demanding the right to send their children to university. These people welcomed the report, at least as they understood it from the press reports and endorsements.

On 13 June 1968, the day after the committee's report was tabled in the Ontario legislature, the *Toronto Globe and Mail* ran a lead editorial entitled 'No Dust-gatherer This.' It went on to say that 'Judge Emmett Hall and his crew have set education on its ear, exposed the failures of every educational institution in the province, plunged eagerly and creatively into the future, and undoubtedly occasioned the eruption of fountains of cold sweat throughout the educational establishment.'[23] The same issue of the *Globe* featured the Hall-Dennis report in an article by the paper's education writer, Douglas Sagi, under the headline, 'Report on Schools Asks End of Grades and Formal Tests,' and alongside with pictures of Emmett Hall and Lloyd Dennis, Sagi summarized the 258 recommendations in glowing terms: 'Gone would be all school categories and their titles including elementary and secondary, academic, vocational and commercial; all streams and programs.'[24] The rigid 'Robarts Plan' was to be replaced by Hall-Dennis's new, more flexible scheme. Under this scheme, Sagi explained, 'rather than using, necessarily, the categories of history, geography, biology and every subject known to anyone ever schooled in Ontario, learning would be organized around general areas such as communications, environmental studies and the humanities.' Students would be liberated from the old order of rigid programs with tests and examinations. 'The report recommends a new system of education that would emphasize individual discovery, continuous learning and flexibility of curriculum, buildings and scheduling.'

Similarly, the Toronto *Daily Star*, ever ready to support the cause of liberation, ran a lead editorial on the day after the report appeared with the heading: 'A Radical Program to Liberate our School System.' The editorial went on to interpret the report favourably.

It is the kind of progressive doctrine we have come to expect from Mr. Justice Emmett Hall, whose Royal Commission on Health Services established the case for a medicare plan for all Canada.

In formal terms, the education committee's report recommends a non-graded 12 year system for Ontario Schools with Grade 13 eliminated.

Why should a student be forced into the narrow confines of a rigid course of studies, whether it fits him or not? Why, if he is engaged by the problems of people and society, should he have to struggle with the abstruse requirements of advanced science or mathematics?

The same, of course, applies to the boy or girl who is fascinated by the challenge of chemistry or the purity of mathematics. Their school time would be far better spent developing these interests than labouring over what to them are dull texts in 'useless' subjects.

The school curriculum, as the Hall Committee correctly sees, should be fitted to the individual talent of the student rather than having his abilities hacked and compressed to fit a Procrustean curriculum.[24]

That same day, Thursday, 13 June 1968, the *Star* gave over an entire page to the Hall-Dennis report under the banner: 'The Aim of Education is to Further Man's Search for Truth.' Following a lengthy and laudatory account of the report were two brief biographies of the two leading commissioners. Hall's was titled 'Justice Hall – He's the Man Who Championed Medicare and Truscott.' This theme was echoed in other contemporary commentary on the committee's report; almost every account of that report alluded to Hall's medicare report and to his dissent in Truscott, the two events in his life that defined him in the public mind. Lloyd Dennis was featured as an educational visionary whose progressive views permeated the report.

The comments of the *Globe* and the *Star* were generally typical of the reaction to *Living and Learning*. The major previous changes in Ontario education had taken place under John Robarts, who, as minister of education, had revised the high school program so as to permit students in the trades to complete their secondary school program in four years; those in the academic stream – destined for university – were still required to spend five years in high school. Now the Hall-Dennis report explicitly urged school boards to 'abandon' core elements of traditional education: 'Abandon the practice of assigning homework ... in favor of long-term assignments that invite pupils to make responsible decisions regarding their use of time' (Recommendation 28); 'Abandon the use of class standing, percentage marks, and letter grades in favor of parents and pupil counseling as a method of reporting individual progress' (Recommendation 74); 'Abandon the use of formal examinations except where the experience would be of value to students planning to attend universities where formal examinations may still be in use' (Recommendation 75). Such an approach was touted in the interest of 'liberating' the student from the current 'rigid' practices which were stifling the creative capacities of primary and secondary students.

All of this bracing program of educational change was enthusiastically endorsed by the province's teachers, as well as the opposition education critics in the legislature. Walter Pitman for the New Democratic Party, a former lecturer at Ryerson Polytechnic Institute, warmly applauded the main recommendations. He said that 'this is one of the most important documents ever tabled in this House in the course of education.'[26] Liberal leader Robert Nixon, a former teacher, tried to be critical but was not able to find a major point with which he disagreed. He was especially delighted to see the recommendation that French-language instruction be instituted in the first four years of school.

SECOND THOUGHTS

But gradually, as people began to read the report and think about the sweeping nature of the proposed reforms, voices of dissent began to be heard. Some professors of education and other educational professionals took aim at the basic premise of the report, which appeared to be that the teacher and the curriculum should not structure learning along the traditional lines of educational instruction. At one point the report asked the rhetorical question: 'Should all pupils be taught by means of logically organized and separate courses in traditional subjects as reading, spelling, arithmetic, history, science, literature and grammar, or should all pupils enjoy the stimulation of lively ideas and be given ample opportunity to discuss them, with the satisfaction of learning by discovery?' The answer was clearly obvious, especially when the reader was told that 'traditional courses lead to a deadening routine.'[27]

The report consisted of a running dialogue between the traditional and modern schools of educational instruction. But the report was clear about which side it was on and threw down the gauntlet: 'The traditional school was largely concerned with what the teacher taught and how effective he was in conducting an orderly class. The modern school is more concerned with what the pupils learn, why and how they learn, and whether they will continue to be disposed to learn.' However unsatisfactory traditional education may have been – and there was much that was wrong with it – most observers of the educational scene in Ontario could scarcely recognize it from the caricature presented in the Hall-Dennis report.

The rejection of structured courses prompted the committee to propose an amorphous curriculum with a minimum of structure in order to meet the individual needs of pupils. Its report made no attempt to say what those needs were – except in the most general terms, such as his or her 'total environment.' To most critics, the flaw in this line of thinking emerged in the discussion of the curriculum. There, the report claimed that 'A good curriculum must meet the needs and expressed desires of pupils.'[28] There was no conception of legitimate or illegitimate needs, or of the distinction between needs and desires.

The Hall-Dennis report compared education to a voyage. After denigrating formal structured courses, the report said: 'On the other hand, it would be confusing to send pupils on voyages of discovery over one vast ocean of knowledge. The study of man, or a curriculum embracing all life, is too formidable a sea for students to navigate without charts of some sort.'[29] This concession to common sense prompted the commission to propose a 'broad design' in place of traditional subject matters, such as history or science. In their place the committee recommended three 'areas of emphasis': 'Communications,' 'Environmental Studies,' and 'Humanities.' The teacher's task was to ensure that the child received a 'balanced learning experience;' he or she should do this by discouraging 'the development of any one interest at the expense of others.'[30]

But, under the program of studies recommended in the Hall-Dennis report, critics argued that students were sent off onto a voyage of discovery without the benefit of detailed maps or charts. If they encountered shoals or reefs en route, it was expected that they would overcome them and benefit from the encounter. No thought was given to the possibility that they might founder; they might have no way of knowing where they were going or indeed when they arrived at their destination.

The committee's resolute reluctance to impose a structure on the educational process led it to overlook content. A good example of this can be found in the section where the report accepted several items from the Hope commission on education in Ontario. The Hall-Dennis committee endorsed nine aims of the Hope report. The first one was 'to develop capacity to apprehend and practise basic virtues.'[31] The committee viewed this aim as desirable but added the comment: the first aim 'needs to be made definite by designating just what virtues the school, and more precisely, the public school, can and should develop.' Unfortunately, the committee did not feel competent to provide the missing virtues by name. Could it not, some observed wryly, have gone on to suggest, as a minimum, 'honesty' and 'respect for the rights of minorities,' to say nothing of other virtues?

The absence of content led the committee to reject a fair measure of form as well. The report said, for example, that 'a considerable number of children have a gift for imaginative and poetic language, and they must be encouraged. Others will see the potentialities of advanced skills in the use of language; they may aim at Fowler's "spare and vivid precision of educated speech," or may see how labour in writing can make a sentence immediately and easily clear to the reader ... They, too, must be encouraged. But all that is required of most pupils is simple clarity and accuracy in expression and comprehension.'[32]

Why, demanded the critics, was it too much to expect that students be made to attain the level of competence recommended by Fowler? The implication appeared to be that some students are by nature capable of learning fine and graceful writing while others, less fortunate, are condemned to a lower level of competence. Surely the normal inclination to mediocrity could be overcome by forceful teaching, to the permanent benefit of the student and society at large. Furthermore, how could students hope to express themselves clearly and accurately without being taught the structure of a good sentence and a good paragraph? Readers of the Hall-Dennis report were led to believe that students would assimilate this information through the process of 'discovery.'

Perhaps the biggest deficiency of the Hall-Dennis report, in the eyes of its critics, was that it demanded the impossible of both teachers and students. Maybe, as one observer confided to this author, if all teachers were as capable as Lloyd Dennis was of instilling enthusiasm, the report could have been successful. But one wonders if it was just a question of teachers. How many students at the elementary and secondary level were capable of responding to this open invitation to discovery with the minimum of structure?

The Hall-Dennis report found favour among the teachers of teachers. And so it should have, for the progressive philosophy of education that drove the report was very much in fashion throughout the teachers' colleges of the province. A large number of the submissions to the Hall-Dennis committee originated in the teachers' colleges, which embraced the report and set about instilling its philosophy into the minds of the rising generation of teachers.

The report was also well received by elementary school teachers: 'Teachers at this level had long been exposed to progressive currents, which had not been determinedly countered even during he 1950s, and by 1968 ... the leadership from the Department of Education was unequivocally in progressive hands.'[33] As R.D. Gidney has noted, deputy minister McCarthy's influence was 'critical, not only because of the ambience he created within the department but because of oft-reiterated, forthright, and forceful expression of his own views.'[34] McCarthy summarized his private views on what the undergraduate school should look like in a presentation to the committee. His comments were reported as follows: 'In describing how a non-graded elementary program could be organized, Dr. McCarthy stated that he would eliminate grades, courses divided by grades, formal examinations, marks, report cards, promotion as it has been practiced, and would substitute a flexible program of continuous pupil progress related to the individual's rate of learning, his readiness, and his mastery of the program, with evaluation shared by the pupils, and with reporting practices which described progress in the program and which involved greater use of parent-teacher interviews.'[35] As Gidney has noted, 'such sentiments would echo through page after page of the Hall-Dennis Report.' But, Gidney emphasizes, 'the effect was simply to *endorse* an extant view of educational reform already well established in influential quarters, and already articulated by the most powerful figure in the ministry aside from William Davis himself, well before the report was produced.'[36]

William Davis, soon to become premier of the province, embraced the Hall-Dennis report. Not a single recommendation of the Hall-Dennis report came as a surprise to the minister; they were exactly what he and his deputy minister wanted. As Gidney has mused: 'What purpose, then, did the publication of the Hall-Dennis Report serve in the larger scheme of things? Certainly it provided a "bully pulpit" from which to preach a particular approach to education to a wider public, and undoubtedly it gave that approach a degree of legitimacy it might not otherwise have had. But it was hardly of decisive importance to the reorientation of pedagogy and the curriculum that was already under way before its publication and that took place after it. J.R. McCarthy, on the other hand, was. However one assesses his influence throughout the period, whether for praise or blame, his place in its history deserves a measure of recognition now too often accorded to the Hall-Dennis Report itself.'[37]

The psychological expertise of Dr Reva Gerstein, the only psychologist on the committee, was a dominant influence on those aspects of the study concerning 'Today's Child' and 'The learning Experience.' Indeed, not a single presentation came to the committee from any other educational psychologist. Of the thirty expert representations listed in *Living and Learning* – ranging from a submission by Peter Stursberg on the educational practices in India to Marshall McLuhan's on education in the electronic age – one finds five reports from members of the Ontario Department of Education, and not one of these studies attempted to show how the traditional approach could be reformed to eliminate the undesirable practices. Instead, the report recommends a complete revamping of elementary and secondary education in Ontario along the lines espoused by 'progressive' educators.

Marshall McLuhan clearly had a major impact on the committee's thinking. In his remarks to the committee, McLuhan stressed the wisdom of pursuing a 'discovery approach' in education. He questioned explicitly 'the value of having fixed goals for education, and suggested that pupils be given opportunities to look at problems for themselves, and to discover new patterns, new possibilities, and new answers.'[38] This philosophy of education clearly permeated *Living and Learning*. Similarly, Dr J.R. Suchman, acting director of elementary and secondary research in the United States Office of Education, stressed in his brief the method of inquiry as a learning process. He emphasized, in particular, 'the need for teachers to avoid giving answers to questions raised during pupil inquiry; the teacher should give no more help than is needed to enable the pupil to continue the process of inquiry.'

The one question that continued to tantalize those who knew Emmett Hall – a thoroughly practical and realistic man – was how could he have become one of the major authors of such an unrealistic report? Did he really have a central role on this committee, as he had on the Health

Services commission? There can be little doubt that he read and digested the numerous briefs which individuals and groups presented for the consideration of the committee. And he emphatically endorsed the recommendations. But the Hall-Dennis committee included among its twenty-four members eight professional educators – three of whom, J.K. Crossley, M.B. Parnall, and E.J. Quick, were closely tied to the Ontario Department of Education – and the forceful Reva Gerstein. This solid core of professional educators, hand-picked by J.R. McCarthy, was already deeply familiar with the material that came before the committee, and they played a large role in determining what recognized educational authorities – from John Dewey to Ivan Illich, from Paul Goodman to Bruno Bettleheim – came to the attention of their colleagues. All of these authorities were proponents of 'progressive' education. No one has suggested that the professional educators misled the committee, but the mere fact that they were several strides ahead of Hall and a number of other members of the committee gave them an advantage. But Emmett Hall was clearly open to the blandishments of progressive education. He delighted in the concepts of education as a child-centred voyage and favoured the abandonment of class structures and grading procedures. No one had to drag him kicking and screaming into the fray. He was a full, if not a dominant, participant.

Hall had strong views on education and he had expressed those views publicly on many occasions. On one such occasion, when he was awarded the Glendon College Public Service award on 22 January 1969, he warned that recent trends toward scientific and technological education ran the risk of contributing to the 'cult of materialism.'[39] He went on to say that 'the world has seen the rise of materialism as a by-product and companion of the Industrial Revolution with the consequent shoving back or overshadowing of the Christian Judaic traditions of freedom of the individual aided and abetted in many educational institutions and educational systems of the west.' It was a theme that he had enunciated years before in Saskatoon when speaking to nurses at St Paul's Hospital. And it was a theme he repeated on 1 October 1971 when he was installed as chancellor of the University of Guelph. On that occasion he said:

... the educational aims of a society may be formulated in terms of noble ideals such as the respect and understanding of all mankind, the self-realization of the individual, and a national identity, achieving himself in a position to make a living adequate to meet his needs ... But a danger lurks in the shadows.

Unless a people is on its guard, the economic demands of society can be made to determine what is done in education. The society whose educational system gives priority to the economic over the spiritual and emotional needs of man defines its citizens in terms of economic units and in so doing debases them. There is a dignity and nobility of man that has nothing to do with economic considerations. The development of this dignity and nobility is one of education's tasks.[40]

That was vintage Hall, calling attention to the higher responsibilities of education, but the thoughts ran against the spirit of the age. For the major thrust of post-war governments in the West was towards more education as a means of providing greater material benefits through science and technology. More specialization earlier became the cry from industry. Many industrialists and government spokesmen clearly believed that 'the advance of industry and technology was intimately bound up with the expansion of education,'[41] in short, that education should serve the ends of the emerging technological society. 'The larger the pool of literate, schooled citizens,' the mantra became, 'the greater the possibilities of industrial, technological, and scientific progress.'[42] As one leading American educator observed: 'In the 1960s, all this was happening on a global scale. In the advanced industrial countries of the West, the tide seemed likely to sweep away structures painfully erected over the centuries.'[43] Above all, education was now seen as an 'investment.' President John F. Kennedy made this point in a message to Congress in 1963: 'This nation is committed to greater advancement in economic growth, and recent research has shown that one of the most beneficial of all such investments is education, accounting for some forty percent of the nation's growth and productivity in recent years. In the new age of science and space, improved education is essential to give meaning to our national purpose and power. It requires skilled manpower and brainpower to match the power of totalitarian discipline. It requires a scientific effort which demonstrates the superiority of freedom.'[44] Kennedy's successor as president, Lyndon Johnson, took up the same theme and urged American businessmen in 1965 'to support expenditures for education on the ground that they were a good investment.'[45] Clearly, there was a growing tendency, among leading figures both in government and in industry, to view education's role as that of providing skilled workers, be they scientists or tradesmen. This ethos ran diametrically counter to the Hall-Dennis committee's findings and recommendations. It eschewed the notion that schools should be dominated by any given ethos, especially by an industrial and technological one. As R.D. Gidney has written, 'the emphasis of the [Hall-Dennis] report fell almost exclusively on education for personal fulfilment. Education was about "self-realization" and not about fitting individuals for predetermined economic or social roles. In this respect, Hall-Dennis reflected the anti-technocratic, anti-traditionalist, romantic impulses of the 1960s.'[46] The Hall-Dennis report did not exclude the possibility of producing scientists or technologists; but students should move in this direction at their own pace and by dint of self-motivation, not compelled to do so by an imposed agenda that stressed the need for 'skilled scientists' and 'skilled workers.' Above all, the educational curriculum, regardless of the demands of industry, should not be structured to produce students with 'marketable skills.' Not surprisingly, therefore, the Hall-Dennis report ran smack into a wall of opposition from industry and governments were sent scurrying for cover.

For the editors of Ontario's daily newspapers, their initial approval of *Living and Learning* soon came to haunt them as students, teachers, and parents came to be increasingly dissatisfied with the product of a loosely structured educational system. In November 1976 a high school valedictorian in Toronto made front-page headlines for saying that his diploma meant nothing because he could barely read or write English, thanks, he said, to the Hall-Dennis reforms. As the products of the new, 'permissive' system began to appear on the university campuses, most universities throughout the province instituted remedial courses in English grammar and composition. However well-meaning the Hall-Dennis report and recommendations may have appeared in 1968, they clearly had not produced better students.

The problem may well have been errors in the underlying progressive philosophy of education which pervaded the report. The most outspoken critic of the report was James Daly, a historian at MacMaster University in Hamilton, Ontario. He wrote and circulated a pamphlet entitled *Education or Molasses?*[47] in which he excoriated the report as 'a bucket of molasses, sticky sentiment couched in wretched prose.' In chapter 2 of his pamphlet, 'The Ghost of John Dewey,' Daly summed up the 'central assertions' of the report in the following words: 'Poor performance by children is the fault of the system or the teacher, not the child; learning is a pleasant experience – unpleasantness makes learning more difficult; punishment is seldom or never justified, and corporal punishment never; students should be given a maximum of choice in what they will learn; the purpose of education is not to introduce the child into the customs and tradition of the adult world, but into those of a world which will be inconceivably different – that is, the purpose of education is to prepare the young for world of Change.'[48] Daly's stinging rebuke was quickly taken up by teachers who began to see their ability to control classes slip away from them. And, as they watched their pupils opting for the easy way out of the process under the new and exciting 'child centred' learning, they became outraged. In short order the teachers, especially in the higher levels, began to fight back.

The report had recommended that students be permitted a greater latitude in choosing courses and that they be permitted to advance even though they were 'unable to make progress in all the disciplines.' In this regard, the report stated that 'it must be recognized that there are many children who have special gifts in music art or drama, but who have no particular interest in the sciences or mathematics or other academic disciplines. The curriculum must provide for their progress and for graduation with emphasis in their specialities.' This meant that children at the primary and secondary levels of education could claim greater interest in some areas of study and thus avoid others; it is safe to say that this generous premise has led a large number of children to avoid more difficult but essential disciplines such as English grammar and composition, as well as languages, especially French.

The crucial fault has been in the incompatible principles of the Hall-Dennis report: it recommended an end to a structured, mandatory course of instruction and in its stead a program based on individual student choice. This necessarily meant that students would take the easiest courses available and avoid the basics. It was clearly a case of too much butter and too little bread. Hall responded impatiently to the charge that the report of his committee initiated a trend away from the basics. But the facts of the matter confirmed the worst fears of the report's critics: students were, indeed, designing programs of study for themselves that avoided the tougher disciplines, such as French-language instruction. And the universities were reaping the results: students inadequately prepared to handle university courses.

Dorothy Dunn, an adviser to the committee, admitted a year or so after the report was adopted that the Hall-Dennis committee erred in not stating the obvious, that is to say, in not stressing reading, writing, and basic skills. 'But there was never any intention,' she insists, 'that the Hall-Dennis Committee sought to minimize the paramount importance of these fundamental skills.'[49] The practical results appeared, however, to be just that – neglect of the basics, for whatever reason.

CONCLUSION

When the work of the committee had ended – the many revisions and changes in format agreed upon – the committee co-chairs sent the report to the printers with the instruction that they wanted it released on 10 June 1968, exactly three years to the day on which they had been appointed to undertake the study. The printers were given eight weeks to print and bind the report. So far as Hall and Dennis were concerned, that was sufficient time. Neither pretended to know anything about the problems of printing a report which contained numerous colour pictures and several charts; all that mattered to them was that they had given their word to William Davis that the report would be in his hands on 10 June 1968.

When the report appeared to be slow in coming, Hall telephoned the printer in Toronto and ordered him in no uncertain terms to have the report ready or else 'heads would roll.'[50] The printer, naturally upset by such bluster, called Davis's office and pleaded with Claire Westcott to intercede with Justice Hall and explain that the report involved a complicated process of graphic design and lithography which required the services of Hugh S. Newton and Company, an editorial and graphic design firm. Westcott consulted with the minister, who affirmed that he was in no special hurry for the report; as far as he was concerned, there was no specific deadline. Westcott attempted to calm the impatient Supreme Court justice, but to little avail. Hall insisted that the report be ready on the date that he had promised it. And it *was* ready and in his hands on 10 June. He presented a copy to the minister on 12 June 1968.

The Hall-Dennis committee cost the people of Ontario a total of $697,137; Justice Hall received an honorarium of $10,000 for his work, in addition to his expenses. Strictly speaking, Justice Hall should not have received an honorarium for his efforts because judges are precluded from augmenting their salaries by 'moonlighting.' He told the author that when he got the cheque he had to do some 'fancy footwork' with Revenue Canada in order to let him keep it. But keep it he did. And, while he appreciated receiving that stipend, he enjoyed even more the perquisites – the travel and per diem expense account – that went with the task. Throughout the three years of the Hall-Dennis committee hearings, Emmett Hall went first-class even though the Ontario government regulations specified economy class for such undertakings; William Davis had to adjust the policy because Hall refused to go economy.[51] His total expenses at the end of the study were

$15,704. The total costs for all other members of the committee including stipends and per diem allowances were $191,965, or approximately $8,000 each.[52]

The Hall-Dennis committee travelled widely. Besides holding hearings throughout Ontario, it undertook a large number of comparative-education 'visits': twenty-four in Ontario, fourteen in the United States, three in the British Isles, and one each in Greece, Israel, Japan, the Netherlands, Belgium, Switzerland, France, the Soviet Union, Sweden, Denmark, the Philippines, and Taiwan. Not all twenty-four members of the committee went to all of these countries; the normal practice was to split the committee into groups and divide up the locations among the groups. This did not satisfy the desires of everyone, especially when the time came to decide who would go to Japan. It was on occasions like this that Hall's tact and ability to flatter and persuade came into prominence.

As with the personnel on other studies and committees and commissions he was involved with, members of the Hall-Dennis committee came to respect and love Emmett Hall despite the fact that he worked them hard on occasion. As Lloyd Dennis wrote at the end of his term as co-chairman of the committee: 'I owe to you, sir, a great personal debt. Your trust in me afforded me a much deeper involvement than I had the right to expect. Your leadership, wisdom and understanding proved an inspiration for me on countless occasions, and I only hope that my response to your encouragement has not fallen too short of your expectations.'[53]

Looking back over more than thirty years since the adoption of the Hall-Dennis report, one finds few traces of a favourable imprint. To all intents and purposes, the Hall-Dennis report contributed very little in the way of positive results to the cause of education in Ontario. Moreover, it had the immediate effect of stirring up a hornets' nest and things have not quite settled down yet. It was, unfortunately, not one of Emmett Hall's finest hours. Indeed, he was surprised and hurt at the criticism the report received. It never dawned on him that the initial newspaper accolades would soon turn sour and that he and his committee colleagues would be vilified in some quarters. And, as time went on, fewer and fewer people had a kind word to say for *Living and Learning*. Even so, Hall remained – until the end of his life – unrepentantly enthusiastic about the principles and the general thrust of this unworkable and seriously flawed scheme of educational reform.

One final point. The website for the Ontario Institute for Studies in

Education has today (September 2003) an attractively presented item entitled 'Hall-Dennis Legacy.' The site features a picture of one June Newhart, who offers a series of seminars called: 'Facets of Learning: A Spiritual Site of Exploration, Discovery and Spirituality.' Ms Newhart is billed as having taught 'spiritual philosophy and metaphysics for over twenty years.' Among her seminars are the following: 'The Role Dreams Play in the Healing Process of Body, Mind and Spirit'; 'The Uncanny Accuracy of Precognitive Dreaming'; and 'A Dream State Created Through Guided Fantasy.' This is the Hall-Dennis legacy? Perhaps, but Emmett Hall would weep to know.

7

In the Supreme Court of Canada

At the time of his appointment to the Supreme Court of Canada on 23 November 1962 – it was one of Prime Minister Diefenbaker's last judicial appointments before the defeat of his government in the election of 1963 – Emmett Hall was just two weeks past his sixty-fourth birthday. He was sworn in as a puisne judge on 10 January 1963. From that date until the last day of February 1973, when he retired from the bench, he sat on 582 cases and wrote 118 judgments (almost twelve each year) of which 28 were dissenting opinions. As one might expect, he was more visible in some areas of the law than in others. For example, he wrote twenty-six judgments in criminal cases and sixteen in motor-vehicle accident cases. He also played an important role in hospital and medical-practice cases, as well as in cases relating to native claims, but he was less visible in matters of constitutional law. This range of cases reflected his experience in the practice of the law as well as his years on the Saskatchewan bench.

A new judge's first year on the bench is normally spent trying to assess his or her new colleagues, some of whom are known to the new member of the Court only through their recorded judgments. Through his work on the Canadian Bar Association, Hall knew well some of the Supreme Court justices – such as Patrick Kerwin, John Cartwright, and Ronald Martland – but not the others. Patrick Kerwin was chief justice at the time Hall joined the Court but he was to die on 2 February 1963, less than a month after Hall was sworn in. Robert Taschereau, appointed to the Court in 1943, was the senior judge upon the death of Chief Justice Kerwin and was appointed chief justice on 22 April 1963. The general practice has been to appoint the senior judge as chief justice. This tradition has been broken only four times in the history of the Court – first, in 1906, with the appointment of Sir Charles Fitzpatrick; second, in 1924, when Francis Anglin was appointed; third, in 1973, when Justice Bora Laskin was appointed over Justice Martland; and, finally, in 2000, when Justice Beverley McLachlin was appointed chief justice upon the retirement of Chief Justice Antonio Lamer the same year (the most senior judge at the time was Justice Claire L'Heureux-Dubé).

The freshman justice attempted to gauge his new judicial colleagues by chatting with them informally and by reading a few of their recent Court judgments. He soon felt comfortable and began to settle into his new position. Yet, while he got along well with the other justices, it was not until Justice Wishart Spence was appointed on 11 June 1963, to fill the vacancy caused by Chief Justice Kerwin's death, that Hall found a truly kindred spirit on the Supreme Court of Canada. From that time to the end of his term on the court, the names of Hall and Spence were to appear together, frequently in dissent. The two justices welcomed a truly kindred colleague on the elevation of Bora Laskin from the Ontario Court of Appeal in 1970.

CRIMINAL JURISPRUDENCE

The first case on which Hall sat as a Supreme Court of Canada judge was that of *Wright, McDermott and Feeley v. The Queen.*[1] The three appellants had been acquitted in May 1961 of the charge of conspiring to commit an indictable offence, namely, of attempting to bribe a police officer for information regarding the date and times when the police planned to raid a certain illegal gambling house. Having failed in its first attempt to convict the trio, the crown proceeded to prosecute the three men in March 1962 on a second charge relating to a conspiracy to effect the unlawful purpose of obtaining from a police officer information which it was his duty not to divulge. Defence counsel immediately objected that the second charge contained the first charge on which the appellants had been acquitted. The trial judge allowed the charge to stand and the jury convicted the three men. The Supreme Court majority, led by Justice Wilfred Judson, agreed with the Court of Appeal and dismissed the appeal against the conviction on the second charge. Hall and Cartwright concluded, in dissent, that the trial judge should have ruled that *res judicata* had been established, that is, that the second charge was indeed embodied in the first charge and, hence, had been determined when the accused were acquitted of the first charge. In other words, they proceeded by asking whether there were one or two conspiracies. The answer to them was clear: there was only one and it had been ruled on in the earlier trial and so the second charge was disposed in the first. Drawing support from United States Supreme Court precedents, Hall and Cartwright stated that the judge should have stopped the proceedings once he ruled that the matter had been previously determined.

This was not the last time that Hall drew support in criminal matters from United States Supreme Court decisions. He believed that the American criminal process had some advantages over the Canadian, especially in the area of procedure, and saw no reason why those advantages could not properly be made a part of the Canadian criminal process. This was especially true in the area of illegally obtained evidence, the area where Hall made his most important contribution to the development of criminal jurisprudence.

'Before the adoption of the *Charter of Rights* in 1982,' Peter Hogg has written, 'Canadian courts followed the rule of the English common law that evidence obtained by illegal means was admissible if relevant.'[2] Hall leaned towards the American practice of excluding all evidence obtained in violation of the Bill of Rights. The United States Supreme Court went beyond the English common law rule by interpreting the United States constitutional provision relating to due process of the law as to exclude all illegally obtained evidence.[3] Advocates of this 'absolute exclusion' rule on the Supreme Court of Canada – one was Bora Laskin, appointed chief justice in 1973 – had never been able to command majority support. Hall was no longer on the Court when the *Hogan*[4] case, which raised this issue in the context of the Canadian Bill of Rights, came to the Supreme Court of Canada in 1975; in that case, the Court majority of seven rejected Chief Justice Laskin's and Justice Spence's efforts to adopt the absolute exclusion rule. And so, despite the Canadian Bill of Rights provision respecting the right to counsel, the common law rule remained in force throughout Canada. And the rule still remains in force – at least in part – for section 24 of the Canadian Charter of Rights and Freedoms states: 'Where in proceeding under this section, (1), a court concludes that evidence was obtained in a manner that infringed or denied any rights or freedoms guaranteed by this

Charter, the evidence shall be excluded if it is established that, having regard to all the circumstances, the admission of it in the proceedings would bring the administration of justice into disrepute.' For our purposes here, it is sufficient to say that, before the Charter, the refusal to allow an accused to see his or her lawyer before taking the breathalizer would not have disqualified the evidence obtained.[5] It was against this kind of procedure that many Canadian judges were opposed, but they were stymied by the absence of formal statutory authority to disallow evidence so obtained.

But, in the pre-Charter era, the Supreme Court of Canada, in part at least aided by Justice Hall, did make a significant advance in the matter of evidence. Writing for the Court in *Piché v. The Queen*,[6] Hall wrote that it was time for the Supreme Court of Canada to clear up the confusion surrounding *exculpatory* and *inculpatory* statements in evidence. An inculpatory statement is one that contains an admission of fault, whereas an exculpatory statement contains no such admission. It is easy to see that inculpatory statements which might have been extracted involuntarily from an accused could amount to self-incrimination, which the law of evidence protects against. Until *Piché*, a court was required to determine whether statements made to an official were of one or the other kind. In *Piché*, Hall said: 'In my view the time is opportune for this Court to say that the admission in evidence of all statements made by an accused to persons in authority, whether inculpatory or exculpatory, is governed by the same rule and thus put to an end the continuing controversy and necessary evaluation by trial judges of every such statement which the Crown proposes to use in chief or on cross-examination as either being inculpatory or exculpatory.'[7] Hall concluded for the Court that there 'is no distinction to be drawn between inculpatory and exculpatory statements as such in so far as their admissibility in evidence when tendered by the Crown.'[8]

The problem of evidence in criminal cases preoccupied Hall throughout his career on the bench. As with all judges, he believed strongly that the onus of proof was on the crown and that the proof had to be strong. In the *Klippert*[9] case, where the Supreme Court majority upheld the conviction of a man as a dangerous sexual offender, Justice Hall was not satisfied that the evidence was sufficiently strong to warrant sentencing Klippert to preventive detention. To his mind, the evidence simply did not support the claim that he was dangerous. Klippert was an acknowledged homosexual who had a record of previous convictions on sexual charges. Two psychiatrists testified at the trial that Klippert was indeed likely to commit further sexual offences of the same kind – that is, with other consenting male adults. At no time had he ever caused injury or pain to any one and was judged not likely to do so in the future.

The Court majority judgment was written by Justice Gérald Fauteux. It claimed that, as revised in 1961, the Criminal Code definition of 'dangerous sexual offender' obliged the court to take into account the *likelihood* of the future commission of sexual offences. Prior to this change, the crown had to show that there had been actual injury to others. On this basis, the majority concluded that Klippert could indeed be sentenced to preventive detention. This meant that he was to be sentenced to imprisonment for an indefinite period of time, until, that is, he showed evidence that he had learned to control his sexual impulses. The thought of sentencing a man such as Klippert – or anyone for that matter – to an indefinite prison term troubled Justice Hall.

Hall and Cartwright dissented on the grounds that the intent and object of the new sections of the Criminal Code dealing with dangerous sexual offenders were to protect people from becoming the victims of those who fail to control their sexual impulses and thus are a source of public danger. As Hall noted in his reasons for judgment: 'The finding that the appellant is a dangerous sexual offender cannot stand, it would be directly contrary to the evidence.'[10] At times like this, Hall tended to assume the role of defence counsel on the bench rather than as an impartial appeal judge, as one former law clerk put it. It is improper for appeal court judges to retry the case on appeal; their task is to review the procedures of the lower courts and to decide whether those procedures were properly followed. That is why it is said that justice resides as much in the procedures followed as in the results reached at trial. Hall, however, had difficulty remembering at times, such as in *Klippert*, that he was not a trial judge but an appeal court judge. Let the crown prove, he urged, beyond a reasonable doubt that Klippert was likely to cause a danger. Try as he and Justice Cartwright might, the Court majority would not agree. The one judge who could have tipped the scales in Klippert's behalf, Justice Spence, concurred with Justice Fauteux. This came as a surprise to both Hall and Cartwright, for they thought that Spence, of all the members of the Court, would have gone with them in this case. Spence was not usually persuaded by the narrow technical reasoning that Fauteux favoured but on this occasion he was.

Hall could only speculate, later, that the nature of the offence was so abhorrent to Spence that he could not join with him and Cartwright in their dissent.

However much Hall and Cartwright were disappointed in not being able to persuade the Court in this case, they took satisfaction in the fact that their dissent played a small part in prompting the Parliament of Canada to amend the Criminal Code in 1968 to remove homosexual acts between consenting adults as a crime. Speaking precisely, Klippert had not been convicted of being a homosexual; he was convicted as 'a dangerous sexual offender.' But the central repeated activity for which he was convicted involved homosexuality. Under the amended Criminal Code, it is highly unlikely that Klippert would be charged today – however repetitious his habits – let alone sentenced as a habitual criminal. He was eventually paroled in July 1971.

Two years after the decision in *Klippert*, Hall was with the majority in the case of *Mendick v. The Queen*,[11] which also involved preventive detention. This time he persuaded four other judges to agree that the evidence presented in support of the charge that Mendick should be sentenced to prison as a dangerous offender was not sufficient. The Court majority ruled that Mendick was a habitual criminal but the crown had not shown beyond a reasonable doubt that it was necessary for the protection of the public that the accused be sentenced to preventive detention.

This victory was short-lived, however, for the following year, in *Sanders v. The Queen*,[12] Hall found himself once again in dissent in a case involving preventive detention. Francis Sanders was found to be a criminal sexual psychopath in April 1958 and was sentenced to preventive detention. At the time of sentencing, he signed a waiver of his right to appeal; as a result, he went to prison without having his case reviewed by a higher court. However, while in prison, Sanders made several futile applications between 1964 to 1967 to have the preventive-detention sentence set aside. In 1967 the British Columbia Court of Appeal finally granted him leave to apply for a writ of habeas corpus with certiorari in aid to quash the warrant of the committal. Prior to amendments to the Criminal Code in 1964–5 which granted appeals as a right from the provincial courts of appeal when those courts deny a writ of habeas corpus, Sanders was obliged to live by his waiver of appeal signed in 1958. The Supreme Court of British Columbia refused to grant the writ of habeas corpus with certiorari and Sanders appealed to the Supreme Court of Canada. His case was heard by a full Court, with Chief Justice Cartwright presiding, on 2 June 1969. The Court's judgment was delivered on 7 October of the same year. The decision was 5–4 against Sanders. Justice Hall was with Chief Justice Cartwright and justices Spence and Pigeon in dissent.

The Court majority judgment was delivered by Justice Martland, who ruled that Sanders had no grounds upon which to appeal for a review of his conviction in light of the Criminal Code provision (682) which barred the courts from granting certiorari after a defendant failed to appeal his conviction. The majority saw no irregularity in the trial proceedings and no grounds for sustaining a request for review of Sanders's conviction. The purpose of certiorari is to allow for a higher court to determine whether an order or conviction of a lower court had been made within its jurisdiction and according to the law. An error of procedure or law could thus be detected by a higher court and a remedy instituted. In the present case, the Court majority said that 'the appellant had appeared before the magistrate. He pleaded guilty to the charge under s. 149. Upon his conviction for that offence, the court which had convicted him was empowered and required, upon application (by the Crown Attorney), to hear the additional evidence as to whether or not the appellant was a criminal sexual psychopath, and to impose the sentence accordingly. No further plea in relation to this inquiry was necessary.'[13]

Justice Martland and the Court majority ruled that section 682 of the Criminal Code prevented review of Sanders's conviction. Justice Hall dissented vigorously, claiming that section 682 did indeed preclude review by way of certiorari but, he and the chief justice insisted, *all* of the provisions of that section of the Code had to be fulfilled; in the view of the court minority, they had not been fulfilled in this case. Hall paraphrased the majority's position in the following terms: 'The view that this section (682) denies the right to remove the order in question here requires holding a person convicted in a proceeding which is in law a nullity without recourse by *certiorari* when that person might have appealed and it is one I cannot accept.'[14] With characteristic directness, Hall concluded: 'Section 682 does not, in my opinion achieve that result. I refuse to impute such an intention to Parliament. I believe that when Parliament said "where the defendant appeared and pleaded and the merits were tried," it meant a lawful trial or hearing and not a proceeding which was in law a nullity.'[15] But Hall's view of the matter was a dissenting one and hence of no benefit to Sanders. It was far from the last time that he would find himself in such a position.

The following year, Hall sat on one of the most contentious cases to come before the Supreme Court of Canada in several decades. That was the case of John Wray.[16] Shortly after noon on Saturday, 27 March 1968, Donald Comrie was shot through the heart in the front office of Knoll's Service Station in Otonabee, Ontario. Whoever had murdered Comrie had taken all the cash from the register – later determined to amount to $55. No one witnessed the shooting, but a young boy of twelve years of age, John Frish, a nephew of the service station owner, heard a 'crack' and when he ran to the front office he saw Comrie lying on his face dead. Through the window the boy saw a man with a rifle running away from the scene of the murder. The bullet that had caused the death of Comrie was recovered by the coroner and ballistic experts later identified it as having been fired from a rifle which police found in a swampy wooded area adjoining the Fyfe road, about fifteen miles from the scene of the crime. Police traced the rifle to James Albert Wray, who testified that he had noticed it had been missing for several days but he had not reported it to the police or to his insurance company. The evidence linking John Wray, brother of James Wray, was all circumstantial and Justice Henderson, who presided at the jury trial, directed a verdict of not guilty. The crown appealed on the ground that the trial judge erred in preventing the crown attorney from introducing certain evidence. Justice Henderson had used his discretion to exclude a statement by James Wray which he felt was unfair and unjust to the accused. The crown alleged that the trial judge had gone beyond the limits of his discretion.

The evidence that the crown attempted to introduce arose out of the following circumstances. On 4 June 1968, shortly after 10:00 A.M., Inspector Lidstone of the Ontario Provincial Police drove up to John Wray's home and asked Wray to come with him to police headquarters in Peterborough. From that time until 7:18 P.M. of the same day – more than nine hours – Wray was questioned continuously by the police and a man named Jurems, a private investigator, who was acting for and with the police, and in the end he signed a statement which consisted of answers to certain written questions relating to the murder of Donald Comrie on the previous 23 March. If the statement had been admitted, it would clearly have been evidence on which the jury could have convicted Wray of the charge of non-capital murder.[1]

The incriminating statement ended with Wray telling the police where the rifle was. The questions were Inspector Lidstone's:

Q. What happened to the gun?
A. I threw it in the swamp.
Q. Where?
A. Near Omemee.
Q. Will you try and show us the spot?
A. Yes.
Q. Is there anything else you wish to add to this, John?
A. Not now, thank you.

At 7:25 that evening, the police set out with Wray in a police car and were directed by the respondent to the place where, as a result of Wray's directions, the police found the rifle the following day.

Wray's family became concerned when John had been taken to police headquarters and retained the legal service of Charles Gordon, a Peterborough lawyer. Gordon attempted all through the afternoon to contact John Wray by telephone, but the police failed to return his repeated calls. When asked during the trial why he had not returned Gordon's calls, Inspector Lidstone replied: 'We did not want to take a chance that Mr. Wray as a result of speaking to Mr. Gordon wouldn't take the police out to where the gun was found.'[17] The trial judge immediately cleared the court of the jury and public and in a lengthy *voir dire* – a procedure designed to establish whether a certain item of evidence can be admitted in open court – he ruled that the statement signed by the respondent was legally inadmissible because it had not been made voluntarily.

The crown appealed on the ground that the trial judge erred in law in refusing to allow the crown attorney to adduce evidence as to the part played by Wray in the finding of the murder weapon. The Supreme Court majority judgments were written by Justice Martland and Justice Judson. Justice Martland stated emphatically: 'I am not aware of any judicial authority in this country or in England which supports the proposition that a trial judge has a discretion to exclude admissible evidence because, in his opinion, its admission would be calculated to bring the administration of justice into disrepute.'[18] He then proceeded to cite the Privy Council precedents, beginning with the 1955 judgment in *Kuruma v. The Queen*,[19] where Lord Goddard ruled that 'the test to be applied in considering whether evidence is admissible is whether it is relevant to the matters in issue. If it is, it is admissible and the court is not concerned with how the evidence was obtained.'

Chief Justice Cartwright explained that 'the underlying reason for the rule that an involuntary confession shall not be admitted is the supposed danger that it may be untrue.'[20] More important for the chief justice was the fact that an involuntary statement may lead an accused to incriminate himself. 'It would indeed be a strange result if, being the law that no accused is bound to incriminate himself and that he is to be protected from having to testify at an inquest, a preliminary hearing or a trial, he could nonetheless be forced by the police or others in authority to make a statement which could then be given in evidence against him.'[21]

The chief justice then reviewed the British and Canadian precedents and showed that they were not as unambiguous as the Court majority alleged. He preferred to accept the interpretation of the Ontario Court of Appeal. The importance of the matter was underlined by the fact that the British Columbia Court of Appeal had taken a view contrary to the Ontario Court of Appeal. It became mandatory, therefore, for the Supreme Court of Canada to settle the matter as clearly and unequivocally as possible. Cartwright, Hall, and Spence wanted to adopt the interpretation of the Ontario Court of Appeal and validate the trial judge's interpretation of his discretion. The Court majority, led by justices Martland and Judson, argued for the adoption of the British Columbia Court of Appeal interpretation which would deny such discretion.

The debate in conference – as Chief Justice Cartwright and Justice Hall later both told the author – was heated and protracted. The strict constructionist justices such as Martland and Judson were vehement in their support for the Goddard view. Hall, Cartwright, and Spence were just as vehement in opposition to that view. The chief justice noted frequently that the discretionary power at issue was based not on statutory powers but on judicial decisions; it was proper for justices of the Supreme Court of Canada to resolve the issue without being fettered unduly by precedents, he contended.

To be stymied by precedent, or *stare decisis*, was a long-festering irritant for Hall. It was no coincidence that this issue was the theme he chose for his address before the John White Society at Osgoode Hall Law School in 1971. On that occasion he began by noting approvingly that the House of Lords had itself declared in 1966 that it would no longer be bound by previous judgments.[22] He cited Lord Gardner, who had then announced that 'too rigid adherence to precedent may lead to injustice in a particular case and also unduly restrict the future development of the law.'[23] He also proceeded to cite the words of the current minister of justice of Canada, Mark MacGuigan, to the effect that *stare decisis* 'both in Canada and in England ... has been a protective screen behind which judges legislated in silence and secrecy.'[24] After reviewing a list of Supreme Court of Canada decisions where a number of justices had indicated that there should be a due but not subservient respect for past judgments of the Judicial Committee – especially following the end of appeals in 1949 – Hall said: 'It is not now open to question that the Supreme Court of Canada is not now bound rigidly by [*stare decisis*] and the way is open to depart from previous decisions.'[25] The problem, he insisted, was how far the courts should go in departing from the course charted by past decisions. To what extent should judges become activists? 'Do judges make law or merely apply it, should judges pursue a policy of judicial activism, which of course can be either a liberal or conservative posture, or should they pursue a policy of judicial restraint?'[26] As to whether judges in fact make laws, he was emphatic: 'I can tell you that the judiciary does contribute to changing the laws because I have participated in making changes in such cases as *Cahoon v. Franks,*[27] *Piché v. The Queen,*[28] and *Ares v. Venner,*[29] to name some.' He felt that the courts were in the front lines of legal reform arising out of specific cases such as *Wray*. The courts could not wait for the law reform commissions to come forth with their recommendations; they had a task to perform and real people depended on them to decide matters of extreme importance. Warming to his subject, Hall showed the full measure of his judicial activism when he rejected the contention 'widely accepted by the bench and bar in Canada,' that a judge must not, in reaching his or her decision, take into consideration political and social issues or public policy and opinion. 'Traditionally,' he reminded his audience, 'the common law grew and became a civilizing force in our society only because it considered social, political and economic fact.'[30] Citing Lord Denning, Justice Hall said in conclusion that those judges who bind themselves rigidly by precedent or *stare decisis* effectively hide behind their predecessors, 'however wrong they are and whatever injustice they inflict.'[31]

HALL AND JUDSON

Some friendships on the court were strained as a result of the *Wray* case but others were cemented even more strongly – between Cartwright, Hall, and Spence – and commitments to divergent judicial philosophies became more deeply felt. Hall always had difficulty comprehending the strict-constructionist approach of some of his colleagues. He disliked, for that reason, to be placed with Judson on an appeal panel. As one of Hall's law clerks observed, 'Judson would ask straight off before the reasons of appeal were barely stated whether the Court had jurisdiction.'[32] This approach struck Hall as backwards and unduly narrow. It is simply too easy for a court, he thought, to claim that it does not have jurisdiction. For Hall, the only approach was to see if an injustice had been done and, if so, find a way to correct it.

In the *Wray* case, Judson dismissed the power of the courts to employ 'judicial discretion permitting the exclusion of relevant evidence, in this case highly relevant evidence, on the ground of unfairness to the accused.'[33] Above all, he rejected Cartwright's and Hall's contention that the problem of discretionary power could properly be settled by courts. 'If this law is to be changed, a simple amendment to the *Canada Evidence Act* would be sufficient,'[34] Judson maintained. He thus saw only a legal problem, the solution to which was to be a statutory corrective. Hall and the Court minority saw a man being sent to jail on evidence unlawfully obtained.

Justice Hall's dissenting judgment in the *Wray* case contained several pointed rhetorical questions. After stating his agreement with the chief justice, he asked: 'Are courts of appeal going to claim unlimited discretion to interfere with the discretion lawfully possessed and judicially applied by trial judges and is this court going to claim an ultimate discretion to weigh and, if necessary, find wanting that measure of discretion which reposes initially in the trial judge or in the Court of Appeal?'[35] He insisted on knowing whether the Supreme Court of Canada was going 'to set up some standard by which the discretion of the trial judge is to be weighed on some imaginary scale calibrated to meet the circumstances of each individual case?' He answered his own questions with the claim that 'surely the established rule is that if the discretion has been judicially exercised by the trial judge, it is not subject to review or to being weighed on appeal.'[36]

For Hall, there was no point in saying that the trial judge had discretion and then demand, when he or she exercised it, that it must meet some imaginary standard. No one in the majority denied that the trial judge had acted properly in conducting a *voir dire* and that he did have discretion. Hall's point was quite simple: how can justices of appeal assess a trial judge's exercise of discretion when they were not present at the *voir dire*?

Hall was determined to uphold the maximum procedural safeguards in the criminal process. He did not attempt to make the task of convicting a guilty person more difficult. But he would not countenance short cuts in the criminal process, especially when there were other means available. As he said in this case: 'The rifle was admissible in evidence as an exhibit apart altogether from the statement because the ballistic expert testified that it was from that rifle that the bullet which killed Donald Comrie came. No part of the statement was, therefore, necessary to identify the rifle as the murder weapon.'[37]

In conference, Justice Hall made it clear in no uncertain terms that he was unimpressed with the reasoning of the Court majority – especially Judson's. 'How can they be so blind,' he exclaimed in exasperation to Ken Campbell, the court administrator, shortly after one conference on the *Wray* case. It was so patently clear to Hall, and Cartwright, and Spence that it was perfectly correct for a trial judge to exercise his discretion in such a manner – they, surely, would have done exactly the same thing. The appeal was accordingly allowed and a new trial directed. The damaging statement was admitted and Wray was convicted and sentenced to penitentiary for the non-capital murder of Donald Comrie.

It might prove useful at this point – as an aid in understanding Hall's view of his judicial function – to contrast him with Justice Judson. A glimpse of the difference of approach emerged in the *Wray* case but the contrast between the two judges is even more pronounced when their judgments over a period of time, are subjected to statistical analysis. As Sidney Peck has demonstrated in his scalogram analysis of the Supreme Court of Canada for the period Emmett Hall served on the Court, the two were almost polar opposites.[38] In criminal appeals, Peck shows that 'Cartwright, Hall and Spence JJ. voted affirmatively [in favour of the accused] in over eighty percent of the cases in which they participated.' On the other hand, 'Taschereau, C.J., and Abbott, Judson and Fauteux JJ. voted negatively [against the accused] in over eighty per cent of the cases in which they participated.'[39] Peck's scalogram shows conclusively that Hall was a core part of a group of judges on the Court whose judgments in criminal cases revealed them to be 'very pro-accused,' in contrast to the 'highly pro-Crown' group of which Judson was a central member.[40] Peck's study of the Supreme Court also indicates the basis for Hall's deep disagreement with Chief Justice Fauteux, who frequently sided with Judson. Peck writes: 'Mr Justice Fauteux voted negatively in all appeals involving jurisdiction in which he participated, holding that the court had jurisdiction to hear four appeals brought by the Crown, and no jurisdiction to hear three appeals brought by the accused.'[41] He shared with Judson the conviction that it should be difficult to appeal cases to the Supreme Court of Canada. Hall felt otherwise and saw the position of Fauteux and Judson as a kind of obstructionism. His belief was that a criminal accused should have relatively easy access to the highest court in the land. As a result, he frequently locked horns with Judson and Fauteux. According to Peck, Judson, 'whose voting pattern is highly in favour of the Crown in both taxation and criminal law appeals, is the only justice whose voting pattern is classified as "highly pro" [pro-government in tax cases and pro-crown in criminal cases] on two scales.'[42]

Shortly after his appointment to the Supreme Court of Canada in 1963 – less than two weeks after coming to the Court – Hall sat on a five-person bench in the case of *John Mazur v. Imperial Investment Corporation*.[43] On that occasion he wrote his first dissenting judgment. The case cannot be considered a major one, but it does illustrate the antithetical approaches of Hall and Judson.

The case came on appeal to the Supreme Court of Canada as of right because it was a civil suit involving more than $10,000. (Until the Supreme Court Act was revised in 1975, all civil cases involving more than $10,000 could go on appeal to the Supreme Court of Canada as of right. Such cases must now receive the leave of the Court.) The *Mazur* case came on appeal from the Appellate Division of the Supreme Court of Alberta, which had confirmed the judgment of the trial judge and increased the amount which Mazur owed on a promissory note held by Imperial Investment Corporation. Mazur appealed on two grounds: that the finance company was not a holder in due course; and that the note was signed blank and delivered subject to conditions which were not fulfilled.

John Mazur had signed a promissory note as a marker for the accommodation of a friend named Karraja. Karraja was the owner of a twelve-ton Mack tandem truck. Early in 1958, he told James Sheddy, the owner of a company known as A.C. Car Sales and Services, that he wished to raise money on his truck. Sheddy checked Karraja's credit rating with Imperial Investment Corporation, which claimed that Karraja was not a good risk. Sheddy suggested that Karraja get someone to act as a third party; he accordingly asked Mazur to let him use his name and credit to obtain the loan from the finance company.

The finance company approved of Mazur as a suitable risk. Mazur then went to Sheddy's office where he signed a customer's statement giving particulars of his assets, a conditional sales contract, and a promissory note. Mazur testified in court that there was no writing on the conditional sales contract when he signed it. As for the promissory note, he said at the trial that it was blank; he did not read it but just signed on the line. He did admit that he knew what he was signing; he had had many dealings with finance companies over the years.

Sheddy presented the conditional sales contract and the promissory note to the finance company. The conditional sales contract purported to sell the truck for a price of $18,500 with a down payment in cash of $6,500, leaving an unpaid cash balance of $12,000. The finance charges were added, bringing the total to $14,326.96, which was to be payable in seventeen instalments of $797 and a final instalment of $777.96. (It appeared in court that Sheddy had filled in the first part of the document down to the $12,000 balance, and that the remainder of the form was filled in at the office of the finance company.) The promissory note was filled in with a typewriter in accordance with the conditional sales contract, and this also had been done in the finance company office.

The documents appeared to indicate a bona fide sale but in fact the sale was completely fictitious to the three parties involved; it was, in reality, a scheme designed to have the finance company discount a note. 'The fraud of all three is obvious but, in addition, Sheddy kept the proceeds of the discount for his own use,' Justice Judson stated in his judgment.[44] Justice Judson wrote the Court majority judgment denying Mazur's appeal. Judson reasoned that Mazur had known for three months that the figure on the contract was $12,000 and not $10,000, as Karraja and Mazur claimed. 'Mazur said,' Judson observed, 'that he understood that the figure was $10,000 but, against this, he was in possession of the completed contract and the booklet of payments (from the finance company) showing that the figure was $12,000 and he made no protest.'[45] Judson was accordingly not sympathetic to Mazur's claim that the larger figure constituted a failure to meet the oral conditions. And Mazur's failure to complain was sufficient in Judson's mind to lead him to conclude that Mazur could, in effect, be said to be a knowing party to the increased figure.

Justice Cartwright (and Hall in his concurring dissent) saw the matter differently. Cartwright wrote: 'It is clear that Mazur placed his signature on the blank printed form of note and delivered it to Sheddy in order that it might be converted into a promissory note. It is also clear that Mazur became a party to the note prior to its completion and consequently he is liable on it only if it was filled up within a reasonable time and "strictly in accordance with the authority given." It was, no doubt, filled up within a reasonable time but it seems to me that the authority given by Mazur to Sheddy was limited to filling it up ... for such amount was necessary to yield $10,000 to Karraja. In fact the note was filled up for $14,326.96, which was the amount required to yield not $10,000 but $12,000.'[46]

Under these conditions, Cartwright continued, 'the note, not having been filled up strictly in accordance with the authority given but actually in contravention thereof in the respect just mentioned, never became an enforceable note at all.' To Cartwright's way of thinking, it was clear that 'authority to fill up a note for the amount of $10,000 plus incidental charges, is exceeded when the note is filled up for the amount of $12,000 plus incidental charges.'[47]

Justice Hall, on the other hand, found something missing in the trial and in the Alberta Court of Appeal proceedings. He wrote in his dissent:

I would like to comment on an important aspect of the case which I think influenced the learned trial judge and the Court of Appeal and was absent in this Court, and which, accepting the findings of the learned trial judge as to credibility, brings me to a conclusion opposite to that reached in the Courts below. The crucial fact in this case, in my judgment, is that the promissory note sued on bore only the signature of the appellant, Mazur, unless it came into the possession of the respondent. It is obvious from reading the judgment of Riley J. that he predicated his finding that the respondent became the holder in due course of the note upon the view that the appellant had not satisfied the onus of proving that the note was not complete and regular on its face when delivered to the respondent (The Imperial Investment Corporation).[48]

Hall found that there was an element of uncertainty on this point at the Court of Appeal, as well. 'On the argument before this Court,' he went on to say, 'it was conceded that the document bore only the signature of the appellant when it came into the possession of the respondent. It is perhaps because this outright admission was not made to Riley J. and the Court of Appeal that both Riley J. and the Chief Justice of Alberta relied so strongly on s. 31 of the *Bills of Exchange Act* and not on s. 32(1).'[49]

Section 32(1) of the Bills of Exchange Act clearly states that any enforceable agreement must be 'strictly in accordance with the authority given.' It was an easy matter to establish, Hall claimed, that this important condition had not been met, especially since the trial judge said that Sheddy was not a credible witness. The combined testimony, therefore, of both Karraja and Mazur as to the correct amount agreed upon was reasonable and persuasive.

Another case five years later, *Dirk Hoogendoorn v. Greening Metal Products and Screening Equipment Co.*,[50] demonstrates the difference in approach of Hall and Judson even more clearly than *Mazur*. In this instance, however, justices Hall and Cartwright are in the majority while Justice Judson dissents along with Justice Ritchie. The facts of the case were as follows. The Greening Metal company entered into a collective agreement with the United Steelworkers of America, Local 6266, to provide a compulsory deduction of union dues. Hoogendoorn refused to sign the form authorizing the company to deduct the dues from his salary. He was accordingly fired at the insistence of the union. Later, Hoogendoorn was reinstated after his lawyer had shown to the satisfaction of the company management that the provisions relating to deduction of dues were applicable only to new employees and not to those in the employment of the company at the time of the agreement. Upon the instigation of the union, the agreement was subsequently amended to make the terms applicable to all present and past employees.

But Hoogendoorn persisted in his refusal to sign the payroll-deduction authorization. The other employees called a 'wildcat strike' in protest over the continued employment of Hoogendoorn. The union and the company management agreed to submit the matter to arbitration. Hoogendoorn was not notified of the hearing; nor was he present at it himself or represented by another. He moved before Justice Campbell Grant in the Supreme Court of Ontario, to quash the award. His motion was dismissed. He appealed to the Court of Appeal against the dismissal. His appeal was denied.

The Supreme Court of Canada granted leave to appeal from the Ontario Court of Appeal's judgment. The only issue before the Supreme Court of Canada was whether Hoogendoorn was entitled to notice of and representation at the arbitration hearing. The union argued that Hoogendoorn had no right to be present because the matter under arbitration was a 'policy grievance' for the purpose of obtaining a decision whether the employer company was in violation of an agreement which applied to all employees. The majority of the Ontario Court of Appeal accepted the union's point of view and dismissed the appeal.

The Supreme Court of Canada majority, which included Hall, allowed the appeal. Hall wrote in his judgment that 'it is obvious that the proceeding was aimed entirely at securing Hoogendoorn's dismissal. The learned arbitrator correctly understood the situation for he concluded his award by saying: "If Mr. Hoogendoorn fails to comply, then I direct that the Company exercise its powers as an employer and discharge him!" The majority of the Court of Appeal recognized the impropriety of this direction and ordered that it be deleted from the award.'[51]

The sole purpose of the arbitration hearing, Hall noted, was to secure the dismissal of Hoogendoorn and nothing else; for the union to claim otherwise was a fiction. There was no other issue before the arbitrator. Hall said: 'The proceeding was aimed at getting rid of Hoogendoorn as an employee because of his refusal either to join the Union or pay the dues. It cannot be said that Hoogendoorn was being represented by the Union in the arbitration proceeding. The Union actively took a position completely adverse to Hoogendoorn. It wanted him dismissed.'[52]

For Hall and the majority, the real issue 'was whether natural justice was done by proceeding in his absence and without notice to him.'[53] Hall claimed that the standards of natural justice had not been done and cited a list of precedents which supported his claim. The Court allowed Hoogendoorn's appeal and quashed the arbitrator's award.

Justice Judson, speaking in dissent for himself and Justice Ritchie, took the opposite view. He agreed with the Ontario Court of Appeal majority. His understanding of the Ontario Labour Relations Act (1960) led him to conclude that 'no individual employee is entitled as of right to be present during bargaining or at the conclusion of such an agreement.'[54] He refused to accept the suggestion of Hoogendoorn's counsel that there was no bargaining taking place but a dismissal hearing under the guise of settling a 'policy grievance.' For Judson, there was no violation of natural justice because the 'rights or interests of Hoogendoorn were not in issue'[55] at the arbitration hearing. He noted that the 'arbitration procedure has been attacked as a sham battle designed to secure the dismissal of one man. This, I do not accept.'[56] Emmett Hall and the majority, however, saw what they believed was a sham in this instance. Hall and Chief Justice Cartwright and Justice Spence believed that, if Hoogendoorn had not persistently refused to sign the authorization form, the hearing would not have been held in the first place.

The human side of legal issues always tended to catch Hall's attention, even where he could do little to resolve the issue. Consider the case of Robert Kinnaird in 1963.[57] Robert Kinnaird had contracted dermatitis as a result of his employment as a painter and was granted compensation by the British Columbia Workmen's Compensation Board from February 1945 until February 1947. He was then informed of termination of compensation and advised to seek work of a clerical nature. At this time, there was no medical-appeal provision in the Workmen's Compensation Act of British Columbia; the act was revised to include such a procedure in 1955. In 1956 Kinnaird applied to the Board, under the new medical-appeal procedures, to be examined by a specialist and his application was granted. A few weeks later, the board informed Kinnaird that it had received the judgment of his specialist and that the board had reviewed Kinnaird's case in the light of the specialist's report and had concluded that no change be made in its earlier recommendation.

Kinnaird made an application for a writ of *mandamus* with *certiorari* in aid to quash the decision of the board. The application was dismissed and Kinnaird appealed to the British Columbia Court of Appeal, which ruled against him. Justice Thomas R. Berger argued that the board had 'declined jurisdiction' because it failed to notify him of its decision regarding the matters contained in the specialist's certificate. There was no doubt that the board did not do this. But, as Justice Roland Ritchie said in his judgment when the case reached the Supreme Court of Canada: 'In my opinion it would have been more humane and more businesslike for the Board to have furnished the appellant with a copy of the certificate and an explanation of its decision, I am nevertheless unable to find that the provisions of s. 54A (9) give the workman a right to anything more from the Board than a notification in writing of its decision, and it seems to me that the Board complied with this section.'[58] A 'more humane' approach, unfortunately, was beyond the Court's jurisdiction to require.

Justice Hall wrote a short concurring judgment in this case in which he expressed his irritation both at what the Workmen's Compensation Board had done and at the means it had employed. For him, the specialist's certificate, which revealed Kinnaird's condition and unsuitability for work as well as the fact that he had suffered several coronary attacks, was sufficient indication that something should be done by way of compensation for Kinnaird. All Emmett Hall could do was add to Justice Ritchie's judgment. 'I am impelled, however, to say, that this workman does not appear to have received the substantial justice which s. 79 of the *Workmen's Compensation Act* of British Columbia contemplates. Section 79 reads: "The decision of the Board shall be upon the real merits and justice of the case, and it is not bound to follow strict legal precedent.'"[59] What troubled him was that the 'courts are without power to review the merits of the case on *certiorari*. The legislature has given the Board unlimited discretion not subject to appeal or judicial review as long as the Board acts within its jurisdiction.'[60] These comments lend credence to the suspicions that Emmett Hall's view of the judicial function was anything but deferential to the legislature.

COUNSEL FOR INNOCENT VICTIMS

In the light of his early involvement in insurance cases, it is not surprising to find that Emmett Hall wrote judgments in sixteen automobile-negligence cases. In these sixteen judgments, he sided with the individual, not the insurance company, especially when the injured victim was a child. In the case of *O'Brien v. Mailhot*,[61] for example, Hall was the lone dissenter. The case involved a young boy, Patrick O'Brien, aged ten and a half years, of Thetford Mines, Quebec. On 13 March 1958 Patrick was on his way home from St Patrick's High School when he was struck by a car driven by Ernest Mailhot. Mailhot had stopped his car in the inside lane next to a bus but back from the intersection on the signal of a traffic police officer. After several children had crossed the street, the police officer apparently gave the signal for the traffic to proceed through the intersection. When the front of Mailhot's car came abreast of the front of the bus, Mailhot saw young O'Brien and attempted to stop his car, which was going at approximately ten miles per hour; unfortunately, he was unable to stop in time and struck the boy, who was left partially crippled. The evidence of witnesses as to the distance Mailhot was from the intersection, the speed he was travelling, and when O'Brien entered his path was all contradictory and inconclusive. The boy's father, E.W. O'Brien, sued Mailhot for $75,000.

The trial judge held that both Mailhot and O'Brien were at fault and responsible. He assessed the damages at $26,941.80 and ruled that Mailhot pay O'Brien the sum of $8,980.60 with interest. The Quebec Appeal Court confirmed this judgment and the Supreme Court of Canada agreed. Justice Hall dissented for three clearly stated reasons. First, Mailhot knew that the intersection in question was in a school zone and that at the time pupils were leaving the school premises and using the intersection. Second, the O'Brien boy was in the pedestrian crosswalk when he was struck. The accident left him permanently injured for life – he walked with a limp. Third, a man named Louis

Donovan was sitting at the wheel of his car on the east side of Notre Dame north of Dumais (the intersection in question) waiting for his daughter to take her home for lunch. The O'Brien boy was right behind as she started to cross. Seeing her father, she ran towards her father's car. She had not reached her father before young O'Brien was struck. Justice Hall made a great deal out of the fact that other children – and especially Ellen Donovan – were in the crosswalk immediately prior to Patrick O'Brien's accident. His conclusion was that Mailhot was negligent in not seeing either Ellen Donovan or Patrick O'Brien, as he admitted at the trial. The fact of the matter, for Justice Hall, was that he *should have seen* them.

The Quebec Motor Vehicle Act stated: 'Whenever loss or damage is sustained by any person by reason of a motor vehicle on a public highway, the burden of proof that such loss or damage did not arise through the negligence or improper conduct of the owner or driver of such motor vehicle shall be upon such owner or driver.'[62] The trial judge claimed that, in the present case, the burden of proof did not apply. 'In this he was completely in error,' Hall retorted. The Court of Appeal applied the section but by a majority judgment held that Mailhot had successfully rebutted the presumption. Hall could not agree with that conclusion. To him, Mailhot 'was under a heavy duty to be on the lookout for school children who might emerge from in front of the bus. Had he been keeping the lookout which the special circumstances then existing demanded, he would have seen the boy before the vehicle was actually in contact with him.'[63]

Because of his experience in private practice with negligence suits, Emmett Hall demonstrated a special sensitivity in cases involving injuries to children. This was borne out six years later in *Freedman v. City of Côte St Luc*,[64] when, once again, he dissented in circumstances similar to those of *O'Brien*. On 7 August 1964 Michael Freedman, aged six, was struck by a truck belonging to the city of Côte Saint-Luc and driven by Raymond Gagné, a city employee. Gagné struck Freedman while he was running through an intersection; Gagné's vision was partially obscured by a parked mail truck. He claimed at trial that he was unable to see young Freedman in time to stop before hitting him. The trial judge found Gagné guilty of negligence. The judge claimed that Gagné had not demonstrated successfully that he had exercised reasonable care in operating his truck. The Highway Victims Indemnity Act of Quebec places the onus on the driver in such circumstances to show that he exercised due caution and control. Freedman was accordingly awarded

$11,067.40 in damages; the verdict was upheld in the Superior Court but was reversed by the Quebec Court of Appeal.

The Supreme Court of Canada confirmed the judgment of the Quebec Court of Appeal; the court majority's judgment was delivered by Justice Abbott. 'Gagné was proceeding,' Abbott observed, 'at a legal and moderate speed in approaching the intersection and had his car under such control that he was able to bring it to a stop before he had completely crossed the intersection.'[65] In his considered view, there was no negligence.

Unlike Abbott and the majority, Justice Hall began by assessing the injury sustained by Freedman. 'The boy was hit by the right front corner of the box and sustained injury to his head. The injury was relatively severe and resulted in permanent partial incapacity agreed to by all parties as 10 per cent.'[66] He then reviewed Gagné's trial testimony and concluded that Gagné had sufficient visibility to see anyone entering the intersection. In obvious sympathy with the young boy, Hall carefully pieced together the facts from Gagné's testimony: 'He (Gagné) was going from 15 to 20 miles an hour or from 22 to 30 feet a second. He says the boy ran out. The six year old boy could not run at a speed of more than 5 or 6 miles an hour. It would take the boy from 2 to 4 seconds to arrive at the point where he was struck according to Gagné.'[67] He concluded in short order: 'I can see no reason why the boy was not seen by Gagné if Gagné had been keeping a proper lookout. In a 2-second interval the truck would have traveled a minimum of 44 to 60 feet, the boy from 14 to 18 feet. If the boy was struck at or near the point where the blood was seen on the pavement, he must have been within the intersection on his diagonal course a minimum of three seconds in which time the truck travelled from 66 to 90 feet, and he from 21 to 24 feet.'[68] What he was doing, in fact, was retrying the case and acting as counsel for the injured boy. Not everyone agrees that it is proper for an appellate court judge to do that but such concerns made little difference to Emmett Hall. He frequently ignored the established procedure and took upon himself the role of counsel of last resort, however inappropriate this conduct was in the eyes of some members of the Court.

In the other case,[69] also from Quebec, Hall was more successful in persuading his colleagues to uphold the claim of an injured child. This was the kind of case he especially liked: it involved a child and a Montreal city bus. The Montreal Transportation Commission attempted to avoid its responsibility on a technicality, the very thing that rankled Hall most.

On 16 April 1956 Michel Methôt, aged seven years, was struck by a bus belonging to the Montreal Transportation Commission. Three days later, on 19 April, notice of the accident was given to the Transportation Commission as required by statute. This, however, makes proceedings in such cases subject to certain provisions of the charter of the city of Montreal. Six months later, on 18 October 1956, René Methôt, Michel's father, brought an action against the Montreal Transportation Commission claiming $16,946.94 personally and $81,000 in his capacity as tutor of his son. The Transportation Commission argued that, according to the city charter provisions, a suit against the commission must be brought within six months of the date of the accident. And since the accident occurred on 16 April, the Methôts were prohibited from pressing for damages. The Quebec Superior Court rejected the arguments of the Transportation Commission and ordered it to pay René Methôt $4,536.94 personally and $16,200 in his capacity as tutor of his son Michel. The Quebec Court of Appeal accepted the arguments of the Montreal Transportation Commission and ruled that the Methôts were too late in bringing suit against the commission.

Chief Justice Fauteux wrote in his judgment, after reviewing the terms of the Montreal city charter, that 'the prescription only began to run from the day on which the Commission actually received the notice of April 19.'[70] The unanimous Supreme Court reversed the Quebec Court of Appeal and restored the trial court judgment. Hall wrote a lengthy concurring judgment and was sufficiently persuasive as to win the concurrence of Justice Judson – a rare event during Hall's ten years on the Supreme Court of Canada. Hall began, as was his custom in such cases, with a thorough study of the relevant portions of the Montreal city charter, just as other members of the Court had done. But he then established, with a list of Canadian authorities, that 'it is settled law that statutes of limitations are to be construed strictly.'[71] The right to sue was, for Hall, a 'vested right' which could not be taken away easily; in this case, the onus of proof that a statute provides for the abrogation of that right rested, in Hall's mind, squarely on the defendant, the Transportation Commission. Not only did the commission fail to prove its case conclusively, but Emmett Hall's meticulous searchings into Quebec's unreported cases paid off. He found a 1948 case, *Le Cité de Québec v. Dame Magna Vézina Berubé*, in which the Quebec Court of Appeal had ruled that the prescription clause begins after the receipt by the commission of the notice of accident. Not only that, he found that the *Berubé* decision was based on a 1921 Supreme Court of Canada judgment. As he said in his judgment with obvious delight: 'It appears that the Court of Appeal overlooked its own judgment in the *City of Quebec v. Berubé* and the judgment of this court in *United Typewriter*.'[72]

The truly remarkable feature of this case was that, when it was tried in the two lower courts, neither of the controlling precedents cited by Hall had been referred to either in the court judgments or in the factums. Not only had two lower courts overlooked the precedents, but even the lawyers for Methôt had overlooked them. Small wonder that Judson concurred with Hall. The latter revelled in the fact that his doggedness – and that of Henry Kloppenburg, his law clerk – had yielded results. This eye for detail was something that not a few of Hall's contemporaries remembered about him. As Percy Maguire, a long-time Saskatoon law partner, has remarked, 'Hall was very particular about preparation. He was meticulous. He was not as theatrical as Diefenbaker. He was always very careful.'[73] Years after the *Methôt* case, Hall smiled at the thought of the embarrassment Methôt's lawyer must have felt on realizing his oversight.

Hall's sensitivity was not restricted to injuries to children; he was just as concerned about the damages incurred by adults, especially if such injuries left the person permanently disabled. This came out clearly in the case of *Ivan Coso*.[74] Coso was struck by a car driven by Alexander Poulos in Vancouver on 18 September 1965. At the trial, it was ruled that Poulos was wholly responsible for the accident. Justice Wilson of the British Columbia Supreme Court awarded Coso $7,000 in general damages and $973 in special damages. Coso appealed this settlement to the British Columbia Court of Appeal; that court accepted Coso's case for an increase in general damages and raised the amount to $12,000. But it also assessed Coso as 20 per cent responsible for the accident. Coso appealed this judgment and asked for an increase in general damages beyond the $12,000 awarded.

The Supreme Court of Canada ruled, Hall writing for the majority with Justice Abbott dissenting, that Coso was not 20 per cent at fault and increased the award for general damages from $12,000 to $30,000. What led him and the majority to raise the award for general damages was the nature of the injuries Coso had sustained as well as the impact such injuries would have on his ability to find future employment. Nor would Hall exclude from consideration the prolonged and excruciating pain that Coso suffered in both pre-operative and post-operative hospitalization.

A year after the accident, Coso suffered an attack of phlebitis which was established as resulting from injuries sustained in the accident a year earlier. He was unable to work for an additional seven months. It was obvious to a majority of the Court that the accident had resulted in injuries so permanent as to prevent Coso from undertaking strenuous employment. At the time of the accident, Coso was twenty-nine years of age and a member of the Tunnel and Rock Workers' Union, with the opportunity of making $1,000 a month. Through the negligence of another person, Coso was suddenly deprived of his normal income and employment expectancy; after the accident he could hope only for light work and less income.

Hall accordingly ruled that, 'taking everything into consideration, including his record of earnings for the five-year period preceding the accident, I am of the view that the amount awarded by the Court of Appeal is inordinately low and such a wholly erroneous assessment that this Court is justified in increasing the award for general damages from $12,000 to $30,000.'[75] Once again, it was the humane considerations that led Hall to his conclusions. But it must not be overlooked that the five-man Court in this case included Cartwright as chief justice and Justice Spence. These men always tended to emphasize the humane aspects of such cases.

It would be difficult to find a greater contrast with the judgment of Hall and his majority colleagues than Justice Abbott's brief dissent in *Coso*. Abbott found himself caught in the well-established procedural rule about increasing damages at the appellate court level. He expressed his dilemma in his brief dissent: 'It is trite law, of course, that, as to the quantum of damages, a second appellate Court will not, except in very exceptional circumstances, interfere with the amounts fixed by the first appellate Court where they differ from the damages assessed by the trial judge. In my opinion, such exceptional circumstances have not been established in the present case and I would dismiss the appeal with costs.'[76]

CONSTITUTIONAL CASES

Constitutional law was not one of Emmett Hall's areas of strength; it is frequently the special interest of law professors or former law professors who become judges. Not surprisingly, therefore, he was enthusiastic over the appointment of Justice Bora Laskin to the Supreme Court of Canada in 1970. Not only did Hall find Laskin a kindred spirit in a wide variety of libertarian matters, but he was relieved to have the company of one of the leading constitutional lawyers in Canada. Although Hall was never subservient to Laskin's views, he concurred with his constitutional judgments in almost every instance. The grounds of agreement with Bora Laskin were rooted in the conviction they both shared that the 'constitution is what the judges say it is.' This well-known American dictum was enunciated by Chief Justice Charles Evans Hughes in 1907.[77] And Hall, in his speech to the John White Society in 1971, claimed that it 'applies with equal force to Canada.' It should be noted, however, that Hughes's dictum has always been controversial in the United States.[78] And, while it has become widely embraced in Canada, it remains an American and not a British proposition. No British judge would have so boldly staked a claim to tell Parliament that his or her court was 'the final arbiter in constitutional matters.' It is here that Hall revealed the limits of his formal legal education. If he had studied the judicial history of the United States more closely, he would have discovered that the Hughes claim to interpretive supremacy has remained a subject of heated controversy in the literature to the present day.[79] That said, Hall's embrace of the Hughes doctrine is indicative of how the pre-Charter Court had begun to lean in the direction of American practice and away from the British practice. Subsequently, with the adoption in 1982 of the Canadian Charter of Rights and Freedoms, that tendency became even more pronounced. Had Emmett Hall remained on the Supreme Court after 1982, there is no doubt that he would have embraced with enthusiasm the new judicial activism. He hinted at his own activism when he suggested that 'the judicial function should be one of active assistance in the progressive development of the law.'[80] There was no question in his mind that both lawyers and judges were called upon to be 'cause pleaders': men and women driven by the desire and determination to eliminate poverty and inequalities in society by way of the power of the law. Speaking to the Canadian Law Teachers at McGill University in June 1972, eight months before he retired from the bench, the subject of 'Law and Social Rights,' he drew on Morris Ginsberg's statement in *On Justice in Society* that 'the central core of the idea of justice [is] the exclusion of arbitrariness and more particularly the exclusion of arbitrary power. Hence the enormous importance of the growth of legality, the emergence of the notion that persons are under the rule of law and not of men.'[81] As lawyers, Hall stressed, 'we must use our skill to act as lobbyists, drafting legislation and pressing for its enactment,' with a view to eliminating the conditions of poverty and social inequality that breed disorder and injustice.[82] With the determination to make a difference, Emmett Hall took up – in the company of Bora Laskin – the new challenges presented in constitutional cases.

One of the most challenging constitutional cases to come to the Court during Hall's tenure was the *Breathalizer Reference* of May 1970. Under Rule 55 of the Supreme Court Act, the governor-in-council (that is, the cabinet) is empowered to submit to the Supreme Court important questions of law or fact concerning five general areas:

a) the interpretation of the British North America Acts;
b) the constitutionality or interpretation of any federal or provincial legislation;
c) the appellate jurisdiction as to educational matters, by the British North America Act 1867, or by any other Act or law vested in the Governor in Council;
d) the powers of the Parliament of Canada, or the legislatures of the provinces, or of the respective governments thereof, whether or not the particular power in question has been or is proposed to be exercised; or
e) any other matter, whether or not in the opinion of the Court *ejusdem generis* with the foregoing enumerations, with reference to which the Governor in Council sees fit to submit any such question.[83]

The full Supreme Court is obliged to answer each question submitted; and the Court's opinion or opinions 'shall be pronounced in like manner as in the case of a judgment upon an appeal to the Court.'[84] The Court is also obliged to inform the provincial governments that a reference has been made and that the provincial attorneys general may appear before the Court to argue for or against the issues.

Technically speaking, reference opinions are no more than advisory opinions. In fact, however, they have the same weight as regularly decided cases on appeal. It is a constitutional practice that has had its supporters and detractors over the years. The reference device has on occasion, such as in Manitoba *Chicken and Egg*,[85] involved the Supreme Court in unreal cases. But it also permits important matters to come immediately before the Court for determination as to their constitutionality; the highly contentious 1976 *Anti-Inflation Reference*[86] was an example of such a matter.

The Parliament of Canada passed the Criminal Law Amendment Act, 1968–69[87] in the fall session of 1969. Among the amendments to the Criminal Code were a number of new regulations governing intoxicated drivers. The regulations made a breathalizer test mandatory and stipulated that it was an offence to refuse to give a sample of one's breath when asked to do so by a police officer. The new law also required that an accused person was to be offered a sample of his or her breath in an approved container; this was to permit the accused to defend himself or herself in Court.

Unfortunately, in 1970 the police did not have 'an approved container' in which to give a person a sample of his or her breath. The government was aware of this and, when it proclaimed the new law, it simply left out the three subsections relating to the right to a sample of one's breath for purposes of self-defence. This exclusion caused considerable dismay among the public and confusion throughout the lower courts. The matter came to a head when a British Columbia judge refused to convict a person accused of drunken driving because he had not been given a sample of his breath, and because the failure to implement this provision of the act violated the Canadian Bill of Rights. The British Columbia judge ruled that it was invalid for the federal government to proclaim only portions of laws duly passed by Parliament.

The matter came before the House of Commons and the opposition parties demanded that the confusion be resolved via a reference to the Supreme Court of Canada. Lawyers for the minister of justice, John Turner, eventually acquiesced and the Supreme Court of Canada was asked two questions:[88]

1) Was s.16 of the *Criminal Law Amendment Act* 1968–69, or any portion thereof validly brought into force on the first day of December 1969?
2) If a portion only of section 16 was brought into force, what portion?

The act provided in section 120 that 'this Act or any of the provisions of this Act shall come into force on a day or days to be fixed by proclamation.' The attorney general argued that section 120 permitted the government to exclude from the proclamation section 16 of the act requiring that the police provide an accused with a sample of his or her breath for purpose of self-defence. The Supreme Court ruled in a 5–4 decision that the answer to question one was 'yes'; and to question two, regarding what portion was brought into force, the court ruled that the answer was 'the whole of the section, with the exception of the three subsections 16 (224A) (1) (c) (1); 16(244A) (1) (f) (iii) (A) and 16 (224A) (6) (b).' Justice Judson wrote the major majority judgment, in which Chief Justice Fauteux and Justice Abbott concurred. Justices Hall and Laskin wrote concurring opinions. It was a most unusual alliance, and the minority – justices Ritchie, Spence, Pigeon, and Martland – was just as unlikely. No case in the ten years that Justice Hall served on the Supreme Court of Canada drew such a combination as did this reference.

It was perfectly understandable that Judson, Fauteux, and Abbott would conclude that section 120 of the Criminal Law Amendment Act empowered the government to excise a significant provision from the act; they consistently gave broad deference to Parliament. What was curious was the fact that they were not able to win the support of Justice Martland, who tended to be a strict constructionist of the Judson mould. He, however, wrote a strong opinion rejecting the contention that section 120 permitted the severence of the sample provision from the proclaimed act.

What was even more surprising were the concurring judgments of Hall and Laskin. Hall wrote that 'notwithstanding that in my view the Order in Council proclaiming parts only of s.16 of the *Criminal Law Amendment Act*, 1968–69, may indicate on the part of the executive a failure to live up to the spirit of what was intended by Parliament, I am nevertheless bound to hold that the remedy does not lie with the Courts.'[89] A mild rebuke for the failure of the executive to live up to the spirit of the Act was all he felt he could do to remind the Canadian government that it had erred in this matter.[90] It is clear that Hall agonized over this judgment; he had traditionally demanded that governments live up to the spirit of the law, that ambiguous statutes or policies should benefit the accused. But in this case he excused himself with the statement that 'under our system of parliamentary responsible government, the Executive is answerable to Parliament, and when Parliament, by enacting s.120, gave the Executive a free hand to proclaim "any" of the provisions of the Act ... the responsibility for the results rests with Parliament which has the power to remedy the situation.'[91]

Why did Hall, of all people, not see that the case involved the Canadian Bill of Rights, as the British Columbia Court did and as Justice Ritchie did? Was this not an example of how the Bill of Rights could be 'whittled away,' as he had warned in the past? Were not Canadians being denied the right to defend themselves in this instance? Other than in this case, there is no other occasion in all of Hall's decisions – either in Saskatchewan or in Ottawa – where he acquiesced in a government denial of a procedural fairness.

What made the *Breathalizer* case so important to Canadian civil libertarians was the fact that both the Supreme Court justices and the minister of justice, John Turner, failed to rise to their respective responsibilities under the Canadian Bill of Rights. That 'quasi-constitutional document' imposed (and continues to impose) an explicit obligation on the minister of justice to scrutinize all proposed federal statutes and regulations 'in order to ascertain whether any of the provisions thereof are inconsistent with [the Canadian Bill of Rights].'[92] Turner did not scrutinize the partial proclamation of the Criminal Law Amendment Act, 1968–69 in light of the Canadian Bill of Rights, as he was obliged to do by the act. In addition, the Bill of Rights imposes a similar obligation on all Canadian judges to bring the Bill of Rights to bear on their own initiative. The only Supreme Court justice to do this was Justice Ritchie in dissent. It was doubly troubling to see the Court fail to apply the Bill of Rights in this case because the British Columbia Supreme Court had ruled that the partial promulgation of the breathalizer offended the Canadian Bill of Rights.

'Diefenbaker thought I had lost my marbles,' Hall said years later with a chuckle.[93] But Diefenbaker had a point. How could Hall, of all people on the Court, have acquiesced in the government's failure to promulgate those aspects of the law that were clearly intended by Parliament to assist the accused? This conduct was all the more remarkable for a man who had always been vigilant to see that an accused person received every benefit of due procedure. His son, John, speculated that it was because his father had been so deeply involved in alcohol-related automobile-accident cases that he was prepared to look aside where the government lapsed in its efforts to correct the evil of drunken driving.[94] There is no question that Hall was clearly uncomfortable at the conference when he saw that Martland was going to go against the government; he knew that one opinion either way would be crucial. He realized that he had to go with Judson and thus become the swing vote. But still the question remains: Why did he feel he had to vote to support the government in this case? The answer appears to be, as court administrator Ken Campbell put it, 'because John Turner wanted it.' Turner did not want to suffer a setback in this matter and face the wrath of John Diefenbaker in the House of Commons.

According to Campbell, who discussed the matter with him,[95] Hall was particularly sensitive to the politics of the case. In his mind, John Turner was 'the best Attorney-General Canada had in more than fifty years.'[96] He was admired throughout Canada by members of the bar and by the judiciary, and he took a keen interest in the appointments to the provincial superior courts. And, while the prime minister appoints people to the bench, John Turner clearly asserted his influence. The appointments of Thomas Berger to the Supreme Court of British Columbia, of Gerald Le Dain to the Federal Court, and of Bora Laskin to the Supreme Court of Canada were popular with members of the bench and bar of Canada. Turner endeared himself to members of the Canadian bar by keeping in touch with them. He would frequently invite groups of lawyers to Ottawa from the various regions of the country and seek their views on legal or judicial matters. On one such occasion he asked, as was his custom, a group of lawyers from western Canada for criticism of his performance as minister of justice; he wanted to know how he could improve his department. He told the group that he could not rely upon his department staff exclusively because they occasionally failed to keep him informed or to offer constructive criticism. He then told them how, on the occasion of the Supreme Court's decision in the *Breathalizer Reference*, Emmett Hall had called him on the telephone on the day of the judgment and told him how the Court was about to rule. This information, he claimed, enabled him to prepare himself for Diefenbaker's questions in the House of Commons. It was, of course, thoroughly improper for a justice of the Supreme Court to make such a call. When told of Turner's comments, Hall vehemently denied that he had called. 'Wait till I see John Turner,' he told the author. It is not known whether he ever confronted Turner on the issue.[97]

John Turner was lucky on this occasion because Parliament adjourned on 26 June for the summer. Diefenbaker did, however, express his annoyance at the Supreme Court for not applying the Bill of Rights in the *Breathalizer Reference*. It was not one of Hall's better judgments. Nor, indeed, was it one of Bora Laskin's better judgments, and for many of the same reasons. It is worth noting that the government of Canada has never, to this day, attempted to procure 'an approved container' by which one accused of driving over the limit can defend him or herself in court. It was Emmett Hall's belief that the government would obtain such a device shortly after the proclamation of the breathalizer law. But why bother, when the Supreme Court of Canada effectively said it did not have to?

Two years after leaving the Supreme Court of Canada, Hall delivered a ringing endorsement of the Canadian Bill of Rights in a speech before the convocation of the Law Society of Upper Canada. After warning that the Bill of Rights was on a 'steep slope to near oblivion,'[98] Hall pleaded for the younger generation of lawyers to encourage Parliament to 'enact a Charter of Human Rights for all Canada' as federal and provincial politicians wrangled over a constitutional-amendment process. Little did he realize then that it would take another seven years before the Charter of Rights and Freedoms would give judges the tools of judicial activism he so strongly supported. Armed with the Charter, the courts now had the power to reach not only federal areas of jurisdiction, as was the case with the Bill of Rights, but all levels of Canadian Society.

One important constitutional case in which Justice Hall participated but did not write an opinion was the *Manitoba Egg Reference*.[99] As Paul Weiler has observed, 'many of our worst constitutional decisions have come from references and this case did not prove an exception to that rule.'[100] Weiler's critical comment on the *Manitoba Egg Reference* was justified when one considers that it was perhaps a perfect example of abuse of the reference process because it was a politically contrived manoeuvre. The case arose out of the following events. Farmers in Ontario in 1970 were producing a surplus of cheap eggs while farmers in Quebec were producing a surplus of cheap chickens. Naturally, egg producers in Ontario attempted to take advantage of the needs in Quebec, while, at the same time, chicken producers in Quebec eyed the potentially lucrative market in Ontario. However, the politically influential but less efficient egg and poultry producers in Ontario and Quebec prevailed upon their respective governments to enact protective legislation that would control the marketing, at fixed prices, of all chickens sold in Ontario and all eggs sold in Quebec, whether coming from inside or outside the province.

Unfortunately for some other provinces, such as Manitoba, the Quebec and Ontario marketing boards began to give preference to eggs and chickens produced within their own boundaries. The result was an effective embargo on eggs from other provinces such as Manitoba. And so Manitoba had to find a way of getting this problem into the courts, where it felt confident that the Ontario-Quebec marketing arrangement would be ruled unconstitutional since the courts have long denied provinces the right to restrict interprovincial trade. The ploy the Manitoba government resorted to was to copy almost verbatim the Quebec legislation and introduce it into its own legislature. The legislation was designed to control the marketing of eggs produced outside the province. The Manitoba government then referred the legislation to its own provincial Court of Appeal for a judgment as to its constitutionality. Not unexpectedly – indeed, to the government's delight – the Manitoba Court of Appeal ruled unanimously that the proposed legislation was unconstitutional.

The government of Manitoba then appealed this judgment to the Supreme Court of Canada, as it was fully entitled to do under Rule 55 of the Supreme Court Act. This was the only way Manitoba could have the Supreme Court of Canada rule, by clear implication, the Ontario and Quebec marketing schemes unconstitutional. To no one's surprise, the Supreme Court of Canada ruled the Manitoba marketing legislation unconstitutional. In doing so, the Supreme Court was fully aware that it was being used as an instrument by which egg and poultry producers in Manitoba were settling a score with producers in Quebec and Ontario.

It was a simple matter for the Supreme Court of Canada to reach the conclusion of unconstitutionality in this reference since the marketing scheme was an explicit violation of the long-established interpretation of section 91(2) of the British North America Act; that section confers on the federal government the exclusive regulation of trade and commerce. Justice Laskin wrote one of the three judgments in this case and Hall concurred in it. Laskin concluded that, while it is well established that the federal Parliament has the exclusive jurisdiction over trade and commerce, this 'does not mean that, in the absence of federal legislation, a province is incompetent to impose any regulation upon transactions in goods produced therein and between persons therein simply because the regulation may have an effect upon ultimate export of the goods from the province, whether in their original or in some processed form.'[101] What bothered Laskin – and presumably Hall – was that the province of Manitoba did not provide the necessary relevant information upon which the Court could assess the reasonableness of the Manitoba scheme. And there is no doubt that this oversight was deliberate. Manitoba wanted the Supreme Court to make its proposed scheme *ultra vires* and so went out of its way to make its own worse case. Manitoba did not ask the Court to judge whether the economic circumstances in Manitoba warranted such marketing arrangements; it asked the Court to rule whether such arrangements in general were constitutional. And, of course, Ontario and Quebec had no way of presenting an account of economic conditions which supported their marketing schemes because their acts were not, in fact, before the Court. They did not appear as intervenors. This case was a blatant misuse of the reference formula and both Laskin and Hall, while seeing through the charade, came close to dissenting. In the final analysis, however, they felt compelled to agree to dismiss the appeal.

There can be no doubt that Hall respected the constitutional expertise of Bora Laskin, for Laskin came to the Court as one of the leading authorities in Canada on constitutional matters; he was the author of the leading casebook on the subject and was much admired and respected throughout the bar and bench of Canada for his knowledge of constitutional law. But Hall's respect for Bora Laskin's constitutional expertise did not mean that he deferred to his judgment in all constitutional matters. In one constitutional case, Emmett Hall departed from one of Laskin's Ontario Court of Appeal judgments.[102] In that case Laskin (at the time a member of the Ontario Court of Appeal) had written that the federal Winding-up Act rendered portions of the Ontario Insurance Act invalid. Hall not only disagreed with this but stated in his judgment: 'In my view, sections 58 and 59 of the (Ontario) Insurance Act are, in pith and substance, valid provincial legislation'; and, as if this were not pointed enough, he went on to say that 's.165(1) of the Winding-up Act is ultra vires Parliament; an intrusion into a field of legislative power reserved exclusively to the provinces.'[103]

This kind of issue did not arise while Hall and Laskin were on the Court together. If it had, it would have been intersting to see whether Justice Laskin could have persuaded Emmett Hall to adopt his strong centralist view of the Canadian federal system, a view that he had expressed throughout his scholarly writings and that he was to reassert in the 1976 Anti-Inflation Reference, three years after Hall had left the bench. Of course, Justice Bora Laskin would not have been able to sit on an appeal from one of his Ontario court judgments. But, surely, the two would have had many long discussions in private over the issues raised by the case. There is no question that Hall talked frequently and at length with Laskin about such matters. Yet, since Hall participated in only a few constitutional cases, one cannot establish conclusively his view on federalism. What little material there is, however, leads to the conclusion that on most matters – Canadian Bill of Rights issues and the criminal law apart – Hall, unlike Laskin, was a champion of provincial rights, a decentralist.

HOSPITALS AND MEDICAL NEGLIGENCE

In view of Hall's long involvement with hospitals and the medical profession, it comes as no surprise that he paid special attention to cases involving allegations against hospital and medical negligence. During his time on the Supreme Court of Canada, he played an important part in five such cases, beginning with *University Hospital Board v. Lepine* in 1966.[104] He wrote the judgment for a unanimous Supreme Court in this case, which came on appeal from the Alberta Court of Appeal. Gerald Lepine, an Indian who resided at Hay River in the Northwest Territories, was an epileptic who had suffered a series of epilepsy seizures on the night of 16 and 17 July 1962, in the King Edward Hotel in Edmonton. At 4:45 A.M. on 17 July, Lepine's physician, Dr George Monckton, told police to take Lepine, who had been threatening to commit suicide, to the University Hospital. Lepine was admitted and placed in Room 402, which was on the fourth floor of the hospital. He was kept in that room from 17 July to 23 July. On two occasions during this period, he was moved to a room near the nurses' station where he could be supervised more carefully. During his time in hospital, Lepine suffered twenty-eight epileptic seizures; of these seizures, about eight or nine were *grand mal* and some seventeen automatisms. He was able to wander out of his room as far as the X-ray room on the same floor of the hospital. In the early hours of the morning of 24 July, Lepine became agitated and noisy. The night supervisor, Nurse Collins, remained with Lepine until 7:30 A.M. that morning; she then had him transferred to a room adjoining the nurse's station for even more careful supervision. Lepine had two other attacks shortly after being brought to the room. He climbed over the side of his bed and had difficulty with his speech.

The nurse reported the matter to Dr Shea; he prescribed sedation, which was given to Lepine early that morning. Later that morning, Lepine sat up in bed and spoke in a rapid voice, claiming that 'that is the man.' He was obviously troubled about something but was incoherent and spoke with difficulty. At 8:00 A.M., Dr Shea visited Lepine and found him to be acting quite normally. Lepine had no recollection of the events of the night before. By this time, he had been returned to Room 402 and placed under normal supervision. At 9:05 A.M., the day nurse left his room to check his chart and when she returned ten minutes later Lepine was nowhere to be found.

The Edmonton police were notified and, within half an hour of his disappearance, they found Lepine wandering along Saskatchewan Drive towards 116th Street; he was dressed in a housecoat, pyjamas, and socks with no shoes. He told the police officers: 'The nuts in the hospital have a bomb.' Police escorted Lepine back to the hospital, where he was handed over to the care of an orderly who was to escort him back to his room. Lepine bolted away from the orderly and ran out the main door of the hospital, knocking over as he went a little girl. Three police officers and the orderly pursued him and quickly caught him. Lepine was hysterical and yelled for the police to shoot him as they attempted to subdue him. With difficulty, the police escorted him to his bed, which was located near the window in Room 402. The three police officers remained with Lepine while the orderly went to get Dr Monckton.

Lepine was permitted to go to the washroom, which was located in a room off the ward. When he came out, he met Dr Monckton coming in. The doctor asked him how he felt and Lepine answered, 'Just fine, Doctor.' He then made his way towards his bed but, as he approached it, he veered quickly in the direction of a chair near the window. He jumped on the chair and dove out the window, injuring himself in the fall, before a police officer could apprehend him. Once he was back in custody, the police shackled Lepine to the bed to prevent him from making any more sudden manoeuvres.

Lepine's family urged him to bring an action against the University Hospital and Dr George Monckton for negligence. The trial judge dismissed the complaint against the doctor but allowed the claim against the hospital. The hospital was ordered to pay Lepine $46,689.50. The Alberta Court of Appeal dismissed the hospital's appeal, allowed Lepine's claim against Dr Monckton, and apportioned blame equally between the hospital and Dr Monckton. Lawyers for Lepine argued that Dr Monckton should have placed Lepine in a psychiatric ward in view of his mental condition throughout the days Lepine was in hospital prior to his jump from Room 402.

Hall was caught between his instinctive support for people such as Lepine and the realization that there had to be a limit to which a hospital and a doctor could be held negligent in cases such as the one before the Court. Of all the members of the Court, he alone had the experience to deal with the case – given his time on the board of St Paul's Hospital in Saskatoon – and he knew that the Court was relying on his assessment of all the details.

Justice Hall proceeded cautiously, acknowledging that 'this is one of those "hard cases" which could easily make bad law unless one adheres to established principles of responsibility in the face of the actual situation as it developed and moved to a rapid and unexpected climax when Lepine emerged from the bathroom, having given no prior sign of wanting to destroy himself.'[105] Hall accordingly went in search of the principle upon which to decide this case. 'One principle emerges,' he concluded, 'upon which there is universal agreement, namely, that whether or not an act of omission is negligent must be judged not by its consequences alone but also by considering whether a reasonable person should have anticipated that what happened might be a natural result of that act or omission.'[106]

Reading the judgment in this case, one can almost feel the discomfort Emmett Hall experienced in arriving at the conclusion that neither the doctor nor the hospital was negligent in this case; his instinctive sympathy was clearly with Lepine but, after carefully considering 'the duty which a doctor and a specialist such as Dr. Monckton owes to his patient and the duty which a hospital owes to a given patient as an individual,' he concluded that Lepine's action 'was not an event which a reasonable man would have foreseen.'[107] Lepine's act of desperation was impulsive and impossible to foresee; to hold doctors and hospitals responsible for such acts would 'make doctors and hospitals insurers against all such hazards which they are not.'[108] Hall participated in this case shortly after submitting his final report on health services, after, that is, an exhaustive examination of all aspects of medical care throughout Canada. From a consideration of health care in broad, general terms, Hall suddenly found himself immersed in a case that took him directly inside the practice of medicine in a specific instance. He struggled to be fair to both Lepine and his doctor as well as the hospital, and he reached his conclusions while affirming that he would not accept less than the highest standards of responsibility from doctors and hospitals. He returned to these convictions in several other cases over which he was to preside in the Supreme Court.

In *Ares v. Venner*,[109] a case involving not only medical negligence but an important matter of evidence law, Justice Hall wrote for a unanimous Court. On 21 February 1965 George Ares, a twenty-one-year-old arts student at St John's College in Edmonton, fell while skiing in Jasper Park and suffered a severe comminuted fracture of both the tibula and the fibula of his right leg, about five inches below the knee. The Jasper Ski Patrol took Ares immediately to Seton Hospital in Jasper, run by the Sisters of Charity of St Vincent de Paul.

On being admitted to the hospital, Ares was placed under the care of Dr Albert Venner, a specialist in internal medicine and a Jasper medical practitioner. The doctor put Ares in surgery where he reduced the fracture and applied a plaster cast which extended from the toes to the upper thigh. The procedures were fully completed by 6:00 P.M. – two hours after Ares had suffered the accident. The next morning, Dr Venner visited Ares; later that evening, he split the cast approximately eight inches. The nurse's report records that Ares's toes were numb, swollen, and blue and that there was no movement in the toes. Later that same day, Ares told the doctor and the attending nurse that he had no feeling in his foot; he could not move his toes nor could he feel pinpricks or pinching. He complained of pain and expressed concern that his toes were swollen and blue. Ares's condition continued unchanged throughout the next day, Tuesday, with the exception that his toes were cool.

The following day, Dr Venner split the cast to the knee and examined Ares's leg; that evening, he split the cast the entire length. During the night, Venner visited Ares and decided, on account of the complications, to send Ares to the University Hospital in Edmonton. Upon arrival at the University Hospital, Dr John C. Callaghan, a cardiovascular specialist, had Ares's leg X-rayed and arteriograms taken. He found evidence of spasm in the deep branches of the blood vessels in what is known as the fascial compartments. He decided that Ares required the attention of an orthopaedic specialist and immediately turned over Ares to the care of Dr Bernard C. Johnston. Dr Johnston took Ares immediately to the operating room where he performed a fasciotomy and applied a padded bivalved cast, one that was split on both sides in order to facilitate removal.

The angiogram that Dr Callaghan had ordered taken revealed that Ares's leg circulation was blocked, at the point of fracture. Despite the attention of both Dr Callaghan and Dr Johnston, the condition of Ares's leg continued to worsen. After additional arteriograms were taken and following consultation with another doctor, Dr Rostrup, the doctors concluded that the leg would have to be amputated below the knee. The doctors found that the muscle of Ares's leg below the knee was dead from lack of blood. It was the judgment of the team of doctors that, if they did not amputate Ares's leg, 'he would end up with a sort of living insensitive leg.'

Following his release on crutches, George Ares brought action against Dr Venner and the Seton Hospital, claiming negligence. The case was tried before Mr Justice M.B. O'Byrne of the Trial Division of the Alberta Supreme Court, who found Dr Venner negligent and ordered him to pay $29,407.13. He dismissed the action against the hospital. Dr Venner appealed the decision to the Alberta Court of Appeal; and Ares cross-appealed the dismissal of action against the hospital.[110] The Alberta Court of Appeal dismissed the complaint against the hospital and set aside the finding of liability of Dr Venner but ordered a new trial of the doctor.

Ares appealed to the Supreme Court of Canada and Dr Venner cross-appealed, claiming dismissal of the action rather than a new trial as ordered by the Alberta Court of Appeal. At the original trial, Mr Justice O'Byrne found that the case was one of 'circulatory impairment,' all the classic signs of which were present clearly and early. The established medical procedure in such cases is for the attending physician to seek the aid of a specialist. Dr Venner did not do that in this instance. The judge said that Dr Venner 'was, in my judgment, concerned more with maintaining the good fracture reduction he had obtained than with the maintenance of good circulation. This led to irreparable damage ... I am satisfied that [Dr Venner's] decision was not the result of exercising the average standard and he is therefore liable for the resulting damages.'[111]

Hall agreed with the trial judge and claimed that the 'finding of negligence, supported as it is by the evidence, should not be disturbed.'[112] But the main legal issue in this case was with the admissibility of notes made by the nurses who attended Ares while he was in Seton Hospital. Dr Venner's lawyer objected to those notes being used as evidence, claiming that they were in effect hearsay and hence, according to the established rule, inadmissible in court. Since those notes contained the damaging evidence about the condition of Ares's leg early in the affair, they were of crucial importance. What compounded the use of these notes was the fact that the lawyers for Dr Venner did not call to the stand for cross-examination any of the nurses who had written the reports and who were in court at the trial.

The Supreme Court of Canada was called upon to settle the important question of the status of such medical records. Justice Hall accordingly reviewed the trial judge's assessment of the law relating to the admissibility of evidence as well as the authorities he used in coming to the conclusion that the notes were admissible. With the concurrence of his colleagues, Hall said that 'the Court should deal with the issue as a matter of law and settle the practice in respect of hospital records and nurses' notes as being either admissible and *prima facie* evidence of the truth of the statement made therein or not admissible as being excluded by the hearsay rule.'[113] What was at issue here from the legal point of view was the uncertainty that surrounded the status of the hearsay rule. The authorities – mainly British – were divided; some said that Parliament was the proper authority to clarify the status of hearsay evidence;

others, such as Lord Donovan in *Myers v. Director of Public Prosecutions*,[114] called for a judicial resolution of the ambiguous status of hearsay evidence. Lord Donovan reasoned that 'the common law is moulded by judges and it is still their province to serve the interests of those it binds. Particularly is this so in the field of procedural law.'[115]

The line of reasoning presented by Lord Donovan appealed to Hall's brand of judicial activism. He stated that, 'although the views of Lords Donovan and Pearce are those of the minority in *Myers*, I am of the opinion that this Court should adopt and follow the minority view.'[116] Justice Hall won the unanimous support of his Supreme Court colleagues on this point. He concluded: 'Hospital records, including nurses' notes, made contemporaneously by someone having a personal knowledge of the matters then being recorded and under a duty to make the entry or record should be received in evidence as *prima facie* proof of the facts stated therein.'[117] But he made it clear that such evidence, like any other, was open to challenge on cross-examination. The general issue of the status of hospital records was thus resolved and Ares's appeal was allowed, restoring the judgment of Justice O'Byrne.

The last medical case that Justice Hall wrote for the Court was tried in May 1971, two years before he retired from the Supreme Court of Canada. The case of the *Toronto General Hospital v. Matthews*[118] involved the vicarious liability of the Toronto General Hospital for the actions of Dr Porteous, an anaesthetist who assisted Dr R.L. Matthews during heart surgery. Both the trial and appeal courts of Ontario agreed that, since Dr Porteous was a fulltime member of the hospital staff, the hospital was vicariously liable for his negligence. Justice John Aylesworth of the Ontario Court of Appeal, reviewing the relevant precedents, concluded that if it is possible to hold a hospital vicariously liable for the actions of a nurse – as the Supreme Court had done explicitly in 1938[119] – then, by extension of the principle in that circumstance, the court could hold a hospital vicariously liable for the negligent actions of a doctor who was a full-time member of the staff. Hall and the Supreme Court of Canada found no difficulty in accepting this view and accordingly agreed with the Ontario Court of Appeal and dismissed the appeal.

It is important not to overlook the fact that, by the date of the *Toronto General Hospital* case, Emmett Hall had close personal contact with two practising physicians, his son, Dr John Hall – at the time chief of orthopaedic surgery at the Hospital for Sick Children in Toronto – and his grandson, Dr John Wedge – also an orthopaedic surgeon and at the time a professor of medicine at the University of Saskatchewan Medical

School in Saskatoon. Justice Hall frequently consulted his son and grandson as to proper medical procedures. He expected the highest sense of duty and responsibility from the medical profession.

THE TRIAL OF STEVEN TRUSCOTT[120]

Newspapers throughout the country carried the news in headlines. The Toronto *Star* proclaimed in bold print: 'SUPREME COURT CONFIRMS TRUSCOTT'S CONVICTION, 8–1.'[121] The Saskatoon *Star-Phoenix* headline read: 'TRUSCOTT LOSES FREEDOM BID BY SUPREME COURT DECISION.' Under a picture of Justice Hall was the caption 'lone dissenter.'[122] No judgment Emmett Hall ever wrote propelled him into such public prominence as did his dissenting opinion in the Truscott case. He became an instant hero for some while his brother justices became heartless old men. Letters to the editors of daily newspapers across the country flooded in, praising the dissenting judge and criticizing the Court majority. It just did not seem right to the public at large that a young boy could be convicted of murder. And Justice Hall's powerful dissenting voice gave credence to those widespread misgivings.

Few trials in Canadian history were followed across the nation as closely as the appeal of Steven Truscott before the Supreme Court of Canada in 1966.[123] Actually, the Supreme Court case of Steven Truscott was not an appeal in the normal sense of the term. The Supreme Court had denied Truscott formal leave to appeal in February 1960. The trial held in 1966 was a reference case submitted by the governor general-in-council under Rule 55 of the Supreme Court Act. Prime Minister Pearson had been pressured by the opposition into referring the case to the Supreme Court. Isabel Lebourdais's book *The Trial of Steven Truscott*[124] played a large role in prodding the opposition and in informing the public about the case. The question asked in this instance was: 'Had an Appeal by Steven Murray Truscott been made to the Supreme Court of Canada, as is now permitted by Section 597A of the Criminal Code of Canada, what disposition would the Court have made of such an appeal on a consideration of the existing Record and such further evidence as the Court, in its discretion, may receive and consider?' The revised Criminal Code section referred to in the question provided that a person who had been sentenced to death and whose conviction was confirmed by a Court of Appeal may appeal to the Supreme Court of Canada on any ground of law or fact or mixed law and fact. This new provision came into effect on 13 July 1961, seventeen months after Trusctott's appeal was denied. The Court was being asked in this reference to say what it would have said had such a right of appeal been available to Truscott a year earlier.

Steven Truscott was tried by Justice R.I. Ferguson with a jury in Goderich, Ontario, on 16 September 1959, at the age of fourteen and a half years for the murder of Lynne Harper, a girl of not quite thirteen. The jury returned a verdict of guilty on 30 September with a recommendation for mercy. Justice Ferguson sentenced Truscott to hang. The conviction was unanimously upheld by the Ontario Court of Appeal; on the same day, 21 January 1960, the conviction was commuted by the crown to a term of life imprisonment. The refusal of the Supreme Court of Canada to hear the Truscott appeal was announced in February 1960. At that time the Supreme Court had jurisdiction to entertain an appeal on two grounds only: a) where there was dissent by a judge of the Court of Appeal on any question of law (there was no such dissent in the Court of Appeal); or b) on any question of law with leave of the Court. Since the first avenue was not open to the Court, it had to look to the second. It did so and found no question of law in doubt at either the appeal or trial level. The appeal panel, composed of Chief Justice Kerwin and justices Locke, Cartwright, Martland, and Judson, unanimously agreed that under the law at the time there was no basis for an appeal to the full Court.

When a case comes before the Supreme Court, it does so either as of right or with leave of the Court. A panel of three Supreme Court Justices hears the application for appeal with leave and decides whether there is merit to the appeal. (Prior to the abolition of capital punishment in 1976, cases punishable by death – like *Truscott* – required a panel of five justices.) If a simple majority of justices agree that there is reason to believe that an error in law had been made at the trial or at the appeal, leave to appeal to the Supreme Court will be granted. Final appeal courts are traditionally reluctant to grant leave to review convictions pronounced by juries and which have been upheld by the provincial courts of appeal. The revised Criminal Code provisions covering the appeal to the Supreme Court of those sentenced to death made such appeals as of right. Furthermore, what was of crucial importance in the Truscott case was the new provisions which allowed the Supreme Court to hear the appeal of questions of fact or evidence and not only of law. Under this procedure, the Supreme Court acquired the authority to call witnesses and review new evidence. Truscott took advantage of this opportunity and gave evidence before the Supreme Court; he had not given evidence at his trial.

The Court ruled in an 8-to-1 decision that, notwithstanding the new evidence and the testimony of Truscott himself, the jury decision must be upheld. The majority decision was a joint opinion by eight members of the Court and announced by Justice Cartwright. No gentler man ever donned a judicial gown than John Cartwright and it hurt him deeply to be in the majority in this case but he saw no alternative. Only Hall seemed to have had the defence counsel's eye for the kind of irregularity that occurred at the Truscott trial, or, at least, so he thought. And he objected in no uncertain terms in a ringing dissent. He was in his element in *Truscott* because the Court was, in fact, retrying Truscott, not simply hearing an appeal.

He was annoyed by the judgment and remained so to the end of his life. He had reason to believe that at least two of his judicial colleagues would join him in dissent; several members of the Court talked with him on the telephone, pledging support, the night before he left for a holiday in the United States. 'When I got back, they had changed their minds. What happened I will never know,' he brooded more than a decade later. When I posed this matter to Justice Douglas Abbott after he had left the bench, the former justice bristled: 'Nonsense, Emmett Hall never had any support on the Court for his stand in Truscott. He was grandstanding, that's all!'[125] This view of Hall as a 'grandstander' was shared by several members of the Supreme Court who preferred that justices of the high Court maintain a low and uncontroversial profile.

Justice Hall was fully aware that a large part of the problem in the Truscott case was that all justices of the Court – except himself and Spence – had been members of the Court when the appeal arrived in 1960. In essence, some felt that the Court was now, in 1966, being asked to judge the wisdom of not having heard the case six years previous, that is, to sit in judgment on its own prior judgment of refusal to grant appeal. An acquittal or direction to hold a new trial would have amounted to an admission of poor judgment in refusing Truscott's appeal in 1960. But, for Emmett Hall, this was irrelevant. All that mattered was that there was an injustice and it needed to be corrected.

In his long dissent, Justice Hall subjected the evidence and trial procedure to an intense scrutiny which mirrored the meticulous care with which he prepared the defence in his own cases. It was the same tenacious approach he brought to bear on all criminal cases. He announced his conclusions in the following crisp and unequivocal words: 'Having considered the case fully, I believe that the conviction should be quashed and a new trial directed. I take the view that the trial was not conducted according to law. Even the guiltiest criminal must be tried according to law. That does not mean that I consider Truscott guilty or innocent.'[126] The fact that Truscott had been convicted exclusively on circumstantial evidence prompted Hall – the old defence lawyer – to subject the behaviour of crown counsel and the trial judge to careful examination. What he found, he did not like. 'I find that there were grave errors in the trial brought about principally by crown counsel's method in trying to establish guilt and by the learned trial judge's failure to appreciate that the course being followed by the Crown would necessarily involve the jury being led away from an objective appraisal of the evidence for and against the prisoner.'[127] Step by step, Hall reviewed the evidence and trial procedures and concluded that the Truscott trial was a bad trial and he asserted with full conviction: 'A bad trial remains a bad trial.'[128] What could be more unequivocal than that? And the nation understood that kind of language.

John Diefenbaker, leader of the opposition at the time, said that Truscott should be released on parole without delay. 'He certainly is not going to benefit by further incarceration,' he announced in the House of Commons. But parole was not granted.

Meanwhile, letters and telegrams poured in to Justice Hall from all across Canada – letters from practising lawyers, from housewives, from old and young. And even a few letters from cranks.[129] One woman in St Catharines, Ontario, said in a handwritten letter: 'After reading the article "Supreme Court Dissenter" in the Toronto *Star*, Friday, May 5, I was compelled to write you a few lines in appreciation of your decision concerning Steven Truscott. Canada needs and wants more men like you in our Canadian courts. You are more than worthy of the position you hold. I have great admiration and respect for you. God bless you.' In a heated letter condemning the Ontario attorney general, Arthur Wishart, for statements praising the Canadian criminal process, a Winnipeg lawyer wrote: 'I have waited some time Justice Hall to allow my choler to abate before expressing my admiration of your stand. Perhaps I have not waited long enough but I think it equally important you should know you are not alone.'

By and large, the letters were similar to one, neatly typed, from a young woman in Toronto who wrote:

> I felt that I must write to you concerning your decision in the Supreme Court hearing on the case of Steven Truscott.

Although one reads the details of the enquiry in the newspapers, and listens to the radio and television reports, it is difficult to be objective. Opinions of experts at the hearing seemed to be so opposite. May I say though that I could not help but agree with your dissenting conclusions.

As you so ably expressed it, and how I believe I have interpreted it, the question in point was not truly one of guilt or innocence, but whether in the first place the trial had been in true agreement with Canadian jurisprudence.

The people seemed to be fully aware of the issues and took the time to write. And, while Hall revelled in expressions of approval from important men and women, those from ordinary people pleased him the most. But some letters, such as the following, upset him:

I would like to state my disapproval of so-called justice in Canada. I have never seen too much of it around; unless you have the thing that means the most, MONEY.

The Supreme Court judgment of the Steven Truscott case so far as a lot of people including myself is concerned, this only serves one purpose that is: that Justice does not exist in Canada.

I am not saying that this boy is either guilty or innocent because even though I feel he is innocent, I don't really know. But I do feel and know that something very funny is going on; someone is covering for someone.

Who is that someone? An RCMP Officer, a big man around town; or the judge that allowed a fake trial and seemed to state without any doubt that Steven was guilty, by allowing something to be said, that shouldn't have been said.

Canada needs men like you Mr. Hall, desperately. But I'm ashamed to say there are very few in our country.

This kind of letter displeased him because it gave the impression that people were over-reacting to one decision and casting doubt upon the whole criminal and judicial process; he certainly had no intention of prompting that kind of thinking, however much he disagreed with the majority decision in the Truscott case. Another letter in the same vein stated: 'I wish to relate how I admire and respect your attitude in the Truscott situation. Without mercy there is no justice. Your colleagues seem to be tyrants. I recommend they mend their ways. There is no bigger man than one who would stop to help a child. We are proud of men like you.'

One of the most curious letters Hall received was from London, Ontario:

I have read with much interest your judgment in the Steven Truscott case. It is incredible that only one of nine Supreme Court Judges could recognize a faulty trial. Thank you very much for pointing out the many reasons why there should be another trial. A friend of mine has recently discovered that she is an automatic writer. She does not go into a trance – just sits down with a piece of paper and a pencil. I asked her to consult her contact about Steven Truscott whom I have always believed innocent. The answer was as follows: Steven Truscott did not kill Lynne Harper. She got in a car, was taken for a ride, went swimming, and on the way home, was attacked on a roadside or in a ditch and died very suddenly in the arms of her attacker. She was then carried or dragged into the woods where she was found. The name given was [deleted] who lived in the area and who worked part-time in a garage in Clinton, if I remember correctly. Neither my friend or I had ever heard the name before and we do not know that district. Her contact told her not to become involved as she would not be believed and that any evidence had long since disappeared. I have promised not to disclose her name. I am giving you the information with her permission.

A few letters disapproved of Hall's dissenting opinion and claimed that he had been duped by 'public relations types such as Berton and LeBourdais.' Those letters did not bother him, but it rankled him greatly when a lawyer practising a thousand miles or more from the scene of the crime said, 'What was Hall up to? We all know Truscott was as guilty as hell.' To this, Hall retorted: 'How can a lawyer make such a statement? He should know better. He didn't see the evidence, I did. Has he forgotten that every accused person is entitled to a fair trial?' It took some time before his annoyance subsided.

Editorial comment throughout the country was uniformly favourable to Justice Hall's dissent. The *Prairie Messenger*, a Catholic Sunday newspaper, ran an editorial on 10 May entitled 'Heartless Decision.' It stated:

The Supreme Court's decision to uphold the 1959 conviction and life sentence of Steven Truscott must strike the public as singularly heartless. Now 22, Truscott has spent the past eight years in Collin's Bay Penitentiary where he was sent at 14 for the alleged sex slaying of Lynne Harper, 12, near Clinton, Ontario. Noting, and grateful for, Mr. Justice Hall's dissent, the public through its elected members of parliament, should continue to press for Truscott's release. What purpose can several more years of confinement possibly serve? While the Supreme Court's integrity must be assumed, does it not appear either callous or vindictive on the part of society to allow the rigor of the law to hold sway? Steven Truscott should be declared a free man by an act of parliament.

The Montreal *Star* editorial for 5 May 1967 reviewed the steps that had led to the Supreme Court hearing.

We shall consider later what may now be done by the government. For the moment, we should like it to be remembered that extraordinary steps were taken to ensure a thorough review of this case seven years after the event. In the words of Solicitor General Pennell, the government took into consideration 'the widespread concern as to whether there was a miscarriage of justice in the conviction' ... The fact that one of the nine judges dissented will impress many people and perhaps help to confirm their view that there was indeed a miscarriage of justice. But it should be noted that Mr. Justice Hall would not have found Steven Truscott innocent; he would have ordered a new trial. Nothing is served by attempting to analyze his reasons for judgment, or those of the majority itself. They have been arrived at after a careful reading of the original trial record and the hearing of new evidence, something the public has, of course, been unable to do.

It was a cautious and responsible comment which pleased Hall. But he did not want to see the administration of justice or his brother justices subjected to ridicule or disrespect in the press. An editorial in the Toronto *Star* for the same day left him uneasy: 'Only the one dissenter, Mr. Justice Emmett Hall, was concerned over the numerous serious errors made by the trial judge in summarizing the evidence for the jury. He considered they called for a new trial. The others did not. One thir.g, however, is clear enough. This case has done damage to public confidence in the administration of justice. The original trial at Goderich showed that the lynching spirit could fare as easily in an Ontario courtroom as in Alabama or Mississippi – and that responsible officials would do as little to control it.' And if this were not sufficiently intemperate, the editorial concluded with the stinging indictment of the trial jury: 'It also demonstrated that the much-quoted rule that a man is considered innocent until he is proven guilty is not always honoured in our jury rooms.' Such hysterical remarks did nothing to reassure the Canadian people about the fairness of the justice system. It simply would not do to paint the other eight justices in a bad light or to robe them in the gowns of hard-hearted executioners.

There is no doubt that the Truscott affair was a troubling event that touched the lives of Canadians from coast to coast. Everyone seemed to have an opinion on Truscott's guilt or innocence and a large majority sided with Justice Hall. His dissent was a blister and called into focus the Canadian criminal process. To the average citizen, the implications were clear: Steven Truscott had been wrongfully convicted. Everyone was asking: How could a child of fourteen be tried as an adult and convicted to hang on circumstantial evidence? And the recent rash of reversals of capital convictions – of David Milgard, Donald Marshall, and Guy-Paul Morin – have done little to put to rest the doubts surrounding Truscott's conviction for the murder of Lynn Harper. To no one's surprise, Steven Truscott, who was released from jail on 21 October 1969, has begun the process to have his conviction overturned and his good name restored to him. Central to his petition is the dissenting judgment of Justice Emmett Hall.

A SAD SIDEBAR

Chief Justice Robert Taschereau was in a poor state of health throughout the *Truscott Reference* and the Court held its breath frequently for fear that the press would detect his deteriorating condition and make an issue out of it. Justice Cartwright sat next to him throughout the hearing and when the chief justice muttered an incomprehensible question, Cartwright would interject immediately: 'Yes, I too, would like to ask counsel that question.' He would then proceed to ask an entirely different question.

Many on the court thought that Taschereau should have stepped down before the Truscott case. His health had been bad for several years and he appeared too weak to preside over a Court confronted by such an important matter of criminal justice. Hall himself remained firm in the conviction that Taschereau's poor health had no impact on the outcome of the proceedings. Yet he was one of those who had wanted him to resign, fearing that the entire Court or the administration of justice might be brought into disrepute if, in the heat of the intense public attention surrounding the Truscott case, Taschereau's condition became public knowledge.

By the mid-1960s, the chief justice's slide into alcoholism had been a subject of *sotto voce* conversation among the members of the Court for a long time, and the same was true of his reputation for extramarital escapades. Until the *Truscott* case, few newspapers bothered to cover Supreme Court proceedings or report its judgments; there was no Supreme Court press corps, as there has been in the United States for generations. But, with the increase in media scrutiny – now called 'investigative journalism' – not a few members of the Court became concerned about Taschereau's plight and the reputation of the Court and its members. The Supreme Court administrative officer, Kenneth Campbell, was close to Chief Justice Taschereau and fully conscious of his failing condition.[130] He attempted gently and discreetly (as was his manner) to have Taschereau resign. He was clearly becoming an embarrassment to the Court. Since the chief justice was required in the absence of the governor general to assume the role from time to time of acting governor general, the matter assumed special urgency. Ken Campbell kept two letters in his pocket for months, one addressed to the minister of justice, Pierre Elliott Trudeau, and the other addressed to Prime Minister Lester Pearson. They were unsigned letters of resignation. Campbell was ready at the first indication that the chief justice was prepared to resign to place those letters before him for his signature.

Several members of the Court, Hall among them, urged Campbell to persuade Robert Taschereau to resign. Campbell and others had tried repeatedly in 1966 to secure Taschereau's resignation but all attempts were unsuccessful. Members of the Court were greatly relieved by the failure of the press to see Taschereau's condition during the Truscott trial; if members of the press did see it, they discreetly refrained from mentioning it in their accounts of the Court proceedings. Campbell admired and liked the chief justice and attempted to shield him as much as possible. He kept after the chief justice through the summer of 1967, reminding him of the enormous responsibilities the office carried and how frail he was becoming – he had developed double cataracts and the work of the Court was clearly getting to him; far from giving leadership, he was rarely able to function fully as a member of the Court.

In 1967, Chief Justice Taschereau received an invitation to attend a gathering of chief justices from around the world to be held at Lausanne, Switzerland. When the invitation arrived, Ken Campbell showed it to Taschereau with the comment that it would probably be a waste of time for the chief justice to go. 'No,' replied Taschereau, 'I'd like to go. You get the travel advance, the tickets and I'll go.' Ken Campbell tried to dissuade him but to no avail; he insisted on going. Campbell reluctantly made the flight and accommodation arrangements, even to the extent of having a Canadian embassy official meet the chief justice in Lausanne and help him to get settled in his hotel room.

When Taschereau returned from the conference, Campbell and other members of the Supreme Court asked the chief justice how he enjoyed the meetings. Taschereau dismissed all such enquiries with an evasive mumble. He let it be known that he did not want to discuss the matter. This attitude, of course, annoyed Campbell and he set out to find out what bothered the chief justice at the conference. Campbell's enquiries through contacts in the Department of External Affairs revealed that the chief justice had never left his room throughout the three days he was there.

A few days after his return, it dawned on the chief justice that it was expected of him to submit a report to the minister of justice, Pierre Trudeau. He called Campbell to his office and told him to write a brief report for him. Campbell asked the chief justice if he had brought back any conference papers; if so, he could use them as a basis for his report. 'No' replied Chief Justice Taschereau, 'I don't have any papers or anything like that. But you write up something for me and I'll sign it.'

Ken Campbell was visibly startled by the request but dutifully set about, with only a copy of the conference agenda to go on, to write a report of the conference. 'I dreamed up the darndest bunch of lies,' he later recalled, 'free and frank discussion – all that sort of thing; a bunch of garbage, you never saw anything like it.'[131] The chief justice read the report and signed it with the comment that 'it would do the trick.' Campbell sent the report to Pierre Trudeau the next day. A few days later, a letter arrived for the chief justice; it was a letter of acknowledgment from the minister of justice stating how pleased he was to have the report and to learn that the chief justice had found it a profitable experience. Ken Campbell was convinced to the very end that Trudeau never really saw the report and that if anyone in the Department of Justice read it, they did so in the most cursory fashion.

Whenever Taschereau became melancholy, he would tell Campbell that he was going to resign. 'I'd like to see John [Cartwright] get a chance to become Chief Justice,' he would say. But he never gave any indication when he would actually resign. Campbell continued to keep the undated letters of resignation with him at all times in anticipation of the moment when Taschereau would actually make the decision to resign. Campbell had even taken the initiative to work out with the Department of Justice the details of Taschereau's retirement benefits.

The time finally arrived on a hot July evening in the summer of 1967. Ken Campbell was at home when the telephone rang. It was the chief justice, he had just returned from a fishing trip. 'I'm going to resign, Ken. Will you prepare something for me to sign?' Campbell could tell from his voice that Taschereau had been drinking but hoped that his decision to resign would hold firm this time. He told the chief justice that he would type out the necessary letters himself and bring them that evening to Taschereau's apartment for his signature. At 10 P.M. that evening Campbell arrived at the small bachelor apartment – Taschereau lived alone in Ottawa, his wife having returned to Quebec some years earlier – and found it a shambles, empty liquor bottles, dirty pots and pans, and unfinished meals and newspapers strewn about.

Taschereau, dressed in an old, soiled dressing gown over a pair of shorts with tattered slippers on his feet, let Campbell into his apart-ment. 'He looked like hell,' Campbell recalled later. He asked Campbell if he wanted a drink; Campbell declined and told him that he had the letters of resignation for the chief justice's signature. Taschereau took the letters, sat down in an armchair, and read them several times; as he did, tears began to flow. He sat there staring at the letters with tears running down his stubbled gray, emaciated cheeks, looking years older than his seventy years. Ken Campbell sat opposite on the sofa with a lump in his throat 'the size of your fist.' He felt sorry for the chief justice, a man who had served his country well as a member of the Supreme Court of Canada since 1940. But Campbell knew that Taschereau had to sign those letters. Without saying a word, he placed a pen in front of the chief justice. A few moments later, Taschereau signed in a shaking hand the two letters of resignation. He put down the pen and looked at Campbell and said: 'Now will you have a drink with me?' 'I certainly will, sir,' replied Campbell.

The reaction throughout the Court at the word of Taschereau's resig-nation was one of enormous relief mingled with sadness for the retiring chief justice, for Robert Taschereau had been an outstanding jurist throughout most of his career on the Supreme Court of Canada. It was only in his last years – worn down by loneliness since the separation from his wife – that he began to fail. And there is no easy or graceful procedure for removing a man from the bench. The retirement age for Supreme Court Justices is seventy-five. Taschereau still had five years to serve. To remove him from the bench would have required a joint address of both Houses of Parliament and it would have disgraced him for the rest of his life.

Taschereau left Ottawa shortly after his resignation. He was never to return. He died at Quebec City on 24 November 1979. Justice Hall along with Ken Campbell accompanied John Turner to the funeral.

IN DEFENCE OF NATIVE PEOPLES

One of Hall's chief interests while a justice of the Supreme Court of Canada was the condition of Canada's native peoples. He had believed for a long time that Canadian Indians and Inuit had suffered at the hands of governments and bureaucrats, noting on one occasion the 'lamentable history of Canada's dealings with Indians in disregard of treaties made with them.'[132] During his ten-year tenure on the Supreme Court of Canada, Hall wrote six judgments in cases involving native peoples. In his first case, that of *Prince and Myron v. The Queen*,[133] he wrote for a unanimous Court that the appeals of Prince and Myron should be allowed.

Rufus Prince and Robert Myron had been charged with unlawfully hunting big game by means of night lights, contrary to section 31 of the Manitoba Game and Fisheries Act. The two were treaty Indians and were hunting deer for food on lands to which they had the right of access. They were acquitted at the trial before Magistrate Bruce McDonald, who ruled that a spotlight used by the defendants was not a night light within the meaning of section 31(1) of the Game and Fisheries Act of Manitoba; the 'night lights' referred to there meant an object rather than a method of hunting. And, since the land was rightly accessible to Indians, he dismissed the charges against them. The Manitoba Court of Appeal rejected Magistrate Macdonald's interpretation of 'night lights' and directed that a conviction be entered and imposed. Justices Schultz and Samuel Freedman dissented.

Justice Hall reviewed the Manitoba Game and Fisheries Act and concluded that the 'sole question for determination is whether the word "hunt" as used in s. 72(1) of the *Game and Fisheries Act* in regard to Indians is ambiguous in any way or subject to the limitations contained in s. 31(1) of the said Act.'[134] The entire Supreme Court of Canada was persuaded that the word 'hunt' must be understood as it is defined by the *Oxford English Dictionary*, that is, as: 'the act of chasing wild animals for the purpose of catching or killing them; to chase for food or sport; to scour a district in pursuit of game.'[135] Hall concluded for the Court that the word is 'not ambiguous nor subject to any of the limitations which s. 31(1) imposes on the non-Indian.'[136] This judgment constituted a major confirmation of the right of Indians to hunt for food and served notice to provincial governments – the provinces of Quebec and Alberta filed factums in this case and were represented by counsel at the hearings – that they could not easily infringe the rights of Canadian Indians.

In another case the same year, *Sikyea v. The Queen*,[137] Hall wrote the unanimous Court judgment denying the appeal of an Indian who was convicted of violating the Migratory Birds Convention Act, 1952. Michael Sikyea, a treaty Indian, was found guilty by a justice of the peace in the Northwest Territories of unlawfully killing a migratory bird (a mallard duck) out of season on 7 May 1962, in an area designated by Canadian Migratory Bird Regulations as a sanctuary.

Sikyea admitted killing the duck for food but claimed that under Treaty No. 11, signed by the government of Canada and the natives of the area in 1921, he was entitled to hunt and shoot ducks for food regardless of any regulations or legislation, whether in season or not. Justice Jack Sissons of the Territorial Court was persuaded by Sikyea's arguments and set aside the conviction; Justice Sissons also expressed a doubt as to whether the duck was wild or domestic. The Northwest Territories Court of Appeal reversed Sisson's ruling and restored Sikyea's conviction, which he appealed to the Supreme Court of Canada.

Justice Hall began by studying the terms of the Migratory Birds Convention Act, 1952 and of regulation 5(1)(a) of the Migratory Birds Regulations and found that they were clear and unambiguous. He dismissed Sissons's doubts as to whether the duck was wild or domestic; he had little difficulty agreeing with the Territorial Court of Appeal that the duck was indeed wild and was protected by the Migratory Act. He took issue directly with Justice Sissons: 'There appears to be no room for doubt that a mallard is a species of wild duck within the meaning of the *Migratory Birds Convention Act* and under the circumstances the doubts expressed by Sissons J. are only consistent with his having erroneously formed the opinion that a wild duck which has once been tamed or confined and is later found at large in the nesting area at a time when it would be likely to nest is not then a "wild duck" within the meaning of the statute. The contrary is the case. A wild duck which has once been tamed or confined reverts, on escaping, to being a wild duck in the eyes of the law.'[138] Hall, accordingly, dismissed the appeal.

Justice Jack Sissons was a colourful and outspoken judge of the

Northwest Territories. He became so thoroughly a champion of Inuit and Indian rights that he frequently found himself in conflict with higher courts. In his memoirs, Sissons wrote: 'In the summer of 1962 I added a stuffed duck to the ornaments in my office at Yellowknife. It looked like an ordinary mallard, and a member of the Supreme Court told me privately that it was just a fifty-cent duck and too much fuss was being made of it.'[139] Little did that unidentified Supreme Court justice know that 'the duck was used as evidence in the prosecution of Michael Sikyea, a treaty Indian of the Yellowknife district who was convicted by a magistrate of hunting out of season, contrary to the Migratory Birds Convention Act. I was away at the time and the matter was brought to my attention by an Indian agent who felt pretty indignant about it. This bureaucratic harassment of Sikyea was a violation of his human rights. For an Indian or Eskimo the very first right is the right to hunt for food. I shared the indignation of the Indian agent and ordered a new trial in the territorial court.'[140] However flamboyant Sissons may have appeared, it is obvious from his memoirs that he had a deep understanding of how the native peoples of the north felt about their ancestral rights. 'The villain of the piece,' he wrote, 'is the Migratory Birds Convention of 1916, [sic: 1921] an international treaty between Canada and the United States. It was told to me by an Indian agent that a few years ago a government official spoke to a local chief and told him shooting ducks in the spring was contrary to the Migratory Birds Convention. The chief asked what was this convention? It was a treaty between Canada and the United States. Did the Indians sign the treaty? No. "Then," declared the chief, "we shoot the ducks."'[141]

Hall was not prepared to go as far as Sissons in extending gaming privileges to native peoples, as was evident again in the case of *Sigeareak v. The Queen.*[142] Sigeareak, an Inuit who lived at Whale Cove, an Inuit settlement on the west coast of Hudson Bay midway between Churchill and Chesterfield Inlet, was charged under section 15(1)(a) of the Game Ordinance of the Northwest Territory of having killed and abandoned parts of three cariboo fit for human consumption at a point two miles from an abandoned cabin on the north shore at the mouth of the Wilson River, Northwest Territories. The Game Ordinance was validly enacted legislation passed by commissioner-in-council pursuant to powers conferred by section 13 of the Northwest Territories Act, 1952.

Sigeareak was tried initially before P.B. Parker, a police magistrate, under section 466(b) of the Criminal Code of Canada at Whale Cove on 26 and 27 February 1965. Magistrate Parker, holding that he was bound by the judgment of Justice Sissons of the Territorial Court in *Regina v. Kallooar*,[143] dismissed the charge on the grounds that the Game Ordinance did not apply to an Inuit.

The minister of justice of Canada applied to the magistrate to state a case under section 734 of the Criminal Code of Canada. (This was a provision by which the crown could have a lower court verdict reviewed on specific questions of law.) Magistrate Parker stated the case, concluding with the following question: 'Was I right in holding that the *Game Ordinance* and particularly Section 15(1)(a) thereof does not apply to Eskimos?' The appeal, by way of stated case, was heard by Sissons, who adhered to his two earlier judgments – *Kogogolak*[144] and *Kallooar* – and answered the key question in the affirmative, thereby upholding the acquittal of Sigeareak. The judgment of the Territorial Court was appealed to the Court of Appeal for the Northwest Territories[145] and it was reversed. Sigeareak appealed this decision to the Supreme Court of Canada; it was heard by a full Court on 5 May 1966. The judgment of the Supreme Court was unanimous and was written by Justice Hall. The Court ruled that Sigeareak's appeal should be dismissed, thereby confirming the judgment and order of the Territorial Court of Appeal.

Sigeareak's main line of argument throughout had been that the Royal Proclamation of 1793 applied to Indians and Inuit in the area in question and that it was still in effect notwithstanding the Northwest Territories Act and the Game Ordinance. Hall's judgment accordingly began with a perusal of the Royal Proclamation and the letters patent granted in 1670 to the Hudson's Bay Company. In the Court's view, the 'Proclamation specifically excludes territory granted to the Hudson's Bay Company and there can be no question that the region in question was within the area granted to Hudson's Bay Company. Accordingly, the Proclamation does not and never did apply in the region in question and the judgments (of Sissons) to the contrary are not good law.'[146]

As to whether the Game Ordinance applied to Inuit, Hall wrote, the authority of Parliament to legislate for the Northwest Territories was unquestionable; so too was the power of the commissioner-in-council to pass the Game Ordinance as an extension of parliamentary authority. Nor was there any doubt that the cariboo killed and abandoned were barren-ground cariboo; they were game and hence were killed in violation of the Game Ordinance.

The Court took explicit care to set aside Sissons's judgments in the leading precedents in order to clear up any ambiguity. Hall wrote: 'I think it desirable to say specifically that insofar as *Regina v. Kallooar* and

Regina v. Kogogolak hold that the *Game Ordinance* does not apply to Indians and Eskimos in the Northwest Territories, they are not good law and must be taken as having been overruled.'[147] So much for Sissons's efforts to restore to the native peoples of the Northwest Territories an unqualified and unrestricted right to hunt without interference from white men's laws. The long-established rights of conquest and dispossession confirmed the practice of regulating the fishing and hunting of native peoples.

This is not to say that Hall was insensitive to the rights of native peoples; nothing could be further from the truth. He believed that, if governments were going to regulate by law the customary ways of our native peoples, they must do so according to law and unambiguously; any ambiguity in law would go to the benefit of Indians and Inuit. The Supreme Court of Canada made this clear in the *Drybones*[148] decision. But, as we see in the *Daniels*[149] case, Hall and other members of the Court – Spence and Cartwright – were not always in the majority in cases involving native hunting rights.

Paul Daniels, of Chemahawin Indian Reserve, in Manitoba, was charged on 3 July 1964 with unlawfully possessing migratory game birds when the possession of such birds was prohibited by the Migratory Birds Convention Act. Daniels was convicted by Police Magistrate Neil McPhee at The Pas, Manitoba. He appealed this conviction and was tried anew in the County Court by Judge J.W. Thompson, who allowed the appeal and acquitted the accused.

The crown appealed this judgment to the Manitoba Court of Appeal. The Court of Appeal, with Justice Freedman dissenting, allowed the appeal and restored the conviction of Daniels. Daniels appealed that judgment to the Supreme Court of Canada and his case was heard by a full Court on 20 November 1967. In a 5–4 decision, the Supreme Court of Canada ruled that the Manitoba Court of Appeal judgment should stand – Daniels was indeed guilty of violating the Migratory Birds Convention Act. The four justices who dissented were Chief Justice Cartwright and justices Hall, Spence, and Ritchie.

The Court majority, led by Justice Judson, held that paragraph 13 of the agreement made on 14 December 1929 between the government of Canada and the government of Manitoba (approved by statutes of the United Kingdom Parliament, the Parliament of Canada, and the legislature of Manitoba) did not exempt Paul Daniels from the terms of the Migratory Birds Convention Act. Justice Pigeon, in a concurring opinion, wrote that the case called for the application of the rule of construction that Parliament is not presumed to legislate in breach of a treaty or in any manner inconsistent with the comity of nations and the established rules of international law.

Chief Justice Cartwright wrote, in dissent, that the 1929 agreement did not cut down or deny the right of hunting which paragraph 13 said, in plain and unequivocal words, the Indians were to have. The rights given to the Indians by those words had been, the chief justice stressed, enshrined in the constitution since 1930 and given the force of law 'notwithstanding anything in ... any Act of the Parliament of Canada.' He reasoned that there was no basis for the Court to insert after the word 'Canada' a phrase such as 'except the *The Migratory Birds Convention Act.*'[150]

Justice Hall wrote the longest judgment upholding the rights of Indians in Manitoba to hunt for food. He noted that the words of paragraph 13 of the agreement ('which the Province hereby assures to them') did not have the effect of limiting the rights thereby accorded to the Indians to provincial rights, but rather constituted *additional* assurance of the general rights described in that paragraph.

Hall said, that in virtue of section 1 of the British North America Act, 1930, giving the agreement the force of law 'notwithstanding anything in ... any Act of the Parliament of Canada,' the agreement took precedence over the Migratory Birds Convention Act and any regulations made under that act.[151] The result was that those enactments relating to migratory birds did not apply to Indians in Manitoba when they were engaged in hunting migratory birds for food in areas of the province set out in paragraph 13. In reaching these conclusions, Hall agreed with the dissenting reasons of Justice Freedman of the Manitoba Court of Appeal.

It is in *Daniels* that Hall refers to 'the lamentable history of Canada's dealings with Indians in disregard of treaties made with them.'[152] For him, the terms of the British North America Act were decisive because 'Parliament cannot legislate in contravention of the British North America Act.'[153]

The fair treatment of Canadian native peoples was a cause Hall brooded over. His knowledge of Saskatchewan history and the plight of its native population made him especially sensitive to the rights and privileges of Canadian native peoples. In *Daniels*, he was clearly annoyed at the Court majority's narrow and (in his view) unfair reading of an agreement. One can see from this judgment his frustration with the blundering of governments which led time and again to a violation of native hunting rights. For these reasons, he was delighted by the decision of the Supreme Court of Canada in the case of Joseph Drybones.[154]

Drybones, an Indian of the Northwest Territories, was found intoxicated in the lobby of the Old Stope Hotel in Yellowknife on 8 April 1967 and charged in violation of section 94(b) of the Indian Act. This section states that 'an Indian who (a) has intoxicants in his possession, (b) is intoxicated, or (c) makes or manufactures intoxicants off a reserve, is guilty of an offence and is liable on summary conviction to a fine of not less than ten dollars and not more than fifty dollars or to imprisonment for a term not exceeding three months or to both fine and imprisonment.'

Drybones pleaded guilty before Magistrate John Anderson-Thompson and was fined $10. Upon appeal to the Territorial Court, Drybones was instructed by his lawyer, Thomas Berger, to change his plea to not guilty. His counsel then argued that the Indian Act was discriminatory and in violation of the Canadian Bill of Rights. Justice William G. Morrow quashed the conviction and agreed that the Indian Act discriminated against Indians. Justice Morrow argued that, since it was not an offence for anyone except an Indian to be intoxicated otherwise than in a public place, the Indian Act denied the 'equality before the law' guaranteed by the Canadian Bill of Rights.

The Supreme Court of Canada in a 6–3 decision agreed with Morrow and the Territorial Court of Appeal. Justice Ritchie, speaking for the majority, wrote:

> I am, therefore, of opinion that an individual is denied equality before the law if it is made an offence punishable at law, on account of his race, for him to do something which his fellow Canadians are free to do without having committed any offence or having been made subject to any penalty. It is only necessary for the purpose of deciding this case for me to say that in my opinion Section 94 (b) of the Indian Act is a law of Canada which creates such an offence and that it can only be construed in such a manner that its application would operate so as to abrogate, abridge or infringe one of the rights declared and recognized by the Bill of Rights. For the reasons which I have indicated I am therefore of opinion that section 94(b) is inoperative.[155]

It was obvious even to the casual reader that this decision had all the earmarks of a major new dimension in Canadian jurisprudence. The calm with which the Canadian legal community received the decision was more akin to the calm one meets at the centre of a storm.

A synopsis of what would undoubtedly follow from this landmark decision was contained in the dissents of Chief Justice Cartwright and justices Abbott and Pigeon. Justice Pigeon's dissent was the longest of the three and raised a number of thorny problems which the judiciary and Parliament would have to confront if the implications of the decision were to prevail. He reasoned as follows: 'If one of the effects of the Canadian Bill of Rights is to render inoperative all legal provisions whereby Indians as such are not dealt with in the same way as the general public, the conclusion is inescapable that Parliament, by the enactment of the Bill, has not only fundamentally altered the status of the Indians in that indirect fashion but has also made any future use of federal legislative authority over them subject to the requirement of expressly declaring every time that the law shall operate notwithstanding the Canadian Bill of Rights. I find it very difficult to believe that Parliament so intended when enacting the Bill.'[156] Pigeon thought that the majority was rushing headlong into broad construction and warned of the danger ahead. 'In the present case, the judgments below hold in effect that Parliament in enacting the Bill has implicitly repealed not only a large part of the Indian Act but also the fundamental principle that the duty of the courts is to apply the law as written and they are in no case authorized to fail to give effect to the clearly expressed will of Parliament.' Driving the point home, Pigeon continued: 'It would be a radical departure from this basic British constitutional rule to enact that henceforth the courts are to declare inoperative all enactments that are considered as not in conformity with some legal principle stated in very general language, or rather merely enumerated without any definition.'[157] This clearly valid objection was what must have made Chief Justice Cartwright draw back from his lone dissent in the 1963 case of *Robertson and Rosetanni v. The Queen*,[158] where he argued that the Canadian Bill of Rights rendered the Lord's Day Act inoperative as infringing the free exercise of religion. In one of those rare moments in legal history, the chief justice openly confessed in the *Drybones* case that he had erred in his dissenting judgment in *Robertson and Rosetanni*.

What gives the *Drybones* case extrajudicial force is the fact that it is almost identical to a 1962 case decided by the Supreme Court of British Columbia. In the case of *Regina v. Gonzales*,[159] the British Columbia Supreme Court ruled that the Canadian Bill of Rights did not render the discriminatory clauses of the Indian Act inoperative. It was thought by some that the *Drybones* decision was one of the most important civil liberties decision in Canadian history, almost on a par with famous American case of *Brown v. the Board of Education*, 1953.[160] As Hall stated in his concurring opinion, 'the social situations in *Brown v. The Board of Education* and in the instant case are, of course, very different, but the basic philosophic concept is the same.'

But by far the most important aspect of the *Drybones* decision was that the Supreme Court of Canada confronted, for the first time, the question that had been tantalizing Canadian jurisprudence since the enactment of the Canadian Bill of Rights in 1960. That question was: How ought the courts to treat the Bill of Rights? Was it meant simply as a guide to judicial construction? Or did it provide the courts the authority to enforce fundamental freedoms throughout Canada? Justice Davey of the British Columbia Supreme Court, and the dissenting justices of the Supreme Court of Canada in the *Drybones* case, argued that the Canadian Bill of Rights was intended merely to provide a canon or rule of interpretation. Justice Ritchie and five others on the Supreme Court of Canada rejected this reasoning, claiming that the Davey view appeared to strike at the very foundations of the Bill of Rights and to convert it from its apparent character as a statutory declaration of fundamental human rights and freedoms into being little more than a rule for the construction of federal statutes.[161]

Ritchie drew upon Chief Justice Cartwright's dissent in the *Robertson and Rosetanni* case for support, especially where the Chief Justice disagreed with Justice Davey's view. In that opinion, Chief Justice Cartwright reasoned that 'it is plain that the Canadian Bill of Rights is to apply to all laws of Canada already in existence at the time it came into force as well as to those thereafter enacted. In my opinion where there is irreconcilable conflict between another Act of Parliament and the Canadian Bill of Rights, the latter must prevail.'[162] In order to escape the force of the Bill of Rights, Justice Ritchie noted that Parliament must declare that the act shall operate notwithstanding the *Canadian Bill of Rights*.'

However happy the *Drybones* decision made Canadian civil libertarians at the time, the Supreme Court of Canada later backed away from the energetic enforcement of the Bill of Rights, much to Hall's disappointment.[163] But, as Chief Justice Bora Laskin had observed long before he came to the bench, the Bill of Rights did not formally invite Canadian judges to strike down as unconstitutional statutes or procedures that offend the terms of the statute. For, however much the

Canadian Bill of Rights was viewed by some as 'a quasi-constitutional document,' it lacked teeth. As we have already seen, it instructed the courts to 'construe or apply' and 'construe and apply' the rights listed in the document.[164] As well, the *Bill of Rights* is an ordinary act of the Parliament of Canada and it applies only to the federal area of constitutional jurisdiction. Its reach excluded all provincal and municipal areas of law, making the focus very narrow. The Canadian Bill of Rights remains in force today even after the constitutional entrenchment of the Charter of Rights and Freedoms. It is superseded only where the Charter's terms supersede the terms of the Bill of Rights.[165]

Emmett Hall's concern with the rights of Canada's native peoples converged in two major cases towards the end of his term on the court, *Calder*[166] and *Lavell*.[167] In the first, Frank Calder and other members of the Nisga'a Tribal Council and four Indian bands in British Columbia brought an action against the attorney general of British Columbia claiming that the aboriginal title to their tribal territory – consisting of 1,000 square miles in and around the Nasa River valley, in northwestern British Columbia – had never been lawfully extinguished. The Indian claim was dismissed at the trial and the British Columbia Court of Appeal rejected the appeal. The case came with leave to the Supreme Court of Canada in the fall of 1971. The Court handed down its judgment on 31 January 1973; it ruled in a 4–3 decision that the appeal should be dismissed, thereby affirming the Court of Appeal ruling. The majority judgment was written by Justice Judson. Justices Hall, Spence, and Laskin dissented.

The Nisga'a argued that their claim to the property in question arose out of aboriginal occupation and that recognition of such a right is well established in English law. Furthermore, they contended that no treaty or contract with the crown or the Hudson's Bay Company had ever been entered into with respect to the area by anyone on behalf of the Nisga'a nation. Within the area, there are a number of reserves but they amount to only a small part of the total band; the Nisga'a did not agree to or accept the creation of these reserves. The Nisga'a further argued that they held title to the lands by virtue of Royal Proclamation of 1763, which extended protection to all Indians living under the sovereignty of the British crown. The proclamation stated: 'And whereas it is just and reasonable, and essential to our Interest, and the Security of our Colonies, that the several Nations or Tribes of Indians with whom We are connected, and who live under our Protection, should not be molested or disturbed in the Possession of such Parts of our Dominions

224 Aggressive in Pursuit: The Life of Justice Emmett Hall

and Territories as, not having been ceded to or purchased by Us, are reserved to them, or any of them, as their Hunting Grounds.'[168]

Justice Judson said that, on the basis of *St. Catherines Milling and Lumber Co. v. The Queen*,[169] 'the Crown had at all times a present proprietary estate, which title, after confederation, was in the Province, by virtue of s. 109 of the B.N.A. Act. The Indian title was a mere burden upon that title which, following the cession of the lands under treaty, was extinguished.'[170] Judson reasoned further that 'the Nishga bands represented by the appellants were not any of the several nations or tribes of Indians who lived under British protection and were outside the scope of the Proclamation.'[171] The territory now comprising British Columbia did not come under British sovereignty until the Treaty of Oregon in 1846. When the colony of British Columbia was established in 1858, the Nisga'a territory became part of it. It entered into Confederation in 1871, bringing with it all the territory including the Nisga'a lands. And, on the basis of the *St. Catherines Milling* judgment, Justice Judson ruled that the Proclamation of 1763 had been superseded in 1871 when British Columbia entered Confederation.

But Judson had a great deal more difficulty in disposing of the Nisga'a claim to title by virtue of their having occupied the territory for centuries. He acknowledged not only the fact of occupancy but also the fact this occupancy was the basis of the claim to ownership.[172] However, he said, the British Columbia courts ruled that this right or title had been lawfully extinguished when British Columbia set apart reserves for Indians upon entry into Confederation. Indeed, title was extinguished before Confederation, in 1858 and 1861; Justice Judson showed that the Indian territories had been specifically dealt with and acquired by the crown in those years. Judson concluded that 'the sovereign authority elected to exercise complete domination over the lands in question adverse to any right of occupancy which the Nishga Tribe might have had, when, by legislation, it opened up such lands for settlement, subject to the reserves of land set aside for Indian occupation.'[173]

Justice Hall, in a lengthy judgment in which Spence and Laskin concurred, wrote that the Nisga'a did have title to the lands in question because, contrary to the court majority, this title had never been lawfully extinguished. He began by showing that, unlike most other Indian tribes throughout Canada, the Nisga'a had never entered into a treaty or deed of surrender with anyone; nor had they ever been conquered.

For Hall, the question was clear: Did the crown lawfully extinguish the Nisga'a title to the lands in question? He noted that the Nisga'a were not challenging the right of the crown to extinguish their title; nor were they seeking compensation for loss of title. His judgment contained long citations from the trial court transcripts, the purpose of which was to show that the trial judge's efforts to relate the Nisga'a concept of ownership of real property to the conventional common law elements of ownership was inhibited by 'a preoccupation with the traditional *indicia* of ownership.'[174] He pointed out that Lord Haldane had cautioned against just such a problem many years earlier. The trial judge 'overlooked that possession is of itself proof of ownership. *Prima facie*, therefore, the Nishgas are the owners of the lands that have been in their possession from time immemorial and, therefore, the burden of establishing that their right has been extinguished rests squarely on the respondent.'[175] There was no doubt in his mind that the evidence supported the claim that the Nisga'a possessed the lands in question. But he was concerned about the manner in which title to the lands was alleged to have been extinguished, if, indeed, they had ever been formally extinguished. He then went on to show that there were treaties with Indians in British Columbia and the Northwest Territories after Confederation; Treaty No. 8, for example, was made in 1889. 'Surely the Canadian treaties, made with much solemnity on behalf of the Crown, were intended to extinguish the Indian title. What other purpose did they serve?'[176] He further noted that the Proclamation of 1763 did indeed serve as a Magna Carta for Indians. 'The Proclamation,' he said, 'must be regarded as a fundamental document upon which any just determination of original rights rests.'[177] That proclamation was pertinent to the case and the Supreme Court had never directly dealt with it. The time had come, he said, to do so. He began by showing how the British Columbia Court of Appeal registered conflicting views on the matter. The main British Columbia precedent was *Regina v. White and Bob* in 1965. In that decision the court majority, led by justices F.A. Sheppard and Arthur Lord, claimed that the proclamation did not apply to Vancouver Island. But Justice T.G. Norris claimed that it did: 'The royal proclamation of 1763 was declatory and confirmatory of the aboriginal rights and applied to Vancouver Island.'[178]

The trial judge in the *Calder* case had adopted the court majority's opinion in *White and Bob*. Hall claimed that, in his view, 'the opinion of Sheppard in *White and Bob* was based on incomplete research as to the state of knowledge of the existence of the land mass between the Rocky Mountains and the Pacific Ocean in 1763.'[179] This led him into an extensive review of the history of that part of British Columbia as well as a close scrutiny of the proclamation. He concluded at length that it 'cannot be challenged that while the west coast lands were mostly unexplored as of 1763 they were certainly known to exist and that fact is borne out by the wording of the paragraph in the Proclamation previously quoted.'[180]

The previous steps were merely prelude to the next important question: 'Were the rights either at common law or under the Proclamation extinguished?'[181] He insisted that, once aboriginal title is established, then it must be proven that this title was lawfully extinguished. The evidence clearly established the aboriginal title to the lands, to the Court minority's satisfaction. Was this title extinguished and, if so, how? The 'how' of extinguishment was very important to him. 'It [Indian title] being a legal right, it could not thereafter be extinguished except by surrender to the Crown by competent legislative authority, and then only by specific legislation.'[182]

Hall looked for clear and plain legislation confirming extinguishment and could find none. Above all, he concluded, the respondent attorney general of British Columbia had failed to prove that the crown had in fact extinguished Indian title. 'There is no such proof in the case at bar; no legislation to that effect.'[183] Hall was here reminding the government that more than inference from past acts was required to establish *de jure* extinguishment; the Privy Council precedents all made that clear. By implication, the attorney general of British Columbia was asking the Court to demand that the Nisga'a prove that their land claims were not extinguished by the crown. In Hall's view, this was backwards: the 'onus of proving' rested on the crown to prove that these claims had been extinguished.

The respondent had rested his case on what was done by governors James Douglas and Frederick Seymour and the Council of British Columbia. Calder and his associates argued that neither Douglas nor Seymour nor the Council of the colony of British Columbia had the authority to extinguish Indian title. And Hall agreed with this. After reviewing the relevant commissions, enactments and ordinances presented on behalf of the respondent, he concluded:

If in any of the Proclamations or actions of Douglas, Seymour or of the Council of the Colony of British Columbia there are elements which the respondent says extinguish by implication the Indian title, then it is obvious from the Commission of the Governor and from the Instructions under which the Governor was required to observe and neither the Commission nor the Instructions contain any power or authorization to extinguish the Indian title, then it follows logically that if any attempt was made to extinguish the title it was beyond the power of the Governor or of the Council to do so and, therefore, *ultra vires*.[184]

The Supreme Court panel of seven justices split three against the appeal and three in favour of it, with one, Justice Pigeon, ruling against Calder on technical grounds. Justice Hall's judgment in the *Calder* case, in many respects, meant more to him than his dissent in *Truscott*. How he wished it could have been the majority judgment; he could think of no better way to end his career as a judge than to see a long-standing injustice to native peoples corrected. But he was denied that pleasure because Justice Pigeon ruled that Calder's appeal should be denied on the ground that he had not followed the provincial Crown Procedure Act's requirement that any party bringing action against the provincial crown must first obtain the provincial government's permission to do so.[185] This was particularly upsetting because of the wide public importance of the issues attached to the case. Pigeon's approach could not have been further from his; to Hall, it represented a legal manoeuvre that avoided the central issue.

Did Hall's *Calder* judgment have any appreciable impact on subsequent negotiations with native peoples in Canada? The plaque under the bust of Emmett Hall at the University of Saskatchewan College of Law lists his judgment in *Calder* as one of his achievements and claims that it has 'formed the basis for Indian land claims' in Canada ever since. This may well be true, for Prime Minister Pierre Trudeau met with Frank Calder on 8 August 1973 and discussed the issue of land claims at great length. The *Calder* case must surely have been a topic of their conversation.[186] Shortly after that meeting, Daniel Raunet has reported, the minister of Indian affairs, Jean Chrétien, 'announced a complete about-face on the land claims issue.' After heated discussion in Parliament of the *Calder* case,[187] the government of Canada promised that negotiations would be opened with all groups which had never signed treaties and were still using their traditional territories. The minister was careful, however, not to promise any land concessions, settling for a vague formula that stated his willingness 'to deal with claims related to the loss of traditional use and occupancy of lands where Native title has never been extinguished by treaty or superseded by law.'[188] This reformulation of government policy clearly reflected the sentiments of Hall's *Calder* judgment but neither Trudeau nor

Chrétien ever retreated from the general policy statement made by the prime minister on the subject of native land claims in August 1969. At that time, Trudeau said:

> But aboriginal rights, this really means saying, 'We were here before you. You came and you took the land from us and perhaps you cheated us by giving us some worthless things in return for vast expanses of land and we want to reopen this question. We want you to preserve our aboriginal rights and to restore them to us.' And our answer ... our answer is 'No.' If we think of restoring aboriginal rights to the Indians, well what about the French who were defeated at the Plains of Abraham? Shouldn't we restore rights to them? And what about the Acadians who were deported – shouldn't we compensate for this? And what about the other Canadians, the immigrants? What about the Japanese Canadians who were so badly treated at the end or during the last war? What can we do to redeem the past? I can only say as President Kennedy said when he was asked about what he would do to compensate for the injustices that the Negroes had received in American society. We will be just in our time. This is all we can do. We must be just today.[189]

Despite these reservations, Sidney L. Harring has observed that 'since 1973, when the Supreme Court of Canada in *Calder* first recognized aboriginal title as a legal right derived from the Indians' historic occupation of their tribal lands, and, nine years later, with the patriation of the Canadian constitution with its recognition of "existing aboriginal rights," there have been significant changes in the basic doctrine of the Canadian law of aboriginal rights along with a renewed interest by legal scholars in these matters.'[190]

However effective or ineffective Hall's *Calder* judgment may have been, one thing is clear: he had championed the cause of Canadian native peoples – on and off the bench – for many years, and he welcomed the opportunity to do something about it in his capacity as a judge. It was one subject that he often spoke about off the bench. In January 1969, for example, he spoke to the Women's Canadian Club in Ottawa on 'Social Justice: Safeguard of Human Rights.'[191] A major theme of this talk was the poor treatment of Canadian native peoples. He asked, pointedly, 'Is the Indian on or off the reserve free? Free in the social and economic sense that he may talk and work in dignity? We all know the answer.' He argued forcefully against an education that would lead to native assimilation and extinction. 'Today's Indians are descendants of the oldest residents of Canada,' he reminded his audience, 'whose traditional cultures have been made increasingly inoperative in the changing environment of the individual in society and who, in the historical process of European settlement and development, have not acquired the technological, economic, and political skills necessary to share in the affluent society.'[192] What was required, he said, was innovative educational programs that would 'facilitate a successful and rewarding economic, social and cultural integration of both individuals and communities of Indian ancestry.'[193] He made a similar passionate plea on behalf of Canadian Inuit, whose conditions he described as 'inhuman.' After noting the deplorable infant mortality rate and the abysmal living conditions throughout many Inuit communities, he called for serious social-welfare reforms in the interests of human rights. 'I said what I believe in the *Health Charter for Canadians* in 1964. I have no desire to add to or to delete from that *Charter*.' Citing Lord Ritchie-Calder, professor of international relations at the University of Edinburgh, Hall concluded that 'freedom begins with breakfast; the emaciated slave dies in the ditch from starvation.' Emmett Hall said much the same thing in his two major non-judicial writings, the *Report of the Royal Commission on Health Services* and *Report of the Provincial Committee on Aims and Objectives of Education in the Schools in Ontario.*

8

More Work in Retirement

The picture of Emmett Hall sitting idle in retirement back home in Saskatoon was, for those who knew him, a difficult one to imagine. Certainly, had he wanted to, he could have settled in and relished his past achievements, which were considerable for any one man. Apart from his contributions to the development of the law, he had established his place as the man responsible for the implementation of a national health-care program in Canada. Clearly, this is the one area in which Emmett Hall's name will be permanently recorded in Canadian history. His monumental royal commission study of 1964 not only led to Canada's universal medicare service but quickly became a classic in the field and is still consulted widely throughout the world.

Yet Hall, a man of unbounded energy, was not one to rest on his laurels in retirement. But what would he do? As much as he enjoyed the occasional trip to faraway places, such as Egypt, he had never liked to lounge on a beach or sit still for very long. There is no question that Belle was anxious for them to return to Saskatoon and take up family life where they had left it before moving to Ottawa and the Supreme Court of Canada. But, whereas most people look forward to resuming in retirement one or more of their hobbies, be it sailing, golfing, reading, or gardening, Hall had no outside interests. His whole life was bound up with the law – with side-forays into education and medicine – the very things that marked his professional life for more than fifty years. Fortunately for him, people knew this and sought him out in retirement. They engaged his services in matters ranging from court reform to 'trains and grains' in the west, a reassessment of health care, and analysis of the impact of free trade on the national health program.

ACADEMIC, LABOUR, AND JUDICIAL MATTERS

Upon retiring from the Supreme Court of Canada at the end of February 1973, and returning to Saskatoon that spring, Hall was scarcely settled in his penthouse apartment on Spadina Crescent when he was called upon 'to examine and assess the entire court structure in Saskatchewan and its utilization and to consider possible measures for the restructuring and re-organization of the courts.'[1] In addition to this broad mandate, he was instructed to make recommendations on the prospects of a unified family court and on a program of continuing education for judges. Hall embraced the challenge readily. His life was the law and he willingly accepted the opportunity to review the court structure of his home province; he knew the courts of Saskatchewan and had a number of ideas about how they might be restructured.

But no sooner had he agreed to undertake this study than Hall was called upon by Premier Allan Blakeney to put out a brush fire relating to the University of Saskatchewan. Until this time, the Regina campus had been administered as an extension of the University of Saskatchwan in Saskatoon. But, as the Regina campus enrolments expanded and as the ambitions of its faculty grew, this arrangement began to chafe and finally issued in a call for full university status for the Regina campus. The NDP government of Allan Blakeney was sympathetic and hastily introduced legislation to sever the campus's ties with Saskatoon and establish an autonomous University of Regina. The public outcry in opposition to the move – especially in Saskatoon – was totally unexpected; the ancestral rivalries between Regina and Saskatoon came quickly to the surface and the government retreated. Blakeney called upon Hall for his advice in the matter, asking him to investigate and report back as quickly as possible. Hall took up the challenge and, after consulting with the parties, especially at the Regina campus, recommended that the government proceed with the plan as initially proposed in the legislation. In doing so, Emmett Hall incurred the enmity of his old friend and sponsor, John G. Diefenbaker, who just happened to be the chancellor of the University of Saskatchewan. From that moment on, there was a frost in the relationship between these old friends. Shortly after he tabled his recommendations, Hall later recalled, Diefenbaker exploded at him: 'What are you doing to my University?' Diefenbaker reminded Hall that the original agreement struck in 1905 was that Regina would get the legislature of the new province and Saskatoon would get the provincial university. Hall knew this, of course, but believed that changing demographics required that Regina have its own fully fledged university. Diefenbaker never forgave him.

After he had weathered this storm and was about to turn his attention to the court reorganization study, Hall received a call from John Munro, the federal minister of labour, asking him to arbitrate a railway strike that had brought the country almost to a complete standstill in the summer of 1973. Fifty-five thousand unionized 'non-operating' workers (those not directly employed in operating trains) across Canada closed down ferries, stranded thousands of summer tourists, and halted grain transportation and manufacturing. Auto-parts companies could not deliver their products to the assembly plants in Ontario, causing layoffs. Two thousand striking railway workers stormed the centre bloc of Parliament, injuring one security guard and breaking windows. After two attempts to settle the strike had failed, Parliament was recalled on 29 August and legislation was passed establishing an arbitration board and ordering workers back to their jobs.

At an emergency meeting of Labour Minister Munro and senior members of his department, one official suggested the name of Emmett Hall, who had just retired from the Supreme Court, as a possible arbitrator. Munro pounced on the suggestion and called Hall immediately. Hall was surprised and flattered by the call but said he was in the midst of an important study of the Saskatchewan court system. Munro pressed on him the urgency of the crisis. Hall replied that he would have to talk with Premier Blakeney first and would get back to the minister promptly. The Saskatchewan premier urged him to take the arbitration; the court reorganization could wait. Hall called Munro and accepted the responsibility to arbitrate the strike even though he reminded the minister that he had acted for the railway companies in the 'featherbedding' dispute of 1957. He felt that he might not be acceptable to the unions. Munro told him not to worry, that he had been sounding out union officials and that he would be accepted. It was Hall's reputation for fairness that continued to win for him the support of these hard-bargaining union leaders. And their trust was not to be misplaced.

Hall received his mandate as arbitrator on 6 September 1973. He immediately called his old friend Ken Campbell in Ottawa and asked him to come on board as his right-hand man. Hall left for Ottawa and met with Campbell the next day and together they put together a staff. One week later, on Friday, 14 September, he began to meet the parties to the dispute. From September to the end of November, the arbitrator held thirty-one meetings: seventeen with the non-operating representatives, nine with the shopcraft unions, and five with representatives of the trainmen. The central issue was, of course, wage rates and pension benefits. Railway workers throughout Canada claimed that their wages had fallen behind those of other workers in allied industries. The railway companies argued that Parliament had frozen their ability to charge their customers and hence they were not in a position to meet the union demands. Initially, the unions had demanded an increase of fifty-five cents an hour in the first year of a contract; later, in 1973, they scaled back the demand to thirty cents an hour, with an increase of 8 per cent the next year of the contract. Hall listened patiently to both sides to this important dispute throughout the thirty-one days of hearings. He had an astonishing capacity to listen to hours of tedious – and frequently repetitive – representations relating to the minutiae of job-security plans and skill and shift differentials. A full range of issues were paraded before the arbitrator: pleadings relating to health and safety matters, paid meal rates, annual vacations, retirement, and isolation-location pay. It quickly became clear to union leaders that this arbitrator was not only listening but was sympathetic to their case. Yet he was not subservient in any way. When, for example, union lawyers claimed that he did not have jurisdiction under his order-in-council to consider the railway company's proposal to reduce train crews, Hall reviewed the relevant statutes and rejected the union arguments.

On matters relating to safety, however, Hall was especially vigilant. The companies pointed out that the unions had agreed that crews be reduced in passenger and yard service operations. Why not extend the same reductions to all freight services? The unions 'produced cogent evidence' that serious accidents had occurred to employees in the caboose through what is called 'slack action, when a conductor or brakeman was thrown violently against or even through the window of the cupola.'[2] On the other hand, Hall noted that there was 'merit in the Companies' proposal. Times and conditions have changed. Technology has improved. The workload of the conductor is much less than it was, his paper-work virtually eliminated. The incidence of "hotboxes" is now minimal.'[3] Nevertheless, after taking all the factors into consideration, he concluded that 'more needs to be done by the Railways in the way of safety measures before implementation of the rule asked for can be decreed.'[4] He urged that the unions and the companies get together and iron out reasonable guidelines.

In the final round of hearings, Hall made a concession to the companies in the way of restructuring and reordering operations in light of the new centralized electronic-terminal systems being developed. He always showed himself prepared to accommodate new technologies and the efficiencies they brought. But, in the matter of money, he gave the unions almost everything they asked for. While the companies grumbled a bit, the unions were delighted with his report. Emmett Hall had shown himself, once again, according to Bob White of the Canadian Labour Congress, 'a friend of the working man.'

Immediately upon completion of this arbitration report, Emmett Hall, to no one's surprise but to the annoyance of Belle, returned to his study of the Saskatchewan court system. His wife was, understandably, resentful that others – no matter how important – still commanded the attention of her husband more than she could; she wanted more quiet time at home with him and their friends, and she thought that she had earned the rest. But Emmett simply could not bring himself to sit still and play bridge. He thrived on work. And so, with characteristic energy, he gave his full attention to court reorganization and, eleven months after submitting his railway-arbitration report, he submitted his court-reorganization report to the government of Saskatchewan, in December 1974, two days before Christmas. The report was a comprehensive examination of the judicial process in Saskatchewan from the level of the justice of the peace to the Court of Appeal. His major criticisms and recommendations were directed towards the magistrates' courts and the district courts. But he also proposed modifications to the family courts of Saskatchewan.

As in other provinces – following the terms of the Constitution Act, 1867 – magistrates in Saskatchewan are appointed by the provincial governments and their salaries are fixed by the lieutenant governor-in-council. At the time of Hall's 1974 report, Saskatchewan magistrates were paid $27,000 per year. Only three other provinces paid their magistrates less than Saskatchewan: Nova Scotia, Prince Edward Island, and Manitoba. Ontario judges of the Provincial Court of Criminal Jurisdiction – the equivalent of magistrates – received $10,000 more per year than their counterparts in Saskatchewan. Hall made no recommendation to increase the salaries of magistrates but did recommend that a chief justice of the magistrates' courts be appointed. The government adopted that recommendation immediately and appointed

Ernest Boychuk, former ombudsman for Saskatchewan, as the first chief judge.

In Hall's view, the magistrates' court was the most important court in the mind of the public; it was in this court that the majority of cases were tried. In 1973–4, the magistrates' courts in Saskatchewan handled 156,620 cases, involving everything from small claims to criminal matters. The provincial treasury received, through fines levied in the magistrates' courts in the same year, $3,456,397.74. The operating costs of those courts for the same time was $860,210.76. Thus, magistrates' court not only 'paid their way' but contributed significantly to the provincial treasury.

The magistrate's jurisdiction and power over sentencing are wide. The magistrate has, in effect, jurisdiction (with consent) to try all indictable offences except those – such as treason, murder, sedition, and so forth – which have been expressly excluded from his or her purview. If conviction follows, a magistrate has power to impose sentences ranging up to life imprisonment. Despite the enormous importance of this level of the judicial hierarchy, magistrates have, by and large, not received much public recognition. As Hall noted in his report: 'With all this tremendous load of work and responsibility the Magistrates Courts are and have been treated throughout Canada, except those in Quebec, more as a branch of the Civil Service than as a necessary and an important component of the Judicial system – an historical outgrowth of the time when it was known as "the police court" and manned by lay Justices of the Peace.'[5]

Hall suggested that the first step towards enhancing the status and reputation of the magistrates' courts would be to discontinue the practice of housing these courts in police buildings. 'There should be a clear separation of the police function from the adjudicative process of the court,' he counselled. The magistrates' court must be viewed, he urged, as the 'peoples court; and the people who pass through it or who work in it are entitled to do so in dignity.'[6] He provided a sketch of the poor conditions under which most magistrates in Saskatchewan worked: 'Except in a few places where the Court has access to facilities in some Provincial Courthouses, the magistrates carry on their judicial functions in an amazing variety of dance halls, legion halls, church basements and other premises which are virtually firetraps with no plumbing, erratic heating, no witness rooms, poor acoustics, all contributing to a lowering in the public mind of the administration of justice as a public function.'[7] The housing provided for magistrates must have reminded him of his first visit, many years ago, to the dilapidated former stable that then housed the Supreme Court of Canada in Ottawa. Hall's report placed a high priority on adequate premises for magistrates.

The major substantive recommendation of his report, however, related to the right, under the Criminal Code, of an accused or the crown to appeal from a magistrate's decision on summary conviction and have a complete rehearing of the case by a district court judge. To Hall, 'the trial *de novo* concept is an historical carry-over from the days of the lay Justices of the Peace. It seems to me an unnecessary duplication of the judicial process in this era of a competent and legally trained bench.'[8] In earlier times, such courts were presided over by laymen, untrained in the law. By the 1970s, however, all magistrates were trained lawyers and hence far more learned in the law.

Hall noted in his report the incongruity of the procedure governing appeals from judges of the magistrates' courts in respect to indictable offences which go direct to the Court of Appeal on the record. These are appeals on matters much graver than those in summary-conviction proceedings. It appeared anomalous to Hall that the appeal as to the lesser offences should be more formal and expensive – involving as it did a complete retrial – than the appeal on convictions that may carry life sentences. The new procedure would, of course, mean that the magistrate's court would become a court of record. This ought to be the case, in Hall's mind, and he saw no problem in establishing such a procedure with the increased cost associated with the move.

The reorganization of the district courts involved matters of an entirely different nature. These courts were established by the District Court Act of Saskatchewan[9] and their judges were appointed by the federal government, which also paid their salaries, as prescribed by the Constitution Act, 1867. The Saskatchewan Act provided for eighteen judges, with jurisdiction throughout the province in twenty-one judicial centres. These courts were inferior courts subject to the overall supervision of the Court of Queen's Bench. The rules relating to pleadings, practice and procedure, and process and forms in the Court of Queen's Bench also apply in the district courts. District court judges had, at the time, jurisdiction in a wide variety of civil matters, such as contract, torts, and recovery of personal property under $5,000. They did not have jurisdiction over matters relating to title to land, libel, slander, and actions against a justice of the peace or any other peace officer.

Hall was fully conscious of the fact that he was conducting an inquiry into court structure at a time when there was considerable discussion throughout the country of the need for a unified family court system. The general proposal being considered at the time in several provinces was for a single large court – in effect an amalgamation of the district court, the provincial family courts, and the Court of Queen's Bench – with various sections responsible for different subjects. The proposals were aimed principally, although not exclusively, at eliminating the problems confronting divorce and matrimonial cases. Under the prevailing arrangement, parties had to go to at least two different courts to secure a divorce and to arrange custody and support matters; in the first instance, one had to go to the Court of Queen's Bench and, in the second, to the provincial family court. This necessarily meant duplication and, hence, increased costs to litigants.

Hall gave the question of amalgamation serious thought and careful study; he was aware that it was favoured widely throughout the county and district courts of Ontario and in several other provinces. He noted that the Ontario Law Reform Commission had rejected the proposal. At length, he came to the decision to recommend against amalgamation on the ground that it would take the section 96 courts – courts staffed by judges appointed by the federal government – further away from the people. 'To abolish the District Court by having it and its judges absorbed into the Queen's Bench would leave only the Magistrate's Courts really accessible to the average citizen and would result in a demand to give the Magistrates much of the jurisdiction now reposing in the District Court when the Magistrate's Courts were already overloaded, particularly if the Unified Family Court proposal is implemented *as I think it should be* and given the extended jurisdiction recommended in my interim report.'[10] He also recommended that a chief judge be appointed for the district courts, with the supervisory functions then performed by the chief justice of the Court of Queen's Bench. Finally, Hall recommended that the district court judge be given jurisdiction to try actions in divorce and matrimonial cases – as was the practice in British Columbia, Alberta, Ontario, and Manitoba. They should also be made local judges of the Queen's Bench.

Emmett Hall, in the course of his many inquiries, only once issued an interim report; he always felt that he would have more effect if he issued a single, comprehensive final one. The one exception was an interim report on the concept of a unified family court for Saskatchewan which he submitted to Roy J. Romanow, attorney general of the province, on 18 November 1974,[11] a little more than a month before he submitted his final report on court reorganization. Much effort went into this interm report. He conferred with the Canadian Law Reform Commission and especially with Julien D. Payne, project director of the family law project for the commission. He studied the mass of material on the question of a unified family court which Payne made available to him. He consulted as well Justice Thomas Berger of the Supreme Court of British Columbia and spent two days observing the inauguration of the British Columbia pilot project. He travelled to Edmonton and northern Alberta to observe the family court in operation there.

Not content with examining the Canadian proposals and practices, Hall went to England and consulted with Lord Scarman, former chairman of the English Law Commission, and several others actively involved in family court administration. He was at this time in his seventy-sixth year, when most people would be enjoying their retirement. But not Emmett Hall. He undertook the rigours of travel, as we shall see, into his eighties on behalf of charitable causes.

In his interim report, Hall drew attention to the recommendation of the Saskatchewan section of the family law committee of the Canadian Bar Association. Both the Saskatchewan section and the national CBA had recommended the establishment of at least one pilot project so as to test the most effective means for providing facilities and services. The Saskatchewan bar's recommendation, however, proposed that the district court be vested with exclusive jurisdiction over all family law matters. Hall agreed with the Saskatchewan bar's diagnosis of the problem and the need for a solution. But he disagreed with the recommendation. 'It is my firm opinion,' he wrote, 'that for Saskatchewan a Unified Family Court should be sited in the *Provincial Court* rather than in the District Court,'[12] although he was prepared to permit district court judges to try divorce and matrimonial cases, as we saw earlier.

The main reason why he proposed that the magistrate's court be the place for a unified family court was because in his view a partnership between that court and the province's Social Service Department was essential and such a partnership could be accomplished only in the less structured climate of a magistrate's court. 'The joint concern of the legal and the social workers must be integrated into a court that aims to deal successfully with family problems.'[13] Hall was apparently concerned that these family problems be resolved within the community and not merely through the legal process. In other words, he saw family-law problems more as social than legal problems and he believed that they were better resolved in an informal atmosphere.

One major characteristic of Hall's recommendation was to keep the appointment of family court judges under the jurisdiction of the provincial government. He noted in his report that the magistrates' court was already the court in which jurisdiction under the Juvenile Delinquents Act was exercised; this matter was an aspect of family law. He recommended that the new family court be the court where summary conviction offences such as assaults involving the members of the family, including child beating and other interspousal offences of a criminal nature, were tried.

But Hall made it clear by implication that some family law matters – such as divorce – should be tried in *two* courts. This was one of the major defects of the present system that his recommendations did not remove, to the surprise of many. As we have seen, he advised in his final report that district court judges be given jurisdiction in divorce and other matters. He recognized that this would add greatly to the work load of the district court, but he thought that the courts could bear the load. He also recommended that a family court pilot project be undertaken in Saskatoon as an initial step leading to full provincial implementation. Following the establishment of such a unified court in Saskatoon, the government should establish one in Regina and at later times in larger cities such as Moose Jaw, Prince Albert, Swift Current, and Yorkton.

The remainder of the interim report was given over to details of the pilot project such as where in the Saskatoon courthouse the new family court might be housed and other matters such as court personnel, including the need to appoint judges of 'high personal integrity with a reputation for that integrity throughout the community.'[14]

Hall clearly understood that what compounded the problem of attempting to unify the family court in Canada were the provisions of the British North America Act, 1867, which divided the jurisdiction over the organization of courts and the appointment of judges between the two levels of government. Section 92(14) grants exclusive provincial legislative jurisdiction over 'the administration of Justice in the Province, including the Constitution, Maintenance, and Organization of Provincial Courts, both Civil and of Criminal Jurisdiction, and including Procedure in Civil Matters in those Courts.'[15] The federal government, on the other hand, is given jurisdiction over the appointment of judges 'of the Superior, District and County Courts in each province, except those of the Courts of Probate in Nova Scotia and New Brunswick.'[16] The federal government is also given exclusive jurisdiction over the criminal law of Canada.[17]

Hall took note of these jurisdictional problems in his report: 'Implementation of a Unified Family Court of the kind now being proposed
would entail amendments to many Provincial Statutes, the object of
which would be to give the court jurisdiction in all those matters affect-
ing the family within the competence of the Provincial Legislature. The
Province cannot give its *provincial* judges jurisdiction in divorce or as
regards maintenance and/or custody as incidental thereto, nor in matters, covered by the Criminal Code and certain Federal Statutes, but
even with these Legislatures can confer jurisdiction to a Provincial
Court.'[18] Critics of this proposal viewed the perpetuation of the need to
go to two courts as a major weakness of the Hall program. He was fully
aware of the criticisms he was receiving but he felt that the advantages
of having the family court close to the community outweighed the
disadvantages of two courts. Hall's proposal for a unified family court
was adopted by the government and became a reality in 1978.

One critic of the Hall proposal for a unified family court for
Saskatchewan dismissed it with the comment that Emmett Hall was
'getting on in years.' The implication was that, had he been a younger
man, he would have seen the virtue of a unified family court at the
district court level. The assessment was as inadequate as it was facile.
Emmett Hall continued to possess, as Chief Justice Bora Laskin noted,
'one of the youngest and most innovative minds in Canada.'[19]

One final recommendation of Hall's report on the court structure in
Saskatchewan related to his long-standing concern for native peoples.
Since more than 90 per cent of all charges brought against native people
and those not familiar with the English language are dealt with in
magistrates' courts, Hall saw a need for qualified court attendants and
interpreters. He felt that those who do not understand English plead
guilty to a charge without fully understanding its nature; hence, they
sometimes err in electing one procedure over another without understanding what they are doing. He wanted to see this problem remedied
by the appointment of native court workers.

GRAINS AND TRAINS IN WESTERN CANADA

Shortly after Emmett Hall submitted his final report on court reorganization, Otto Lang, the federal minister of transportation who was also
responsible for the Canadian Wheat Board, commissioned him, under
the Public Inquiries Act, 'to inquire into the rail needs of communities,
the economies of a modernized rail system and the probable conduct of

producers and elevator companies in changing circumstances for the purpose of making recommendations concerning the future role of that portion of the rail network identified for further evaluation.' Hall received able assistance in his task with the appointment of R.H. Cowan of Rosetown, Saskatchewan, Lloyd Stewart of Rock Glen, Saskatchewan, and Rheinhold Lehr of Medicine Hat, Alberta. Two years to the day after he was appointed chief commissioner, Hall completed, on 18 April 1977, a massive report – *Grain and Rail in Western Canada* – on the problems facing grain transportation in the west. The 545-page report consisted of a detailed examination of grain transportation in western Canada and was hailed throughout the west as an economic charter. True to his past performance, the Hall report on grainhandling and transportation on the prairies was a solidly researched and carefully prepared study of a complex problem. His mandate was to come to terms with the major problems of train transportation in western Canada. The difficulties involved in getting Canadian grain to international markets had been with prairie producers from the beginning of grain production in western Canada. Unlike many other grain-producing countries, Canada is almost completely dependent upon rail transport to move grain from where it is grown to where it can be delivered to its customers. The grain-producing prairies of western Canada are almost 800 miles from the nearest port, surrounded by formidable geographic barriers: on the west, the Rocky Mountains; on the north, a waterway normally used only twelve weeks a year; and on the east, the rugged terrain of the Canadian Shield and a river system open only about eight months of each year.

What compounded the problems over the years was the rapid increase in productivity on the part of the prairie grain and oilseed industry. Three years in succession, the production reached almost one billion bushels annually, and yet the transportation facilities – boxcars, terminals, elevators – were the same as they had been fifty years earlier, when production had been significantly lower. This is not to say that grain and rail matters had not been studied in the past. No other aspect of Canadian industry can claim to have received as much official scrutiny as the railway industry. Starting in 1899 with the Sankler commission, there had been no fewer than twelve major federal royal commissions, or inquiries, into the grain industry and grain-transportation problems in Canada. Hall's was to be the thirteenth, and he was determined to see the major problems addressed and remedied.

What became clear from the outset of his investigation was that Hall did not view the problem simply as an economic one which, once solved, would bring benefits to the prairies. For him, the major aspect of the problem was that there were communities that depended on branch lines for vital hospital and school contact with major centres such as Regina, Saskatoon, Prince Albert, and Moose Jaw. He could not blithely, without any overall plan, cut off miles of branch lines because their continued maintenance was costly to the railways. The termination of rail service to remote communities would have more serious consequences than just forcing farmers to truck their grain long distances to elevators in major centres; it could mean the death of some of those towns, such as St Walberg, with a population of 135. With almost 20,000 miles of railway tracks criss-crossing the three prairie provinces, the transportation challenges confronting Hall were dauntingly complex.

The Hall commission held four kinds of public hearings: global hearings, conducted over twenty-five days, where the railway companies, the grain companies, the provincial governments, farm and labour organizations, and so on were invited to express their views; local hearings, which were conducted in seventy-seven small towns throughout the three prairie provinces and through which the commission received 1,180 briefs in ninety days; regional hearings, which were designed to explore the problems in regional terms and at which the commission received 111 briefs in twenty-seven days. Final hearings were held in Saskatoon, Edmonton, and Vancouver; these meetings lasted sixteen days and at them the commission received forty-one briefs.

Before making any recommendations, the Hall commission sketched the history of railway development in western Canada, beginning with the formation of the Canadian Pacific Railway in 1870, when Sir John A. Macdonald had promised a national railway as an inducement to British Columbia to enter Confederation. Afterwards, the rail network of branch lines became important for the expanded wheat production of the prairie provinces. With the increase in both came the increase in grain elevators, where farmers stored and washed their grain in preparation for export. At the time of the commission, there were 3,964 elevators with a storage capacity of 344 million bushels. The peak handling period occurred in 1971–2, when over one billion bushels of grain moved through 4,383 elevators.

Grain was shipped from the prairie elevators to five main port terminals: Thunder Bay, Vancouver, Victoria, Prince Rupert, and Churchill. These terminals had been constructed in 1935, and, unfortunately for the grain industry, their capacity had increased only slightly since then.

For example, the total capacity of terminals in Thunder Bay, Churchill, Prince Rupert, and Vancouver in 1935 was 118.2 million bushels; in 1976 it was only 122.2 million bushels. At the time of Hall's inquiry, the Canadian Wheat Board was conducting an incentive program to encourage the construction of additional storage capacity – sufficient to handle eleven million bushels in Vancouver and three million in Prince Rupert.

The commission gave explicit attention to the social and community implications of railway abandonment by holding,[20] as we have seen, meetings in small towns and villages throughout the prairie provinces. Hall and his colleagues listened intently and sympathetically to the many pleas to continue the branch lines. Yet, at the same time, the evidence was mounting against the practicality of retaining thousands of miles of branch lines to small and economically inefficient towns and hamlets.

Most people agreed with the commission's finding that the railway network was overbuilt in western Canada. Earlier in the century, when the prairie provinces were growing at a rapid rate, rail lines had been laid in virtually every direction and, as Emmett Hall recognized, small hamlets and villages had grown up as a direct result.[21] Since that time, elevator facilities with greatly increased storage capacity had appeared – which meant that fewer elevators were needed. The increase in productivity and the efforts to speed up the delivery of grain rendered the numerous small elevators obsolete.

The commission eventually concluded that many small towns and hamlets were not as dependent on railways as they once were. The advent of cars, trucks, and buses had meant the decline in importance of the train. As the report said: 'Good transportation is a necessary condition for the development and growth of most industries and businesses. It is essential to the social well-being of Canada's population, particularly in the hinterlands of the movement of people and commodities. In the development of Canada during the late 19th and early 20th century, rail transport served practically all purposes in Western Canada. However, with the advent of the motor car, good roads, trucks, buses and aircraft, the transportation patterns have changed dramatically.'[22] In the course of the commission's hearings, Hall came to believe that the greatest benefit to the peoples of the small towns and villages would come through a revitalized community, not through perpetuating antiquated and outdated transportation.

And so the Hall commission concluded, albeit with reluctance, that some of the branch lines had to be phased out of operation. The evidence did not support the claim that all small towns would die if the branch lines were abandoned. 'It is the people and the spirit of the people which gives the community viability, not the railways nor the elevators.' The overriding consideration had to be given to the future transportation requirements of the entire west. These new requirements would have to include, in addition to grain, the needs of forest products, coal, potash, sulphur, minerals, and other agricultural products such as canola. The projected increase in the volume of grain alone was from 690 million bushels to 1,480 million bushels. And the demand for coal owing to the increase in the cost of petroleum was projected to be substantial. Ontario Hydro alone would increase its use of coal from 9.2 million tons in 1977 to 11.5 million in 1978; most of that coal came from the United States but, as that source was depleted or redirected to domestic use, Ontario would require coal from western Canada, principally Alberta. An appropriate rail-delivery system became imperative in the light of the new industrial developmnets. And there was no doubt that 'increase in the movement of the minerals such as sodium sulphate, bentonite, nickel, uranium and others would compete with grain, lumber, potash and sulphur for the rail facilities and capacity available.'[23]

It is clear the Hall report was 'aimed at gaining and regaining for Western Canada a larger portion of the secondary processing industries associated with agriculture.'[24] He was not laying the grounds simply for the delivery of raw materials from the western provinces; he acknowledged the desire of many westerners to establish an integrated economic program of primary and secondary development in western Canada. Predictably enough, newspapers throughout the western provinces hailed the report as a charter for western economic development.

The work of this commission was typical of Emmett Hall inasmuch as he did not interpret his terms of reference narrowly or focus on one small part of a problem and ignore others. In this as in all other commissions he conducted, he took the larger view and always presented integrated and precise solutions. This is why he could say in the concluding pages of his report: 'The Commission examined the operation and economics of the total system and makes recommendations which in the long run lead to the greatest return to the grain producers and the maximum development for individuals and communities in Western Canada.'[25]

His attention was deflected away from the commission's work for a few weeks in the spring of 1976 when his son-in-law, James Wedge, died. The death was not unanticipated, since Wedge had been in a nursing home since 1968 suffering from complications arising out of diabetes. Belle and Emmett Hall generously assisted their daughter with the details of the funeral and consoled their four grandchildren. Once matters were settled, Hall returned to his commission and wrote the final report.

The Hall commission recommended that 2,165 miles of grain-related prairie branch line be abandoned. This process, however, was to proceed as part of a carefully conceived and executed plan. In the first place, it would occur in stages to the year 1981; the report specified precisely which branch lines should be abandoned and when. It also recommended that 11,813 miles of prairie branch lines become part of the basic rail network, guaranteed to the year 2000. This was to ensure capacity for the increased grain, mineral and timber production the commission foresaw. One of the boldest recommendations was the establishment of the Prairie Rail Authority (PRA), which was to be empowered to supervise the use and maintenance of the remaining 2,344 miles of prairie branch lines. It was recommended that this new administrative office be located in western Canada and that to make it independent of the railways, it be funded by the federal government. One of its duties would be to respond to the new demands on rail service as these demands arose. It was also to be vested with the authority to terminate or abandon rail lines after holding public hearings. The chief purpose of the PRA was to oversee the abandonment of some of the branch lines or the incorporation of others into the permanent rail network. But this was not to be another bureaucratic structure, for the new authority was required to be self-liquidating by 1990.

Another major recommendation of the commission was the establishment of a Northern Development Railway department of the Canadian National Railways (CNR). This railway would incorporate the present Northern Alberta Railway (NAR), the Great Slave Lake Railway (GSLR), the Alberta Resources Railway (AAR), and the Athabasca and Sangudo subdivisions of the CNR. The major reason for recommending this consolidation was the belief that 'Western Canada still has a large frontier for development which is becoming increasingly important.'[26] He was convinced that the 'expansion of agriculture and industry in the last frontier is assured; it is only a matter of time and expedience.'[27]

Just as railways had been essential in the past for the opening of the west, so would they be essential in the future. Hall saw the undeveloped area of northwestern Canada – including the northern half of Alberta, the northeast portion of British Columbia, and the western part of the Northwest Territories – as 'the last agricultural frontier in Canada [and] perhaps the largest in the entire world.'[28] It was twice the size of the Federal Republic of Germany, he observed. The only way it could be developed was through rail access since it was virtually inaccessible by sea.

Not surprisingly, Alberta was a chief proponent of northern development and it submitted a proposal for the establishment of a North West Rail Authority. This proposal was quickly countered by the CPR and CNR as beyond the terms of reference of the Hall commission, a tack that was tantamount to telling him that he had not understood his terms of reference. True to form, he confronted the charges of the railways directly.

'We must emphatically disagree,' he wrote in his report, 'with the CP Rail opinion that our terms of reference limited this Commission to consideration "of how best to move grain to export positions." Rationalization of the network for grain gathering and movement is, to be sure, at the forefront of our concerns. Grain movement, however, though certainly prominent and controversial, is by no means the only transportation issue which public policy must confront. Our charge, as we construe it, is to consider any and all proposals, whether they are specific or global in scope, which may have an influence for transportation betterment in Western Canada over the years ahead.'[29]

The railways specifically opposed the Alberta plan for a North West Rail Authority because they believed in the principle that 'established institutions are always best equipped without modification, to address new and unique situations as these arise.'[30] Hall and his colleagues, though ultimately deciding to remain neutral on the Alberta proposal, responded to this contention with the remark: 'We do not share this view. Were it valid, Canada would never have emerged from its colonial cocoon. Central to our thinking, by contrast, is an urgent need for institutional change, adequate to address and resolve the transportation needs of a dynamic society.'[31] On a related matter, the Hall commission gave special consideration – to the chagrin of both the CPR and the CNR – to the suggestion put forward by Alberta that the western provincial governments acquire ownership of all roadbeds in Canada. In the end, however, it did not embrace the idea.

In addition to recommendations on transportation, the Hall commission included specific suggestions relating to provincial compensation for road costs (incurred by municipalities as a result of rail abandonment), to compensation for tax loss (also due to rail abandonment), to the Canadian Wheat Board – the commission recommended that the board play a greater role in grain transportation – and other matters such as flour milling and rapeseed crushing.

The public response to this report was immediate and favourable. On 17 May 1977 an article in the Saskatoon *Star-Phoenix*, headlined 'Farm Leaders Praise Report,' quoted Roy Atkinson, president of the National Farmers Union, as saying that he was pleased with 'the common recommendations.' He was disappointed, however, that Hall had not recommended the nationalization of the country's complete railway system.[32] Other farm groups also voiced their general approval of the recommendations.

Some, such as John Diefenbaker, attempted to make partisan capital out of the Hall report. Diefenbaker, said, for example, with characteristic hyperbole, that the Hall report was 'a blow to the solar plexus of the government.'[33] He took special delight in the fact that the report repudiated, by implication, the suggestion of his arch rival from Saskatchewan, Otto Lang, that users of the rails should shoulder the costs. Lorne Nystrom, the NDP agriculture critic in the House of Commons, urged swift action on the recommendations in order to end the uncertainty throughout many small towns and villages of Saskatchewan 'as to whether they will have mail facilities in the years ahead.'[34]

Otto Lang, the very man who had appointed Hall to undertake the study, was not pleased that the report provided his opposition critics with so much ammunition. On the report's recommendation that the Crow's Nest Pass freight rates remain undisturbed, Lang claimed that the commission had gone beyond its terms of reference and that, in any case, its position was 'not very carefully put.'[35] Nonetheless, he promised he would study the report carefully.

The Edmonton *Journal* was less favourably disposed to the Hall commission's report than the Saskatoon *Star-Phoenix*. In one editorial entitled 'Sacred Cows,' the *Journal* claimed that however useful the Hall report might be, 'it does not have such stature that free copies should be provided for every hotel room bedside table.'[36] But it went on to caution the Conservative Party not to join 'the chorus of compliments against the Hall report,' especially on the Crow's Nest rates issue. 'Much-maligned Transport Minister Otto Lang has always said that the benefit now enjoyed by Prairie grain farmers through the subsidized

Crowsnest rate should continue – but not necessarily through the Crowsnest rate.'[37]

The main criticism of the Hall commission's recommendations came from the United Grain Growers (UGG). president Mac Runciman called the recommendations relating to the Crow's Nest rates 'fuzzy.'[38] He was especially critical of the report's silence on the disposition of those rail lines which were subject to review. 'This was the whole point of the study, but there are no new approaches.'[39] Runciman termed as 'shallow' the commission's analysis of the problem of higher freight rates on livestock than on grain shipped from the prairies. In the final analysis, Runciman claimed, the Hall commission placed too much faith in government intervention and not enough in the marketplace as the means of solving economic problems. Emmett Hall was not impressed with the critics of his report. He was especially unimpressed with Runciman's suggestion that the forces of the marketplace be the main avenue of economic reform. He had lived too long on the prairies not to know how fickle those forces could be.

One of the sharpest objections to the Hall commission's recommendations came from an Ontario economist writing for the Ontario Economic Council. A. Abouchar, in *An Economic Analysis of the Hall Commission Report*, took issue with the fundamental proposition underlying the Hall Report. The report, he said, rested on the proposition that 'the unique Canadian situation is unlike any other major grain growing and exporting country. Canada is absolutely dependent on rail transportation to move grain from where it is grown to export position.'[40] This alleged unique characteristic of grain production necessitated the continuation of government subsidies. As the Hall commission had noted: 'The government must continue to subsidize the transportation of export grain and that the full cost, as deemed by the Commission on the Costs of Transporting Grain by Rail, must not be imposed on the producer. The contribution Western grain makes to Canada's balance of payments position demands that a substantial part of any increase be borne by the federal government in the National interest.'[41] Abouchar responded: 'Apart from questioning the uniqueness of Canada's position – the U.S., the U.S.S.R., Argentina and Australia, the world's other major grain producers, quickly come to mind as sharing Canada's dependence upon railroads for their grain export – one has to ask: "so what? Why does this mean that transportation for export should be subsidized?"'[42] Abouchar went on to suggest that there were any number of other industries that could quality for public financial assistance if one were to accept the Hall commission's basic economic principle. He also asked why, if rail transport was to be subsidized by the federal treasury, the government should not also increase its subsidization of the road construction that would be required with the abandonment of rail lines.

Abouchar was not the only economist to cast doubts on the Hall commission's recommendations. To Manitoba economist Greg Mason, the 'recommendations are either unexceptional (dredging operations in harbours), or politically palatable only to western interests.'[43] Mason went on to suggest the 'examination of policy options is at best superficial, and one is left with the impression that the report sacrifices rigour for politics.'[44] He was particularly critical of the suggestion to establish a Prairie Rail Authority. In Mason's mind, the existing institutions – such as the Canadian Grain Commission – were quite capable of handling any of the proposed changes to rail lines and the location of future elevators. 'In sum, the Prairie Rail Authority overlaps with existing agencies and is given no clear duties. As such, it can only serve to obscure what is already an institutionally congested area.'[45] And why, asked Mason, establish another agency whose operating costs would 'unlikely to be less that $100 million per year'? 'Clearly a commission of inquiry has a duty to explain why increased subsidies are due an industry declining in importance to Canada's export revenues and why a new agency will relieve the grain producer, handler and shipper of the costs associated with the present system.'[46] These were not the kind of comments Emmett Hall wanted to hear, especially from western-based economists.

When Lang came to implement some of the provisions, he did not follow the report. Hall had recommended that, upon abandonment of a rail line, the roadbed should pass to the provincial crown for disposition after consultation with interested parties. Lang announced, to the chagrin of Gordon MacMurchy, the Saskatchewan minister in charge of transportation, that the roadbeds would revert to the federal government.[47] Nor did Lang accept the recommendation to establish a Prairie Rail Authority. Even though the Hall commission had built in provisions for the self-liquidation of the PRA by 1990, Lang saw it as a threat to the minister's power over grain and rail development and tended to agree with economists like Greg Mason that the PRA was unnecessary. But, over a period of time, many of the Hall commission's recommendations with respect to the abandonment of branch lines were adopted. As Transport Canada has observed: 'The Hall Commission grew out of

the agricultural industry's concern over terminals and branch line clo-
sures, and its findings resulted in a realignment of elevator and rail
systems.'[48]

One of the first acts of the short-lived Progressive Conservative government of Joe Clark was to appoint Emmett Hall in 1979, now eighty-one
years of age, to review the state of health services throughout the
country. The appointment was greeted with applause by all parties,
except by his wife. But he was not to be stopped. No sooner had he
begun his review, however, than the Canadian voters ousted Joe Clark
and his Progressive Conservative government and returned Pierre
Trudeau and the Liberals. When the government changed, Hall immediately ceased his review and sought an interview with Prime Minister
Trudeau and Monique Bégin, minister of health and welfare. The new
government instructed him to continue his review under the original
terms of reference, with this confirmation firmly in hand, he returned to
the task. Thus, once again – as in the Royal Commission on Health
Services – Hall found himself undertaking an assignment for a different
government than the one that had initiated it.

With the capable research assistance of Professor Malcolm Taylor of
York University and Dr Alice Girard of Montreal – two of his former
Health Services colleagues – Hall set about to retrace the steps he had
taken twenty years earlier. His chief responsibility was to consider 'the
extent to which the goals of the Charter of Health for Canadians have been
met.'[49] Hall held hearings in all the provinces and major cities of Canada;
he received and digested some 450 briefs on all aspects of the problem.
The climate this time was noticeably more favourable to medicare. As
Emmett Hall reported: 'I found no one, not any Government or individual, not the Medical Profession nor any organization, not in favor of
medicare. There were differences of opinion, it is true, on how it should
be organized and provided, but no one wanted it terminated.'[50]

The central focus of the report that he submitted to Monique Bégin on
29 August 1980[51] was stated in chapter 3: 'The Dominant Issues.' After
1977, when the federal Parliament substituted block funding for conditional grants,[52] problems arose in several provinces: some doctors became dissatisfied with the fee schedules and began to bill patients a fee
in excess of the fee schedule, and others opted out of the scheme
entirely. While Hall was emphatic in his opposition to extra-billing, he

was just as emphatic that doctors be adequately compensated for their efforts.[53] And they were not, in his view, receiving adequate income relative to other professions. He recommended, accordingly, that in the event of deadlock between the provincial medical associations and the provincial governments over fees, the dispute should be submitted to binding arbitration. Needless to say, this recommendation was not favourably received throughout the medical profession. For those doctors who did not wish to participate in the medicare scheme, they should, Hall's report concluded, have the right to operate outside the service, but they should not derive *any* benefits from that service. Doctors who decided to opt out of medicare would be required to provide the full range of billing services at their own expense and, of course, be prepared to assume responsibility for bad debts.

The public response to the Medicare Review report was generally favourable.[54] The Toronto *Globe and Mail* endorsed the report in an editorial and urged action. The *Globe* especially liked the recommendation relating to binding arbitration. It called that recommendation 'a prescription for justice for both patients and doctors.'[55] The federal minister of health, Monique Bégin, praised the recommendations and promised support. Indeed, the Trudeau government viewed the report as an endorsement of the fiscal changes introduced in 1977, which had reduced the level of financial support to the provinces. The provincial governments were less enthusiastic since most of the recommendations resulted in an increase in provincial expenditures on health and, in at least three provinces, Ontario, British Columbia, and Alberta, an end to premium payments. Even here, however, the Hall report was cautious and conciliatory: he recommended a gradual elimination of premiums.

Some observers felt that Hall could have been more critical of the way the federal government and the provinces had implemented his 1964 report. The one thing he stressed in that report was the need for universal standards of service throughout the country. The review committee of 1979–80 listened to numerous complaints about the lack of reciprocity between provinces and the difficulty a person had in being reimbursed for expenses incurred while absent from home. Hall recommended that the provincial ministers meet and work out these problems, which were, he said, 'of great annoyance to many Canadians.'[56] The one theme that pervaded the report, however, was that both levels of government must maintain a steady vigilance over the crucial matter of health services for Canadians. Hall firmly believed that his review of medicare in Canada pointed at those areas which needed special attention; they were the areas which must be preserved against erosion if an effective and humane medical scheme was to remain within the reach of all Canadians.

On a personal level, these were difficult days for Emmett Hall, for Belle, who had been ill for some time, was deteriorating throughout the fall of 1980 and her condition worried him greatly. She became worse over the winter and summer of 1981 and died in October, eight months short of their sixtieth wedding anniversary. It was a deeply sad time for Emmett, who had depended on Belle as a sounding board and steady rudder for so long. To no one's surprise, he immersed himself in more work as an escape from grief. He soldiered on but not without the constant awareness of Belle's absence. He dined with his daughter, Marian – now a justice of the Saskatchewan Court of Queen's Bench – several times a week; but, still, he was terribly lonely.

THE LAST ACT

During the heated national debate over Prime Minister Brian Mulroney's plan to sign a free trade agreement with the United States in the late 1980s, critics, especially in the NDP, claimed that such an agreement would threaten Canada's health care system. At age ninety, Emmett Hall once again found himself in the national spotlight. In order to scotch the charges that free trade would adversely affect medicare, the federal government sought Hall's advice. He obligingly reassured the public that free trade would in no way impugn the national health care system. His comments did much to silence the most vocal critics, though some of them circulated rumours that Hall had become senile and incapable of comprehending the complexities of the free trade initiative. That was nonsense, for Emmett Hall remained mentally alert and lucid right up to hours before he died.

Hall's sense of duty was especially acute when it came to assisting causes that touched the lives of those most in need. In 1984, at the age of eighty-six, he accepted an invitation to become president of Children's Village Canada, an organization founded in 1968 by Hermann Gmeiner, an Austrian, with the aim of providing funding for housing for indigent children throughout the world. Emmett Hall took up the responsibility to preside over the Canadian branch of the organization, which had been established in 1970. He continued to travel to Ottawa each year to chair the annual meetings of *Children's Village Canada* until his ninetieth year, when he could no longer face the stress of travel.

Emmett Matthew Hall died in Saskatoon on 12 November 1995, at the age of ninety-seven. His funeral was held on Wednesday, 15 November, at St Paul's Cathedral in Saskatoon and was attended by an overflow crowd of dignitaries and friends from across Canada. The front benches were occupied by Premier Roy Romanow, Lieutenant Governor Jack Wiebe, Chief Justice Donald MacPherson of the Saskatchewan Court of Queen's Bench, and several federal cabinet ministers, including Ralph Goodale and Diane Marleau.[57] Hall was survived by his daughter, Madam Justice Marian Wedge, now retired from the Saskatchewan Court of Queen's Bench, his son, Dr John Hall, a professor of medicine at Harvard Medical School, twelve grandchildren, and eight great-grandchildren. His coffin was escorted into the cathedral by a phalanx of twelve priests, including his brother, Father Anthony Hall, beneath an honour guard of Knights of Columbus with swords drawn. The homily was preached by Monsignor Len Morand, who resisted the trend to parade Emmett Hall's long list of honours: 'If he were to wear all his medals, he would look like a Russian General. So we won't do that.'[58] Morand simply compared Emmett to Moses: 'While on the Supreme Court, he interpreted the law to serve the common good and lead the country to the promised land. Working on land claims, he led the Natives to their promised land.' Others, such as retired British Columbia Supreme Court Justice Thomas Berger, praised him as 'one of Canada's greatest sons.' And Bob White, president of the Canadian Labour Congress, called Hall a visionary who 'was a friend to working people. The Canadian labour movement will miss him.' The accolades came from a wide spectrum of the Canadian public, giving testimony to the extent of his influence and legacy.

One final anecdote. This story of the life of Emmett Hall has been intimately associated with the life and career of John Diefenbaker. The two were classmates at law school and life-long friends; Diefenbaker as prime minister appointed Hall to the bench in Saskatchewan and in Ottawa. Hall never ceased to acknowledge the debt he owed to his old friend. Who would have thought that Diefenbaker would throw a pall over Hall's last years? Shortly before he died, Diefenbaker struck Emmett's name off the list of pallbearers for his funeral. Hall was deeply hurt. But Belle was enraged not only at the hurt to her husband but also by the knowledge that Diefenbaker had had his second wife, Olive, who had predeceased him, exhumed and brought to Saskatoon for burial beside him. This was the ultimate slight to the memory of her old friend, Edna, Diefenbaker's first wife, who had put so much energy and sacrifice into her husband's political career. Belle knew how Edna had stood by him through those long desolate years in the political wilderness. And she resented Diefenbaker for this final slight to Edna. Neither Emmett nor anyone else was ever to know the reason for the slight.

As Dennis Gruending has related, when Diefenbaker was buried on the grounds of the University of Saskatchewan on 22 August 1979, Hall – with tears in his eyes – watched the pageantry unfold from his penthouse balcony on Spadina Crescent across the river from the university. When asked why he wasn't there, he replied: 'You don't go where you aren't invited.' It was a sad commentary on John Diefenbaker that he would do such a thing to an old friend. But the friendship between Hall and Diefenbaker had begun to decline as far back as 1973 and Hall's University of Regina report. Indeed, one could say that there never was a depth to their friendship; no one ever got that close to Diefenbaker – he always kept a certain distance from even those who called him their friend, such as Emmett Hall. But, then again, John George Diefenbaker was a dull mirror of a man: he could not abide reflecting the greatness of others. That is why he distrusted wiser men and treated them with suspicion. Even those as devoted to him as Alvin Hamilton were kept at arm's length.[59] Perhaps, in his last years, as he receded further from public view at a time when Emmett Hall was still being sought out and accorded the glow of public prominence and approval, Diefenbaker saw Emmett Hall as a rival, as one who deflected attention away from himself. Two lives that began in the warmth of youthful friendship ended with the sting of petty estrangement. It was a hurt that Emmett Hall took to his grave. And it need not have happened.[60]

Epilogue

I chose 'Aggressive in Pursuit' as the title of this biography of Emmett Hall because it captured, I thought, the essential personality trait of the man. I resisted a suggestion that the title should be 'Aggressive in the Pursuit of Justice' because – although true – it would have narrowed the focus too much. For Emmett Hall was aggressive in everything he did and undertook: whether as a school board or hospital trustee, as a royal commissioner or arbitrator, or as a defence counsel or judge. He felt passionately about the issues he was involved in at any given moment. And he expressed his convictions aggressively. He was a man of temper and frequently let that temper loose upon his colleagues and adversaries. But it always puzzled him that people would take it personally. On one occasion during the final preparation of the Health Services report, he exploded at one of his staff for not producing a section of the report on time. When the person returned later crestfallen and offered to resign, Hall was nonplussed. He had difficulty believing that persons who were the object of his dressing downs took them personally. And he never held grudges against people with whom he had been at loggerheads on any given issue. He was in every sense a strong man complete with a forceful personality.

One of the issues he felt passionate about was the role of lawyers as social and political reformers. Indeed, many of his public non-judicial statements could be subsumed under the rubric 'Addresses to Lawyers to Awaken to the True Scope of Their Profession.' He saw lawyers as social activists by virtue of their calling to the law. No other group shared, he believed, the intimate contact with social problems that lawyers had, and no other group had the opportunity to see the diverse issues and problems of humanity so clearly. On one occasion, when addressing students and faculty at the University of Toronto Law School, he said: 'I am suggesting to you that we as lawyers have a responsibility to see that ... needed reforms are brought about even though they do not concern us directly in that part of our criminal justice system we have traditionally thought our own.'[1] As Louis Brandeis had warned, he reminded his audience, 'the greatest dangers to liberty lurk in insidious encroachment by men of zeal, well-meaning but without understanding.' A legal education should provide lawyers with the understanding by which to effect the necessary social and political reforms. Without their assistance, reformers become frustrated and seek extrajudicial or revolutionary means of bringing about reforms, he insisted. He pleaded for lawyers to shed the image – all too readily ascribed to them – of being agents of an unjust social and political order. Lawyers must be aggressive and take their place at the forefront of reform. 'We must use our skill to act as lobbyists, drafting legislation and pressing for its enactment.'[2] He saw injustice 'as the inevitable breeder of disorder.' It is found, he continued, 'where there is discrimination, poverty, ignorance, slum conditions; where there is suppression of legitimate protest and the refusal to redress old wrongs and inequalities, and by perpetuating old and worn out discriminatory practices, whether in business, government or education.'[3] He never ceased to draw attention to the plight of the 'sub-culture [that lives] in every province; they are of all ages, but principally quite young or growing old; many fatherless; many uneducated, both old and young; many deserted wives with dependent children.'[4]

Emmett Hall's life was one long advocacy on behalf of the indigent and disadvantaged, especially among Canada's native population. His achievements bear testimony to this aggressive advocacy. No one doubts that he has left his mark upon the national life of Canada. He conducted one of the most successful royal commissions in our history and set in place a national health care system of which Canadians are fiercely proud. He did not fear to speak out or shout his convictions. He aggressively defended his health care program in numerous speeches across the country, to the chagrin of many people. He vigorously championed the cause of native land claims in his *Calder* decision. And he was heard throughout Parliament and throughout Canada. Emmett Matthew Hall served his country well and continues to deserve the public gratitude of the nation.

But there was another side to Emmett Hall and that was his enormous personal generosity. Few will ever know the full extent of his generosity because he kept it private and never spoke of it. In addition to his financial support to members of his extended family – which was considerable – he came to the assistance of countless people personally unknown to him. His charity went far beyond sitting on boards and agencies of charitable causes. His private papers are sprinkled with letters addressed 'To My Anonymous Benefactor.' Letters from young nursing students thanking him for financial support, testimonials from others to whom he had given financial aid in one form or another, are found buried deep within his papers. He never achieved great wealth but he gave generously from what he had. He was, as many people would attest, a 'soft touch.' As his priest brother Tony would affirm, Emmett Hall lived his Catholic faith, and it was that faith – with its core principle of charity – which motivated his generosity. One of his contemporaries, Hal Rees, said of him: 'He was never the kind of guy who was trying to build houses or make money that way. He was too good a student of the law so I don't think he ever wanted to bother with that sort of thing ... it wasn't the situation it is now where every lawyer is building houses and castles and hotels.'[5] In the world, Hall was aggressive, but in the privacy of his den he was a gentle and compassionate man few outside his family would ever come to know and which this biographer could glimpse only *a longe*. Every effort to intrude into that private redoubt was deflected with a fearsome frown reflecting his public demeanour.

Notes

1 FROM SAINT-COLUMBAN TO SASKATOON

1 All information relating to Emmett Hall's family and early years was
provided by Justice Hall in a series of interviews over more than ten years.
Transcripts of these sources have been filed in the Hall Papers with the
Saskatchewan Archives, University of Saskatchewan. See also Dennis
Gruending, *Emmett Hall: Establishment Radical*.

2 Emmett had two older brothers, John and Mike. He had two younger
brothers, James and Tony. His sisters were Anne, Alice, Virginia, Eva,
Eileen, and Helen.

3 For a sympathetic account of those dreadful days, see Anthony Trollope,
Castle Richmond.

4 Stephen Leacock, *Montreal*, 224.

5 Ibid., 224–6. Cannon submitted his report calling for the abolition of
aldermanic government and the establishment of 'commission government' on 12 Dec. 1909.

6 For much of the material on the early period in Saskatoon, I am indebted
to Wilbur N. Lepp, local history librarian, Saskatoon Public Library. I am
also deeply grateful to Professor Donald Kerr, University of Saskatchewan, for giving me a copy of his unpublished paper on early Saskatoon,
entitled 'Psychology of the Boomtime: Saskatoon, 1905–1913.'

7 Saskatoon *Phoenix*, 18 Feb. 1911, 16.

8 Ibid., 9 Oct. 1909, 12; 17 March 1910, 8; 12 Nov. 1910, 8; 12 April 1912, 1.

9 Ibid., 5 Jan. 1911, 8.

10 Ibid., 18 April 1911, 1.

11 Ibid., 24 Oct. 1912, 14.

12 Manitoba's dispute over religious schools led twice to the Judicial Committee of the Privy Council. See *Winnipeg v. Barrett*, (1892) AC 445 and
Brophy v. Attorney General for Manitoba, (1895) AC 202.

13 Pamphlet, Scott Papers, AS, G. 10, 1905–9, 8.

14 Patrick Kyba, 'Race, Religion, and Resources: J.T.M. Anderson and the
Conservative Party of Sackatchewan,' in Gordon Barnhart, ed.,
Saskatchewan Premiers in the Twentieth Century.

15 See W.L. Morton, *The Kingdom of Canada*, 380. See also W.L. Morton,
Manitoba: A History, 380.

16 Interview with Douglas Schmeiser, Saskatoon, September 1976.

17 The tragic story of this pandemic is told in detail in Gina Kolata, 'FLU: The
Story of the Great Influenza Pandemic of 1918 and the Search for the Virus
That Caused It.'

18 The Saskatoon *Daily Star* carried stories on the flu from 2 Oct. 1918
through 24 Nov. 1918. See 19 November: 'Deaths Have Reached 163 in
Saskatoon.'

19 *The Sheaf: Graduation Number, April, 1919*, 218–19.

20 Ibid., 260.

21 RSC.7–8 Geo. V, c. 21.

22 *Report of the Soldier Settlement Board* (Ottawa, 1921), 105.

23 *The Soldier Settlement Act* was eventually challenged in the district court
before Justice A.H. Bence. See *In Re Soldier Settlement Act*, (1939) 2 W.W.R.
199. Bence ruled that the act was valid under section 95 of the *British North
America Act, 1867*, as well as under the 'peace, order and good government' clause. 'The reestablishment of civil life after the war of many
thousands of soldiers was a national emergency' (202).

24 Ibid., 44.

25 J.K. Johnson, ed., *The Canadian Directory of Parliament: 1867–1967* (Ottawa:
Public Archives of Canada 1968).

26 Dennis Gruening, *Emmett Hall: Establishment Radical*, 17.

27 Interview with the author, Toronto, 30 Dec. 1976.

2 AT THE BAR OF SASKATCHEWAN

1 *Glenn and Babb v. Schofield*, S.C.R., (1928), 210.

2 R.S.S., 1920, c. 169.

3 R.S.S. 1920, c. 170.

4 *Schofield v. Glenn and Babb*, 1927, 2 W.W.R. 186.

5   Ibid., 186.
6   Ibid., 187.
7   Saskatoon *Star*, 6 March 1928, 1.
8   For a general history of the Supreme Court of Canada, see James G. Snell and Frederick Vaughan, *The Supreme Court of Canada: History of the Institution*.
9   For an account of the controversy surrounding the establishment of the Supreme Court of Canada, see Frederick Vaughan, 'The Birthpangs of the Supreme Court of Canada.'
10 Ibid., 211.
11 Ibid.
12 Goronwy Rees, *The Great Slump*, 66–7.
13 Ibid., 67.
14 J. L. Granatstein, *Twentieth Century Canada*, 214–15.
15 Ibid., 216.
16 Interview with Professor Colwyn Wiliams, Saskatoon, 25 Aug. 1971, Hall Paper. I am using a transcript of the taped interview with Hall's corrections. 35.
17 Interview with author, Ottawa, 10 June 1974.
18 These letters are reprinted in Dennis Gruending, Emmett Hall: *Establishment Radical*, 23.
19 See, the London *Evening Free Press*, 21 Jan. 1926, for a first-page account of the 'First Canadian Ku Klux Burial Here.' The story pictured a group of robed Klansmen and a fiery cross at the graveside of a dead colleague.
20 See Constance Backhouse, *Colour-Coded*, 173.
21 Patrick Kbya, *Alvin: A Biography of the Honourable Alvin Hamilton*, 12. For a fuller account of this matter, see Patrick Kyba, 'Ballots and Burning Crosses,' in Norman Ward and Duff Spafford, ed., *Politics: Saskatchewan*. See also William Calderwood, 'Pulpit, Press and Political Reactions to the Ku Klux Klan in Saskatchewan,' in Susan M. Trofimenkoff, ed., *The Twenties in Western Canada*, 191.
22 Ibid.
23 Hall to Vaughan, 22 May 1970, Hall Papers. In this letter Emmett Hall added: 'I can say without any hesitation that Mr. Diefenbaker was never associated with the Klan. His interest at this particular time, circa 1929, was Federal and he did not take part in the 1929 election.' Actually, John Diefenbaker was a candidate for Prince Albert in the 1929 provincial election and was defeated by Thomas Clayton Davis by 415 votes. See *Directory of Saskatchewan Ministries: Members of the Legislative Assembly and Elections, 1905–1953*.

24 Backhouse, *Colour-Coded*, 368n.110.

25 Ibid.

26 See *Yee Clun v. the City of Regina* (1925) 4 D.L.R. 1015; 3 W.W.R. 714. See Constance Backhouse's discussion of this case in *Colour-Coded*, 150–72.

27 See Raymond J.A. Huel, 'J.J. Maloney,' in John E. Foster, ed., *The Developing West*.

28 R.S.C. 1990, c. C-34.

29 *Criminal Code and Other Selected Statutes of Canada*, (1927), 34.

30 Ibid., s. 136, 35.

31 For a discussion of this matter, see, Robert J. Sharpe, *The Last Day, the Last Hour*, 12–13. This famous trial took place one year after the Dealtry trial and is not exactly parallel because General Currie brought a civil action for damages. But it contains instructive information relating to libel cases in the late 1920s.

32 For a full account of J.J. Maloney's activities in Saskatchewan, see Raymond J.A. Huel, 'J.J. Maloney,' in John E. Foster, ed., *The Developing West*, 219.

33 Cited in ibid., 225.

34 Ibid., 227.

35 *Boucher v. His Majesty the King*, (1951) S.C.R. 265.

36 Ronald Liversedge, *Recollections of the On to Ottawa Trek*, Victor Hoar, ed., viii.

37 Ibid., 206.

38 Ibid., 194–216.

39 Ibid., 202.

40 Ibid., 215.

41 Ibid., 220.

42 Charge, King' Bench, Criminal Docket, 1922–47, 345–77.

43 Winnipeg *Free Press*, 2 July 1935, 1 and 4; and Regina *Leader*, 2 July 1935, 1.

44 Interview with the author, Guelph, 25 May 1975.

45 See, Winnipeg *Free Press*, 2 July 1935, 1 and 4; Regina *Leader*, 2 July 1935, 1.

46 Saskatoon *Star-Phoenix*, 7 May 1935, 8.

47 Cited in David Ricardo Williams, *Just Lawyers*.

48 Saskatoon *Star-Phoenix*, 10 Aug. 1938, 3.

49 *Wegeler v. Craig and Charmbury* (1937) W.W.R. 513.

50 Saskatoon *Star-Phoenix*, 8 Oct. 1937, 3.

51 Interview with Professor Colwyn Williams, 21. I am using a transcription of the taped interview with Emmett Hall's corrections.

52 Ibid.

53 Ibid., 22.

54 See *Lloyd v. Milton and Derkson*, (1938) 1 W.W.R. 95.

55 *Lloyd v. Milton Derkson*, (1937) 3 W.W.R. 504.

56 *Lloyd v. Derkson*, (1938) S.C.R. 315.

57 *Derkson v. Lloyd*, (1938) S.C.R. 315.

58 See Saskatoon *Star-Phoenix*, 26 Feb. 1938, 3.

59 Saskatoon *Star-Phoenix*, 12 Oct. 1936, 10.

60 The ideological confusions of those pre-war days surfaced late in 1939 when Father Anthony Hall, Emmett's younger brother, returned from theological studies in Rome. The young priest had nothing but praise for Mussolini and expanded at length on his many achievements. Those views were duly reported in the Saskatoon *Star-Phoenix*, much to the later embarrassment of the Hall family.

61 Saskatoon *Star-Phoenix*, 8 Sept. 1939, 3.

62 Ibid., 1 Sept. 1939, editorial.

63 Ibid., 11 Sept. 1939, 7.

64 M.J. Coldwell succeeded Woodsworth as parliamentary leader of the CCF in 1940.

65 In addition to Emmett, the surviving children of James and Alice Hall at the time of her death were: Mrs A. Tomczak, M.H. Hall, James S. Hall [HQ Canadian Army overseas], Mrs G.M. O'Reilly, Mrs Denis Rowley, Mrs A.E.W. Paterson, Rev. A.W. Hall, and Mrs J.J. Scissons.

66 *Giesbrecht v. Wolfe*, (1944) 1 W.W.R. 634.

67 'Documentary Evidence Filed in Case of Contested Will Here; Ashley Questioned,' Saskatoon *Star-Phoenix*, 13 May 1952, 1.

68 'Handwriting Expert Surprise Witness in Will Case Here, Defence Gets Adjournment,' Saskatoon *Star-Phoenix*, 14 May 1952, 3.

69 Ibid., 15.

70 Saskatoon *Star-Phoenix*, 15 May 1952, 3.

71 Ibid., 28 May 1952, 3.

72 *In the Surrogate Court of the Judicial District of Saskatoon, in the Estate of Lily May Taylor, late of Saskatoon, in the Province of Saskatchewan, Widow, Deceased*. I am grateful to Illa Knudsen, deputy local registrar, Federal Court, Judicial Centre of Saskatoon, Saskatoon, for assistance in locating the files relating to this case.

73 Saskatoon *Star-Phoenix*, 4 Sept. 1952.

74 Unless otherwise noted, material for this case comes from notes on the case in the Hall Papers as well as from interviews with Justice Hall. The case is reported as *In re Beck* (1951) 3 W.W.R. (NS) 92 K.B. For two accounts of the Beck trial, see 'Judge Quashes Sale of Becks Lands, Advertising Methods Said Improper,' Saskatoon *Star-Phoenix*, 11 April 1951, 3;

'Body of Kaspar Beck, Central Figure in Tax Case Found Hanging in Garage,' ibid., 10 Aug. 1951, 3.

75 'Did the Income Tax Kill Kaspar Beck?' McKenzie Porter, *Maclean's*, 15 July 1951, 41.

76 Ibid.

77 Execution Act, R.S.S., 1930, c. 65, s. 20.

78 See 'John Petlock Continues to Elude Police,' Saskatoon *Star-Phoenix*, story, 3 Sept. 1955, 1.

79 See 'Petlock Caught in Edmonton,' Saskatoon *Star-Phoenix*, 5 Sept. 1955, 2.

80 Robert McKercher, cited by Dennis Gruending in *Emmett Hall: Establishment Radical*, 40.

81 Interview with Douglas Schmeiser, Saskatoon, 23 June 1976.

82 Cited by Dennis Gruending, in *Emmett Hall: Establishment Radical*, 33.

83 Ibid., 46.

84 Not only did Belle have an eye for decoration, she could, on occasion, deliver unsolicited observations with a sharp comment. Shortly after Emmett had been installed as chancellor of the University of Guelph in 1971, she walked through the newly decorated bachelor President's House on campus, took one look around, and said: 'Right out of Eaton's catalogue.'

85 Dennis Gruending, *Emmett Hall: Establishment Radical*, 47.

86 Ibid.

87 Ibid., 49.

3 LEGAL AND POLITICAL AMBITIONS

1 Tucker to author, 31 October 1977, Hall Papers, University of Saskatchewan Archives, Saskatoon.

2 Ibid.

3 Ibid., 3.

4 Ibid.

5 Ibid., 4. Tucker was careful to say not that Hall's anger with Jimmy Gardiner was the *only* reason for his leaving the Liberals for the Conservatives but that it played an important part in his decision. It is interesting that Hall rarely spoke about Gardiner. All efforts by the author to draw him out on the subject of Gardiner's pervasive influence in Saskatchewan politics were met with a look of annoyance and the shake of his head.

6 Dennis Gruending, *Emmett Hall: Establishment Radical*, 55.

7 Hall to author, 22 May 1970, 2, Hall Papers.

8 Saskatoon *Star Phoenix*, 10 Oct. 1947.

9 Ibid., 23 June 1948.

10 Report of the *Royal Commission on Dominion-Provincial Relations*, 197.

11 Radio Address, CFQC, 23 April 1948, 3, Hall Papers.

12 Saskatoon *Star-Phoenix*, 15 Jan. 1947, editorial.

13 Radio Address, CFQC, 23 April 1949, 4–5, Hall Papers.

14 Eric Knowles, Saskatoon *Star-Phoenix*, 24 July 1947.

15 See David E. Smith, 'Membership in the Saskatchewan Legislative Assembly,' Norman Ward and Duff Spafford, ed., in *Politics: Saskatchewan*, 179.

16 Interview with author, Toronto, 12 June 1974.

17 Emmett Hall did seek, 'half-heartedly,' he said years later, a Tory nomination in the 1957 general election. On this occasion he lost to Harry Jones, who went on to become a Progressive Conservative member of Parliament. It is interesting to speculate how Hall's career would have turned out had he been successful in winning the nomination. He almost certainly would not have become chief justice of the Court of Queen's Bench.

18 Radio Address, 'Playing Politics with the Outlook Dam Project,' 23 Feb. 1949, 2.

19 Ibid., 3–4.

20 Ibid.

21 Ibid.

22 *Report of the Royal Commission on the South Saskatchewan River Project*, Thomas H. Hogg, chairman (appointed Aug. 24, 1951: report tabled 29 Oct. 1952).

23 Cited by Hall in radio address, 'The Outlook Power Irrigation Project,' 9 Feb. 1953.

24 Ibid.

25 Ibid., 4.

26 Ibid.

27 Ibid., 5.

4 ON THE BENCH OF SASKATCHEWAN

1 Hall to author, 18 Jan. 1977. Information on the matter of Hall's appointment to the bench and his schedule during the first weeks after his appointment comes from this letter.

2 The annual salary of the chief justice of the Court of Queen's Bench in 1957 was $18,500. Hall to author, 18 Jan. 1977.

3 Diefenbaker to Hall, 25 Oct. 1957, Hall Papers.

4 Hall to Jackett, 7 Oct. 1957, Hall Papers.
5 Hall to author, 18 Jan. 1977.
6 Ibid.
7 Letter from Roy S. Meldrum, deputy attorney general, 11 Aug. 1960, file no. 3085 G 3290 G, Hall Papers (in the author's possession).
8 Roy S. Meldrum to Judge McFadden, 11 Aug. 1960, Department of the Attorney General, file no. 3085 G 3296 G, Hall Papers.
9 Roy S. Meldrum to Judge McFadden, 11 Aug. 1960, Department of the Attorney General, file no. 3085 G 3290 G, Hall Papers.
10 R.A. Walker, attorney general, to Hall, 15 July 1960, Hall Papers. Italics in the original.
11 Hall to E.D. Fulton, 15 Aug. 1960, 2, Hall Papers.
12 Ibid.
13 Ibid.
14 R.A. Walker to Hall, 19 Aug. 1960, Hall Papers.
15 Ibid., 1.
16 Ibid., 2
17 Ibid.
18 *Re Sklar and Sklar*, (1958) 26 W.W.R. 184.
19 R.S.C. (1952) c. 14.
20 *Williams v. Leggett and Leggett* (1951), 4 W.W.R. 455.
21 *Re Sklar and Sklar*, 187.
22 *A.G. for Quebec and the Royal Bank v. Love and A.G. for Canada*, (1928) A.C. 187.
23 *Regina v. Hnedish*, (1958) 26 W.W.R. 685; 29 C.R. 347 (Sask., Q.B.)
24 Ibid., 689.
25 *Rex v. Hammond*, (1941) 28 Cr. App. R. 84 (1941) 3 All E.R. 318.
26 Ibid., 688.
27 Ibid. Ten years later, as a member of the Supreme Court of Canada, Emmett Hall found himself in dissent, with justices Spence and Pigeon, in just such an opportunity to settle this issue. See *DeClercq v. The Queen*, (1968) S.C.R. 902.
28 *Regina v. Phillips*, (1958) 26 W.W.R. 315.
29 Ibid., 318.
30 Ibid.
31 Ibid., 319.
32 *Re Elliot; R v. Jackson*, (No. 2) (1959) 29 W.W.R. 579; 125 c.c.c. 354; 31 C.R. 368 (Sask. Q.B.).
33 Ibid., 582.
34 Ibid., 584.

35 *Shumiatcher v. A.G. of Saskatchewan*, (1960), 33. W.W.R. 132; 129 C.C.C. 267; 34 C.R. 152 (Sask. Q.B.).
36 Ibid., 133 (W.W.R.).
37 Hall was notified of his appointment as chief justice of Saskatchewan by D.S. Maxwell, deputy minister of the Department of Justice. The telegram read simply: 'The Honourable E.M. Hall, Chief Justice of the Court of Queen's Bench, Court House, Regina, Sask. You have been appointed Chief Justice of Saskatchewan effective March first. Writing.' Signed 'D.S. Maxwell.' Hall's was not the only appointment on that occasion, for Diefenbaker appointed five other chief justices on the same day. New chief justices were appointed for Quebec, Manitoba, and Alberta. In Quebec, Associate Chief Justice William B. Scott became chief justice of the Superior Court; Lucien Tremblay was appointed as chief justice of the Quebec Court of Queen's Bench; in Alberta, Justice Sydney Bruce Smith was elevated to chief justice of Alberta. In Manitoba, Judge Calvert Charlton Miller was elevated to chief justice of the Appeal Court.
38 *Shumiatcher v. A.G. of Saskatchewan*, (1962) 39 W.W.R. 577.
39 Ibid., 578.
40 Ibid.
41 Ibid., 579.
42 Hall to Diefenbaker, 20 June 1962, Diefenbaker Papers, Diefenbaker Centre Archives, University of Saskatchewan.
43 Peter Russell, *The Judiciary in Canada*, 342.
44 Ibid., 343.
45 *Regina v. Drybones*, (1970) S.C.R. 282.
46 Peter W. Hogg, *Constitutional Law of Canada*, 188–9.
47 *Thomas v. Thomas* (1961) 36 W.W.R. 23.
48 R.S.S. 1953, c. 352.
49 *Thomas v. Thomas*, 27 at 26.
50 Ibid., 28.

5 THE BIRTH OF NATIONAL MEDICARE

1 *Financial Post*, 24 Nov. 1956, 19.
2 *Report of the Conciliation Board*, 17 Dec. 1956.
3 Ibid., 34–34A.
4 Ibid., 34A.
5 'Kellock Royal Commission Report,' in *Canadian Pacific Spanner*, special supplement, February 1958, 9.

6 The Warren commission on the assassination of President Kennedy was a notable exception.

7 See Allan Manson and David Mullan, ed., *Commissions of Inquiry.*

8 *Report of the Attorney General's Committee on the Appellate Jurisdiction of the Supreme Court of Ontario,* Hon. Arthur Kelly, chairman, Toronto, 10 March 1977.

9 A.P. Herbert, *Mild and Bitter,* 37.

10 'Royal Commissions as Part of the Legislative Process,' unpublished paper, Hall Papers.

11 Ibid., 12.

12 The full title of the report is *House of Commons Standing Committee on Justice and Legal Affairs: Sub-committee on the Penitentiary System in Canada,* 1977.

13 Saskatoon *Star-Phoenix,* 12 Jan. 1961.

14 Interview with author, Ottawa, 19 Nov. 1971.

15 Interview with Professor Colwyn Williams, Saskatoon, 25 Aug. 1971, 36, Hall Papers.

16 Ibid.

17 Interview with T.C. Douglas, Ottawa, 19 Nov. 1971.

18 Hall to Diefenbaker, 12 April 1958, Diefenbaker Papers.

19 Diefenbaker to Hall, 21 April 1958, Hall Papers.

20 Diefenbaker to Hall, 27 May 1961, Hall Papers.

21 For a full account of the role played by Saskatchewan in bringing medicare to Canada, see C. Stuart Houston, *Steps on the Road to Medicare.*

22 Material for this part of the story is from interviews with Bernard Blishen, Emmett Hall, and several others connected with the commission.

23 Wallace McCutcheon resigned from the commission when he was appointed to the Senate on 19 Aug. 1962.

24 Interview with author, Guelph, 10 Jan. 1976.

25 Ibid.

26 Vancouver *Sun,* 21 Feb. 1962.

27 House of Commons *Debates,* 19 Feb. 1962, 999.

28 'Doctors Give the Needle to Commission Hearings,' Toronto *Globe and Mail,* 16 May 1962, 22.

29 *Submission of the Canadian Medical Association to the Royal Commission on Health Services,* Toronto, 16 May 1962, 7–8.

30 Malcolm G. Taylor, *Insuring National Health Care,* 139. Taylor has written a comprehensive account of the seven decisions that led to the establishment of the Canadian health insurance system. See his *Health Insurance and Canadian Public Policy.*

31 P.E. Bryden, *Planners and Politicians,* 130.

32 Cited in ibid., 130.

33 *Submission of the Canadian Medical Association to the Royal Commission on Health Services*, Toronto, 16 May 1962, 7.

34 'Anesthetists Rebuked by Judge during Health Hearings,' Toronto *Globe and Mail*, 24 March 1962.

35 Interview with Professor J.J. Madden, a member of the commission's pool of economic advisers, Guelph, 20 Sept. 1972. When Hall met privately with commission staff, he used to give vent to his opinions, often in colourful language.

36 *Report of the Royal Commission on Health Services*, 1965, 19.

37 Ibid., 11.

38 Ibid., 13.

39 Ibid.

40 Ibid.

41 Ibid., 14–15. Italics in the original.

42 Ibid., 4.

43 Toronto *Telegram*, 19 Feb. 1965.

44 *Time Magazine*, 31 July 1964, 9.

45 P.E. Bryden, *Planners and Politicians*, 133.

46 Pearson Papers, MG, 26 N2, 115: Old Age Security (2), address by L.B. Pearson on 'The Nation's Business,' 4 Oct. 1961, Cited in P.E. Bryden, *Planners and Politicians*, 69.

47 For an extensive discussion of the matter of timing and election strategy, see P.E. Bryden *Planners and Politicians*, 134–9.

48 Pearson to Hall, 7 Jan. 1965, Hall Papers.

49 Saskatoon *Star-Phoenix*, 23 July 1964.

50 Ibid.

51 Montreal *Star*, 19 Feb. 1964, 4.

52 Toronto *Globe and Mail*, 19 Feb. 1965, 12.

53 'Implications of a Health Charter for Canadians,' mimeo, 1, Hall Papers.

54 Diehl to Hall, 23 April 1965, Hall Papers.

55 Citation of the Public Health Association of the United States, 3 Nov. 1966, Hall Papers.

56 Donald Fraser Memorial Lecture, Edmonton, 1 June 1965, 13.

57 Ibid., 14.

58 Ibid.

59 MacPherson paper, mimeo, 2; Hall Papers.

60 Ibid., 4–5.

61 Ibid., 2.

62 Ibid., 10.

63 Ibid.,16.

64 Ibid.

65 Cited in Walter Stewart, *The Life and Political Times of Tommy Douglas*, 211.
66 The vote on third reading was 177 to 2 in favour. See, *House of Commons, Journals*, 8 Dec. 1966, 1125–7.
67 *Senate Debates*, 13 Dec. 1966, 1238.
68 Ibid.
69 Ibid.
70 Ibid., 1266.

6 REFORMING EDUCATION IN ONTARIO

1 See W.G. Fleming, *Education*.
2 R.D. Gidney, *From Hope to Harris*, 3.
3 For an excellent overview of the history of these royal commissions, see ibid.
4 Ivan Illich, *Deschooling Society*.
5 Ivan Illich, *Celebration of Awareness*.
6 W.G. Fleming, *Education*, 307–8.
7 Hilda Neatby, *So Little for the Mind*.
8 For a retelling of this story see James Pitsula, 'The Courage of Her Convictions,' 26.
9 W.G. Fleming, *Education*, 189–90.
10 R.D. Gidney, *From Hope to Harris*, 67–8.
11 Dorothy Dunn was a good friend of Father Anthony Hall, Emmett's youngest brother. Some people have come to believe that this association with Father Anthony prompted the recommendation.
12 Dennis Gruending, *Emmett Hall: Establishment Radical*, 104.
13 John Hall to Hall, December 1965, Hall Papers.
14 *Living and Learning*, 4.
15 Eric W. Riker, 'Teachers, Trustees and Policy,' cited in Gidney, *From Hope to Harris*. 76.
16 Ibid.
17 *Living and Learning*, 9. As one reads this report today, thirty-five years after it was written, it is interesting to see that all students are referred to as 'he' or 'his' and teachers are almost always referred to as 'he.'
18 Ibid., 9n.27.
19 Robert T. Dixon, *Catholic Education and Politics in Onatrio*, vol. 4, 45.
20 Ibid.
21 For a discussion of this reversal and the friendship of Cardinal Carter and Premier Davis, see ibid., 236.
22 Ibid., 75.
23 Toronto *Globe and Mail*, 13 June 1968, 1.

24 Ibid.
25 Toronto *Star*, 13 June 1968, editorial.
26 Toronto *Globe and Mail*, 13 June 1968, 11.
27 *Living and Learning*, 69.
28 Ibid., 75.
29 Ibid., 77.
30 Ibid., 75.
31 Ibid., 70.
32 Ibid., 77.
33 Ibid., 223.
34 R.D. Gidney, *From Hope to Harris*, 76.
35 Ibid., 76–7.
36 Ibid., 77.
37 Ibid., 77.
38 Ibid., 210.
39 Speech delivered at Glendon College Public Service Award Dinner, 22 Jan. 1969, Hall Papers.
40 Address to Convocation, University of Guelph, 11 Oct. 1971.
41 Robert M. Hutchins, *The Learning Society*, 5.
42 Ibid., 5–6.
43 Ibid., 9.
44 Ibid., 6.
45 Ibid., 5.
46 R.D. Gidney, *From Hope to Harris*, 72.
47 James Daly, *Education or Molasses?*
48 Ibid., 8.
49 Interview with author, Toronto, 22 Jan. 1976.
50 I am grateful to Clare Westcott, Queen's Park, Toronto, for details relating to these matters. Interviews with author, Toronto 10 Feb. 1977.
51 Ibid.
52 The total costs of the commission came to $697,137.
53 Dennis to Hall, Hall Papers.

7 IN THE SUPREME COURT OF CANADA

1 *Wright, McDermott and Feeley v. The Queen*, (1963) S.C.R. 539.
2 Peter W. Hogg, *The Constitutional Law of Canada*, 931–2.
3 For an account of the process leading up to the adoption of the absolute-exclusion rule in the United States, see M. Glenn Abernathy, *Civil Liberties under the Constitution*, 131–40.
4 *Hogan v. The Queen*, (1975) 2 S.C.R. 574.

5　See *Hogan v. The Queen* (1975) 2 S.C.R. 574, and contrast with *R v. Manninen* (1987) 1 S.C.R. 1233. For a discussion of the development of the exclusionary rule, see Rainer Knopff and F.L. Morton, *Charter Politics*, 50–7.

6　*Piche v. The Queen*, (1971) S.C.R. 23.

7　Ibid., 36.

8　Ibid., 40.

9　*Klippert v. The Queen*, (1967) S.C.R. 822.

10　Ibid., 831.

11　*Mendick v. The Queen*, (1969) S.C.R. 865.

12　*Sanders v. The Queen*, (1970) S.C.R. 109 at 152.

13　Ibid, 157.

14　Ibid., 165.

15　Ibid.

16　*Regina v. Wray*, (1971) S.C.R. 272; 11 D.L.R. (3d) 673.

17　Ibid.

18　Ibid., 277.

19　*Kuruma v. The Queen*, (1955) A.C. 197.

20　*Wray*, 277.

21　Ibid., 279.

22　'Paper prepared for delivery to the John white Society,' Osgoode Hall Law School, Toronto, 29 Sept. 1971, Hall Papers. The House of Lords announcement was made on 26 July 1966: House of Lords *Debates*, col. 677.

23　Ibid., 3.

24　Ibid.,

25　Ibid., 4.

26　Ibid., 9.

27　(1967) S.C.R. 455.

28　(1971) S.C.R. 23.

29　(1970) S.C.R. 608.

30　'Paper prepared for delivery to the John White Society,' 14.

31　Ibid., 18.

32　I am grateful to Professor Neil Brooks, Hall's law clerk during the 1970–1 term, for this observation. Emmett Hall was partly instrumental in having the Supreme Court of Canada provide each judge with a law clerk; his lobbying was eventually successful. In addition to Brooks, Hall's law clerks were: William Corbett, 1967–8 term; Steven Gill, 1968–9 term; Henry Kloppenburg, 1971–2 term; and Bill Estey, 1972–3 term.

33　Ibid. Wray, 299.

34　Ibid.

35 Ibid., 303.
36 Ibid.
37 Ibid., 304.
38 S.R. Peck, 'Scalogram Analysis of the Supreme Court of Canada,' *Canadian Bar Review*, vol. 45 (1967).
39 Ibid., 283.
40 Ibid., 282.
41 Ibid., 284.
42 Ibid., 285–6.
43 *Mazur v. Imperial Investment Corporation*, (1963) S.C.R. 281, 290.
44 Ibid., 284.
45 Ibid., 285.
46 Ibid., 289.
47 Ibid., 290.
48 Ibid., 290–1.
49 Ibid.
50 *Hoogendoorn v. Greening Metal Products and Screening Equipment Company et al.* (1968) S.C.R. 30.
51 Ibid., 38.
52 Ibid., 39.
53 Ibid.
54 Ibid., 34.
55 Ibid., 35.
56 Ibid.
57 *Re Kinnaird v. Workmen's Compensation Board*, (1963) S.C.R. 239.
58 Ibid., 243.
59 Ibid., 246.
60 Ibid.
61 *O'Brien v. Mailhot*, (1966) S.C.R. 171, 176.
62 R.S.Q. 1941, c. 142, s. 53.
63 *O'Brien*, 179.
64 *Freedman v. City of Cote St. Luc*, (1972) S.C.R. 216.
65 Ibid., 219.
66 Ibid., 220.
67 Ibid., 222.
68 Ibid.
69 *Methôt v. Montreal Transportation Commission* (1972) S.C.R. 387.
70 Ibid., 392.
71 Ibid., 397.

72 Ibid., 407.

73 Gruending, *Establishment Radical*, 34.

74 *Coso v. Poulos* (1969) S.C.R. 757.

75 Ibid, 764.

76 Ibid.

77 Chief Justice Hughes made this famous remark in a speech to the Chamber of Commerce in Elmira, N.Y., 3 May 1907. For a discussion of Hughes's judicial philosophy, see G. Edward White, *The American Judicial Tradition: Profiles of Leading American Judges*, 206–9.

78 See Christopher Wolfe, *The Rise of Modern Judicial Review: From Constitutional Interpretation to Judge-made Law.*

79 'Paper prepared for delivery to the meeting of the Association of Canadian Law Teachers,' Montreal, 7 June 1972, 1.

80 Ibid., 3.

81 Ibid., 4.

82 Ibid.

83 *Supreme Court Act*, R.S.C. 1962, c. 259, s. 55.

84 Ibid.

85 *A.G. for Manitoba v. Manitoba Egg and Poultry Association et al.*, (1971) S.C.R. 689.

86 *Anti-Inflation Reference*, (1976) 2 S.C.R. 373.

87 *In the Matter of a Reference by the Governor General in Council concerning the Proclamation of Section 16 of the Criminal Law Amendment Act*, 1968–1969, (1970) S.C.R. 777 [hereinafter *Breathalizer Reference*].

88 Ibid., 783.

89 Ibid., 784.

90 For an extensive discussion of Hall's opinion in the *Breathalizer* case, see Frederick Vaughan, 'Emmett Matthew Hall: The Activist as Justice,' *Osgoode Hall Law Journal*, 425.

91 *Breathalizer Reference*, 785.

92 *The Canadian Bill of Rights*, s. 3. For a discussion of this issue, see Peter W. Hogg, *Constitutional Law of Canada*, 790–1.

93 Interview with the author, Toronto, 21 Oct. 1976.

94 Interview with the author, Toronto, 30 Dec. 1976.

95 Interview with the author, Ottawa, 24 June 1974.

96 Ibid.

97 The author is reluctant to reveal the source of this anecdote (contained in a taped interview) but is thoroughly convinced of its veracity.

98 Toronto, 22 March 1975, 7.

99 *A.G. for Manitoba Egg & Poultry Assn.* (1971) S.C.R. 689.

100 Paul Weiler, *In the Last Resort*, 262.

101 *A.G. for Manitoba.*

102 *A.G. for Ontario v. Policyholders of Wentworth Insurance*, (1969) S.C.R. 779, 793.

103 Ibid.

104 *University Hospital Board v. Lepine* (1966) S.C.R., 561.

105 Ibid., 579.

106 Ibid.

107 Ibid., 588.

108 Ibid.

109 *Ares v. Venner*, (1970) S.C.R. 608.

110 *Ares v. Venner*, (1969) 70 W.W.R. 96.

111 *Ares v. Venner*, (1970) S.C.R. 615.

112 Ibid.

113 Ibid.

114 *Myers v. the Director of Public Prosecution*, (1965) A.C. 1001; (1964) A11 E.R. 881.

115 *Ares v. Venner*, (1970) S.C.R. 625–6.

116 Ibid.

117 Ibid., 626.

118 *Toronto General Hospital v. Matthews*, (1972) S.C.R. 435.

119 *Sisters of St. Joseph v. Fleming*, (1938) S.C.R. 172.

120 *In the Matter of a Reference re: Steven Murray Truscott*, (1967) S.C.R. 309 [hereinafter *Truscott Reference*].

121 *Toronto Star*, 4 May 1967.

122 Saskatoon *Star-Phoenix*, 5 May 1967.

123 *Truscott Reference*, 309.

124 Isabel Le Bourdais, *The Trial of Steven Truscott.*

125 Interview with Mr Justice Abbott, Ottawa, 28 Oct. 1970.

126 *Truscott Reference*, 383.

127 Ibid., 384.

128 Ibid., 390.

129 Letters to Justice Hall on Truscott trial, Hall Papers. I have deliberately excluded the names of the writers.

130 I am grateful to Ken Campbell for much of the material contained here. Interview with the author, Ottawa, 21 June 1974.

131 Ibid.

132 *Daniels v. White and the Queen*, (1968) S.C.R. 517, 531; 2 D.L.R. (3rd) 1; 64 W.W.R. 385.

133 *Prince and Myron v. The Queen*, (1964) S.C.R. 81.

134 Ibid., 84.
135 Ibid.
136 Ibid., 85.
137 *Sikyea v. The Queen*, (1964) S.C.R. 642.
138 Ibid., 646.
139 Jack Sissons, *Judge of the Far North*, 150.
140 Ibid.
141 Ibid., 151.
142 *Sigeareak v. The Queen*, (1966) S.C.R. 645.
143 *Regina v. Kallooar*, (1964) 50 W.W.R. 602.
144 *Kogogolak v. The Queen*, (1959) 28 W.W.R. 376; 31 C.R. 12.
145 (1966) 55 W.W.R. 1; 55 D.L.R. (2d) 29.
146 *Sigeareak*, 517.
147 Ibid., 652.
148 *Regina v. Drybones* (1970) S.C.R. 282; 71 W.W.R. 161; 9 D.L.R. (3d) 473.
149 *Daniels*, 517.
150 Ibid., 522.
151 Ibid., 530.
152 Ibid., 531.
153 Ibid., 523.
154 *Drybones*.
155 Ibid., 297.
156 Ibid., 304.
157 Ibid., 305.
158 (1963) S.C.R. 651; 41 D.L.R. (2d) 485.
159 *Regina v. Gonzales*, (1962) 37 W.W.R. 257; 132 C.C.C. 237.
160 *Brown v. the Board of Education of Topeka, Kansas*, (1953) 347 U.S. 483.
161 *Regina v. Gonzales*, 294.
162 Ibid.
163 There was a valid concern throughout the legal community that the *Dry-bones* decision could backfire and, as Peter Hogg notes, 'cast doubt on all the provisions of the *Indian Act*, and on the whole principle of a special regime of law for Indians.' Peter Hogg, *Constitutional Law of Canada*, 669.
164 For a good discussion of the limitations of the Canadian Bill of Rights, see William E. Conklin, *Images of a Constitution*, especially chapter 5.
165 See Peter Hogg, 'A Comparison of the Canadian Bill of Rights and Freedoms with the Canadian Bill of Rights,' in Walter S. Tarnopolsky and Gerald A. Beaudoin, ed., *The Canadian Charter of Rights and Freedoms: Commentary*.
166 *Calder et al. v. A.G. for British Columbia*, (1973) S.C.R. 313.

167 *A.G. For Canada v. Lavell; Isaac et al. v. Bedard*, (1974) S.C.R. 1349.
168 *Calder*, 323.
169 *St. Catherine's Milling and Lumber Company v. The Queen*, (1889) 14 A.C. 46.
170 *Calder*, 320.
171 Ibid., 325.
172 Ibid., 328.
173 Ibid., 344.
174 Ibid., 372.
175 Ibid., 375.
176 Ibid., 394.
177 Ibid., 395.
178 *Regina v. White and Bob*, (1965) 52 W.W.R. 218.
179 *Calder*, 297.
180 Ibid., 401.
181 Ibid.
182 Ibid., 402.
183 Ibid., 404.
184 Ibid., 412.
185 For a discussion of this case in the wider context of British Columbia history, see Paul Tennant, *Aboriginal Peoples and Politics*. See also Daniel Raunet, *Without Surrender, Without Consent: A History of the Nishga Land Claims*.
186 I am grateful to Professor Douglas Sanders, University of British Columbia Law School, for information on this point. He reports: 'An adviser in Trudeau's office said that Trudeau (after all, a law professor) had read the three decisions in the case and had been more impressed by Hall's reasoning than Judson's.' E-mail to the author, 30 Oct. 2003.
187 See House of Commons Debates, 15 April 1973, 3207.
188 Raunet, *Without Surrender, Without Consent*, 161.
189 Cited in ibid., 150.
190 Sidney L. Harring, *White Man's Law: Native People in Nineteenth-Century Canadian Jurisprudence*, 15.
191 'Social Justice: Safeguard of Human Rights,' 15 Jan. 1969. Hall papers.
192 Ibid., 8–9.
193 Ibid., 9.

8 MORE WORK IN RETIREMENT

1 Emmett Matthew Hall, *Report of the Survey of the Court Structure in Saskatchewan*, 23 Dec. 1974.

2 *Railways Arbitration 1973: Report of the Arbitrator*, 77.
3 Ibid.
4 Ibid., 81.
5 Ibid., 15.
6 Ibid., 16.
7 Ibid., 17.
8 Ibid., 23.
9 R.S.S. 1965, 74.
10 *Report of the Survey of the Court Structure in Saskatchewan*, 34. Emphasis in original.
11 *Interim Report for a Unified Family Court*, 18 Nov. 1974.
12 Ibid., 6.
13 Ibid.
14 Ibid., 10.
15 British North America Act, s. 92 (14).
16 Ibid., s. 96.
17 Ibid., s. 91 (24).
18 *Interim Report for a Unified Family Court*, 18.
19 Speech at the University of Guelph, on the inauguration of Emmett Hall as chancellor, 11 Oct. 1971.
20 See Report of the Grain Handling and Transportation Commission, *Grain and Rail in Western Canada*, vol. 1, 'Social and Community Implications of Railroad Abandonment,' 75–7.
21 Ibid.
22 Ibid., 76.
23 Ibid., 64.
24 Ibid., 83.
25 Ibid., 52.
26 Ibid., 106.
27 Ibid.
28 Ibid.
29 Ibid., 118.
30 Ibid., 119.
31 Ibid.
32 Saskatoon *Star-Phoenix*, 17 May 1977. For a good account of the report, see Lawrence Thoner, '2,165 Mile Rail Abandonment Urged,' Saskatoon, *Star-Phoenix*, 16 May 1977.
33 Ibid., 2 June 1977.
34 Ibid.
35 Ibid., 17 May 1977. See, for the same day, the Saskatoon *Star-Phoenix*

article by Fred Harrison, 'Lang Upset but Opposition Lauds Crowsnest Proposal,' 8.

36 Edmonton *Journal*, 7 June 1977.

37 Ibid.

38 'Hall Disappoints U.G.G. Head,' Saskatoon *Star-Phoenix*, 18 May 1977.

39 Ibid.

40 *Grain and Rail in Western Canada*, vol. I, 2.

41 Ibid., vol. I, 336.

42 A. Abouchar, *An Economic Analysis of the Hall Commission Report*, 33.

43 Greg Mason, *The Report of the Grain Handling and Transportation Commission [Hall Report]: An Economic Analysis*, 240.

44 Ibid.

45 Ibid., 241.

46 Ibid., 242.

47 Ibid., 2 June 1977

48 Transport Canada. *Grain Handling and Transportation Commission, 1975–77*.

49 *Canada's National-Provincial Health Program for the 1980s* , 2.

50 Ibid.

51 *Canada's National-Provincial Health Program for the 1980s*, 3.

52 *Federal-Provincial Fiscal Arrangements and Established Programs Financing, 1977* (R.S.C. 1980).

53 *Medicare Review*, 27.

54 For assessments of the Hall report, see Pran Manga, 'Arbitration and the Medical Profession,' 670; Lee Soderstrom, 'Extra-billing and Cost-sharing,' 103; and John Horn, and Glen Beck, 'Medical Fee Determination,' 107.

55 Toronto *Globe and Mail*, 17 Sept. 1980.

56 *Review Report*, 40.

57 For an account of the funeral, see, Dan Zakreski, 'The Good Fight Over, Hall Goes to His Rest,' Saskatoon *Star-Phoenix*, 15 Nov. 1995, A1.

58 Ibid., A2.

59 See Patrick Kyba, *Alvin: A Biography of the Honourable Alvin Hamilton*, 317, where he reports: Diefenbaker 'continued to refer to Hamilton as 'Young Alvin' long after 'Young Alvin' had become a grandfather, he savaged Hamilton's proposals often in cabinet and occasionally in public and, after encouraging Hamilton to run for the leadership in 1967, he refused to stay out of the race even though he knew that his entry would likely ruin Hamilton's chance of success.'

60 According to the Diefenbaker Centre archives, Diefenbaker struck Hall's name off the list in 1976 with the note in his own hand: 'no longer on the bench.' The Diefenbaker Centre archivist explains the excision: 'Several

other people seem to be crossed off the list for the same reason; that they no longer hold the position they had previously occupied.' But Emmett Hall's relationship to John Diefenbaker went back sixty years; it is hard to believe that he would exclude Emmett Hall for that reason. Jason Tyler Caldwell to author, 7 July 2003, Hall Papers.

Bibliography

PRIVATE PAPERS

Hall Papers, University of Saskatchewan, Saskatoon, Saskatchewan.
Diefenbaker Papers, Diefenbaker Centre, University of Saskatchewan, Saskatoon, Saskatchewan.

INTERVIEWS

The Honourable Douglas Abbott, Ottawa.
Mr Kenneth Campbell, Ottawa.
The Honourable John R. Cartwright, Ottawa.
The Right Honourable John G. Diefenbaker, Ottawa.
The Honourable D.C. Douglas, Ottawa.
Dr John Hall, Toronto.
Professor Douglas Schmeiser, Saskatoon.

BOOKS AND ARTICLES

Abernathy, M. Glenn. *Civil Liberties under the Constitution*, 2nd ed. New York: Dodd, Mead and Company, 1972.
Abouchar, A. *An Economic Analysis of the Hall Commission Report*. Toronto: Ontario Economic Council, 1977.
Backhouse, Constance, *Colour-Coded: A Legal History of Racism in Canada: 1900–*

1950. Toronto: University of Toronto Press Osgoode Society for Canadian Legal History, 1999.

Barnhart, Gordon, ed. *Saskatchewan Premiers of the Twentieth Century*. Regina: Canadian Plains Research Centre, 2004.

Blishen, Bernard R. *Doctors and Doctrines: The Ideology of Medicare in Canada*. Toronto: University of Toronto Press, 1969.

Bryden, P.E., *Planners and Politicians: Liberal Politics and Social Policy, 1957–1968*. Montreal and Kingston: McGill-Queen's University Press, 1997.

Canada's National-Provincial Health Program for the 1980s. Ottawa: Department of National Health and Welfare, 1980.

Canadian Medical Association. *Submission of the Canadian Medical Association to the Royal Commission on Health Services*, Toronto, 16 May 1962, Ottawa, 1962.

Conklin, William E., *Images of a Constitution*. Toronto: University of Toronto Press, 1989.

Daly, James. *Education or Molasses? A Critical Look at the Hall-Dennis Report*. Ancaster, Ont.: Cromlech Press, 1969.

Dixon, Robert T., *Catholic Education and Politics in Ontario, 1964–2001: Volume IV*. Toronto: Catholic Foundation of Ontario, 2003.

Duncan, Kirsty, *Hunting the 1918 Flu: One Scientist's Search for a Killer Virus*. Toronto: University of Toronto Press, 2002.

Fleming, W.G. *Education: Ontario's Preoccupation*. Toronto: University of Toronto Press 1972.

Foster, John E. *The Developing West*. Edmonton: University of Alberta Press, 1983.

Gidney, R.D. *From Hope to Harris: Reshaping Ontario's Schools* Toronto: University of Toronto Press, 1999.

Grain and Rail in Western Canada. Report of the Grain Handling and Transportation Commission. Ottawa: Ministry of Supply and Services, 1977.

Granatstein, J.L., *Twentieth Century Canada*, 2nd ed. Toronto: McGraw-Hill, 1986.

Gruending, Dennis. *Emmett Hall: Establishment Radical*. Toronto: Macmillan, 1985.

Hall, Emmett Matthew. 'Lawyers and Canadian Criminal Law in the Seventies.' Law Society of Upper Canada *Gazette*, vol. 5, no. 1 (March 1971): 25.

Harring, Sidney L. *White Man's Law: Native People in Nineteenth-Century Canadian Jurisprudence*. Toronto: University of Toronto Press/Osgoode Society for Canadian Legal History, 1998.

Herbert, A.P. *Mild and Bitter*. London: Methuen, 1963.

Hogg, Peter W. *Constitutional Law of Canada*. Toronto: Carswell, 1992.

Hogg, Thomas H. *Report of the Royal Commission on the South Saskatchewan River Project*. Ottawa: King's Printer, 1952.

Horn, John, and Gen Beck. 'Medical Fee Determination,' *Canadian Public Policy/analyse politique*, vol. 7, no. 2 (1981): 107.

Houston, Stuart. *Steps on the Road to Medicare: Why Saskatchewan Led the Way*. Montreal and Kingston: McGill-Queen's University Press, 2003.

Huel, Raymond J.A. 'J.J. Maloney: How the West Was Saved from Rome, Quebec and Liberals,' in John E. Foster, ed., *The Developing West*. Edmonton: University of Alberta Press, 1983.

Hutchins, Robert Maynard. *The Learning Society*. New York: Frederick A. Praeger, 1968.

Illich, Ivan. *Celebration of Awareness: A Call for Institutional Revolution*. New York: Doubleday, 1970.

– *Deschooling Society*. New York: Harper and Row, 1970.

Kerr, Donald. 'Psychology of Boomtime: Saskatoon, 1905–1913.' Unpublished paper. Hall Papers.

Knopff, Rainer, and F.L. Morton. *Charter Politics*. Scarborough, Ont.: Nelson Canada, 1992.

Kolata, Gina. *FLU: The Story of the Great Influenza Pandemic of 1918 and the Search for the Virus That Caused It*. New York: Simon and Schuster, 1999.

Kyba, Patrick. *Alvin: A Biography of the Honourable Alvin Hamilton, P.C.* Regina: Canadian Plains Research Centre, 1989.

– 'Ballots and Burning Crosses,' in Norman Ward and Duff, eds, *Politics: Saskatchewan*. Toronto: Longmans Canada, 1968.

– 'Race, Religion and Resources: J.T.M. Anderson and the Conservative Party of Saskatchewan,' in Gordon Barnhart, ed., *Saskatchewan Premiers of the Twentieth Century*. Regina: Canadian Plains Research Centre, 2004.

Leacock, Stephen. *Montreal*. New York: Doubleday, Doran 1944.

Lebourdais, Isabel. *The Trial of Steven Truscott*. Toronto: McClelland and Stewart, 1966.

Liversedge, Ronald. *Recollections of the On to Ottawa Trek*, ed. Victor Hoar. Toronto: McClelland and Stewart, 1973.

McLachlin, Chief Justice Beverley. 'The Charter of Rights and Freedoms: A Judicial Perspective. *University of British Columbia Law Review*, vol. 23, no. 3 (1989): 579.

Manga, Pran. 'Arbitration and the Medical Profession: A Comment on the Hall Report,' *Canadian Public Policy/analyse politique*, vol. 6, no. 4 (1980): 127–32.

Manson, Allan, and David Mullan, eds. *Commissions of Inquiry: Praise or Reappraise?* Toronto: Irwin Law, 2003.

Mason, Greg. 'The Royal Commission on Health Services.' *Canadian Public Policy/Analyse Politique*, vol. 4. (1978).

Morton, W.L., *The Kingdom of Canada*. Toronto: McClelland and Stewart, 1977.

– *Manitoba: A History*. Toronto: University of Toronto Press, 1957.

Neatby, Hilda. *So Little for the Mind*. Toronto: Clark, Irwin, 1953.

Pitsula, James. 'The Courage of Her Convictions.' *The Beaver*, October/November 2003, 26–31.

Porter, McKenzie. 'Did the Income Tax Kill Kaspar Beck?' *Macleans Magazine*, 15 July 1951.

Raunet, Daniel. *Without Surrender, Without Consent: A History of the Nishga Land Claims*. Vancouver and Toronto: Douglas and McIntyre, 1984.

Rees, Goronwy. *The Great Slump*. New York: Harper and Row, 1970.

Report of the Provincial Committee on the Aims and Objectives in the Schools of Ontario. Toronto: Department of Education, 1968.

Report of the Royal Commission on Health Services. Ottawa: Queen's Printer, 1964, 1965.

Riker, Eric W. *Teachers, Trustees and Policy: The Politics of Education in Ontario, 1945–1975*. PhD dissertation, University of Toronto, 1981.

Russell, Peter. *The Judiciary in Canada: The Third Branch of Government*. Toronto: McGraw-Hill-Ryerson, 1987.

Scarman, Sir Leslie. *English Law: The New Dimension*. London: Stevens and Sons, 1974.

Sharpe, Robert J. *The Longest Day, the Last Hour: The Currie Libel Trial*. Toronto: University of Toronto Press/Osgoode Society for Canadian Legal History, 1988.

– and Kent Roach. *Brian Dickson: A Judge's Journey*. Toronto: University of Toronto Press/Osgoode Society for Canadian Legal History, 2003.

Sissons, Jack. *Judge of the Far North*. Toronto: McClelland and Stewart, 1968.

Smith, David E. 'Membership in the Saskatchewan Legislative Assembly: 1905–1966,' in Norman Ward and Duff Spafford, eds, *Politics: Saskatchewan* (Toronto: Longmans, 1968).

Snell, James G., and Frederick Vaughan. *The Supreme Court of Canada: History of the Institution*. Toronto: University of Toronto Press/Osgoode Society for Canadian Legal History, 1985.

Soderstrom, Lee. 'Extra-billing and Cost-sharing,' *Canadian Public Policy/ analyse politique*, vol. 7, no. 3 (1981): 103.

Stewart, Walter, *The Life and Political Times of Tommy Douglas*. Toronto: McArthur, 2003.

– *MJ: The Life and Times of M.J. Coldwell*. Toronto: Stoddart, 2000.

Tarnopolsky, Walter, and Gerald A. Beaudoin, eds. *The Canadian Charter of Rights and Freedoms: Commentary*. Toronto: Carswell, 1982.

Taylor, Malcolm G., *Health Insurance and Canadian Public Policy*. Montreal: McGill-Queen's University Press, 1987.

– *Insuring National Health Care: The Canadian Experience*. Chapel Hill: University of North Carolina Press, 1990.

Tennant, Paul. *Aboriginal Peoples and Politics*. Vancouver: University of British Columbia Press, 1990.

Trofimenkoff, Susan M., ed. *The Twenties in Western Canada*. Ottawa: National Museums of Canada, 1972.

Vanderbilt, Arthur. 'The Law Center.' *American Bar Association Journal*, vol. 32 (1946), 569.

Vaughan, Frederick. 'The Birthpangs of the Supreme Court of Canada.' *American Review of Canadian Studies*, vol. 26, no. 2 (Summer, 1986): 125–38.

– 'Emmett Hall: The Activist as Justice.' *Osgoode Hall Law Journal*, vol. 10, no. 2 (1972): 425.

Weiler, Paul. *In The Last Resort*. Toronto: Carswell-Methuen, 1974.

Wechsler, Herbert. 'Towards Neutral Principles of Constitutional Law.' *Harvard Law Review*, vol. 73, no. 1 (1959): 1–35.

White, G. Edward. *The American Judicial Tradition: Profiles of Leading American Judges*. New York: Oxford University Press, 1976.

Williams, Colwyn. Transcript of an interview with Emmett Hall, Saskatoon, 25 Aug. 1971.

Williams, David Ricardo. *Duff: A Life in the Law*. Vancouver: University of British Columbia Press/Osgoode Society for Canadian Legal History, 1984.

– *Just Lawyers*. Toronto: University of Toronto Press/Osgoode Society for Canadian Legal History, 1995.

Index

PUBLICATIONS OF THE OSGOODE SOCIETY FOR
CANADIAN LEGAL HISTORY

1981 David H. Flaherty, ed., *Essays in the History of Canadian Law: Volume I*
1982 Marion MacRae and Anthony Adamson, *Cornerstones of Order: Court-houses and Town Halls of Ontario, 1784–1914*
1983 David H. Flaherty, ed., *Essays in the History of Canadian Law: Volume II*
1984 Patrick Brode, *Sir John Beverley Robinson: Bone and Sinew of the Compact*
       David Williams, *Duff: A Life in the Law*
1985 James Snell and Frederick Vaughan, *The Supreme Court of Canada: History of the Institution*
1986 Paul Romney, *Mr Attorney: The Attorney General for Ontario in Court, Cabinet, and Legislature, 1791–1899*
       Martin Friedland, *The Case of Valentine Shortis: A True Story of Crime and Politics in Canada*
1987 C. Ian Kyer and Jerome Bickenbach, *The Fiercest Debate: Cecil A. Wright, the Benchers, and Legal Education in Ontario, 1923–1957*
1988 Robert Sharpe, *The Last Day, the Last Hour: The Currie Libel Trial* John D. Arnup, *Middleton: The Beloved Judge*
1989 Desmond Brown, *The Genesis of the Canadian Criminal Code of 1892*
       Patrick Brode, *The Odyssey of John Anderson*
1990 Philip Girard and Jim Phillips, eds., *Essays in the History of Canadian Law: Volume III – Nova Scotia*
       Carol Wilton, ed., *Essays in the History of Canadian Law: Volume IV – Beyond the Law: Lawyers and Business in Canada, 1830–1930*
1991 Constance Backhouse, *Petticoats and Prejudice: Women and Law in Nineteenth- Century Canada*
1992 Brendan O'Brien, *Speedy Justice: The Tragic Last Voyage of His Majesty's Vessel* Speedy
       Robert Fraser, ed., *Provincial Justice: Upper Canadian Legal Portraits from the Dictionary of Canadian Biography*
1993 Greg Marquis, *Policing Canada's Century: A History of the Canadian Association of Chiefs of Police*
       F. Murray Greenwood, *Legacies of Fear: Law and Politics in Quebec in the Era of the French Revolution*
1994 Patrick Boyer, *A Passion for Justice: The Legacy of James Chalmers McRuer*
       Charles Pullen, *The Life and Times of Arthur Maloney: The Last of the Tribunes*
       Jim Phillips, Tina Loo, and Susan Lewthwaite, eds., *Essays in the History of Canadian Law: Volume V – Crime and Criminal Justice*
       Brian Young, *The Politics of Codification: The Lower Canadian Civil Code of 1866*
1995 David Williams, *Just Lawyers: Seven Portraits*

Hamar Foster and John McLaren, eds., *Essays in the History of Canadian Law: Volume VI – British Columbia and the Yukon*

W.H. Morrow, ed., *Northern Justice: The Memoirs of Mr Justice William G. Morrow*

Beverley Boissery, *A Deep Sense of Wrong: The Treason Trials and Transportation to New South Wales of Lower Canadian Rebels after the 1838 Rebellion*

1996 Carol Wilton, ed., *Essays in the History of Canadian Law: Volume VII – Inside the Law: Canadian Law Firms in Historical Perspective*

William Kaplan, *Bad Judgment: The Case of Mr Justice Leo A. Landreville*

F. Murray Greenwood and Barry Wright, eds., *Canadian State Trials: Volume I – Law, Politics, and Security Measures, 1608–1837*

1997 James W. St.G. Walker, *'Race,' Rights, and the Law in the Supreme Court of Canada: Historical Case Studies*

Lori Chambers, *Married Women and Property Law in Victorian Ontario*

Patrick Brode, *Casual Slaughters and Accidental Judgments: Canadian War Crimes and Prosecutions, 1944–1948*

Ian Bushnell, *A History of the Federal Court of Canada, 1875–1992*

1998 Sidney Harring, *White Man's Law: Native People in Nineteenth-Century Canadian Jurisprudence*

Peter Oliver, *'Terror to Evil-Doers': Prisons and Punishments in Nineteenth-Century Ontario*

1999 Constance Backhouse, *Colour-Coded: A Legal History of Racism in Canada, 1900–1950*

G. Blaine Baker and Jim Phillips, eds., *Essays in the History of Canadian Law: Volume VIII – In Honour of R.C.B. Risk*

Richard W. Pound, *Chief Justice W.R. Jackett: By the Law of the Land*

David Vanek, *Fulfilment: Memoirs of a Criminal Court Judge*

2000 Barry Cahill, *The Thousandth Man: A Biography of James McGregor Stewart*

A.B. McKillop, *The Spinster and the Prophet: Florence Deeks, H.G. Wells, and the Mystery of the Purloined Past*

Beverley Boissery and F. Murray Greenwood, *Uncertain Justice: Canadian Women and Capital Punishment*

Bruce Ziff, *Unforeseen Legacies: Reuben Wells Leonard and the Leonard Foundation Trust*

2001 Ellen Anderson, *Judging Bertha Wilson: Law as Large as Life*

Judy Fudge and Eric Tucker, *Labour before the Law: The Regulation of Workers' Collective Action in Canada, 1900–1948*

Laurel Sefton MacDowell, *Renegade Lawyer: The Life of J.L. Cohen*

2002 John T. Saywell, *The Lawmakers: Judicial Power and the Shaping of Canadian Federalism*

Patrick Brode, *Courted and Abandoned: Seduction in Canadian Law*

David Murray, *Colonial Justice: Justice, Morality, and Crime in the Niagara District, 1791–1849*

F. Murray Greenwood and Barry Wright, *Canadian State Trials, Volume II: Rebellion and Invasion in the Canadas, 1837–1839*

2003 Robert Sharpe and Kent Roach, Brian Dickson: *A Judge's Journey*

Jerry Bannister, *The Rule of the Admirals: Law, Custom, and Naval Government in Newfoundland, 1699–1832*

George Finlayson, John J. Robinette, Peerless Mentor: *An Appreciation*

Peter Oliver, *The Conventional Man: The Diaries of Ontario Chief Justice Robert A. Harrison, 1856–1878*

2004 Philip Girard, Jim Phillips, and Barry Cahill, *The Supreme Court of Nova Scotia, 1754–2004: From Imperial Bastion to Provincial Oracle.*

Frederick Vaughan, *Aggressive in Pursuit: The Life of Justice Emmett Hall*